A CELEBRATION OF POETS

EAST
GRADES K-6
FALL 2015

creativeCOMMUNICATION
A CELEBRATION OF TODAY'S WRITERS

A Celebration of Poets
East
Grades K-6
Fall 2015

An anthology compiled by Creative Communication, Inc.

Published by:

creativeCOMMUNICATION

A CELEBRATION OF TODAY'S WRITERS

PO BOX 303 · SMITHFIELD, UTAH 84335
TEL. 435-713-4411 · WWW.POETICPOWER.COM

Authors are responsible for the originality of the writing submitted.

Thank you to our student artists whose work is featured on the cover:
Genevieve Wu - Grade 5, Laura Wang - Grade 6, Robert Hunter - Grade 8, Audrey Han - Grade 3, Nasim Dalirifar - Grade 9, Jacob Wong - Grade 12, Cassandra Fernandez de Aenlle - Grade 12, Haley Sellmeyer - Grade 2, Yihan Wu - Grade 9, Shiyi Huang - Grade 12, Landon Tinsley - Kindergarten, Pranav Sitaraman - Grade 3, and Xinyi Zhang - Grade 3.
To have your art considered for our next book cover, go to www.celebratingart.com.

ISBN: 978-1-60050-718-2

FOREWORD

Dear Reader:

In the forward to the anthology last spring, I mentioned one of my favorite writers, John Tobias, whose most famous poem, "Reflections On a Gift of Watermelon Pickle Received From a Friend Called Felicity," featured in the book by the same title, has been published well over a million times. As a writer he has been published by numerous magazines including *The New Yorker*, and had had his plays produced in 15 countries. I shared with him a copy of the Spring 2015 edition and wanted to share with you, our readers, his comments.

Thank you for sharing your "Celebration" anthology. A Celebration indeed – I find its mix of young voices expressing their yearnings, self-discoveries, responses to nature, to change, to death, and all other outer and inner forces that strongly affect them a fascinating window into the future of writing as they explore the power of language linked to metaphor, counterpointed imagery, rhythm, music, and tough minded insights.

It is you who have given them and their teachers the impetus and courage to try their wings and risk disappointment…to fall down and get up again and keep at it…to accept the need to re-write and improve and simplify and learn when less is more, and how to create a synergy that stays with the reader long after the piece has been read.

Thank you again for all you do and have done to keep writing alive and flourishing.

No, John. Thank you.

I am a teacher and have been the Editor at Creative Communication for over 20 years. I firmly believe in what we do in promoting writing in our schools. But when an accomplished, professional writer validates my belief in our mission, then all is well.

Sincerely,

Thomas Worthen, Ph.D.
Editor
Creative Communication

WRITING CONTESTS!

Enter our next POETRY contest!
Enter our next ESSAY contest!

Why should I enter?
Win prizes and get published! Each year thousands of dollars in prizes are awarded throughout North America. The top writers in each division receive a monetary award and a free book that includes their published poem or essay. Entries of merit are also selected to be published in our anthology.

Who may enter?
There are four divisions in the poetry contest. The poetry divisions are grades K-3, 4-6, 7-9, and 10-12. There are three divisions in the essay contest. The essay divisions are grades 4-6, 7-9, and 10-12.

What is needed to enter the contest?
To enter the poetry contest send in one original poem, 21 lines or less. To enter the essay contest send in one original non-fiction essay, 100-250 words, on any topic. Please submit each poem and essay with a title, and the following information clearly printed: the writer's name, current grade, home address (optional), school name, school address, teacher's name and teacher's email address (optional). Contact information will only be used to provide information about the contest. For complete contest information go to www.poeticpower.com.

How do I enter?
Enter a poem online at:
www.poeticpower.com
or
Mail your poem to:
Poetry Contest
PO Box 303
Smithfield, UT 84335

Enter an essay online at:
www.poeticpower.com
or
Mail your essay to:
Essay Contest
PO Box 303
Smithfield, UT 84335

When is the deadline?
Poetry contest deadlines are April 7th, August 18th and December 3rd. Essay contest deadlines are February 18th, July 14th, and October 15th. Students can enter one poem and one essay for each spring, summer, and fall contest deadline.

Are there benefits for my teacher?
Yes. Teachers with five or more students published receive a free anthology that includes their students' writing. Teachers may also earn points in our Classroom Rewards program to use towards supplies in their classroom.

For more information please go to our website at **www.poeticpower.com**, email us at editor@poeticpower.com or call 435-713-4411.

TABLE OF CONTENTS

STATES INCLUDED IN THIS EDITION:

CONNECTICUT
DELAWARE
DISTRICT OF COLUMBIA
FLORIDA
GEORGIA
MAINE
MARYLAND
MASSACHUSETTS
NEW HAMPSHIRE
NEW JERSEY
NEW YORK
NORTH CAROLINA
PENNSYLVANIA
RHODE ISLAND
SOUTH CAROLINA
VERMONT
VIRGINIA

Fall 2015 Poetic Achievement Honor Schools

Teachers who had fifteen or more poets accepted to be published

The following schools are recognized as receiving a "Poetic Achievement Award." This award is given to schools who have a large number of entries of which over fifty percent are accepted for publication. With hundreds of schools entering our contest, only a small percent of these schools are honored with this award. The purpose of this award is to recognize schools with excellent Language Arts programs. This award qualifies these schools to receive a complimentary copy of this anthology.

Academy of Greatness & Excellence
Teaneck, NJ
  Heba Aboubakr*
  Rena Zebi*

Amherst Middle School
Amherst, NH
  Michelle Emmond*

Aston Elementary School
Aston, PA
  Vivienne F. Cameron*

Blackrock School
Coventry, RI
  Linda Cohen
  Michaela L. Keenan*

Boiling Springs Intermediate School
Boiling Springs, SC
  Susan Lyda*
  Wanda Sullivan

Boyce Middle School
Upper St Clair, PA
  Diane Ecker*

Catherine A Dwyer Elementary School
Wharton, NJ
  Rebecca R. Mears
  Nancy Reeves*

Central Park Elementary School
Plantation, FL
  Mark Siegel*

Chickahominy Middle School
Mechanicsville, VA
  Shannon Floyd
  Laurel Floyd
  Kimberly Harrell
  Melissa Ingram-Crouch
  Leigh Rooke

Cooley Springs Fingerville School
Chesnee, SC
  Rita Reams*

Country Day School
Largo, FL
  Janice LeVine
  Belinda Pager

Dawson County Middle School
Dawsonville, GA
Aimee Park*

East Lake Elementary School
Massapequa Park, NY
Kim Cawley*

Elbridge Gale Elementary School
Wellington, FL
Toni Koy*

Ethel M Burke Elementary School
Bellmawr, NJ
Kathy Vespe*

Ettrick Elementary School
Petersburg, VA
Vicki Bowers
Arlene Cary
Bonnie Dance
Lesley Harris
Lynne Johnson
Maria MacLaughlin
Rebecca Traffas

Good Shepherd School
Camp Hill, PA
Cheryl O'Neil*

Hawthorne Christian Academy
Hawthorne, NJ
Mrs. Pollard
Joan Wolff

Heartland Christian Academy
Sebring, FL
Dr. Belinda West*

Hurley Elementary/Middle School
Hurley, VA
Charlotte Ashby*

Immaculate Conception Catholic Regional
School
Cranston, RI
Judith McCusker*

Interboro GATE Program
Prospect Park, PA
Kelly DiLullo*
Joyce Faragasso*

Lake Success Camp
Valley Stream, NY
Dr. Debbie Mayerson*

Long Island School for the Gifted
Huntington Station, NY
Natalie Hatami*

Marie Curie Institute
Amsterdam, NY
Jerilynn Einarsson
Diana L. Giardino*
Jennifer Satas
Linda Sawicki*

Medway Middle School
Medway, ME
Patricia McKinnon*

Memorial School
Bedford, NH
Cheri Schmitt*

Murray Middle School
Stuart, FL
Mark A. Fisher*
Carol Forbes*

Oak Ridge Elementary School
Harleysville, PA
Ross Pollack*
Jill Schumacher
Karah Ziff*

Oakdale-Bohemia Middle School
Oakdale, NY
Patty Alway*
Kay O'Rourke-Kowalski

Paul L Dunbar Middle School for Innovation
Lynchburg, VA
Brittany Clark-Slaughter*
Jennie Howell
Contessa Johnson

Pocopson Elementary School
West Chester, PA
David Lichter*

Public School 114 Ryder Elementary
Brooklyn, NY
Elaine E. Rowe*

Public School 131
Brooklyn, NY
Anita Betances*

Riverside Middle School
Riverside, NJ
Lori Wareham*

Roosevelt Elementary School
Rahway, NJ
Deborah Prakapas*

Saint Pauls Middle School
Saint Pauls, NC
Ilyssa Greene*
Donald Weller*

Spring Creek Elementary School
Bonita Springs, FL
Jamie Fleming*

St Anselm Elementary School
Philadelphia, PA
Ruth McIntyre*
Freda M. Tait*
Miss Wolfe

St John Neumann Regional Catholic School
Lilburn, GA
Barbara Sneed*

St Jude School
Mountaintop, PA
Marilyn Baran*

St Mary Magdalen Catholic School
Altamonte Springs, FL
Debbie Kelly*

St Michael the Archangel Regional School
Clayton, NJ
Sr. Bianca Camilleri*
Mr. Joe Williams

Tarpon Springs Middle School
Tarpon Springs, FL
Crisy Mathews*

Walker Memorial Academy
Avon Park, FL
Sharon Coldren*

Windsor Learning Academy
Tampa, FL
Miss Annette
Miss Brenda
Cynthia Cornelius
Miss Lisset
Miss Melissa

Top Ten Winners

List of Top Ten Winners for Fall 2015; listed alphabetically

Darwin Baker	Grade 3	Van Rensselaer Elementary School	IN
Ian Eld	Grade 3	Oak Ridge Elementary School	PA
Georgia Mae Fosth	Grade 3	St Stephen Lutheran School	CA
Sanaa Gotora	Grade 1	Valentine Hills Elementary School	MN
Sarah Henches	Grade 3	Lincoln Park Elementary School	NJ
Soraya Kamath	Grade 2	Public School 333 Manhattan School for Children	NY
Lulu King	Grade 3	S Ray Lowder Elementary School	NC
Annabella Lozano	Grade 1	Birkes Elementary School	TX
Austin Paturzo	Grade 3	Oak Ridge Elementary School	PA
Margalit Salkin	Grade 3	Campbell Hall School	CA
Samantha Bradley	Grade 6	Franklin Township Elementary School	NJ
Mari Cheng	Grade 5	Zervas Elementary School	MA
Taylor Horton-Raymond	Grade 4	Outley Elementary School	TX
Suzi Peter	Grade 6	Cedar Bluff Middle School	TN
Sarah Ramsdell	Grade 6	Tarpon Springs Middle School	FL
Brad Roe	Grade 6	Dr Dyer Intermediate School	WI
Calvin Weng	Grade 6	Banting Middle School	BC
Laynie Williamson	Grade 5	Foothill Elementary School	CO
Jennifer Xia	Grade 6	Kennedy Jr High School	IL
Alyssa Yin	Grade 6	Chinese American International School	CA

All Top Ten Winners may also be seen at www.poeticpower.com

Growing Up

Growing up is not always easy to do
So, take your time and get to know you
You are only young once before it's gone
Enjoy your youth before life moves on

No doubt, you will make many mistakes
If you find yourself lost, put on the brakes
Always accept counsel when there is an issue
Because if you listen, it can be very beneficial

Sometimes your attitude may not always be good
Just don't forget, it's because you
feel misunderstood
When your friends try to get you to break a rule
Remember doing the right thing, is what is cool

Growing up is not always easy to do
But if you accept the love, you will make it through
So try and try as hard as you can
Because before you know it, you will be a woman or man
Taylor Horton-Raymond, Grade 4

Away

Away you went with countless family portraits
sloppily drawn in crayon,
and the pink overalls with butterflies
that I wanted to keep forever.
Gone, in the time it took for me to blow out
the candles on my birthday cake.

Away you went with my business Barbie dolls,
my role models at age six,
and a storybook filled with fairy tales
that inspired me to write my own.
You disappeared for good when I thought
you'd be back by recess.

Away you went with my tricycle
that took me to distant lands,
and my coloring book filled with Disney characters,
where I unleashed my imagination.
Gone, leaving me to deal with the harsh
realities of the world.
Suzi Peter, Grade 6

Winter's Night

Midnight stroll in paradise,
The world awash in silver light,
Icicles glimmer like diamonds,
The moon giving an iridescent glow,
A sprinkle of stars across the sky,
A gentle breeze flowing through the air,
The beauty of it bringing peace to my heart.
Calvin Weng, Grade 6

My World

My world is full of wonders, excitement, and joy,
With our imagination we construct the finest toy,
Here we look at the star's shimmer, shining bright,
We see deep colors painting the never-ending night,
This is my world.

My world is an adventure, the voyage of a generation,
Tragedy and humor, victory and loss, all a creation,
We explore the deep ocean, making it up as we go,
Like a writer we record our tales and see them glow,
This is my world.

My world is a place of innocence, where children stay,
Here they glance at their first home, walk, talk, and play,
They are snowflakes and in the breeze they dance,
A child blossoms like a flower, and then they prance,
Because this is where the children grow and learn,
This is my world.
Jennifer Xia, Grade 6

The Box

My heart is a box and only I hold the key,
Inside I keep things of value to me,
This box is kept locked most of the time,
But when it is open I am defined,
Everything in it I hold down inside,
Some of these things are just there to hide,
This box is my secrets, my deepest fears,
Sometimes I forget that these things are here,
The contents of my box will never be known,
No secret is shared, no fear is shown,
When Good seems wrong and Evil right,
My box will be here for courage and might,
The key to this box is the key to my heart,
And together the world will be mine to impart...
Samantha Bradley, Grade 6

Seasons

Ice crystals drifting
Softly falls on fading grass
Cold water hardens

Young animals born
Beasts are soon awakening
Slush is now forming

Blazing sun appears
The warm breeze swims through the air
Water refreshes

Colored leaves falling
Crunching sounds beneath our feet
Soon deer disappear
Brad Roe, Grade 6

Halloween

It's Halloween night
Get ready for fun
But better watch out
Because here they come!

The ghosts and goblins
Get ready to haunt
They're sneaky and scary
Looking to taunt

The witches cackle with delight
While making the raven stew
With werewolf hair and bear claws
The potion will surely get to you

But don't forget the vampires
With their blood sucking love
And ghostly pale white skin
They can take you from above

Go trick or treating
Have some fun
But better watch out
Because here they come
BOO!

Laynie Williamson, Grade 5

In the Morning

Strung between leaves
droplets of dew
form a pearl necklace
in the morning.

Fatal and invisible
threads weave
innocently between twigs
in the morning.

Silent and cunning
floating like a scrap of silk
dropped from the clouds
in the morning.

A home for eight legs
a funeral for all those without
it dangles beautifully
in the morning.

Alyssa Yin, Grade 6

The Foal of Souls

Races, from soul to soul,
helping you gallop
past your worries,
like galloping
past schools
of dust.
And if your heart
is overflowing
with tears,
the foal of souls
will take you
on her back
to the place
known for cheers.
Dreams
love her.
Nightmares
are scared of her.
Safeness
is the blanket
that she provides.

Georgia Mae Fosth, Grade 3

My Dog, Toby

Toby used to be a puppy,
But now he is old.
He used to sleep a lot,
And now he sleeps more.
Toby used to run across the couch,
And jump on my dad.
But now he doesn't hardly run.
One time Toby pulled me through the grass
With his leash,
But now he only walks.
Toby used to be my cuddle-pillow,
But now it hurts him to cuddle.
I know I might not have Toby for long.
So I will give him healthy treats
And lots of hugs.

Darwin Baker, Grade 3

To All Who Served

The flag waves in the air
Showing our freedom
Showing our pride
Our fighting spirit.

Courage runs through the veins of those
Who fight for the love of country,
To defend our freedom
A priceless debt.

The ultimate sacrifice
That soldier pays
A tear rolls down our cheeks,
Grieving at the grave.

To all who have served
Today we honor you for
You have defended our freedom,
And we salute you.

Sarah Ramsdell, Grade 6

Special Art

I pick my paintbrush up again
And begin from the start
But I do not start over.
I always like my art.

Sometimes I draw abstract
Sometimes I draw what's known
Sometimes my lines are colorful
And go off on their own.

My art is always special
It always looks so good
Even if I do it "wrong"
It looks the way it should

I draw blooms and headphones
I draw fantastic vessels
But no matter what I draw
My art is always special

Mari Cheng, Grade 5

The City of Light

This is a sad time, I'm here to say.
I will never forget the events of this day.
Paris is a city I've always wanted to see,
But now it's a place that frightens me.
I feel helpless; all I can do is cry.
The people of Paris are strong,
They will survive this tragedy.
Love, not hate, is the only remedy.

Lulu King, Grade 3

A Funny Thing Happened on Christmas Eve

A funny thing happened on Christmas Eve,
I was coming home from Nanie's, fiddling with my sleeve.
I could hear the radio blasting my sister's favorite song,
Hearing Frosty the Snowman all night long.
Finally, I arrived at my house,
Not a creature was stirring, not even a mouse.
I rushed upstairs, and leaped to my bed,
Closed my eyes, and tried to rest my head.
"Grace?" I called at about 10:09,
"I'm awake!" she called, "By the way, I'm just fine!"
We rushed down the fourteen stairs, and then through the way,
He stepped out of the chimney, and sniffed the warm air.
His hair was whiter than I'd seen anywhere.
My sister looked at me, and I smiled at myself,
There, dancing, was my Elf on the Shelf.
He placed all the presents under the tree,
Some were for Grace, and some were for me.
Not eight, but nine reindeer pulled his sleigh,
And crossed the night sky in a graceful way;
We couldn't wait for Christmas day.

Sarah Henches, Grade 3

The Life of Writing

When I first got my pencil
My arm was shivering
Fear
Hope had gotten trapped
In somebody else's mind
I put my pencil on my paper
Fear was crawling up my spine
I started to write my first word
I felt like I was going to burst into tears
I don't know how much fear I have left in me
But I don't like fear
I feel like my arm is a fish
And words are sharks
Suddenly fear flashes off
I start finishing my poem
I drop my pencil
My poem is finally finished
But I know I'm going to make more poems
Each better and better

Austin Paturzo, Grade 3

SwiftySwatt

My shadow wears.
A neon pink sequined dress.
A guitar that keeps alive and knows where I go.
A hip hop jacket that moves my body to the beat.
Her hair is like a glitter bomb.
Sleek and bouncy.
My shadow is a dance performer.
It's powerful voice explodes.
Heart big as the world.
Creating miracles in all it touches.

Annabella Lozano, Grade 1

Why

When I look up at the sky,
I wonder why.
Why we live, why we die.

Why do we hope, why do we dream.
Because it makes everything seem ...
Fine, when it's not.

Why do people hate, why do people isolate.
Perhaps it makes them feel special and strong
But, in the end, it really is wrong.

My question is why.
Why we live and why we die.

Margalit Salkin, Grade 3

Dance

I walked in.
I saw all the people staring at me.
I tried to keep my scared-ness in,
But then I was embarrassed.

I have never done,
Such a big performance, I thought.
We were awesome.
And when I saw all of the audience clapping at me,
I thought I was as brave as a soldier.

Soraya Kamath, Grade 2

Bonfire

Wood stacked
The fire flashes
Flames tremble
Then come with a blast
A mountain of heat
As my dad watches

Down bottom
Blood red coals
I gaze at the flashing flames
As the crackle of the wood bellows
Ash dashes and darts
All around me
A temple of heat
Burning down
As my dad watches

The fire
Just like a dragon
Breathing fire
The fire dozes
Warmth moves out
As the fire dies

Ian Eld, Grade 3

My America
America the fairest, the greatest of all.
A free country,
Free entry for all.
The land that stands tall
bold and beautiful.
The land that is a breath of fresh air
for everyone out there.
The world is cheering for America.
Its a land where dreams come true.
A land where ideas come through.
Where the sky is forever blue.
There is love, there is laughter,
there is an all ever after.
Oh how I love,
My country, my America.
Sanaa Gotora, Grade 1

Grades 4-5-6
High Merit Poems

Flower in Winter

In October the air turned cool
In November it started to get cold
In December the snow started falling down
We didn't like the cold, truth be told

The frigid air stung
We started sneezing
When the heater wasn't on
We started freezing

But signs of spring
They came all right
Our hope grew big
Our heart became light

Green grass breaking through snow
The leaves began growing back
Flowers bloomed on that pear tree
One flower, then two, then a whole pack.

We know in February it'll turn warmer
In March the lion turns to lamb
In April we can wear T-shirts again
And in May spring will soon be over, like BAM
Olivia Duan, Grade 5

Oh Pizza

Oh pizza, oh pizza, so good and so salty to my tongue.
I feel rainbows leap over my tongue as the cheese lands.
My taste buds go crazy with delight
When the bite goes down my throat.
I daydream of crust, cheese, and sauce.

Those tasty toppings like
tomatoes, bacon, pepperoni, and olives
It's like toppings on a hot fudge sundae.
Oh greasy grease, you are so shiny
The slice makes my hands slippery

Although you make me thirsty, I still want more.
Although you make me full, I still want more.
Although you might burn my tongue,
I want you even more.

Pizza, you are a blanket layering my tongue.
The smell of you pizza
makes my stomach growl like a bear,
I am happy that you are my life pizza.
I want to eat you pizza, 24/7.
Oh pizza, oh pizza
Welcome home.
Jeremiah Miller, Grade 5

Falling for All

Fall season is here.
Crisp air and Halloween decorations everywhere.
People walk spider-dressed dogs,
Jack-o'-lanterns sit on porches.

There are falling leaves,
And children jump into piles of them.
The skies are blue and the sun is shining
And yet the air is chilling.

When the moon comes out to play,
I retreat inside to a warm fire.
I sit down and think,
"What a wonderful season fall is!"

And when I fall asleep,
I dream about pumpkins, ghosts, and skeletons,
And wait
For Halloween to come.

I feel energetic in the morning.
It's Halloween! The day is cold, and the night is even colder,
Yet people flood the streets,
In search of some tricks and some treats.
Jacob Schmelzer, Grade 6

Run Like the Wind

It's time for the meet,
I jump to my feet.
We arrive at the course,
my throat is hoarse.

I am nervous beyond thought,
even though I know everything I've been taught.
The pre-whistle blows,
wow, I have to go.

I'm at the line,
it's almost time.
The canon fires with a bump,
we start to run with a jump.

All the racers race to the hill,
I push ahead with all my will.
I emerge in first place,
Where I hope to stay throughout this race.

I put on a final burst of speed,
to cross the line is what I need.
I spin around and see I'm first,
I won the race with the final burst.
Nicole Susie, Grade 6

Family

My family is very sweet,
We love to eat tasty treats.
All of us like to laugh and play,
We could do this every day.
Sometimes my house is crazy,
And sometimes we are very lazy.
Please, please listen to me,
That's what we always see.
Watching my brothers go munch, munch,
Waiting to go to lunch, lunch.
Sitting silly and hard to find,
My family and me don't really mind.
I love my family so very much,
Even though we're not a big bunch.
Makayla Gardner, Grade 5

Soccer Shot

My favorite sport is soccer,
I am not a good goal blocker.
But out on the big soccer field,
The goalie is like a shield.
Swiss! A great shot at the goal,
And the whistle gives a blow.
A goal is scored for the team,
Now that's quite a great soccer dream.
Once you made the awesome score,
You really feel like you soar,
While the crowd gives a loud roar,
Of happiness in the great outdoors.
I don't exactly play on a team,
But it is really my true soccer dream.
Nazarii Klymiuk, Grade 5

Baseball

I love to play the sport baseball.
I like to play it in the fall.
Nothing will compare to the thrill.
You will never forget the feel.
I am really good at shortstop.
My glove seems to always pop.
I love the sound of the alloy bat.
It always makes a good TAT.
While you wait you cheer on your team.
If you strikeout don't pout or scream.
Baseball is a wonderful sport.
You can play it even if you're short.
If you end up winning the game.
You will never have any shame.
Brandon Boling, Grade 5

Going to Jasper

Early morning ride, we're going to Jasper.
Allyson and I are having a blast.
Loading up the car, it's time to leave.
I wish we could stay and play.
Basilisa Hall, Grade 6

Mind of a Mad Scientist

mind of a mad scientist
thinks like a cell
so complex and precise
no hair like Einstein
but a brain like so
a mind
crammed
tired
bright
hopeful
a mind
to change the world
with just one thought
a mind
Einstein
Bell
Curie
mind of a mad scientist
Catherine Mowry, Grade 6

Me, Myself, and I

I celebrate myself
in all that I am
Like a great oak
strong I stand
I sing in the air
and my voice floats away
I fight to win
and write my heart's song
My words float
from my mind to my pen
I am a smart individual
and let it all go
I am fragile
and break like snow
I have insecurities
but I love who I am
I celebrate myself
In all that I can
Rayne Elling, Grade 5

The Cat

With the woman, holding him
On top of her colorful bed,
The cat purrs
As softly as a mouse.
The woman says,
"It's almost time for bed."
The cat still purrs
As he gently goes to sleep.
The woman
Puts him down, beside her
On her bed and says,
"Goodnight, Midnight."
As the black cat purrs
Riley Troxell, Grade 4

My Mouth

I love my mouth
My mouth is mine
I use it all the time
I love my mouth

I love my mouth
I use it for emotion
For friends and family
I love my mouth

I love my mouth
It helps me smile
I use it to speak
I love my mouth
Allison Reitz, Grade 6

Island Paradise

Island paradise I want to visit,
palms so tall but I won't hit it,
I'd like a mango for an Island snack,
but today I have to pack,

I'd like to surfboard on the sea,
a surfboard champion I'd like to be,
I want to practice to be great,
to be great it's never too late,

beautiful hotel on the beach,
sometimes they serve me a peach,
island peaches I really love,
the world surfboard champion I'll be above.
Lilian Ali, Grade 4

My Feet

My feet take me to see special places
To see all the pretty faces
They help me run with all my friends
This is what my feet do for me

When we hear the whistle to go
No one runs crooked or slow
We always try our best and we run hard
This is what my feet do for me

They help me play my favorite sport
I run up and down the court
My feet control the ball and kick it far
This is what my feet do for me
Gabriella Sherman, Grade 6

Winter

The roads paved with ice
Frost giants are not scarce here
Harsh breezes again
Ainsley Allen, Grade 6

Freedom

Freedom. What a simple thing.
What a tough thing
To reach where I am
Today.
Soar high like a bird
Never giving up
Flying, ever-so persisting
To escape the clutches of imprisonment
Imprisoned. Alone. Frightened.
Removed from the ones you love.
Escape
A beautiful concept
Flying, soaring
You're a majestic eagle, gliding away from
Imprisonment, slavery
Returning to your family,
As home beckons you back,
You reach your longed-for destination,
Rejoicing! What a simple thing.
What a tough thing to reach
Where I am today.

Peyton Hand, Grade 6

Hooray!

Today is the day
When my stomach says hooray!
I'm about to eat
Some twisted, tangy wings

Oh my heart sings
Today is the day
I get my crunchy candy
To nibble on all day long

In my mind
I'm still singing that song

Until I come upon
Something sour
And it parches my lips
For about an hour

But in the end
It is still all okay
Hooray!

Keyana Martin, Grade 6

Thanksgiving

Thanksgiving
I see my family
I smell happy smells
I hear my family talk
I taste the turkey
I touch my presents
Thanksgiving

Chaz Elliott, Grade 6

I Know It's Halloween

I know it's Halloween when
It starts to get cold outside
People wear jackets
And drink warm milk.

I know it's Halloween when
Leaves, orange and red,
Fall off the trees
And land on the ground.

I know it's Halloween when
Children go shopping
For Halloween costumes so they
Can go trick or treating, door to door.

Yes, it's Halloween when
It is cold outside,
Leaves fall off the trees,
And children go trick or treating.

Clairece Shackelford, Grade 6

Changing Seasons

Spring is coming.
Birds are singing.
Flowers are blooming.
Grass is shining.

Summer is waiting.
Perfect for swimming.
Vacation is coming!
But, time is running.

New school year is starting.
Fall is approaching.
Leaves are falling.
Days are shortening.

Winter is starting.
Snow is falling.
New Year is arriving.
My fourth season is ending.

Malaika Niazi, Grade 5

The Stormy Night

In the snowy winter night,
The fog hides the shining stars,
The snow takes a flight,
All over the world.

The snow is silk,
falling in my mouth,
Time for bed come drink your milk,
The snow will still fall,
Till tomorrow dawn,
When the spring starts to bloom.

Riley Dupre, Grade 4

Rainy Day

Fuzzy silence,
A distant haze,
A faded movie, Almost
As if time
Stopped.
A tiny gray Sprout
Creeps up
Above ground.
Bigger, Darker
The clouds spread
Darker thicker and blackened
The tiny plant,
Gathers
The shadows,
Consumes it, revealing
The sun,
Big, bright
Absorbing the sorrow,
Sadness.
Creating marvelous
Joy.

Jayanthi Simhan, Grade 5

It's About Thanksgiving!

It's about staying up all night
talking
eating all night

It's about awesome nights
going to your friends house
staying over

It's about giving thanks
sharing
playing

It's about caring
hanging out with the family
having fun

It's about joyful times
playing video games
crazy activities

It's about the best day ever

Anuj Peri, Grade 5

Parents

P atient and kind
A wesome all the time
R eady and set
E nergy and peppy
N ever ever slumpy
T hat's what they are
S tewards all the time

Madison Del Pizzo, Grade 4

Fish Tank

I look at my fish tank
Oh what a sight I see
Fish of all colors swim by me
Gray, black, yellow and a shark as well
In and out of the decorations they go
Bubbles that really look like snow
Grass so green
I cannot believe what a sight I've seen
Xavier Jacobsen, Grade 5

Winter Lights

White wonderful clean soft snow.
Glittering pine smelling Christmas tree,
Yummy tasty cocoa,
Warm cozy fireplace,
Beautiful twinkling candle light.
Amazing Christmas songs fill the air,
When you hear the songs you know,
Winter is here!
Jaylene Hoang, Grade 4

Samantha

S mart with math
A dventurous when outdoors
M ischievous about family
A nnoyed by my brother
N ice to people
T all like the rest of my family
H ardworking like my grampy
A fraid of heights
Samantha Gagnon, Grade 5

Kaydence

K ind
A mazing
Y ankees
D aring
E vil
N aughty
C laustrophobic
E asy going
Kaydence Pelkey, Grade 5

Feelings

Hearts are red,
The sky is blue,
Friends are sweet,
And so are you.
The sky is blue,
The sun is yellow,
Winter days are cold,
And summer days are mellow.
Abigail Kelly, Grade 6

I Am

I am a Coventry little league baseball player
I wonder if I will get hit
I hear the bat hitting the ball and me rounding first base it was good
I see the ball flying high in the blue sky
I want to hit a home run out of the little league field
I am a Coventry little league baseball player

I pretend to hit the ball in the air
I feel loose when I hit the ball in the air it feels exciting
I touch the bat and ball
I worry about striking out or not getting a good hit
I am a Coventry little league baseball player

I understand if I strikeout or make an error
I say in my head, "hit"
I dream that I get a home run
I try to at least play good
I hope my team will get better and win the playoffs
I am a Coventry little league baseball player
Allen Benevides, Grade 5

I Am

I am a boy and I like baseball
I wonder if I'm good at baseball
I hear all the bats clinking and the pitchers release the ball and the baseball wind
I see bats and baseballs and parents screaming to kids
I want to go to the Major League and play for Boston
I am a boy and I like baseball

I pretend I am in the Major League playing
I feel my glove on my hand and the ball in my glove
I touch my bat and glove
I worry if I strikeout or make a bad fielding error
I am a boy and I like baseball

I understand if I strikeout or make an error
I say nice play to teammates
I dream that I get a home run
I try to get a hit
I hope I get a home run some day in junior baseball
I am a boy and I like baseball
Anthony Benevides, Grade 5

Winter!

Snowy, snowy Christmas night.
Hanging out with my family.
Eating yummy Christmas treats.
Also eating a scrumptious Christmas feast.
Baking sweet cookies and toasting fluffy marshmallows.
Drinking mouthwatering hot chocolate to melt my marshmallow down.
Buying warm clothes for the homeless.
Warm blankets to keep me from getting the flu.
Eating tasty homemade chicken noodle soup.
   A perfect winter day.
Mikayla Jean-Louis, Grade 4

The Elf on the Shelf

An elf was sitting on the shelf.
An elf was sitting by himself.
He was very gay.
He smiled all day.
He's like a Ninja, very stealth.
Vincenzo Varriale, Grade 6

Fat Paws

There was a guy named Santa Claus.
Who had some deer with big, fat, paws.
He had a bad elf,
Who sat on a shelf,
Who let the deer in just because.
Meghan Burton, Grade 6

Shoes

Shoes — all types, all kinds, all colors
Shoes — high heels, flats, tennis shoes
Shoes — leather, suede, cloth
Shoes — green, black, or blue
Shoes — I love shoes
Brooke Harris, Grade 5

Nature Is Dancing

Trees sway from side to
side, butterflies glide, while birds
sing, flowers blooming.
Charlee Letner, Grade 5

Winter

beautiful snowflakes
like shining diamonds at night
glistening like stars
Cassidy Smith, Grade 5

Fall Sparkles

Fall is wonderful
Leaves dazzle in the sunlight
I revel the fall
Laurel Wilson, Grade 6

The Sequoia Tree

Tall and towering
The biggest trees in the world
The Sequoia tree
Michael Kuzminskiy, Grade 5

Summer

Time for bees to buzz
Butterflies drinking nectar
Time for vacation
Mitchell Freshour, Grade 5

Blue

When I think of blue, I think of the seaside and blue birds chirping in the sky.
I think of a big, blue, bouncy-ball making children laugh with joy.
I think of a globe with a lot of blue for the sea,
Or my blue folder with my drawings.
I think of the smell of blueberry pie,
Or the veins that keep me up and running.
Sometimes I feel blue when I'm sad.
Blue is a great big blue shark, swimming in the sea, going CHOMP!
I think of a blue train going choo choooo,
A big, blue, blasting jet plane in the sky,
Or a blue shopping bag with my blue toy race cars.
My two pet fish are blue.
Blue is the color of a magic potion that is filled with evil.
Blue is a diamond shining in the moon light.
Blue is the cover to a book about blue cars going zoom zoom,
A blue butterfly with bright blue wings,
A falling snow flake.
A paint brush with blue paint.
Or my blue eyes.
Nathan Rhoads, Grade 4

Blue

Blue is the color of my nails, painted to match my blue uniform for cheerleading,
The beautiful sent of raspberry markers and forget-me-nots
And the feeling you get when you step on a blue Lego
(Man, does that hurt!),
The pretty blue birds chirping a song just right outside!
And when my blue homework gets handed out,
Oh and my fresh warm blanket just coming from the wash.
The sweet, juicy taste of the blueberries popping juice in your mouth.
I smell the sea salt of the blue ocean crashing up on the sand.
Blue is the look of the spinning blue sky
And the clouds swaying above the earth.
Blue is the color of sadness when someone calls you names,
The beautiful blue of our flag to worship our county!
Blue is the color of our blood running though our body
Blue is the smell and taste of the blue raspberry ices,
Blue is the taste of the blue icing that's on your nose!
Blue is the color of our earth spinning around.
Blue is the color of the blank computer screen.
This is the beautiful color of… Blue!!!!
Makayla DiCarlantonio, Grade 4

Serenity

At dusk the beach was silent,
Except for the waves crashing along the shore.
Little bubbles of sand and water popped and sizzled into nothing.
Seagulls soared in the sky, squawking at each other, looking for food scraps.
In the distance a single boat drifted across the water
as a cool breeze hit against its sail.
Though the beach was abandoned,
there was one red, white and blue bucket
with a small red shovel in it
left behind probably by a child.
Oh, such serenity!
Emily Weiskopf, Grade 6

Coldness

I lay in my house
On a dark black night
It feels like I'm in the Arctic
It's so cold
Then a white snowflake starts to fall
After that, thousands start to fall
I could tell that it was a nice winter night
Ava Santisi, Grade 5

Fall

The season of fall is all around
The leaves are dropping to the ground
Beautiful colors of yellow, orange, and red

Now the trees are bare overhead
When you smell that cool autumn breeze
You know you're at ease
Alexander Omlor, Grade 6

The Beautiful Butterfly

The wings sparkle in the sky
As it gently perches on a branch
And does a quick little prance
They are colorful like the rainbow
And their instincts are fine
As they carelessly fly
Around the world
Melinda Chao, Grade 5

Fall

Fall
Colorful, windy
Jumping, falling leaves, raking
Pumpkins, vacation, spring break, flowers
Blooming, playing, planting
Warm, sunny
Spring
Josephine Mercado, Grade 5

Dilophosaurus

I am a dilophosaurus
Green as a crocodile
I run around and spit acid
I can run faster than a velociraptor
I can eat other dinosaurs
I can be in packs
I am a dilophosaurus
Jaydin Wiggins, Grade 5

A Great Heron

In the last light of the dusk
A great heron
Flies to the big blue lake
All animals get out of its path
For it is the great heron
Adelaide Orsetti, Grade 5

Waiting for My Letter

I am waiting for the judges to see if I had won
a poem contest with my poem and picture I had drawn
I reckon it's going to take a while
in fact, my poem has been sent to a place that is more than a mile
so, I hug on my teddy bear so tight
that I think he might explode since he's so light
I tell my mom and dad that I might burst soon
so, to calm me down, they put on my favorite tune
the next morning when the mail came in at dawn
one of the letters titled, Poem, said that I had won
I tell my parents that I'm so happy, that I can gobble up some blue cheese
so, I ask them, may I enter another poem please
Farhaanah Ahmad Ali, Grade 4

Thanksgiving Is for Fond Memories

T hanksgiving is our favorite holiday.
H aving my family together is fun.
A t the table is where we finish all the turkey.
N ever eat fast because then you will get a stomach ache.
K ind people come to our Thanksgiving party.
S ome of our friends are really silly on this day.
G etting the dessert is fun when you finish the turkey.
I love eating the delicious meal.
V ery happy we are at the table.
I am thankful for Thanksgiving and I will
N ever forgot how much we've ate, and will think of others who don't have food.
G etting the turkey from the market is our joy.
Melany Eyzaguirre, Grade 6

Halloween Night

Halloween night
Halloween night
O Halloween night
On such a night ghouls and goblins
Come out for a fright
On this very night of All Hallow's Eve
Vampires, werewolves, skeletons
And every spooky creature comes out for a trick or treat
Go to the edge of the forest if you want a fright from a gruesome creature
But a word or wise to the brave
If you go to the edge of the forest on Halloween night and see a specter
Be careful because the specter you see might be your own face
Cemile Hasirci, Grade 6

Aries

Son of my mom Pody and my dad Syed
Who loves to play the drums and sports
with my family and with my friends
loves swimming
Who gives my old clothes to those in need
Who fears poisonous spiders, snakes, and never coming back to school
Who'd like to go to Africa to help those in need
Who dreams of being a famous drummer like my dad
A student of Clover Street School
Newton-Campbell
Aries Newton-Campbell, Grade 4

Winter Snow
I love to throw white, winter snow,
My feet sink down very low.
I turn to an ice cube outside,
To stay nice and cozy, I tried.
Fairly fun for friends and I,
It seemed like the snow learned to fly.
My crew is big and strong but few,
And that is a fact that is true,
But do not underestimate us,
Because soon your fort will bust,
And my legion will stand on your dust,
My team has all of my complete trust,
Playing in the winter snow is fun,
But now the snow skirmish is done.
Cameron Jones, Grade 5

Basketball
The players all running
It is quite stunning
The ball goes smack
And backboards crack

They pass the ball
It smacks the wall
The crowds all root
While the players shoot

Half time strikes
The coaches yell yikes
I make baskets
Coaches blow gaskets
Jeremy Brown, Grade 5

Dogs
Dogs everywhere all need our care,
But there's only one dog in mind,
Her name is Lucy Loo but I'm aware,
She is definitely one of a kind,
She has shiny light brown golden hair,
She has a loud low pitched bark,
I really treat her with more care,
When it's food time she's a shark,
I play with her more than modern warfare,
And all the faces she can make,
Silly, happy, and also really square,
At night she always keeps me awake,
She is one of the really rare,
And when she yawns there's an earthquake.
David Loftis, Grade 5

Emma
E xpecting good grades
M arvelous at gymnastics
M exican-American
A nimals are my life!
Emma Canales, Grade 4

Dear Mother
As I look back on my life,
I find myself wondering.
Did I remember to thank you,
for all that you have done for me?
For all of the times you were
by my side to help me
celebrate my successes
and accept my defeats?
Or for teaching me the value
of hard work, judgment,
courage, and honesty?
I wonder if I've ever thanked you
for the simple things
and the laughter.
Jakyah Boykin, Grade 6

The Beach
The gentle water
Washes up to shore
Making a loud crash
As it falls onto the
Soft golden sand
Then
The breeze blows
Quietly
And makes me smile as
I hear children laughing
And splashing each other
In
The crystal clear
WATER
Hannah Mixon, Grade 4

Eat Your Words
long ago
when the saying
"eat your words"
was invented
there was no way you could actually
"eat your words"
until one day —
that marvelous day —
when someone created
something called
ALPHABET SOUP
and from that day forth
you can now
"eat your words"
Daniela Alvear, Grade 5

Saint's Jersey
Black, gold
Run, sweat, play
Awesome to wear important places
Special shirt!
Major Tomeo, Grade 4

Through the Looking Glass
Through the looking glass I saw
something big and, something small
Something pink, and something not
Something bad or so I thought
I was blind but now I'm not
Something good has yet to come

Through the looking glass I've seen
something not so mean
As I looked as I saw
my thoughts began to crawl

Gazing through this magical glass
I begin to change

Things aren't always as they seem
Don't listen to what they say
Ellie Reinhart, Grade 4

Cosmo Is the Best
How I love thee, for he makes me happy
I love him so much that he is my joy
Though he is not that yappy
Yes he is my dog and not just a toy

I hope that all shall love him like I
I shall be ever so tightly shut
If you look upon him and say oh my
For I love him and he is not a mutt

His name might be Cosmo and he's a show
And he is my favorite dog
And when he performs I seem to glow
When he plays and jumps over a log

I do not care what you think
For I love him and we're in sync
Kierra Shillingburg, Grade 5

Soccer
We wear cleats
That we put on our feet
I love soccer

We play with a soccer ball
Not with a football
I love soccer

We play against a team
That we want to cream
I love soccer

The game makes me glad
But sometimes it makes me sad
I love soccer
Alan Arceo, Grade 6

The Beautiful Flower
Madison Aretz
She is a beautiful, enchanting, hibiscus flower.
She is as pretty as the shining night sky.
She loves writing enchanting stories, swimming in the fascinating sea, and being with awesome family members.
Madison Aretz, Grade 6

Purple
The color of ancient kings in the past,
A shade that is built to last

A tone that was once rare on archaic Earth,
A tone now widely regarded with mirth

Many things are the color of me,
But for some, I am all they can see

I am regarded as the mark of magic,
The wash of wizardry, and of valiant victory

When people look for a creative spark,
My red-blue fusion erases their question mark

When leaders hold me in their grip,
I will be sure not to slip

Described as the tint of riches,
And the theme of ambitious wishes

I color the hearts of those in nobility,
And also the souls living in luxury

I will prevail as the pigment of peace,
And the ever-present tinge of wisdom

I am purple
Shana Reddy, Grade 6

French Stripe Red
French Stripe Red is the ink you use to correct.
The glittering fireworks on the 4th of July.
The striped tie your dad wears.

The sparkling ornaments on your Christmas tree.
The smell of apple pie at your Thanksgiving Feast.
The swish, and splash of the cranberry bog.
The autumn breeze rushing through your hair,
or the velvet curtains that fly through the air.

It's the French flag with partners blue and white waving
down to the streets below, watching children play all day
and night.

It's the feeling you get when you want to burst,
or simply the way you feel when you're embarrassed
or hurt.
Taylor DeFlorio, Grade 5

Thanksgiving
It's about cooking
Going to the crowded grocery store
And then having to go back for more

It's about everyone coming
Loud around the house
Nowhere sounds like a mouse

It's about talking to people
Talking to people you haven't seen in years
And putting your glasses up to say cheers

It's about getting hungry
And very voracious
Smelling the turkey and going "Goodness gracious!"

It's about varieties of food on your plate
Salty and sweet
There is so much to eat

It's about being too full
You feel so bloated from the meat
But you have to go in for just one more treat

It's about saying your goodbyes
Feeling sad that it's over
But you are happy tomorrow for leftovers
Madeline Long, Grade 5

When I Am…
When I am fatigued, I am as tired as a grumpy old cat
that has been besieging mice for hours,
running up and down side to side

When I am melancholy, I am like glum Eeyore on a
stormy day being doused with rain

When I am irked, I am like a furious jackhammer
pounding at the ground

When I am joyful, I am like jubilant Penn Web when
he first meets Crash

When I am famished, I am as hungry as a baby bird
waiting for its mother to get back with worms for dinner

When I am moody, I am like a caged tiger that got
its food taken away by a zoo keeper and wants it back
Jack Milewczik, Grade 6

Hunting

The air is cold,
And the ground is bold.

We went over a peak,
And found a little creek.

The grounds is filled with crispy frost,
I hope we don't get lost.

The partridge are drumming,
And we are coming.

I heard a spring,
There he was it is the king.

He had a crown,
But it was a tannish brown.

It was a buck,
Not a duck.

I pulled the trigger,
My dinner just got bigger.
Wyatt Stanley, Grade 5

Ode to Best Friends

We fight, yeah sure, we make up
All the time. It's what we do.

Best friends
We share secrets and
Tell each other everything

Best friends
No matter what people think, we're family
We would do anything for each other

Best friends
You mean the world to me
Even when you let out a secret
I know it was an accident

Best friends
We go together like peanut butter and jelly
We work together like a pencil and paper

Best friends
No matter what people think,
We're family
Ariane Lanes, Grade 5

Winter Dreams

Trees bare down with snow
The grey fox burrows his hole
Cold long nights cast dreams
Sarah Stacy, Grade 6

Hunting

Hunting is a very fun sport,
It is not always very short.
The bullets go out with a "Bang,"
The fight of a buck goes "Clang, Clang."
The White-Tailed deer is what I hunt,
They even sometimes like to grunt.
As smart as whips are the female deer,
They come out when they know it's clear.
The White-Tailed deer runs very fast,
They can also kick with a blast.
I like to hunt in a stand,
We hunt on 1,100 acres of land.
I can also hunt the wild boar,
Or just watch the eagle soar.
Devin Roe, Grade 5

Let Us Thank Those Brave Soldiers

Let us thank those brave soldiers,
 who fought to make men free.
Let us thank those brave soldiers,
 who died for liberty.

They marched upon the dreaded battlefield,
 their faces strong and stern.
And never would they yield,
 lest their country burn.

Let us honor those brave soldiers,
 the living and the slain.
Without those brave soldiers,
 we never would maintain!
Christiana Beaupre, Grade 6

How Fire Became Red

Fire, fire starting white
In the forest of the night.
Keeps us warm and bundled up tight
without a care.

They put it out, with water as
clean as soap. "Let it burn,"
they said, but it was not to be.
Now the fire's red with rage.

Fire, fire starting white
in the forest of the night.
Keeps us warm and bundled up tight
without a care.
Genesis Espaillat, Grade 6

Mary

M erciful
A wesome
R adiant
Y oung
Aaron Henry, Grade 4

Colors

Colors are the world
Colors are us
Without them the world would be sad
We would be dull.

Not as beautiful
That's why you should thank God
For it I have
You should too.

It just wouldn't be the same
Without colors I wouldn't like it
You probably wouldn't too
Just think without colors.

If you woke up with no colors
You wouldn't like it
I wouldn't say I don't
Want a world without colors
You might regret it.
Ashton Bragg, Grade 6

You

You're my love
You're my heart
I love you until
We depart

We're together forever
I know we're broke
But we can make
It as long as
We're together

Grapes are purple
Violets are blue
I turn red
Because of you

You're my love
You're my heart
I love you
Until we depart
Angelina McDowell, Grade 6

A Night Under the Stars

Stars shining bright
on this dark and cold night
a cool summer breeze
don't worry you won't freeze
It's a beautiful sight
because the stars are shining bright
on this beautiful
summer
night under the stars
Deborah John, Grade 5

I Like Trains

I like trains.
Some go fast and some go slow.
Trains travel far and wide.
Trains can't stop.
Trains can only slow down.
Trains take one mile to slow down.
Cameron Upshaw, Grade 4

Friendship

Friendship is like two peas in a pod
It smells like a campfire and s'mores
It tastes like cookies and milk
It sounds like wind and waves
It feels like pajamas and slippers
It lives in my heart and soul
Jordyn Chepolis, Grade 6

Destruction

Destruction is death
It smells like fear
It tastes like sorrow
It sounds like a freight train
It feels like torture
It lives deep in peoples' minds
Matthew Kerstetter, Grade 6

Snowmen Fun

Once a snowman thought he was cool,
But really he was just a fool.
He was having fun,
Being in the sun.
I found him playing in my pool.
Taylor Dill, Grade 6

No Freedom

"I'm free," I say.
Until they catch me at the bay
saying, "hey, you're my slave."
All I want is to feel freedom, but all
I have is this.
Jasmine Padgett, Grade 6

If Kids Ruled School

Let's go on strike kids!
No more homework or schoolwork
Let's only have gym
Let us have recess all day
No more school forever kids!
Andrew O'Malley, Grade 5

Superb Sunny Spring

Flowers like to bloom
In the emerald, fertile grass
On a warm morning
Morrissey Empke, Grade 6

Abigail

An eerie enigmatic voice came from inside the awful abandoned house.
Was it a genuine ghost?
Was it a hazy host?
But no, it was Abigail whose voice was as faint as a mouse.

The legend says that Abigail was maliciously murdered by her merciless mother.
And if you say "come play with me,"
Her gauzy ghost you will see.
She had even frightened the lives of two brothers.

Her vague voice had come again once more.
"Come and play with me,
For your future you will see."
I never came back from behind that door.
Alexis Saleh, Grade 6

Thanksgiving

Thank you for all my ears can hear —
Knock, knock, and knock here comes the Thanksgiving company
Crunch, crunch, crunch there goes parents biting down to the wishbone
Bank, bank the table topples as everyone storms for the repast

Thank you for all my eyes can see —
Pilgrims, pumpkin pie, parade and prayers are to be keepsake
Turkeys in the pen are crispy roasted golden meals a day later
People viewing the Thanksgiving Parade is like watching a diversity of football games

Thank you for all my tongue can taste —
Gravy encompassing mashed potatoes on the colorful plate of repast
Apple pie with burned crust and creamy insides is mouthwatering together
Ending the meal with colorful M&M cookies, nothing is better than that…
Aidan Mallon, Grade 6

Home

The world goes to sleep, but nobody knows who hides in the shadows all alone.
War breaks out, people are fighting.
Citizens are dying, but most of all, many are crying.
Everyone is sacrificing, killing,
and trying to keep their loved ones safe from perishing.
Nobody knows when it will stop or if it will go.
They all know they'll never see home.
Kids are asking "Where's mom and dad?"
But people just answer "You should be glad."
When their family is safe and at rest, people's hearts are beating in their chests.
You never know the dangers of this world; pollution, war, and so many unheard.
You just need to know,
To live your life slow.
Savor the moments, for in these moments you can go home.
Rebecca Blitz, Grade 5

What Freedom Really Is

Freedom is knowing that there is nothing to be afraid of.
Freedom is a feeling so powerful you can hurt it and it will still stand up.
Freedom is a trail you can walk,
A lane to peace.
Jack DeMetrick, Grade 5

Like a Girl, by a Girl
She makes a move around him,
Ha! Someone said.
"You just got beaten by a girl,"
Someone else said.
In sadness,
That girl hangs her head.

He swings, and misses,
You bat like a girl,
Someone replied,
Luckily,
No girl
Was by.

Cooking,
Cleaning,
So called a girl's job,
It's good the women,
Started objecting.

Like a girl, and by a girl,
Is a hurtful phrase,
But it's still used today.
Amanda Cheng, Grade 5

The Moth
When I open my eyes,
I see rain coming down
hard on the window.

Then,
a little moth comes.
It flaps its wings
back and forth,
over and over again.

It stays there and
stares at
me,
wondering
what is inside.

Then the sun comes
and it goes
away,
flapping its
wings
back and forth,
over and over again.
Angie Leung, Grade 5

Winter
Winter is too cold
The wind cuts through my jacket
The hot sun came out later
Branston Justus, Grade 6

Fall Magic
I know it's fall when
Leaves change colors
From green to
Orange and red.

I know it's fall when
People are raking
Leaves into a pile,
And jumping in them.

I know it's fall when
I am standing outside,
Early in the morning,
Feeling the wind blow in my face.

I know it's fall when
I am eating pumpkin pie,
And cooking pumpkin seeds
With my wonderful family.
Cecilia Dieffenthaller, Grade 6

Football
Some say the best sport ever
Some hate it most
Even though you see it coast to coast

But I don't care what they say
I love it, even though I always lose
That's why my team doesn't slay

When you have 14 kids on your team
You don't get off the field
When you tackle someone the play yields

It makes me very tired
Since I'm always playing
I think the league got my coach fired

I always get at least 2 tackles a game
And always hold my block
No kid plays the same
Nicholas Neyland, Grade 6

Spring Has Sprung
Spring has sprung.
Oh, what fun!

Birds are chirping.
Flowers are blooming.
Children are playing.
Rainbows shine.
Colors unite.

Spring has sprung.
Oh, what fun!
Ayah Elzomor, Grade 5

Dark, My Rooster
Dark, oh what a Dark.
He will leave a dash of spark
in your heart.
His feathers are made up of
light brown, black, and gold.
His eyes are black,
and so bright, they could glow in the dark.
Dark once rode in a car.
He once ate a chocolate bar.
He will go to your door to ask for rice.
He never has lice.
Though Dark had a terrible loss,
of his sister Light,
who was the boss,
Dark is my rooster.
When I am sad, he is a booster.
That is why I love Dark
with all my heart.
Denisse Miguel, Grade 6

We All
I, you, me, we're all different.
It does not matter if we are all cute,
All mean,
All nice.
In a way we are all different.
At times in our life when
We will be mad,
Sad,
Teased,
Bullied, upset,
We may also think that
We are unlovable or
Ignored.
We are all wanted and will be
Remembered one day.
So there is no reason to cry,
We all, we all, we all will fall.
But we will always come back.
Nevaeh Smith, Grade 6

Blue
The wing of a blue bird
The sky
The ocean waves
The heavy wind blowing me away
The waves splashing into me
The bird flapping its wings away
A juicy blueberry
A sweet blueberry pie
A cupcake's frosting
A day when no one wants to play with me
I'm the luckiest kid in the world
I have nothing to do
Blue can make you express yourself
Jamir Cuevas, Grade 4

I Am

I am kind
I wonder about the future
I hear the wind blowing
I see the trees lose their leaves
I want to be helpful
I am kind

I pretend with my friends
I feel the cold fall ground
I touch my glasses
I worry about my family
I cry when I get hurt
I am kind

I understand that things sometimes don't go my way
I say good morning
I dream about animals
I try to do my best
I hope to get better grades
I am kind

Robert Cote, Grade 6

White

I walk through the halls peacefully with panache,
not wanting to cause harm,
but no one really notices me.
I am known for my beauty and grace,
I really am,
but I am conservative and secretive.
I peek through the dark, depressing walkways,
and I find everyone staring at me.
I just want to be unnoticed, innocent,
like a blank sheet of paper.
My purity shows through like a shining moon at night,
noticed by everyone and everything,
just because I appear to be good at anything.
I seem to float through the room like a cloud,
With every step,
and people can't get enough of me.
Everyone loves me,
they "ooh" and "ahh,"
saying that I am absolutely, positively, innocently perfect.
White

Anna Cancilla, Grade 6

Memorial

Fight for us
The US army has fought for is all these years
We should give them all cheers
Our brothers, sisters, fathers, mothers
Have died to protect us
I am so glad I can say thanks
To all of those on Memorial Day
So I would like to say
I love you Memorial Day

Gabrielle Wesolowski, Grade 6

My Relationship with Food

I hate a lot of food
Don't you dare conclude
Dessert is better than chitchat
Because it is always true that
Eating is lame
So please don't try to claim
My food tastes kind of good
Because there is a high likelihood
I'm eating something that I hate
Don't try to demonstrate
I like what is on my plate

(Now read the poem from the bottom line up to the top line.)

Isaac Rajagopal, Grade 5

Legs

My legs help me run,
They are always on the move,
Especially when I am having fun
Sometimes my legs need a rest,
Usually at night
When my legs are put to the test

My legs are as good as they get,
Tan and nice and long
Sometimes they will also get licked by my pet
They will be with me forever
Wherever I go
Let's enjoy the lifetime together

Alyssa Papasodero, Grade 6

Where I'm From

I'm from snowy slopes and green grassy fields.
From blue sparkling water and brown dirt fields

I'm from the little t-ball field to the big softball field.
From the little Como field to the big Shark field.

I'm from the little green circles to the big black diamonds.
I'm from the swimming lessons to the big, deep ocean.

I'm from little school in the Burrow to the big school in Mystic.
I'm from the little Judy Moody books to the big chapter books.

That's where I'm from!!!

Carly Constantine, Grade 5

Supper Time

The voice of the lion was silent
It was about to be supper time
There in the grass was a gazelle
It was a sitting duck
The stillness of the lion was magnificent
Suddenly, the lion was sprinting through the grass
And it was supper time!

Michael Robak, Grade 5

Christmas
I see Nick the Elf
I smell a cinnamon pinecone
I hear Santa saying, "ho, ho, ho,"
I taste delicious chocolate chip cookies
I touch all of the presents looking for mine
Christmas
Ryan Zajac, Grade 4

Pandas
P uffy black and white
A nimal is big
N othing is cuter
D ad pandas are big
A n awesome animal
S o cute when babies
Mikaela Abernathy, Grade 5

Rabbits
Rabbits, bunnies, hares,
they're mammals not fish or birds.
Rabbits are cool creatures,
They eat, sleep, and play.
Some walk on leashes, some lick
I love rabbits every day.
Hannah Keep, Grade 4

My Big Family
My family is nice
I have a big family
some of them live in
Virginia and Pennsylvania
I have a sister and
brother that are loving.
Jasmine Patterson, Grade 4

The Macabe Miracle
Eight candles are lit
Delicious latkes in the oven
Hot cookies in my hand
Yummy food in my mouth
The last guest walks through the door
Happy Hanukkah
Isaac Koenigsberg, Grade 4

Ode to Summer
S unny days
U nder a beach umbrella
M agnificent
M akes people happy
E xcellent weather
R ide to the pool and beach
Daniela Munoz, Grade 4

The Siplamario
The siplamario was a feral looking fellow
with a joyful, joyful look in his eyes.
It had a strong love for unique bow ties.
He loved the bright, bright sun light,
but was terrified of night.
This creature was the vanguard and bellwether of the digiloos,
these digiloos hopped like kangaroos.
They went hop, hop, hop.
The siplamario ordered these digiloos to climb up their trees and don't stop till the top!
The siplamario lugged back to his tree too,
carrying his voluminous weight, thinking and regretting what he had just ate.
Snore, snore, snore, what a bore, bore, bore.
Suddenly, there was a knock at the door, door, door.
It was his friends, party, party!
They were so caring, hearty, hearty
They had great fun. They danced around and spun!
They didn't stop till the rise of the sun.
Balloons, balloons galore!
The siplamario couldn't ask for more!
The wily siplamario dozed off and began to snore, snore, snore.
Brianna Maddonni, Grade 6

The Book
A story, a setting, a plot and more; adjectives, nouns and verbs galore!
Emotions are present and bore is alack; but the creepies and crawlies and monsters are back.
The sunrise and twilight, the noon and the eve.
And even the sadness and mourning of bereave.
The happy the joy and the love fills the air.
But the anger and hate lingers everywhere.
Regret and guilt conquer the minds.
Fought by others of their kinds.
Many terrains have been crossed.
Even the lands of the lost.
Things have been seen that are not as they seem.
Flowers and gemstones that shimmer and gleam.
Waterfalls, dragons, gold and the lore.
Oceans, animals, plants at the core.
The sky, the stars, the planets all there.
The distance beyond them gives a scare.
Here lies the place where the inspiration stands.
Inside the magic of the hands.
The typing or writing created the start.
What is read is the book and it comes from the heart.
Morgan Deville, Grade 6

The Brave
Veterans, you are brave.
When the time came, you left your family so America could be free.
When gunshots blocked out all sound, you kept fighting.
When friendships were lost to death, you kept pushing.
When there was nowhere else to run, you didn't hide.
When your struggles got the best of you and tears fell like rain, you gathered your courage
and fought to live another day.
And when the smoke cleared, our flag still waved, showing to all that America is free.
After all...America is home of the brave.
Colten Sakadales, Grade 6

When a Poem Is Written

When a poem is written,
Your thoughts should flow,
Flow from your mind,

Down to your arm,
And though your pen,
Filled with emotion.
When a poem is written,
You may be in silence,
There may be music.
When a poem is written,
Many ideas cross the mind,
Some may be thought to be terrible,
Use every idea,
Fix it later.
When a poem is written,
Your thoughts are expressed,
Your mind is clear,
When a poem is written,
You choose what happens,
It is your story
When a Poem is Written.
Christian Thompson, Grade 6

Most Thankful For

Alive and living
As free as I can be
Allowed to be me

I can go to sleep
Feeling safe and secure
With a roof over my head
To make sure
I am safe

I have a loving family
That makes me happy
They feed me
They clothe me
And gave me a home
They care
They understand
They forgive and forget
And a lot more
But most of all
They love me
And I love them
Jessie Olson, Grade 6

Grandparents Are…

The most thoughtful people I know.
The best hug-givers.
Always thinking of me first.
Always there for me when I need them.
The most loving people ever.
Chloe Oudin, Grade 6

My Hands

I love my hands and you should too
I can do so much with them
I can play video games
I love my hands and you should too

I love my hands and you definitely should
I can catch a football
I can play basketball
I love my hands and you definitely should

I love my hands so much
I can ride a bike
I can draw
I love my hands so much
Joey Cuthbert, Grade 6

Useless Things

A spider without a silky web
A dog with a precious bark
A pencil without lead graphite
A sun without its powerful shine
A clock without its ticking hands
A boat without a long bow
Paint without a small brush
A desk without a chair
Water without a bottle
A picture without a beautiful frame
Scissors without a sharp blade
Tape without a roll
A light without a wall switch
Our world without a sea
Alexander Bardy Jr., Grade 4

Green

It starts as a miniscule seed
underneath a layer of
soft, warm soil
alive and young
ready to grow
expanding up and down
roots, and stems, and leaves
taller taller taller
growing confident
opening up
blooming beautifully
the sun's warmth creating
a flower:
pure happiness
Zoe Dvorin, Grade 6

Mr. Squirrel

Up! up! up! up! up!
Climbs so high he'll touch the sky
Crack! Down goes squirrel.
Emily Creamer, Grade 4

Autumn Breeze

Billowing breeze blowing the leaves,
Creating chills through the air,
Softly skimming from here to there,
Sending tingling feelings down your sleeves.

Down the path a creaking gate,
Clanging flagpoles across the lanes,
Next you hear rattling window panes,
Fall was definitely not late.

Whisking wind and wafting smells,
Soaring spirits in the sky,
Serene and peaceful but oh so high,
Autumn air is absolutely swell.
Emma Sullivan, Grade 6

Halloween

Crackling candy wrappers everywhere
Trick or treat, time to be sweet
Scary costumes can be neat
Freaky ghouls are out for a scare.

Jack-o-lantern lights up the night
Haunted houses are a fright
Full moon could be bright
Black cats wonder in the dark sights.

Halloween decor has some flare
Creepy stories can be eerie
Vampires could make you weary
Monster you have to beware.
Andrea Delgado, Grade 6

The Love of Christmas

Christmas bells everywhere.
Everybody's spreading love and care.
Everyone is dancing with cheer.
Look at how many people are here.
Listening to the bells
and breathing the Christmas smells.
A big Christmas tree
and kids roaming around free.
Ring, ring, ding-a-ling
I just want to hear the bells sing.
Looking up at the stars,
I wonder if Santa is close or far.
Why must this day end when
I love it here with my Christmas friends.
Grace Westin, Grade 4

Soldier

Fight for freedom
Middle East territory
Twenty-four hours a day
For world peace—bravely
Hagen Stamps-Hill, Grade 5

Again and Again
Again and again you do it another time.
You think you're cool because you leave me out.
I'm famished for power. You leave me out again
and again.
It irks me over and over.
I just want the respect I deserve.
I want to be your friend, but you don't care.
I say hi but you push me away.
I'm not as good at soccer, as you leave me out?
I just want an Everyday Hero to help me out.
But I don't have one because you scream and shout.
I just want to be in your group chat, but you push me away.
But now I see it doesn't matter to me because
I'm…
ALL IN!
Madeleine DiGaetano, Grade 6

Merry Christmas!
Pretty bows and wrappings of all sort,
Boxes of size, skinny or short
Placed under the light-up tree
Waiting there for them to see
What Santa left them that night.
Dashing away before the morning light
Piles of them lying there,
Twinkling in the morning glare
But, what's the toy or prize,
Is not the meaning
for Christmas being
so jolly and bright.
Where merry songs whisper throughout the night
And everyone is joyful for all their family and friends
Who are hoping this special night never ends.
Anna Calkins, Grade 5

Thanksgiving
Thank you for all my eyes can see…
holiday cornucopia with oranges, walnuts, and
apples helping hands putting on the lace tablecloth
parades of people barraging in my house for Thanksgiving

Thank you for all my tongue can taste…
mom's scrumptious, creamy pumpkin pie,
crisp apple cider slaking my thirst,
magnificent turkey cooked to perfection.

Thank you for all my nose can smell…
aroma of splendid mashed potatoes, turkey, stuffing,
and pumpkin pie
mouth watering pleasant carmel apples getting
ready to be put on the table.
Emerson Rougey, Grade 6

Two Elements
Water and nature are two different things
Water refreshes you on a hot day
Nature shows you the beauty of the Earth
Even though they are different, they are both elements
They work together to help our home.
Giselle DoCarmo, Grade 4

Create Your Own
A poem is a place that your imagination soars
You can have a land made up of fours
Pirates could attack
There might be a head on your back
There could even be giant boars.
Jewel Hicks, Grade 4

Hanukkah
Hanukkah is blue and silver
Hanukkah smells like gelt and burning candles
Hanukkah tastes like potato latkes and doughnuts
Hanukkah sounds like unwrapping paper
Hanukkah makes me feels happy
Hannah Dunn, Grade 4

Winter Is Coming
Winter is coming
Steamy breath on a cold day
Frozen toes in boots

Winter is coming
Snowflakes falling like white lace
Falling to the ground

Winter is coming
A white blanket on the ground
Made up of soft snow

Winter is coming
Snow angels and snowmen too
Piles of snow on the lawn

Winter is coming
Some warm cocoa after play
Some chicken soup too

Winter is coming
Warm flannel pajamas on
Reading by the fire

Winter is coming
Buried in blankets at night
Another day soon
Kathryn Barrus, Grade 5

Assumption
A bird, but not a bird,
Sat on a tree, but not a tree.
Began to sing, but didn't sing
About the leaves that weren't leaves.
And while the bird, but not a bird,
Began to whistle, but didn't whistle,
About the worms that weren't worms,
I listened, but didn't hear
All the words.
Teysia Tuff, Grade 6

Christmas
C hrist was born
H e's the best
R eindeers on the roof
I t's my favorite holiday
S anta is watching
T he presents are one of the best things
M y family is these
A delicious turkey
S anta gives everybody gifts
Matthew Hurley, Grade 6

The Falcon
Grey winged falcon flying high
Soaring through the midnight sky
Always remembering where to go
Never searching high or low

Gathering prey as food for kin
Remembering where they've always been
Through the trees above the pine
She finds her home in the soft moonshine
Alison Riker, Grade 6

Zip Lining
It was a cold day in October,
The wind was blowing colder,
We were zip lining in the trees,
So many zip lines I see.
The mountains were near,
The leaves were gold,
The valley was yellow and very bold.
I love zip lining in the trees,
Oh how I love the cold, cold breeze.
Emily Chaires, Grade 6

The Full Moon
On the night
Of a full moon
A firefly flew
Into the castle
Where there was
A sense of joy
Seeing the emperor with his children
Cole Hoover, Grade 5

Inspiration
Inspiration is everywhere
On the ground and in the air
So many things are inspirational, like
A photograph from long ago, think of all the mystery inside of it, what the
People were doing or what the photo means if there is a story or memory
Behind it,
Just imagine all the inspiration that one little object brings,
Or an elephant, the way it uses its trunk to pick up food or spray itself to
Cool down,
Just think about if two things so different can both bring so much
Inspiration to people just imagine
All the things in the world that could bring inspiration.
Madi O'Donnell, Grade 4

Yellow
Yellow is the eerie temporary glare of a glow stick in the night mist.
The glint of the setting sun in a raindrop on my bedroom window.
The yellow jacket claiming its territory puncturing your delicate skin
with its painful sting.
The dimpled juicy temptation of a lemon with a sting in my bitten lip.
The rhythmic beat of a tennis ball rebounding off a racket.
Yellow is the sound of mischievous minions wreaking havoc.
Bitter yellow burning flames stench.
A bunch of buttercups filling the room with their heavenly scent.
The sweet nectar getting slurped out of the honey suckle by a buzzing
hummingbird.
Creamy curl of cheese noodles dissolving with taste on my tongue.
Dylan Button, Grade 6

As Free as a Wild Horse
What is freedom I ask myself?
Freedom is a wild horse that roams in the wide open plain.
Freedom is the many stars around the universe glistening on their own.
Freedom is a penguin that can finally be free and take off into the air.
Freedom is like a caged animal that can break loose and explore the wide open world.
Freedom is the American flag that waves in the wind as if it were saying hello.
Freedom is the engine that moves our country forward.
Freedom is the prisoner that finally sees his family.
Freedom is a precious diamond that must be guarded and protected.
Freedom is a new born baby with nothing to trouble about.
Freedom is the statue of liberty standing tall without a fear.
Freedom is me and you with liberty and justice for all.
Colter Kendall, Grade 6

The Little Butterfly
The little Butterfly flaps her wings gently together
As if pounding two powdered donuts together
Her wings flap as delicate as glass
The tips of her wings glow with warmth from the sun while the rest is white as snow
Her little hands are cold as ice
The little butterfly flaps harder and harder, faster and faster as quick as a cat
Trying to seek her destination she flaps more quickly
Until finally she reaches the tree during sunset
And the little butterfly drifts off to sleep
Anaya Teye, Grade 4

Soccer

Cleats stomping,
Sweat dripping,
Crazy running,
Whistles blowing,
Halftime is coming!
Water spilling,
Referees sigh,
As it is a tie,
With a minute on the clock!
The more hard and strong we walk,
The better we will win,
And we try to kick again,
To eventually score and scream!
Together we get ice cream!
Addison Sapp, Grade 5

Animals

A bond did begin,
And I started to grin.
As we rode on that day,
The horse started to neigh.
There never is a barrier
According to the Boston Terrier,
Always without a care,
Chloe never just sits there.
Oh cats, cats, cats
They might be as small as bats.
Yet oh who cares,
Even if they're big as bears!
Whether it is woof, meow, or neigh,
My love for them all will never decay.
Jocelyn Madden, Grade 5

Blue

Freedom
Soaring
Like a bird in the sky
Like a fish in the sea
No limits
No borders
But sadness trickles in
Leaving home
Lost
But free
No fences
No boundaries
Independent and free
Blue
Delaynie McMillan, Grade 6

Spring

The sky is crying
it feeds all that lives
flowers are blooming
Avery Herring, Grade 6

Peaceful Fall

A cool breeze
Triggers falling leaves
Tall trees cover
Leaves and clean air hovers
Birds chirping
Squirrels lurking
Peace in every corner
Animals scatter
Hear a soft
Pitter patter
See color
It is a peaceful fall ya'll
Johanna Foudy, Grade 5

Troubles

There are times when you're in trouble
And no one is around
You turn to your loved ones
Who never let you down.
These are the people
That you can trust most of all.
Some people leave you
And make you fall.
You should always get up
And try again
Just like your mother and father
And loved ones said.
Kayla Robb, Grade 6

Sweet, Sweet Chocolate

I love Chocolate, it is so sweet,
It even gives me a great treat.
I can eat it for breakfast, lunch and dinner
And not worry about ever getting thinner.
It is my true love,
It is as twice as sweet as a dove.
My heart pounds when I get near it
I don't ever have to fear it.
I can eat it cold and
Every time I write it, it is in bold.
I hope chocolate is here to stay
I couldn't live even a day without it!
Caleb Crider, Grade 6

Life Is an Open Door

Life is an open door
for everyone you see
Life is an open door
of opportunity
Life is an open door
for all the world to be
Life is an open door
for all of you and me
Life is an open door
for all eternity
Carvin Watkins, Grade 6

Random Useless Things

A toaster that doesn't work
A water gun that doesn't squirt
A squeaky door
A slippery floor
A two dollar bill
A very dirty pill
A light that won't shine bright
An empty can of sprite
My cousin Peter's pet mouse
My little sister's pink doll house
A winter without white snow
A red sports car that doesn't go
A drone that won't fly very far
Storm Troopers from the Death Star
Jack Panossian, Grade 4

Halloween

Witches flying everywhere,
Some are flying above your hair.
Skeletons and spiders give me fright,
But, I like scaring people through the night.

I get a lot of candy going door to door,
I don't get tired cause I always want more.
Walking around all night with my friends,
Hoping that this night will never end.

When my bag is full of treats,
I run home through the streets.
I gobble up candy until I get sick,
I hope I feel better very quick.
Jack Weaver, Grade 6

My Eyes

My eyes are shaped like almonds
But that doesn't make me frown
They can be many colors
Mine are just brown

My eyes help me play football
They help me with my coordination
Which also comes in handy
When I play on the beach on vacation

My eyes make me smile
They can see colors like green and blue
They are big and round
Without them, what would I do
Matthew McGovern, Grade 6

Night

Night is great so great
Night is beautiful with stars
Night is like moonlight
Anthony Popa, Grade 4

The Paintball War

The first time I went paintballing it was amazing.
I was so excited to finally play paintball.
We made a game plan and we got ready.
Then the host blew the whistle and we were off.
It was so much fun,
My dad and I had so much fun.

Robert Curtis, Grade 6

Sadness

Sadness is a rainy day
It smells like rotten eggs
It tastes like you're biting into a lime
It sounds like your alarm clock when you have to wake up
It feels like slamming the car door on your finger
It lives under a thunderstorm

Ethan Stoltz, Grade 6

Moving Adventure

The day that should've been one of the best.
Turned out to be nearly the worst.
It was my 11th birthday.
When we moved to Orlando.
I had to leave everything in Georgia.
But it all changed when I made new friends.

Samuel Barbosa, Grade 6

Kite Flying at the Beach

There's a chill in the air,
But the weather is windy and fair.
We're at the beach to fly our kite.
If you feel the water its chill will bite.
Now we'll untangle the string, hold on to it tight,
And let our kite take flight.

Victoria Smith, Grade 6

I Love Fall

Fall is a time to jump and play.
Sometimes, some days.
Halloween is a time for getting candy at night.
And sometimes giving your sister a fright!
Fall is a really fun season, it's also a time to jump and play,
It's starting right now, so run and play!

Genaisha McNatt, Grade 6

St. Patrick's Day

I see people with green hair
I smell cabbage
I hear a leprechaun talking when I put up gold
I taste Lucky Charms
I touch a pot of gold when it rains
St. Patrick's Day

Joshua Richardson, Grade 4

My Toad*

I have a toad not so nice
Who says I must wash his toes
I plead loudly saying I've washed them twice.
It says, "Stop pleading my boy and wipe your nose!"

I wish so very much to clean clothes
But I must dust his book.
My toad must watch the Game Of Thrones
While he plays on with its nook.

It says I need to make scones but its belly is much too small
It makes me get the door
My toad says to replace the walls
I say, "We are much too poor."

Grace Pettey, Grade 5
*Inspired by Lewis Carroll

The Baseball Diamond

I play on this diamond every game.
My dream is to play in the big leagues some day.
Signing baseballs will make fans' day.

throwing curve balls to the catcher's mitt
or is it when I make that hit? The bright light on
me like a spotlight.

Here I am on the baseball diamond looking at
all the fans surrounding me and cheering me on.
I tip my hat very proud as I leave.
I hear the roars of the crowd.

Baseball is my life,
I dream of it morning and night.

Anthony Vallaro, Grade 4

Thanksgiving

Thank you for all my eyes can see…
Crispy turkey glowing gold at the table
Hundreds of diversity's of repast on Thanksgiving
Corn dancing with joy as it gets grilled

Thank you for all that I can taste…
Crispy golden turkey that slides down my throat into
my stomach like a slide
Soft, warm, brown walnut cake during tasty dessert
Yellow corn buttered and lightly salted melts in your mouth

Thank you for all that I can hear…
Knock, knock, knock loving grandparents at the door
Sizzle, sizzle, sizzle the corn gets grilled
People talking, enjoy each other's company laughing and playing

Chris Guarnieri, Grade 6

Ode to Bacon

Hello Bacon, you know me.
I'm the one who eats you
Every Saturday.
I smell you baking like
A pig standing in the sun.
With eggs and toast,
I want to grab you and
Eat you all day.
I want to tell you something.
I would do anything for you.
I would carry you to
Your bacon throne.
Anything, just
Anything you want.
Take you out for ice cream,
Or give you icing on a cake.
I crave you Bacon, because you are
Greasy, Crispy, Yummy, Tasty.
That is why I love you, Bacon.
I just L-O-V-E you
Bacon!
Jack Gladstein, Grade 5

The Perfect Spring

Relaxing in the sunny sun,
Letting off steam.
The sky will be bright baby blue,
And my friends and I will be at school.
It will be so cool.
I will be at the park,
While my dog is going to bark.
I will be looking at flowers,
For many and many of hours.
I will be growing,
While my grandma is sewing.
While my brother is booing at the TV,
I will be canoeing in the lake.
While I'm in the pool,
My family will be acting so cool.
It will be a sunny day,
And I will watch the bunnies play.
I love spring,
And you get to play.
This is the end,
And I have to go to bed.
Briana Knight, Grade 4

I Am Genesis!

G enerous at helping my parents
E xcited to play outside with my friends
N ice to my cousins
E ager to learn about Math
S ad when I get hurt
I ntelligent at writing
S cared of strangers that talk to me
Genesis Turrubiartez, Grade 4

Always Waiting

Waiting all alone,
In a castle she once called home,
Our kingdom's princess is asleep,
Still quietly counting sheep,
Waiting for her prince to come,
Sadly he answers to none.

Cursed by an evil queen,
One who no longer hopes nor dreams,
The young princess took both away,
Which is why she simply couldn't stay.

Eternally slumbering,
The queen's voice is still thundering,
Our kingdom long since forgotten,
And we're still down trodden.
Gabby Quattrocchi, Grade 6

Homework

Pencil, paper in my hand,
Time to do my work.
Wait, oh man, I forgot the page number.
What do I do…then I think a minute.
And then I stand, grab my phone,
And start texting with both hands.
Text all my classmates asking if they know.
Then I think, what if they say no?
OH MY WORD.
I just heard a ring,
Thank the Lord they know.
Yes, here you go.
Thank you! So text you later, I have to go.
I take a seat, I turn to the page,
I've done this already, oh well.
Time to play.
Katie Ray, Grade 6

The House Is a Sea of Mysteries

The house is a sea of mysteries,
Be careful not to drown,
Among all of its lies and traps,
Pulling you through locked doors,
The house is a sea of mysteries,
A third floor but no way up,
A closet full of moonbeam jars,
A book in a forgotten tongue,
The house is a sea of mysteries,
Green eyes flickering in the dark,
Your own eyes now betray you,
And you can't control your mind,
Yes, the house is a sea of mysteries,
As hard as you may try,
You will never forget,
The house full of lies.
Linnea Sumpman, Grade 6

The Mirror

In the mirror
I saw such a sight.
Too scary to say
a true, ugly fright.
It has eyes of red
and fangs to match.
Fangs that would scare you
and easily scratch.
Gray skin, that blends with the night.
I shut my eyes closed with all my might.
I swear to you
this is all true.
If you keep asking
I will bite you too!
David Frazer, Grade 4

Dance

Oh, how I love to dance!
I always skip and prance.
It's always super fun!
I'm not pulling a con.
Dancing is not just a fashion.
It's also my great passion!
I love it till the end.
It's my one and only friend.
I will do it till I die.
Till I am dancing in the sky.
Dance has me in a trance.
I will always dance when I have a chance.
I love it with all my heart.
We will never be torn apart.
Messiah Moring, Grade 5

Mom and Dad

Mom and dad
Are the best for
As they take care of
as they buy what
ever we
want we love
our mom and
dad so much mom
and dad
work so hard
for as
mom and dad
will do this
for us
Anisha Abidas, Grade 4

Drizzle Asleep

I watch a swan majestically fly
Butterflies flitting in unison
A drizzle of rain to top it off
To make me slowly fall asleep
Caitlin McManus, Grade 5

Stars

Each star has a special story,
The stars all have their own bright glory.
They are flying so very high,
Way up there in the night sky.
They twinkle all night till early light,
Then they take off for their daily flight.
They hide all day until the night,
And shine all night until it's bright.
Oh what would we do without the stars?
If only we could catch them in jars.
But a star is only a little sun,
Until they fizzle out then they're done.
I will love stars no matter what they are,
Even though they are very far!

Emma Mize, Grade 5

Star Wars

A long, long time ago,
In a galaxy too far to know
In the bright Tatooine sky,
Imperial TIE fighters fly,
But the Jedi are there,
To save worlds everywhere,
With the buzz of light sabers,
They will fight Lord Vader,
Yoda will teach you,
The Sith will try to beat you,
But the Dark Side will flee,
And the Rebels will be worry-free,
A long, long time ago,
In a galaxy too far to know!

Matthew Mills, Grade 5

Semmi

Semmi is my Maltese dog,
At dinner time he becomes a hog.
Semmi is not that big, he's small,
Semmi is like a cotton ball.
After his bath he gets mad,
Semmi will never be too bad.
On our sofa he has a spot,
He likes my daddy's couch a lot.
Semmi has a big black nose,
Be ready, he likes to get up close.
Semmi is 7, a little bit old,
Semmi acts big and super bold.
I love my Semmi, he is my boy,
He will always be my pride and joy.

Jaelyn Charles, Grade 5

I Give Thanks For

I give thanks for…
my caring mom…she stands up for me,
my amazing dad…he makes me laugh,
my loving grandma…she takes care of me.

Melanie Mioduchoski, Grade 4

It Was 9/11

It was 9/11
When the evil came ashore,
To attack the people
And call it a holy war.

Many thousands were injured,
Many thousands are gone.
Many heroes among
Whose courage was strong.

Change is our world now.
And with burned heroes' flesh,
Our flag is furled
And as we in America
Cried, tears red, white, and blue,
From the pain to the heart
I seemed the world died
So as we united,
Our pain and our hearts together,
In one group, our nation stands.

Sandy Molina Velazquez, Grade 6

Volcano Island

Red hot fire flowing
Trees burning
Fast as the wind,
It glides
Every nick and cranny with lava
Burning into the ocean
Destroys the island
Then the volcano falls into the sea

This underwater volcano
Boiling up
As hot as fire,
But only bubbles
Rising to the top
Bubbling, bubbling, bubbling

This volcano
Land or water
It always
Won

Icie Favata, Grade 4

Blue

Blue is flowers in the forest
Blue is blue cars on the road
Blue is a blue the color of my pants
Blue is the color of my shirt
Blue is blue cotton candy
Blue is blueberry lollipops
Blue is blue hair spray
Blue is the ocean in the summer time
Blue is the night sky

Molli Ronan, Grade 4

Horses

Horses are so wild and free,
Horses make me feel care free.
They are black and white or spotted brown,
As we ride my hair falls down.
The steady beat of horses hooves,
When we ride my horse improves.
We're soaring over jumps so far,
I think that I can touch the stars.
Galloping at the speed of light,
His eyes sparkle in the moonlight.
Walk to trot to oh so steady,
Canter to gallop if you're ready.
My fury friends I love you so,
Together we put on a show.

Kylee Keller, Grade 5

Kittens

I was born to love kittens,
They're so soft like my mittens.
I love the cute and cuddly things
I think their feet are made of springs
No matter what color, they are rad,
They could be happy, or even mad.
They could be too short or tall,
They could be chubby or small,
The only thing a kitten does bad,
Is claw and make you scream, "I'm sad."
A kitten can be very sweet,
I do know that they love to eat.
My kitten talks only to me,
When I pet her I feel so free.

Morgan Carver, Grade 5

Reading Books

I open up my book with delight
To read the book with fun and fright
To the character's world I will go
With fun places both high and low
The library is the place to be
To find some books for you and me
There are books as far as the eye can see
Some are sad and some are filled with glee
The books can be a myth or tale
And they are fun to read and tell
The story could be about a crook
Or could teach you how to cook
Whatever book it may be,
Books could make you worry-free!

Michaelyn Knight, Grade 5

Snowdrop

Icy cold snowdrop
grows in the wintry cold snow
shuts in the warm sun

Alexis Hurley, Grade 6

Being Something Else

Looking up at the sky,
Wishing I could be a bird and fly,
Or be a fish,
and swish swish swish,

Could I be,
as tall as a tree?
Or be as pretty as a flower,
sitting in the ground hour after hour?

That seems so right,
But it may give me a great big fright
I could stay me,
And be happy as can be!
Leah Bailey, Grade 4

My Pet

I have a big white furry pet,
He is by far the best one yet.
He likes it when I rub his ears,
He always comes when his name he hears.

Harper is his name,
Frisbee is his game.
His big brown eyes that look at me,
Hoping he will get a walk around the tree.

His great big tongue that licks my face,
He thinks the couch is his very own space.
He is like my very old friend,
I think I will love him until the end.
Mackenzie Bailey, Grade 6

Christmas

Christmas is the best time of the year,
I can't believe that it so near.
I can't wait till the wonderful night,
The house is bright like a light.

The gifts are so nice and sweet,
I love the sweet peppermint treats.
I love the shiny white snow,
I can't wait till the Christmas show.

I love to decorate Christmas trees,
The tree is so beautiful that I see.
I love to eat the candy canes,
I can't wait to go on the Christmas train.
MacKenzie Bauman, Grade 6

I Always Loved You

Makes me always love
He may have left forever
But he never left.
Sydney Shaw, Grade 4

Fall

Fall is near,
Children await the leaves,
The change,
The breeze.
Slowly, slowly
The bright green changes
to Red, Yellow, Orange
Slowly, slowly
They fall
Raked into piles,
Ready to be jumped upon.
Summer bids its farewell,
Heat turns to a brisk chill,
Fall has arrived.
Mahrukh Iftikhar, Grade 6

My Life

I used to have a dog,
but now I don't.
I used to like tanning,
but now I prefer the shade.
I used to like reading,
but now I prefer movies.
I used to have long hair,
but now I have short hair.
I used to have hermit crabs,
but now I don't.
I used to hate broccoli,
but now I love it
I used to have white hair,
but now I have blonde
Victoria Schub, Grade 4

The Girl at the Window

The girl at the window,
So curious and sweet,
You'd love to pay a nice little greet.

The girl at the window,
So friendly and caring,
Just sitting there and staring.

The girl at the window,
So gentle and polite,
Now you're the one staring,
At the curious, sweet, friendly, caring,
Gentle, polite, and plain old
Girl at the window.
Caroline Grubb, Grade 4

The Last Breath

Gently waiting in my bed,
Quick as a gunshot,
Quiet as a humming bird,
The thin air just slipped away.
Julianne Snopkowski, Grade 6

My Head

This is my beloved head
It does not look special at first
But once you go deeper into it
My imagination bursts

I think of pirates walking the plank
And streets of rolling cars
As you can see my imagination
Does not hold any bars

My head also protects me
From any sort of harm
When I see trouble up ahead
It is my alarm

And now you know why my head
Is something I need
Truly the head is something
Very special indeed
Victor Paduano, Grade 6

Spring

Snow is melting here and there
The flowers start to bloom.
Gray winter skies turn cheery bright
The bees around me zoom.

I smell the fragrant blossoms
Then bask in the warm, warm sun.
I gaze up at the wooly clouds
And think "What could be done?"

So I get up and run around
And climb a big oak tree
I fly a kite and roll down hills;
What glorious things to see!

The baby birds, they learn to fly
And joyful songs they sing.
I look at stars and make a wish
And yell out "I love spring!"
Nora Betts, Grade 6

Christmas

My favorite holiday's Christmas,
It's a day I wouldn't want to miss.
We wake up our parents to see
Lots and lots of presents.
It is glowing green,
Full of joy and glee.
It's full of lights and jolly.
We see by the tree my dog, Holly.
The huge bright star on top.
It's so fabulous that I freeze
In my tracks and stop.
Micah Seidel, Grade 5

Basketball

At the tip off, we start to play,
Basketball just makes my day.
A first class point guard is what I am,
I pass it to my teammate, and wham!
He shoots the ball, and swish! He scored,
We call him Brandon, the scoring Lord.
My team is the Mountaineers,
And all we hear are the loud cheers.
If we win every game,
We are sure to be in the Hall of Fame.
On the court, I'm as fast as lightning,
My passes are so accurate, it's frightening.
All these things make basketball fun,
But most of all I like to run.
Jake Diaz, Grade 5

My Legs

My legs are everything
They make me walk
They make me run
My legs are everything

My legs are everything
I can do track
I can do horseback riding
My legs are everything

My legs are everything
They are long
They are useful
My legs are everything
Mia Scogmanillo, Grade 6

My Hands Can...

Catch a softball
My hands can write
And type
And even throw

My hands can hit a home run
And braid my hair
My hands can save a goal
And help me punt a soccer ball

My hands can straighten my hair
And even blow it out
My hands can grip a field hockey stick
And even drive a field hockey ball
Carina Ramirez, Grade 6

Changing Seasons

The faded red leaves,
About to fall off the tree,
Winter is coming.
Megan Wright, Grade 6

Snow

Cold snow
Falling soft
Falling slow
In the night

Bright sun reflecting
Icicles shimmering
Snow crystals connecting
To build a snowball

Bigger, taller
Fatter, wider
Each one's smaller
For a snowman

Let's ride a sled
I know tonight
I'll be so tired I'll want to go to bed
But for now I'm happy

In a fun, snowy land
Anna Boone, Grade 6

I Am

I am a daughter
I wonder if I can be a better sister
I hear my parents
I see my family
I want to see my meme in heaven
I am a daughter

I pretend I am the only child
I feel my family hug me
I touch my puppy
I worry that my parents will die
I cry when I see my family get hurt
I am a daughter

I understand that I am not a perfect person
I say I love you to my parents
I dream we will all live and not die
I try to be good
I hope we will be safe all the time
I am a daughter
Abbigail Perreault, Grade 6

My Loved One

I love you, I love you.
My mother, my mother.
You are my heart.
You are my star.
I hope you never leave me,
And I mean it.
Shine at night,
Hug me tight.
Latisha Breana Brewer, Grade 6

Birds

I like to watch
birds chirping
and flapping.
It makes me
so very happy.
Perched upon the
leafy trees,
swaying in the soft
spring breeze.
I like to watch
them flap and soar
right outside
my backyard door!
Kailly Nocera, Grade 4

Orange

Today, I shall go explore
I shall go where the dinosaurs used to roar
Where the pterodactyl soars
To a place far away
Always meant for another day
It's gutsy indeed
But I need to do the deed
Not for myself
But for everyone
I must lead
I'll go to the unknown
Where the princes and ogres groan
And I shall rule
Aidan Besselman, Grade 6

Tornado of Our Thoughts

Tornado of our thoughts
everyone's biggest fear,
of having all of our
thoughts come at us
like a storm.
your mind rethinking
more and more
about everything
life has had in store,
as you hear the tornado
of your thoughts wishing
that it all would stop.
Lacy Parrish, Grade 6

A Breezy Day at Cocoa Beach

On our way, I see the trees go by,
As I am looking up at the sky.
Today is the day that we will play.
My family and I will be at the beach,
Before the scent of this beautiful speech.
Sand between our toes, sunburned faces,
The smell of the salty breeze, so beautiful.
Oh, how I miss the beach.
Isabella Moreno, Grade 6

Orange

Orange is the color of pencils writing all day.
Orange is the taste of fresh pumpkin pie in the oven.
Orange is the sound of a tiger's roar in the night.
Orange is the smell of a new can of orange paint.
Orange is leaves crunching under my feet.
Orange is traffic cones in the street.
Orange is the dead grass in the yard.
Orange is cheese in the kitchen.
Orange is icing on my birthday cake.
Orange is an owl hooting in the night.
Orange is a campfire roasting hot dogs all day.
Orange is sweet cantaloupe for lunch.
Orange is robins singing in the sun.
Orange is the peaches on the tree.
Orange is fresh nail polish on my hands.
Orange is orange juice in a tall glass.
Orange is orange lollipops from the bank.
Orange is pumpkins in a field.
Orange is a horse's mane flowing in the wind.
Orange is the color of my favorite book in the library.
Orange is a desert in Africa, hot as the sun.

Olivia Lombardo, Grade 4

My Mind Is a Never-Ending Maze

My mind is a maze
Never ends
Never stops
It runs on and on
My mind is a frustrating collection of thoughts
Secrets in every corner
Confusing everyone
My mind has eternal twists and turns
No beginning
No end
My mind is a strange place or is it a thing?
It can't ever be solved
It makes me cry
It makes me smile
It makes me laugh
It makes be growl
Emotions, conflicts, stories
All jumbled up and mixed together
My mind is a maze
Never ends
Never stops

Eujine Kim, Grade 6

Someday

Someday...
Someday I will change.
Someday I will be a good boy.
Someday I will be recognized.
Someday I will be an inventor.
Someday I will get married.
Someday I will have kids.
Someday I hope I will fit in the world.
Someday they will be proud for what I did.
Someday I will learn something new.
Someday I will change the world.
Someday I will invent a machine to help the world.
Someday I will get a better bike.
Someday I will get my license.
Someday I will go to the movies.
Someday I will go to university.
Someday I will take my parents out to eat.
Someday I will find the perfect girl.
Someday I will invent something for my parents.
Someday I will be rich.
Someday...

Israel Flores Segura, Grade 6

Christmas Eve

I walk into this house
On a snowy Christmas Eve.
The tree is a giant
Looking down upon me.
Strung with different color lights
That shine so bright.

I walk into this house
On a snowy Christmas Eve.
The dog is in a dream
And the cats are unseen.
There is a wondrous scent floating in the air
Warming my senses with fresh Christmas fare.

I walk away from this house on a snowy Christmas Eve,
With all my family waving goodbye;
All this excitement for all these things,
I realize is why this night flew by
In a blink of an eye,
And I will walk away feeling
Like the moon at its height in the sky.

Sydni Williams, Grade 6

Journey of Life

Tadpole
Itty bitty and slimy
Slithering, swimming and gliding
Sunbathing on the lily pad waiting for a prey
Hopping, anticipating and swallowing
The green speckled
Frog

Meeta Agarwal, Grade 5

Leif Ericson

Twenty four years old this day
On a strenuous escapade for King Olaf of Norway
Let's take a quest out west to discover new land
He knew the sea like the back of his hand
He loved to sail that's what he did
He relished the sea like it was his kid
This humble man was always on the grid

Theo Demopoulos, Grade 5

Waterfalls
Beautifully clear
flows down the quiet river
with peaceful noises
Jacalyn Leahr, Grade 5

Autumn
Green leaves turning brown
Thanksgiving, Halloween too!
Soon the leaves will fall
Elizabeth Dyer, Grade 6

The Leaf Blower
leaves fall on the ground
the wind blows them all around
like a leaf blower
Jackson Lester, Grade 6

Fall
The leaves are falling
Majestic and colorful
Flying by the sun
Olivia Martinez, Grade 6

My Dog Thelma
Likes fresh ham and cheese
She is shy with different people
She sleeps with me
Natalie Prusiensky, Grade 4

My Dog
Crazy dog barks at night.
My crazy dog likes to lick me.
My dog likes to jump.
Kiley Cannon, Grade 4

First Snow
The snow came last night
making it hard to travel
but great for sledding.
Lorinn Justus, Grade 6

The Season Spring
Waves flow oh so high,
Flowers dance toward the sky,
The wind whispers bye.
Isabel Guerra, Grade 5

Love Is in the Air
Plants are blooming here
Birds are chirping over there —
Love is in the air.
Amelia Alexander, Grade 6

Who I Am
I'm from the picture books I read when I was 5,
I'm from the chapter books I read now,
I'm from the ridiculous plays I put on for my family, to the huge stages where I take a bow,
I'm from the squeak of my tiny rain boots to the screech of my basketball shoes,

I'm from the sadness of missing a shot to learning it's okay to lose
I'm from the yell of my dog Dominic to the bark of my new dog Baloo
I'm from the sky I wished to fly in, to feeling as if I am on the moon

This is where I'm from from the waters and the sand
This is who I want to be
This is who I am.
MacKenzie Pettegrow, Grade 5

I'm From
I'm from catching a touchdown pass in football
I'm from playing madden on my phone 24/7
I'm from eating pasta with my family plate after plate
I'm from running around outside and I am gasping for water
I'm from lying on the couch relaxing dosing off sleeping
I'm from not being patient whatsoever, when will it come!?
I'm from hanging out with my friends to going outside and playing sports
I'm from spending time with my family
I'm from my mom and dad who made me.
Matthew Vingara, Grade 6

Alyssa's Fall Tree
As he is gazing at the children playing, he is also wondering when his leaves will leave him.
The wind is whistling through the air as it is pushing the leaves out of their spots.
He is as sad as a dog who has just lost their owner.
Every day he looks up and waits for the fluffy snow to fall.
Once it falls he won't see his fantastic friends anymore.
Saying goodbye is hard for him because he has only seen them for a sliver of time.
The only thing he likes about fall is the colorful colors floating around him.
The time is soaring around him like a bird who is lost in the woods.
He knows that he will be standing out in the crowd knowing that he is super special.
Alyssa Edgren, Grade 5

Fall Night
In the cool, breezy forest stands a wonderful, bold wolf keeping his cubs safe.
Once it turned to dawn they enjoyed a very delicious meal
in their cozy warm den.
Then they snuggled together in their cozy bed,
under the sparkly twinkling stars.
The stars smiled down at them, while we closed our eyes.
Peaceful…
Alexis Alvarez, Grade 4

Christmas
I see a Christmas tree with such pretty lights sparkling and so bright,
I smell fresh baked cookies from the oven and I bet they taste yummy,
I hear lots of music from our TV and also me opening my presents,
I taste some really yummy food like cookies with white milk and my mom's homemade pie,
What I touch is the wrapping paper when I open my gifts and that's fun,
Christmas.
Miracle Lafferty, Grade 5

My Best Friend Shelby

She is as pretty as a rose
She is as sweet as candy
She is as joyful as a summer day
She is as funny as a monkey
She is as kind as a butterfly
She is as fast as a flying bird
She is as caring as a care bear
She is as colorful as a rainbow
She is as awesome as a bulldog
She is as bright as a star

Charlotte Prevatt, Grade 4

The Little Red Bucket

As the waves crashed,
The shells disappeared.
Seagulls squawked,
And a single red bucket stood in the sand.
It sat there all day and all night.
Many playful children built sandcastles
And swam in the ocean around it.
Some had sand toys and some didn't.
But the red bucket remained.
It was a perfect day for the beach.

Sierra Stone, Grade 6

My Brother

He is as nice as a butterfly
He is as caring as a care bear
He is as funny as a clown
He is as playful as a dog
He is as awesome as a star
He is as strong as a lion
He is as good at singing as a rockstar
He is as fast as a cheetah
He is as trustworthy as a K9 dog
He is my brother and I love him

Carson Logan, Grade 4

Dad

He is as fast as a cheetah
He is as funny as a clown
He is as nice as a panda
He is strong as an elephant
He is as good as Lebron James
He is as tough as a rhino
He is as playful as a puppy
He is as fun as a Slip and Slide
He is as careful as a bear
He is as tall as a tree

Brayden McLeod, Grade 4

Giraffes

Giraffes have long necks
Giraffes eat leaves and have fun
They sleep in the night

Rachel Bonebrake, Grade 4

Winter

Oh yay, yay, yay!
It's a winter day.
There's a lot of stuff to do today.
Like drinking excellent hot chocolate,
While sitting by the cozy fire.
Every day going outside and having a snowball fight,
Seems just about right.
When I want to have fun,
I like to go ice skating or ride a sled,
From sun up 'til sundown and then I go to bed.
Winter is the best because Christmas is coming next.
When it's Christmas, Santa goes to your house,
So you need to be as quiet as a mouse.
I like when my family is always with me,
We can make snow angels, eat yummy cookies, or drink cold milk...you'll see!

There's lots to enjoy in winter!

Richyia Hamilton, Grade 4

Thanksgiving

Thank you for all my ears can hear
Famished bellies rumble waiting for the Thanksgiving feast
"Rumble, rumble"
Immense marching bands tooting and banging their
loud instruments down the long streets of NYC
Crackling leaves crunching like biting into crisp apple pie

Thank you for all my nose can smell
Steamy, savory stuffing smells tasty spiced with spices
The aroma of cinnamon and nutmeg flying through the house
Thanksgiving turkey tanning in the hot oven

Thank you for all my tongue can taste
Mouthwatering pumpkin pie sending me off to Thanksgiving heaven
Sweet candy apples getting stuck in your teeth
Steamy apple cider running down my throat while
wrapped up in several layers of blankets

Gia Keddy, Grade 6

Falling into Winter

Glorious golden light falling to the Earth
Vanishing vibrant vivid swaying hues
Can you guess the clues
It is the season of autumn, for all it's worth!

Now the holidays are coming along
There is Grandparent's Day then Thanksgiving
Thanksgiving is when everyone is feverishly forgiving
Getting to winter is not long.

The wonderful white winter snow starts falling on the city
All the fall leaves turn into beautiful hues then fall off onto the ground
Making a great big mound
Getting close to the time that people talk about the Yeti.

Cara Wright, Grade 6

Useless Things

Elvis without a microphone
Mario without a hat
Rock and roll without the Beatles
A T-rex without teeth
Dracula without fangs
A guitar without strings
A school without students
A building without an entrance
George Harrison without a guitar
Charlie Brown without clumsiness
Sonic being slow
A pencil without lead
Harry Potter without a wand
An Italian without pasta
A musician without an instrument
A hero without justice
Thor without lightning
A tennis player without a racket
A cat without fluff
  Benjamin Saravi, Grade 4

Love Is a Singing Soaring Lark

Love is a singing soaring lark,
 so deep and rich.

Love is a happiness,
 so kind and thoughtful.

Love is a fountain,
 spreading happiness to the world.

Love is an omen,
 of faith and trust.

Love is an orchestra,
 playing the music of life.

Love is a well,
 that never dries.

 Love is life.
  Sasha Hatch, Grade 6

Jumping January

January oh I love January,
What a lovely day,
It's a good time to run and play,
Making snowmen is so much fun,
A lot of clouds and no sun,
The cold air is like a song,
The winter days are not so long,
The moon shows up at night,
And the clouds are out of sight,
The fun days of January will not last,
So be happy with what you have!
  Maria Kryvonos, Grade 4

Wrestling

When the music hits and the crowd cheers,
 the building will shake in crazy fear.
The wrestlers will enter the ring,
 waiting for the bell to ding.

Their costumes are colored and tight,
they have amazing moves they use to fight.
Bodies slam off the rope,
pinning their opponent is their main hope.

I sit and watch on the edge of my seat,
hoping my favorite wrestler won't be beat.
Their moves are astonishing,
 sometimes they even swing.

 The ref counts one.
 The pinning has begun.
 The ref counts two,
  this can't be true.

 The ref counts three,
  this couldn't be.
The wrestler pops up to his feet,
 the champ has been beat.
  Justin Hajdukiewicz, Grade 6

Dying Star

I am old now
People depend on me

This space is my world
But also my deathbed

Once I was a nova
The planets sang me songs of love
Masterful melodies
But not today

My existence is a message in the sand

I feel the persevering pain
Like I am screaming forever
No one listens
Death digging through me
A slave to entropy
Please

Goodbye
 So cold
  So cold
   So
  Maverick Williams, Grade 5

Hair

I love my hair.

It is light brown
Has a little blond
Is a little curly
Keeps my head warm
Looks good straightened

I love my hair.

I always style it
Pull it back with a bow
Brush it when it's tangled
Wash it when it's dirty
Curl it so I look pretty

I love my hair.
  Kelly Snyder, Grade 6

It's About

It's about surfing, waves, boardwalk
Bodyboarding, feet in the sand
Ping-Pong

It's about arcades
Finding shells
Bike rides

It's about 3 months of freedom
Screaming, playing, having fun
Showers every day

It's about sweating
Scoring goals
Getting hurt

It's about the best 3 months of your life!
  Kevin Carson, Grade 5

My Legs

The best part of me are my legs
 They help me run
 They help me walk

My legs are filled with muscles
 They help me stand
 They help me sit

My legs help me dance
 They help me stretch
 They help me turn

My legs are used every day
They are used in many tasks
They are the best part of me
  Natalie O'Brien, Grade 6

Picture Perfect

That feeling when I move my brush,
Across the paper with no rush.
Drawing on the paper of mine,
While sitting in the warm sunshine.
Bright puffy clouds and grassy fields,
Along with birds in the window sill.
Rivers and trees at the mountain,
Is what my picture will contain.
At night I draw a crescent moon,
While making sure it has no gloom.
I paint a city with some cars,
And above them are some bright stars.
I can always paint what I saw,
My favorite hobby is to draw.
Trisha Nguyen, Grade 5

The Only Scarlett

Scarlett is the one I adore,
Taking care of her is a chore.
Sometimes she can make a mess,
Sometimes there is a lot of stress.
When lightning flashes she runs away,
When I find her I say "It's okay."
When it is dark she is my light,
She is the star of starry night.
"Woof!" she says when she wants to play,
I miss her when I am away.
She is very loyal to me,
Empathy is the key.
She is my angel from up above,
I will always give her my love.
Allyson Ward, Grade 5

My Legs

My legs are the best part of me.
They help me grow. They help me
show that I am a fast runner. I am
tall. I am strong.

When I dance, my legs help me.
When I do tricks, they help me dance.
When I ride my bike, I need my legs.
I walk with my legs. I also jog.

My legs help me stand up straight.
My legs help me play my sports.
My legs help me be me.
My legs are the best part of me!
Emily Keaveney, Grade 6

The Beach

Waves crashing by me
Buried treasure in the sand
Breath of salty air
Isabella Bartolacci, Grade 6

Orange

I shall
Explore
Daringly
Leading the way
Like the sun
Picking up rewards
Along the way
Applying caution
To my thoughts
I am quite courageous
But weak
With the sun
Shining on me
Helping me live
I am now alive
Thanks to
The
Sun
Eddie Albert, Grade 6

The Book I Have

The bustling city was big and bold,
but I was told,
that the dangers there are horrid.
So when I sat on a little bench,
cramped with five other people,
I pulled out my book and had a look
and I glanced at the other humans.
They all looked sad
and a little mad
as they looked at their iPhones.
But I was happy
the book I had
was so great
and it wasn't sad
or mad
and I smiled as I read
in the middle of those people
who didn't have a book.
Brooke Murawski, Grade 4

Mother

My mother, my mother
I love you like butter.
You are so sweet,
Like candy and treats.
I'm gonna miss you, when I'm gone.
And that's not far from long.
I hope that you love me,
Just like butterflies and bees.
You are my mother,
And will always be.
Like I said before,
But now I love you,
Like honey in a honey tree.
Deonne Lenora Jinkins, Grade 6

Elements

The wind rustles my hair,
and I am aware,
that tonight is the night of the sky.

The sun burns my skin,
and I am aware,
that the fire will win.

The ground below me starts to shake,
and I am aware,
that the earth will take.

The rain water falls,
and I am aware,
that the water will make its calls.

The elements scatter,
and I am aware,
that nothing else will matter.
Vela Belin, Grade 5

Love

Love is me
Love is you
Love is better
When it's two

I am yours
You are mine
We'll be together
To the end of time

Don't be fake
Keep it real
Love is the way
You make me feel

Love is you
Love is me
Love is
What it's meant to be
Ashlyn Freeman, Grade 6

Ten Years from Today

Not waking up early
No more school
It isn't getting cooler
Living in LA
Beautiful weather
No more snow
Missing the cold
Getting old
Meeting new people
Getting real busy
It's starting to get dizzy
Karla Azucar, Grade 6

Ode to Horror

You creep up on me at night
You press against my mind every second
Without you there would be joy, and light
No sorrow and hate.
Without you,
There would be nothing but light, and life.
No darkness,
No death,
No fear,
No horror.
Andrew Gomez, Grade 6

Dad

He is as funny as a clown
He is as good at sports as Jordan
He is as strong as a gorilla
He is as fast as a cheetah
He is as playful as a puppy
He is as nice as a panda
He is as tall as a giraffe
He is as sneaky as a fox
He is as tough as a rock
He is as fun as a roller coaster
Christopher Rivera, Grade 4

Chris

He is as fast as a cheetah
He is as sneaky as a fox
He is as athletic as Stephen Curry
He is as strong as a tiger
He is as fashionable as a super star
He is as tall as a building
He is as creative as an artist
He is as bright as a star
He is as loud as a T-rex
He is as funny as a hyena
Bailey Teeters, Grade 4

Charlotte

Today is the day when I get to see
the little children who love me.
Today is the day when I move away
from my home web where I stayed.
The children make me feel like a celeb.
Now today when my eggs hatch,
I pray my offspring don't get snatched.
I hope that with their eight little eyes,
they can see they are my prize.
Maryam Rassif, Grade 4

Cherry Blossoms

Cherry blossoms float
Along the creek, pink and white
So peaceful and calm.
Madison Park, Grade 6

Courage

Courage is raising our flag through the glare and smoke of a desperate battle
It smells like the fabric of a tattered flag rising over the horizon
It tastes like the frigid December air
It sounds like the prayer you whisper at your finest hour
It feels like the anxiety you are forced to push aside
It lives in the heart of every man
Michael Nicotera, Grade 6

Thanksgiving Day

The gravy on the hot turkey is looking the best it could be
The aroma from the turkey is making the entire city have a good day
Hearing the wishbone crackle and crinkle, you won, you finally won
Taking the first bite is like biting into heaven
Feeling the cold utensils gives me the shivers
Thanksgiving is over, you are now in the car on your way back to your house.
Andrew Azar, Grade 4

The Beach

The beach
With its warm sand
under your feet.

The beach
A cool breeze
Tickles your face.

The beach
Beautiful blue water
Glistens in the sun.

The beach
the sound of the ocean waves
brushing against the sand.

The beach
Its wonderful sunset
brings my family together...the beach.
Lizzie Kelly, Grade 6

Ash

Ash, the cat.
Always there for you,
well, it's just that…
He's hiding in the closet,
with all the clothes.
Will anyone find him?
I sure do not know.
He's not too wild,
but he does get whiny.
And if you can't find him,
remember, he's tiny.
Now, don't take hours,
looking for him all day.
But I assure you,
he'll be there, I swear.
Rebecca Safra, Grade 6

Believe in Me

I think I can do it.
I know I can prove it.
You don't believe me.
I know you deceive me.
Oh yeah
I know I can do it.
Just try to believe me.
I would if I were you.
Just try to think
About what you would do
I'll try to do it
I know I can make you believe in me
I know I can do it
Just let me believe
I think I can make it to the top
My heart will never stop
Believe in me
I know we can be together forever,
you and me
Meaghan Irwin, Grade 4

Meteor

The massive meteor
In the land of nothing
Nothing but stars and deep black
Passing each one
The weird wonder
No eye has seen me
No one has been me
As rare as a language with 1 speaker
Yes, I am a wonder
Alive but dead
Many moments later, I see it
Something bright in the distance
A large planet, green and blue
Finally, a planet that I can go to
My time has arrived
Joshua Carey, Grade 5

My Senses

I see the brightness of the sun
I smell the summer's flowers
I hear the roar of the beach waves
I feel the hotness of the sand
I taste the sweetness of summer
I think of all the beauty that summer offers

I see the dim light of fall
I smell the fall scents
I hear the raking of leaves
I feel the chilly winds
I taste the pumpkins
I think of the colorful leaves

I see the white, beautiful snow
I smell the cocoa and coffee
I hear children playing with the snow
I feel the coldness of the winter
I taste the sweet baked treats
I think a new year has begun
Sherlyn Perez Aguilar, Grade 6

Spring

Oh spring is coming,
when the flowers bloom,
and the fresh grass of spring springs.

And the smell of
the flowers makes
my heart sing like a bird.

This is when the birds
sing, and my favorite time
of the year when we all
see the animals come to life.

So come spring, come
to light your spring smell
and bring the birds
to sing their songs,
and don't forget
the trees, grass
and your flowers!
Chilali Mancilla, Grade 6

Heartache Dream

Love can be pain
Dreams are destroyed
They may disappear but
They will start over
Where love will be
It will last as a shiny glass
Thinking of the time we spent together
Your breathing will stop
But it was only a heartbroken dream
Veverlin Aguilar Bautista, Grade 6

My Eyes

My eyes are brown
They see the nature in town
They are stunning
And are loving
They help me spot in dance
Take my chance
Shine in the light
When I'm in a fight
They help me write
And gives me might
They make lies
I love my eyes
Olivia Ferranola, Grade 6

Christmas Delight

Christmas is a jolly time
To spend with family with delight
Spending near the cozy fire
Singing song with hearts desire
Up, up, up in the white sky
Down, down where the snowflakes glide
We can make a snowman
We can try!
Achoo achoo
I feel a sneeze
I need to get comfy
Please please please
Rihana Morris, Grade 4

Dance

The small speakers crackle
sound no not sound,
Music bursts out and I can barely hear
the voice of the teacher,
fragile faint instructions in the distance
but I'm already lost in a different world of
movements and rhythm. The dance studio
disappears and I'm in New York,
I see my name in flashing lights
on buildings of all different heights.
Dance just isn't a sport. Dance is an
amazing art, a passion, and a profession.
Ashley A. Anderson, Grade 6

Summer Rocks

Summer is here and I can't wait,
I am going to have so much fun.
I'm going to get everybody,
So we can go to the beach.
Splash, splash splash attack!
I hope summer will never end,
So I don't have to go to school again.
I won't have to do any work,
And all I'm going to do is have sleepovers.
Summer rocks!

Eric Parson, Grade 4

I Am

I am Alex
I wonder when God will take me
I hear animals in the morning
I see my friends
I want a baby brother
I am Alex

I pretend to kill zombies
I feel animals
I touch my cat
I worry when my parents will pass
I cry about my family members who died
I am Alex

I understand friendship
I say, "Good job" to my friends and family
I dream about being an NBA star
I try to be nice
I hope they find a cure for cancer
I am Alex

Alex Jones, Grade 6

Watermelon

Green stripes of
Light and dark
White rind
Turning pinker,
Darker, redder,
Juice running down
My chin
Slurp
Little black seeds
Shining
In my lovely fruit
I take another bite
Flavor-filled bubbles burst
The deepening color
The crispy texture
The juice spreads in my mouth
Suddenly I taste the flavorless rind
Dropping the shell
On my sticky red plate
I extend my hands
And reach for another slice...
Ani Vaughan, Grade 5

Spring/Fall

Spring
warm, beautiful
gardening, hiking, fishing
flowers, leaves, bare trees
raking, jump in leaves
windy, colorful
Fall
Eshan Kumar, Grade 4

Spring

The snow has melted
All the flowers are blooming
The grass is greener.
Stephen Crum, Grade 6

Fall

Leaves, leaves everywhere
Covering the ground with orange
Exposing the trees.
Audrey Sofo, Grade 6

The Sea

The beautiful sea,
Waves that almost touch the sky,
Crash on sugar sand.
Maddie Elliott, Grade 6

Spring

The whistles of wind
The buzzing of working bees
The croaking of frogs
Christopher Joseph Rife, Grade 6

Lonely River

Rushing through the woods
I come and go, days move on
But the river stays
Kate Mikol, Grade 4

Burning Bush

The bush turned darker
darker than the sun and moon
the burning bush stays.
Emma Hurley, Grade 6

Sunny Summer Sun

Hot Sunny Weather
Crabs and fish in the water
Ocean tastes salty
Joelle McElroy, Grade 6

Snowflakes

Covered in white flakes,
Gathering on the damp grass,
Falling with such grace.
Johanna Phillips, Grade 6

Winter

Icy crystals blow
across the glistening sky
over the mountains.
Emily Justus, Grade 6

Trust

Trust is a delicate flower
It takes hard work to grow
But …one false step could completely break it, rot it
Trust is a vile ingredient in the game …Of LIFE
Trust is a key to many things
Trust is the key to Friendship
To Loyalty
To Companionship
To Certainty
To Faith
To Assurance
To Conviction
To Credence
To Reliance
To Reliability
And most of all
Trust is key to…truth, within the secret of trust lays the truth of life
It shows what life would be like with and without it
Trust is a complicated thing
A Question
But to all questions there are answers you just need to know where to look
Nathnael E. Haile, Grade 6

Amazing Autumn

Green leaves change to scarlet, gold and copper
as we say goodbye to tank tops and shorts
and hello to sweaters and boots
The colorful trees paint a picture as real as life
The heavenly scent of baking pumpkin and apple pies
People are raking leaves that were once scattered like objects in a messy room
Delicious, mouthwatering turkey and mashed potatoes with gravy
every Thanksgiving is a flavorful vacation
Acorns are falling loudly on the roof
while people are cozy inside carving Jack-O-Lanterns
and sticking their hands in the gooey insides of the pumpkin
Crackling bonfires are keeping people warm outside
Salty, buttery corn boiling in the pot
as kids jump into piles of raked leaves
People standing in long queues at Starbucks
waiting to have a warm Pumpkin Spice latte
People are picking juicy apples and bright pumpkins to make delicious pies
Squirrels are gathering acorns for the winter
Everybody is getting prepared for winter
People are putting away leggings and Halloween decorations
and taking out puffy coats and Christmas trees
Julianne Ventimiglia, Grade 6

The Tree's Final Time with Friends

Finally the tree had to let go of his pals the leaves.
Since the tree lost his friends, he is sad as a mother bird losing one of her eggs.
He doesn't have as much warmth now and has to hold on to the rest
Of his water supply as the wet ground eventually freezes.
He tries to reach out with his branches to catch his falling friends.
But the tree can't wait to rest all winter long.
Then in the spring his friends will come back one by one.
Liam McNamara, Grade 5

When I Lived in D.R.

I remember playing with my kite
I remember baking cakes with my uncle
I remember collecting avocados from a tree
And playing with my grandma
I remember my room full of toys
I remember my pool
I remember collecting coconuts
Even seeing people climb the coconut tree
I remember leaving to live in the U.S.A.
But my favorite memory's yet to come.
Brianny Luna, Grade 6

Why Be a Bully?

Why be a bully when you can be the
greatest hero in the world
Why be an assailant
When you can help people in need
Instead of bullying them
Why be a bully when
You can do immense things
In life
I should have just said this at the beginning
DON'T BE A BULLY!
Aiden Fremer, Grade 6

Oreo

School in the sun?
A day meant for fun!
City kids free to explore.
What is this animal we implore?
The black and white cow stood proud.
"Moo," she said loud.
Wow, what a sound!
A Queens Zoo legendary treasure.
She weighs 2,000 pounds!
Oreo is a big treasure we found.
Tyler Ferland, Grade 4

Because of You

I once was invincible,
Now all I am is invisible.
I once was brave,
Now all I am is afraid.
I once was confident,
Now all I am is indefinite.
This was all a misshapen,
Not meant to be true.
But now I see,
It was all because of you.
Marielle Mago, Grade 4

Puppies

Puppies are playful
They make me laugh a lot too
They are very cute.
Amanda Puga, Grade 4

I Am

I am a girl who likes playing soccer.
I wonder who will pass to me.
I hear the crowd cheering for me, the coach yelling at me to pass the soccer ball.
I see my teammates passing the ball to each other.
I want to be on offense and get the ball in the goal.
I am a girl who likes playing soccer.

I pretend that I will win the soccer game.
I feel the sweat down my face while I run to the goal.
I touch the ball with my foot.
I worry that the other team will score on the goalie.
I am a girl who likes playing soccer.

I understand that I will miss the championship.
I say "pass, pass I'm open!"
I dream I will get a trophy.
I try to score a goal.
I hope that I win a soccer game for my team.
I am a girl who likes playing soccer.
Mitzie Westgate, Grade 5

Where I'm From

I am from books,
from Tide and Lysol.
I am from the squealing and giggling of siblings.
I am from the magnolia tree,
the bushes in front of our house
I am from breakfast casserole on Christmas mornings and horrible eyesight,
from Laurie and Dan and Jack,
I am from being late and staying up late,
From "Go Wake Forest!" and yes ma'am.
I am from trying your hardest so you can know what you can do.
I'm from Thomasville and Lexington, Arkansas and North Carolina,
BBQ and chocolate shazz.
From the wreck in my dad's car on a rainy night
the scar on his head
and when he told me he was Harry Potter because of it.
I am from the bookshelf in our living room.
Pictures of family, friends, and trips.
Pictures of school, babies, and weddings.
Memories are stored there.
Sidney Briggs, Grade 6

Where I'm From

I am from couches to kitchens and Topps trading cards,
I am from the cushion crack to the dust mites on top of it,
I am from the bushes the trees whose arms I remember is if the were my own.

I am from Boston sports because they're the best at everything,
I'm from football and basketball and buff chicken for life,

I am from playing catch with my brother,
and football with my mom and dad,
but most of all I am from family and that's what matters the most.
Jackson Hayes, Grade 5

Paper Airplane

In the air is where I soar,
Faster than a vicious velociraptor racing for its prey,
With my continuous crafted wings,
And my tip as sharp as a sea urchin's spike,
The wind refreshing me like a hot shower.

All the kid's faces filled with gasps to see how far I go,
Not knowing that my joyful journey will come to a halt.

I drop anchor by crashing,
Into an aromatic arborvitae,
With my
    mangled
      and
        corrupted
          wings

Dessa Kavrakis, Grade 5

Thanksgiving

Thank you for all my eyes can see…
Mashed potatoes look like a puffy cumulous cloud
Turkeys fly right into the oven
Mouth-watering pumpkin pie is like a freshly picked orange

Thank you for all my tongue can taste…
Savory stuffing smelled scrumptious
Golden-brown turkey was a crispy
As a bag of Lays potato chips
Sweet apple cider tingles my tongue
As it slides down my throat

Thank you for all my ears can hear…
Ding! The oven golden turkey is ready to be gobbled up
Cling! The silverware walking all over my China plate
Crackling of the fireplace as winter confronts fall.

Hailey Scheyder, Grade 6

Piano

When your fingers touch the keys, you are invincible.
Getting louder. Crescendo.
  Softening up. Diminuendo.
   A whole path of music notes await.
    Take it.
     Just play it out.
      We're listening.
       Beethoven
        Mozart
         Haydn
          Vince Guaraldi
           So many possibilities.
But every adventure ends with a
  Double
  Bar
  Line.

Maggie Kwan, Grade 4

Revenge

Revenge is love that got stolen away.
It smells like fire, fire burning down a whole house.
It tastes like a hot, hot chili pepper, spicy, yet delicious.
It sounds like a faint whisper in a busy crowd.
It feels like a knife, driven through your back.
It lives in the emptiest hearts and the maddest brains.

Chloe Pugh, Grade 6

A Date

I see a little sparkle. I look into her eyes.
Then her cheeks turn red. Then I know she is shy.
I go up to her one day and ask her for a date.
It must be courage from God,
Or maybe it is just fate.

Alejandro Rivera, Grade 4

Grandparents Are…

Fluffy companions snuggling up next to you.
Bedtime stories read with expression.
Cookies baked with love and compassion.
The feeling inside me when I'm appreciated.
An area of comfort to run to.

Favor Ufondu, Grade 6

Thanksgiving Feast

Looks like a bountiful feast underway
Smells like cranberry sauce, gravy, and clam chowder
Tastes like mouthwatering turkey delicacy
Sounds like festive music and joyful laughter
Feels like a warm and happy family

Andie Zou, Grade 5

Fall

All the leaves that were once green are now brown, yellow, and red.
The bumble bees buzz from flower to flower getting nectar.
The cool wind carries the leaves that are falling.
The squirrels scramble to store food.
You hear the birds singing in the trees.

Ethan Slavin, Grade 5

Frost

Those pure white speckles that drift from the sky,
Each one unique, flying through the sky,
When they do takeoff and reach with open arms for earth,
They are hoping to create the birth,
Of a new winter wonderland.

Sophia Molnar, Grade 5

Love

Love is something you cannot return
Love is something you share
With family, friends, and things important
You share it with God, angels, and passed on family
That's what love is to me

Haillee Roof, Grade 4

Video Games

Video Games
Addictive, awesome
Gamin, scoring, yelling
Cool to play with friends!
Need For Speed
Thomas Duke, Grade 4

Fright Night

Halloween can be very scary!
I once saw a girl dressed as a zombie fairy.
The candy is sweet.
It is an awesome treat.
But there are many tricks so be wary!
Isabella Losada, Grade 4

Batter Became Art

There once was a bat named Sam Heart,
He was very happy and smart.
He loved to play ball,
But he was too small.
So he decided to paint art!
Julianna Olley, Grade 6

The Art of My Soul

The beat of my mind,
The rhythm of my heartbeat,
Flowing through my head,
Like a majestic river,
Music, the art of my soul.
Olivia Whittaker, Grade 6

The Lost Garden

Never to be seen,
Beautiful leaves of the trees,
Glistening water,
Waiting for someone's presence,
To reveal its true beauty!
Elizabeth Wolfe, Grade 6

A Broken Owl

There once was an owl named Tim
He fell right off his limb
He broke a bone
And called for home
But nobody answered him
Joel Kolagani, Grade 5

Blooming Flowers

Flowers awaken,
Yellow like the shining sun,
Planted in the grass,
Pretty as a shooting star,
Graceful as a newborn chick.
Penny Williams, Grade 6

Amazing Autumn

Putting shorts and tank tops back in the attic
bringing pants and sweatshirts back down
Golden pumpkin seeds
are autumn leaves crunching underneath your feet
Jack-o-lanterns light up row by row like city street lights
Succulent flavor of apple cider fills my mouth
Pumpkin guts squish in your hands as you carve your pumpkins
Savory scents of roasted corn make my stomach grumble
Trick-or-treaters dressed so scary giving people a spooky fright

Friends and family come to celebrate Thanksgiving
The aromatic smell of turkey fills my family's noses
My family and I queue up near the food so we can all eat
Feel the crisp chill in the air as you step outside
Exquisite flavor of apple pie sunk into my brain
The wind whistles while it blows leaves off of their trees
Rough pine cones are safety pins poking your hands as you pick them up
The leaves get buried from the snow
Now winter has begun
Ella McNay, Grade 6

Free as a Bird

Some people say they are as free as a bird,
I think I am one of those people.
But, from the things that I have inferred,
I am also not one of those people.

I am not as free as I want to be,
And that is not such a bad thing.
But I am as free as I should be,
And I still feel like a king.

In my mind, my freedom has lifted me higher than any bird has been,
At those times I feel joyous and free.
Other times, freedom is hard to find, not knowing where it's been,
At those times, I feel more trapped than a cat stuck in a tree.

When I am feeling weak and low in the sky,
I can always hear the wind whispering to me,
"It is okay, don't worry, tomorrow is another day, and before I say goodbye,
Always remember to stay high in the sky, and know that you are free."
Ari Gorostiaga, Grade 6

Margaret Mead

Born in December
Always will be remembered, as a great Anthropologist
Born in Philadelphia
Proceeded to the summit of Columbia
Earned her doctorate degree
Famous for her writing, for all to see
Also a deft museum curator of Ethnology
She worked from 1946 to 1969 as a teacher at New School
Married, but never carried by another shrewd soul
She thought no one would remember how she
Showed us her sighting, inspiring words in the months from December.
Madison Kiesel, Grade 4

New York

New York City is my favorite place to go,
I like to eat out and go see a show.
There are lots of shows to go see,
But Spiderman is the best, according to me.

The decorations at Christmas are something to see,
Especially Rockefeller Center, when they light up the tree.
Christmas music is loud and piped through some speakers,
As I run around the park in my new pair of sneakers.

Homeless people sleeping on the streets,
Knowing that they are hungry and have nothing to eat.
I wish they had a home or some place to go,
Because winter is coming and lots of snow.

There are food trucks everywhere, take your pick.
I know you'll be having some chicken on a stick!
As the weeks go and on our way
We will be back for another day.

Landon Magnone, Grade 6

Purple

Smart, but not so smart.
Heart, but not much heart.
I am on top of all,
But trust me, it makes me feel somewhat…small.
Inside I feel diffident.
On the outside I show something different.
Somehow, I am graceful with elegance,
While I try to show my fake intelligence.
I am honored for my looks.
Pure royalty, like in storybooks.
Sometimes I try to be better than all,
But my hopes and dreams crumble and fall.
When I awake, I wish my life was as carefree as my dreams,
Without a crown on my head that twinkles and gleams.
"Gorgeous" and "great leadership" they say.
Why can't I be unnoticed like gray?
My royal wisdom isn't the best.
I just want to be like the rest.
Purple

Alyana Childs, Grade 6

Fall Day

I sit by the fire, warm and cozy
Then I walk past the woods quietly
Soft and white bunnies go around
A crispy and warm fire, then they
Tell fall stories. I look up at the sky
I see it, it looks down on me
And puts on a smile, I look back up
At the sky I put on a smile.
I go walk back home and I watch a movie about fall,
I go to bed just hoping for school again,
I wake up I'm late for school.

Olivia Vera, Grade 4

Grey

Black and white
Dark grey and light grey
Evil and good
Death and life
My life is not black or white
I am not bad or good
No corruption has ever touched me
Yet I am not pure
I am grey
I don't want to be confusing
But I don't want to be easy to decipher
I'll turn the world upside down
Inside out
And bottom up
I want to make the world a better place
And I want to start today
So tomorrow is brighter
And so darkness is not considered bad then too
But is considered a beauty

Alex Teresi, Grade 6

Fall

I can't wait, fall it's starting I see,
fall is the season for me.
A brilliant sight; the leaves falling and trees turning colors,
I go to the pumpkin patch to gather decorations with others.

I'm outside jumping in leaves,
It's so cold that I must wear long sleeves,
Standing out there in the cold my love for fall excites me,
It's a season of happiness I guarantee.

Halloween is here; it's a time of fear,
I am going trick or treating with my peers.
I'm getting ready for Halloween night,
I know I'm going to have a big fright.

I smell the turkey cooking; the pumpkin pie is baking,
Ding, ding the oven rings
It's time for the big feast; my family is here
They are here for thankfulness and cheer.

Anna Clemente, Grade 6

Fall Is So Great

Amazing, cool, and nice weather.
Colorful walks in the park.
Puffy clouds light blue skies and spending time with,
My family on Thanksgiving night.
Playing football games too.
Fall is my favorite season.
Fall is so fun for our family,
Because we get to go to my grama's,
And drink yummy hot cocoa. That's yummy in my tummy.
Toasting marshmallows and piling them in my hot cocoa.
Mmm mmm so good. This is why fall is my favorite season of all!!

Gian Ortiz, Grade 4

Ode to the Heroes of World War II

The strong spectacular heroes,
Rest in peace to the ones who didn't survive the deathblows.
We admire your bravery,
We cry when we hear of your painful woes,
And rejoice when you were released so many years ago.

Some soldiers survived it all,
Others had that one heart-shattering fall.
We honor the dead and the alive,
We pay tribute to the ones who died,
Pity the soldiers of both sides.

They'll be our heroic inspirations
for when we are fighting our demons.
We will remember you forever,
As heroes of the second world war.

Sophia Ly, Grade 6

Things in Nature

Trees swaying in the wind, flowers blooming in the sun
Branches falling on the ground, leaves flowing in the breeze
Bushes growing rapidly, stems shining from the sun
Butterflies flying in the air, bees buzzing happily
Snow falling beautifully, hail thumping on the floor
Ice with ice skaters, crows crowing in the breeze
Birds singing like the wind, rain falling with love
Sleet swimming in the air, bugs underground
Grass growing like a child, weeds running from place to place
Fruit falling off of trees, skies are blue
Clouds are white and fluffy, sun shining down on us
Breeze singing in the night, animals playing with each other
Soil helping plants, music of the trees
Secrets of the wind, water sparkles
Colors glow, stars twinkle
Dreams flow into the sunset

Zakaria Ahmad, Grade 4

Winter Wishes

Amazing, cinnamon and sweet pumpkin scents,
Filling the air and making it smell so scrumptious!
Yum, yum, yum!
Everybody loves the cinnamon and pumpkin scents!
I sit with my family by the hot, cozy fireplace,
Drinking delicious hot chocolate!
We all watch a great Disney movie!
Then we all cuddle up in a warm cozy blanket!
We make sweet s'mores by the fire,
And then eat them, crunch, crunchy, crunch!
I play with my friends,
And we have fun all together!
My dad and I go ice skating,
We have marvelous fun!
Decorations light up the neighborhood, and it's very pretty!
Winter makes my heart sing!

Rachel Battat, Grade 4

The Ninjas in Black

I spot them jumping from tree to tree.
Making the trees shake as they step their branches.
They do so they could get around quicker.
Not so silent but not loud either.
Each and one of them wearing a black cloth
covering their whole body except their eyes.
Carrying a sword on their back for defending and attacking.
They're called Ninjas.
Traveling night and day without resting but
still has plenty of energy to spare.
If they sense an enemy approaching they will get into a formation.
I stepped closer to see more I stepped on a branch by accident.
Their ears hearing as good as a komodo dragon
and their eyes as clear as an eagle's eye,
saw me hidden looking at them.
They all turn and saw me but they knew I was no harm to them.

Waydoh Htoo, Grade 6

The Marks of War

The marching of soldiers off to battle, a great battle,
The chant of the enemy, trying to intimidate us
The sound of gunfire, and the bullets whooshing past us
Friends and foes dropping all around us
The sound of explosions, as explosives detonate
The dust of war, smoke, floating away…
The whoosh of fighter jets and bombers, and the rolling of tanks
The shout of victory, but the sorrow of lost ones
The cries and the funerals of lost friends and family
The marks of war trace the Veterans today
War is never necessary
War is painful in all ways
War must be stopped
War must never come again
War must become a whisper
War must be banished from history!

Reynard Furstenberg, Grade 6

A Piece of Love

A piece of love that is gone,
A piece of love that is still so strong.
That piece of love was my grandfather, Bobby.
A piece of love that is really big.
A piece of love that had two dogs.
A piece of love that loved peanuts.
A piece of love that was always happy.
That piece of love was the strongest,
With a bond that could not break us.

Even if he died and is gone,
He always will be a piece of love for me.
Even if it breaks my heart,
I know it had to be.
I really wish he could have stayed.
But it's time to go on with my day.

Ashley Boone, Grade 6

Sisters
Caring, brave,
quick, helpful,
someone very nice,
encouraging, courageous, inspiring,
generous, giving
a sister
Cherish McCoy, Grade 4

Movies
Funny, boring,
Watching, looking, shaking
They teach lots of lessons,
Raging, clicking, browsing,
Violent, scary,
Video.
Xavier Ivey, Grade 5

Spring Has Sprung
Spring is green
Spring tastes like fresh berries
Spring sounds like rain pouring on the roof
Spring smells like newly cut grass
Spring looks like people flying kites
Spring makes me feel happy
Aiden Stalnaker, Grade 4

I Am
I am kind and a good friend
I wonder why people have two arms
I hear birds chirping
I see the turtles swimming
I want to become an art teacher
I am kind and a good friend
Emily McCullough, Grade 5

Halloween
Gruesome, fun
Scaring, fleeing, trick 'o' treating
Time to dress up
Surprising, tricking, walking
Enchanting, shadow
'O' Hallows Eve
Michelle Taylor, Grade 4

Forest
A cool, sunny afternoon
The trees tower above us
The loam under my feet is soft
The quietness is beautifully peaceful
Gracefully, a bird chases a moth
The happiness inside of me is relaxing.
Jonathan Yoo, Grade 5

The Eye of the Storm
The angry wind howled
As the freezing waves beat against the ice
But most of all there was snow
Falling snow, settled snow, bright shimmering white snowflakes
Drifting, blowing, still snowflakes
Everything covered in white
Blinding white, so bright it will hurt eyes
So cold that it will numb skin
So fresh one can smell the chill in the air
So smooth and clean, it is pure enough to taste
So no one can hear the snow crunch
But then there was silence
Deafening silence
There was a spell over the freshly falling snow so that everything was peaceful
It seemed that the world was holding its breath
And then the breath was let out
The earth came back to life as the eye of the storm passed
Samanyu Kovvuri, Grade 4

Loving Lockwood Avenue
My neighborhood is soft and calm place like a beach
house on Kimset, Fire Island hearing the water douses up to the shore.

My neighborhood is an interesting town when you can
catch a glimpse of the Oak Tree's vibrant red, crisp
yellow, orange and green apparel is drifting onto the
rocky road of Lonely Lockwood Ave with only two houses on the lovely road.

My neighborhood is inviting and beautiful with
immense houses on the Connequot River, hearing boats
zooming by while watching the sunset.

And it is a perfect place to see the beautiful winter
wonderland just like in freezing Antarctica.

And it is an extraordinary town, that I am glad to call
my relaxing and quiet town, home.
Paige Dreyfus, Grade 6

Orange
Smell the fire, feel the heat.
See the bright orange marigolds like waves, dancing in the wind.
Have warm pumpkin pie in the warm pumpkin light.
Hear the tiger roar, like the color orange itself.
Run your finger on a pumpkin and feel the rough skin of an orange.
Taste the marmalade on the warm toast.
Orange is racing cars that were just scrubbed and hear the car motor,
Rrrrrmmmmm, rrrrrrrmmmm.
Hear the sizzling Fanta, like orange juice with bubbles.
Feel the glue, a sticky pond of orange.
A pencil smells like orange, and
So does my bright orange coat.
Smell the beautiful orange
Chrysanthemums, standing straight up tall.
Orange is the color of happiness.
Jacob Shapiro, Grade 4

Rocky the Bulldog

Rocky
Fun, funny, and playful
Who belongs to our family
Who plays with bones, toys, and food
Who experienced sadness, scary, and mad
Who fears fireworks, loud noises, and other dogs
Who accomplished scaring away other dogs
Who feeds on dog food, chicken, and turkey
Who lives in his house, our house, and outside
Who belongs to the class of mammals,
Canis Familiaris
Yair Lopez Vallejo, Grade 6

My State of Maine

Maine is a place with tall pine trees,
with lots of animals for people to see.
The Maine state animal is a big bull moose,
who walks around on his two front hooves.
Sitting there in a tall pine tree singing along for you and me,
Is the Maine state bird, the chickadee.
If you go Downeast, it is lobster in a pot,
but if you break the law, you are going to get caught.
Aroostook County is at the top of the state,
where fur trappers live and Portland people hate.
This is my state, MAINE.

Braden Richard, Grade 5

Holidays and Their Seasons

In fall we have Halloween with pumpkins that glow,
costumes, decorations, and ghosts that glow.
Trick or treating will bring candy, and belly aches, Oh no!

Thanksgiving will come for us all to show,
our love for God and ones we know.
We give thanks for family and friends you know.

And then there is winter with all its snow,
wind will blow and snow will flow,
and before you know it, Christmas aglow.
Hunter Acernese, Grade 6

My Father

You always work so hard to provide.
So that we have the very best in life.
Many times you go in sick, hurt, no matter what.
So we never have to ask for the necessities of life.
You work from sun up to sun down,
So we never go without.
From the sweat of your brow,
to the blood of your knuckles,
you always give 100% of yourself.
Through this you've shown me a father's love.
So I pray you never question your son's love for his father.
Malachi Teague, Grade 6

My Brother Dan

My brother Dan
is the cutest little man.

He has blue eyes and blond hair.
He sits in a high chair if you can keep him in there.

He has a fat little belly,
and sometimes can be very smelly.

He really knows how to scream but
when he smiles it's the cutest thing I've ever seen.
Samantha McGuckin, Grade 4

Ode to Pikachu

Pikachu,
Playful, active, blonde, and hairy,
Who belonged to Diego and Naiade,
Who loved playing and running,
Who experienced love, fun, and freedom,
Who feared strangers, bathing, and yelling,
Who accomplished bringing company in my life,
Who fed on chow, chickens, and rubber,
Who lived in our house, my room, and Naiade's room,
Who belongs to the class of mammals,
Canis Familiaris.
Diego Morales-Pineda, Grade 6

Hands

I like my hands, my hands can do many things
My hands help me write
I like my hands
My hands punch the punching bag
I love my hands
My hand waves goodbye in a right to left motion
I love my hands
Although I have to give them a break I will never fake
How much I love my hands
My hands tie my shoes and eat my favorite foods
I love my hands
James Wright, Grade 6

Nature in Life

The trees are twinkling in the sun.
The roots look like fingers hugging the ground.
The roots were as big as the Grand Canyon.
The trees swayed in the wind.
Clatter clatter I heard a squirrel running up the tree.
The leaves danced while falling off the tree.
The trees looked like they were hugging each other all around.
The ground looks like chocolate with sprinkles on it.
Caw caw a bird is talking.
Scratch scratch a chipmunk is scratching at a tree.
The leaves are as green as summer grass.
Giselle Jeffrey, Grade 4

Don't Give Up

Don't give up,
you can do this!
Believe you can
and you'll get through this
Walk into school with your head held high
And if they say something to you,
you just say goodbye
Be optimistic, the power of positivity
Clearly, they're just acting silly
So, remember if they pick you apart,
just believe in yourself with all your heart.
Holly Tomassi, Grade 6

Candy Canes

Candy canes on the tree,
How they do tempt me.

Candy canes on the ground,
Oh no! They must have fallen down!

Candy canes safe and sound,
Up in the tree, all around.

Candy canes, now don't leave!
Stay up there 'til Christmas Eve!
Sadie Shank, Grade 6

Sun

The sun and the rain
The wind and tranquility
All are opposite
But still the same
Come from the same sky
Come from the same land
Together are one
Mother Nature is queen
God the king
Together as one
But not the same
Grace Hubbard, Grade 6

Hail, America

The veterans risked their lives for us
We must care for them
We must pray for them
We must remember their sacrifice
We must remember their bravery
Fighting through fear
We must never forget their sacrifices,
They have saved our freedom,
We will always honor you
And make sure your sacrifice isn't in vain
We thank you for our freedom.
Zachary Dodgin, Grade 6

Rock Persona

I stand here still as a statue
I stare at the people
Lying here heavy and strong

The cars rolling by
Humans driving and controlling them
Like little boys playing video games

People try to pick me up
A life in me
No heart
All alone day and night
Like a lost boy on the corner

Starving for food
Striving for movement
Stumped for words

Shaping and shifting into different forms
When the weather strikes
Evolving and disintegrating over time
Matthew LoPiccolo, Grade 5

Giant Beast

You stomp
With your big gray feet
Each step making an
Earthquake

Happily living
With your family
Eating grass
And trumping
Out loud

Until a gun sounds
And you fall with a thump
A piece of your heart cut off
For the pleasure and
Beauty of others

A giant beast
Lies there
Never to sound
Again
Siri Mudunuri, Grade 6

Seasons

Fall
Cold, rainy
Leaves falling, raking, sliding
Leaves, dark, parties, green grass
Playing, running, flowers growing
Hot, sunny
Spring
Isis Bragg, Grade 5

Beautiful Diamond

How
Small but
Yet so valuable
Watch this diamond
Sparkle in the sunlight
Its crystal shiny edges sparkle
In the moonlight, it sinks in the
Sand all alone in the darkness
It gets washed upon the
Shore while crashing
Waves may crack it
But this is what
Makes it
Beautiful
Abbie Tanner, Grade 6

Baseball

I really want to hit the ball!
Bang! I did and it hit the wall!
I ran and ran, I made it to third.
Then, I just suddenly heard,
the clink and clack of a baseball bat.
I can tell the crowd is happy with that!
I keep running and running,
I feel like that is very stunning!
He made it all the way to second base,
The other teams players chased and chased!
I'm happy if he makes it home too,
the team yells cause he really flew.
You can tell from the words above,
Baseball is my only love!
Ben Mabry, Grade 5

Football

I love football how about you?
If you don't that's fine, but don't sue.
Maybe you like to tackle or block.
The guys who do this look like rocks.
CRACK! the defense takes out the tight ends.
And that's just how you can defend.
So passing is what you like to do?
Don't get hit, just run to be on cue.
The best part is when you score.
Then you will hear the crowd roar.
You make a touchdown be a clown.
Then you feel just like you own the town.
Then if you win the football game.
That is how you get the fame.
Ethan Collins, Grade 5

Grandparents Are...

A tissue for your tears.
A treat for your taste buds.
A smile for your face.
A hug for your heart.
Lily Eyvazzadeh, Grade 6

My Eyes
My eyes, my eyes
Oh my eyes
Sometimes they lie
But I don't really cry
They show me things that look cool
They help me see when I'm at school

Mine are blue like the sky
But when I'm sad, they turn pink
The tears come and I start to blink
If you try to say goodbye
They will give you the evil eye
My eyes my eyes
Gabriella Marie Brooks, Grade 6

Life Is a Mountain
Life is a mountain
There're ups
There're downs
Life is a mountain
Sometimes life gets rocky
Sometimes smooth
Life is a mountain
You can climb to the top
or stay at the bottom
Life is a mountain
You can jump right off and end it there
or make it memorable and get to the top
Life is a mountain
Sage Grant, Grade 6

Dead Battery
I have taken
your phone
that was in
the room;
you were
probably
saving the battery
for school.

Forgive me,
it was fun
to play games
and text.
Jamaine Rodriguez, Grade 6

Summer Fun
Summer's here at last
With my friends, we will have a blast
We will play and have fun
Water games for everyone
As the light from the sun goes down
A slumber party with all my friends around
What a wonderful day
Aryella Marti, Grade 6

Summer Fun
Splash! I jump in the pool.
I'm having a barbecue.
Swimming and snorkeling what fun.
My mom invited my entire family.
We are a huge, loving, fun family.
It is beach time.
Vacation to the wet water park.
Eating delicious ice cream.
Camping and making yummy smores.
Time for the big July 4th celebration.
Fireworks bursting in the air.
Summer fun everywhere!
Gavriel Molina, Grade 4

9/11
It was the day
when the Twin Towers were very busy loud.
Then something odd came.
It was a plane,
that crashed into the Twin Towers.
It was a sad day.
People were crying.
They are sad now.
They pray for the people
in the Twin Towers.
That was the day of
September 11, 2001.
Emmanuel Segura, Grade 6

Summertime
On the hot sunny day drinking cold drinks,
Having a nice time in the hot weather.
Going to the beach,
Swimming in warm water.
Relaxing and playing outside.
Putting on sunscreen,
To block the intense sun.
Hot hot! Sun blazing.
Bug land invading and coming.
Enjoying surfing, doing barbeques,
And eating sweet fruits.
Summertime is the best!
Mussadiq Malik, Grade 4

Hello New York!
Where the snow falls heavy,
And the cold hits deep.
Where the mountains are high,
And there is a bright blue sky!
Where the taxies go beep,
And no one goes to sleep.
Where the pizza is thin,
The Yankees know how to win!
New York is the best place to be!
You should go and see!
Allyson Giarrusso, Grade 6

One Window
One window is all I need.
To see the world beyond me.
To see what lies in store for me.
To see myself reflect for me.
To see how beautiful I am on the inside.
To see all the adventures there are.
To hear all the birds chirping in my yard.
To look and see my future.
To look inside the world.
To find my inner expression.
To look beyond the troubles in my life.
To see all my family and friends playing.
To see my reflection and my past.
To see my past and future.
To see the people inside.
To know how it feels to be sad.
To know that everything is going to be okay.
To see all the animals playing in my yard.
To see the bus to get on.
To know that I have a beautiful life.
Shayla Miller, Grade 6

Summer Sun
That big and
yellow circle in
the sky is called
the sun. It is
very hot on
summer days.
Some days
you can not
see the
sun because
the clouds
cover it. If
it is not cloudy
be sure to apply
sunscreen. It
will get hot
and you won't
want to get
burnt.
Nico Duarte, Grade 5

The Kiss of Dancing Flowers
The kiss of dancing flowers
it spreads through me with happiness
The kiss of dancing flowers
it fills me with joy
The kiss of dancing flowers
my first kiss at last
The kiss of dancing flowers
it is more than love
The kiss of dancing flowers
it has finally come true
Juliette Coffey, Grade 6

Life

Life is like a flower.
You bloom and grow,
wither and die,
but you will always be beautiful in the process.

Life is like a tightrope.
It takes getting used to.
You will teeter back and forth.
Just when you feel like you're about to fall,
you get the hang of it.

Life is like jumping on a trampoline.
There's ups and downs.
There are times you will fall,
but you get back up and keep going.

Life is like a spinning wheel.
You never know what'll happen next,
or where you'll land.
Just when you think you're at the top,
you fall back down.
But when you think nothing can get worse,
you go right back to the top again.

Sydney Topoleski, Grade 5

Legs

Legs, my beautiful legs
They are so helpful can't you see
Everywhere I go
My legs follow me

They help me kick
When I play
As I walk
I use them every day

They help me with sports
What would I do without soccer
Oh my legs, I hope I never break my amazing legs
I hope they stay with me forever

Kaitlyn Taylor, Grade 6

Sledding with a Snowman

Zooommm!
I was going so fast,
I could not stop!
I think I passed my mom's spot,
But it just would not stop!
The sled was booming and zooming,
And I was afraid.
Then I saw a large white figure standing there,
It was a snowman it gave me a scare!
But he showed me the way back home,
With my family right there,
And that friendly snowman for now on always there.

Cameron Donals, Grade 4

Fall Is in the Air

"Come," said the wind to the leaves one day
"Come" over the meadow and we will play
Put on your dresses of red and gold
For summer is asleep, and the days grow cold*

I always dislike the summers end;
Since I have to pull out that play book once again
The red leaves on a tree are like strawberry jam, falling off a tree
The weather is like a cold Jacuzzi
And the wonderful sunset spreads out like a brilliant star
Tangerine toned leaves, shaped like golden corn flakes
The sky is like a blue crystal sea
Leaves are as crunchy as tortilla chips
A season of descending leaves and hibernating trees
A season for crunching and munching
As well as bonfire flames dancing in the midnight air
That delicious Thanksgiving Day repast, oh so delightful!
A season for listening to racing winds whistling
through sleepy undress branches
And for children chasing the host of whirling, twirling fallen leaves
It's time to say goodbye to summer and hello to autumn fun!!

*"Come Little Leaves" by George Cooper
Heather Stein, Grade 6

The Rainbow

Red is the taste of a sweet juicy cherry
Dancing along your taste buds in a sugary rush
Orange is the blazing rays of the sinking sun
The evening's bursting finale
Yellow is the joy that we carry
Helping us defeat the stress
Green is the smell of sprouting spring fun
A sweet blooming daisy's scent
Blue is the humming morning dew
Making the birds sing
Purple is the silky sunrise mist
Softly rousing you awake
The colorful band arching over you
Takes you on a journey, grasping your wrist

Olivia Costolo, Grade 6

Marco Polo

Marco Polo was the first European to meet the Asian
He would start a quest on any occasion
He was born in Venice, Italy and traveled the Silk Road
And if you read *The Book of Marvels*, that is where he is shown
He was born in 1254, he'd travel land, and he'd travel shore
His journey lasted 24 years
And on his strenuous escapades, he had no fears
He died in 1324
And you know why he did it
Because he relished to explore.
On his adventures, he'd never make a blunder
He'd travel through any storm, any lightning, any thunder

Dylan Smith, Grade 5

Leaf

Red, Orange, Yellow, shots of Green
Watching as they flow
One lay down, far, far from the rest
Different, different from the rest
Thought he was alone, sad, lonely
It started flying, flying, far, far away
It sat down, beside a curb
And thought, and thought, and thought
He realized
"What have I done?"
A frown opened up
What was happening
He was needed, wanted
Back home
He flew there, he tried
To no avail, he was alone
A streak, red flew past
He followed her
She led him
Somewhere new, somewhere old
Home.
Amol Bhingarde, Grade 5

Sky

I wish the sky wouldn't fall
on the people I love most of all
and make them drown in their own doubt
when they don't even have a voice to shout.

They helped me
get to the light
even when
I had no strength to fight

They helped me find
who I am
Though now THEY cram
My life with others

Forgetting all they ever knew about me
I watch them leave
the door where I walked in
they walk out and they scream and shout
at each other for so long and I wonder
Where have they really been?
Genevieve Savage, Grade 5

Lizard

I am a cute lizard
Green as a grassy field
I can walk slowly
I can run fast
I can camouflage
I can bite
I am a cute lizard
Andrea Dorman, Grade 4

Softball

Hitting, bunting
slapping, running
pitcher, catcher
throwing, catching.

Infield, outfield
dugout too
batters, batting
pitchers, pitching.

Balls, strikes, and
walks to all
called by umpires
and sliding for a
safe or out.

Winning, losing
shaking hands
saying the good game
is the softball way.
Virginia Grace Elmore, Grade 5

Force and Motion in Nature

How do birds fly?
That's a question you might ask.
Scientist used to always study.
But all that's in the past.
Now they know the how and why.
They spread their wings to maintain lift,
Then they bring them down.
The flight of a bird is a special gift.
Have you ever heard of a flying squirrel?
All that's just a spoof.
Flying squirrels jump and glide,
Now you know the truth.
Dolphins can swim all through the water,
On their belly, back, and side.
Their smooth skin gives them easy turns,
It's almost like it glides.
Now you know the truth,
About the way things really work.
The way animals survive and move,
From the clouds into the dirt.
Nolen Howard, Grade 5

Python

I am long and slippery
On the prowl I will go
To eat is my main objective
Even in the cold
I change my colors
for disguise I must
Slide fast and quick
Surprise my prey
So I can live for another day
Anthony Salgado, Grade 5

Pomegranates

Pomegranates, Pomegranates
Juicy and sweet,
Pomegranates, Pomegranates,
Great to eat.
Pomegranates, Pomegranates,
So delicious and red!
Pomegranates, Pomegranates,
Can't get them out of my head.
Pomegranates, Pomegranates,
Juicy and sweet.
Pomegranates, Pomegranates,
Oh, boy — What a treat!
Kamel Jabji, Grade 5

My Hands

My hands help me grip
My hands can get hurt
But I can help them heal
For after all the things they do for me
Oh what would I be without my hands
Well, I would not be me without my hands
With them I dance and play
I can play and dance all day
I can accessorize my hands
I can paint my nails
Oh how much I love my hands
I hope you do too
Kaylee Brown, Grade 6

Blue

I am blue
A fish swimming in the sea
A dove flying up above
For blue is free
I am blue
Overwhelmed by sadness
Drowning in sorrow
I am blue
Feeling the wind kiss my face
As I sail into the land
Of independence
I am blue
Anoushka Sinha, Grade 6

Holiday

Christmas trees glow of green
Wherever you're in my house be seen
It has a lot of sharp pine leaves
I'm lucky it doesn't make me sneeze
Christmas is the best holiday
Because I get to decorate in my own way.
Look at my tree!
Christmas trees are best tall
Because while opening presents underneath
I feel so small!
Arina Gavrilenko, Grade 5

The Winter Day

Hurray! Hurray!
It's a winter day.
It is a good day to play.
I build a terrific snowman,
And have an incredible snowball fight.
It's a good day to have yummy hot cocoa.
At night I sit by the cozy fire.
And is an incredible day.
Alex Lemongellow, Grade 4

Owls from Canada

Out of the nest,
Through the tundra,
Into the canyon,
Past the glacier,
Over New York,
In the city,
Above my house,
In my backyard.
Michael Spinelli, Grade 5

Friendship Is…

A friend is kind when we play.
A friend is loyal when we hang.
A friend is caring to me.
A friend is sweet as ice-cream.
A friend is wonderful to me.
A friend is always there.
A friend is loving when I am sad.
A friend is Brenda.
Nylah Coleman, Grade 4

Loved One

My mom, she cooks the best chicken.
It's so finger licking'
I keep on lickin'.
We know that you will go,
We hope you don't,
We all know you won't go soon.
We all love you,
So I love you mom.
Daniel Porter, Grade 6

Fishing with Dad

I like fishing with my dad.
He is the best at fishing,
And I like going with my two brothers,
Once I caught five amazing fish in a row.
They were all the same fish!
I had an excellent time with my dad,
And my two brothers.
Bryce Mann, Grade 4

Ode to French Fries

Oh French fries,
You're the king of my belly.
Your salty taste ties together a meal.
Crispy, salty, Yum, Yum, Yum.
Without you French fries, I would never have fireworks in my mouth.
No other food gets my respect other than you French Fries.

You're 5 STARS, the big leader,
the tasty YUM in my mouth.
When you bring your friend sweet potato fry,
you're DELICIOUS!

You and ketchup are a team.
You and ketchup are best friends.
Your arch enemy hotdog has no chance of beating you!
You don't really need ketchup, you are great by yourself.
Let your saltiness shine like the sun, with no clouds in your way
You're at the top of the menu

When I fall asleep, your sweet and salty taste lingers in my mouth
When I have to say goodbye to you French Fries,
I know I'll see you and eat you again.
French Fries,
Even though you're just a food, you're still the king of my belly!
Parker Mills, Grade 5

Light and Dark

Light is hopeful,
Light is beautiful,
Light is something you should be thankful.

Light can be big,
Light can be small,
but that doesn't matter it is a beautiful call.

Light is the sign of good fate,
Light has a good trait,
Light can go in a peaceful rate.

Dark is hopeless,
Dark is night,
Dark is something that has a bad sight.

Dark can go wrong,
Dark makes a minor song,
Dark is the sadness that goes very long.

There is nothing good about dark, remember it is a very bad mark.

Light is a milestone, but Dark is not, these are words that matter a lot.
Light and Dark will go for ever and they will always be together.
Bhargav Sristy, Grade 5

Ode to My Family

Oh, my family
I love you
From the bottom of my heart.
You're the only thing I need,
My family

I'm wondering,
What's me without you?
Would I even be here, standing on Earth,
Without you?

You are like a mama bear
Taking care of her cubs,
With your love,
With your strength,
And all your care.

You made me,
My family.
I'll do anything,
To be with you.
You're the only thing I need
My family
Veronica Ramos, Grade 5

I'm Growing Up

I'm traveling over high mountains
Going down the deepest oceans
Crossing bridges and jumping waves
Diving into the darkest caves.

I'm growing up, I'm pushing through
I cannot stop to wait for you.

You reach wanting to hold me tight
You fight thinking you are right
But faster and faster I grow
And it's harder than you will know.

I'm growing up, I'm pushing through
I cannot stop to wait for you.

The moments we spend together
My mind will cherish forever
Even if it lasts a minute or two
These memories will carry us through.

I'm growing up, I'm pushing through
And if I stray, you'll be there eternally.
Alma Gaxiola, Grade 4

Winter Has Come

Gentle, soft powder,
Covering the dull dead grass,
Chilling, yet so nice.
Kaylee Hinson, Grade 6

Hands

My hands are important,
They help me in everyday life,
They help me cut potatoes with a knife,
My hands, my hands
Oh you help me so much,
So that I'm not in a rush
Hands help me text my sister
My hands are good with writing,
They are trying,
My hands, my hands
You are so strong
But sometimes you are wrong
Tierney Phillips, Grade 6

The Willow Tree

Sitting there by the creek,
Just waiting,
Not a peep.
Her leaves are falling,
Her branches are throbbing.
She helps the poor,
She nurses the weak.
On the hill you can see her peak.
The thrashing wind makes her happy,
That is the only time she can dance.
Even then she has time to be,
The Willow Tree.
Jillian Zimmerman, Grade 4

Thanksgiving

T urkey that is stuffed
H am on the table
A nd dishes stacked everywhere
N o one leaves the house hungry
K nocks on the door bringing
S miles from people
G iving thanks
I ce cream piled high on pies
V anilla wafers — gather
I n to watch football
N ow we are the stuffed ones
G iving thanks to everyone
Zackary Stacy, Grade 6

I Want to Know

I want to know
Why they treat me this way
because of my skin, my hair my clothes.
I want to know
Are they mad about my good grades?
That teachers like me?
I want to know why y'all stare and laugh
when I walk by.
I've been bullied, pushed, pulled.
Tell me why you don't believe in me.
Mina Fleshman, Grade 6

Love One

Mom is a wonderful word,
because it is the most beautiful word,
I ever heard.
She is like a flower,
she fills my heart with showers.
It is like she has powers.
She is my joy,
she is my pride,
she is my mom,
and I love her,
from deep inside.
Taniya Watson, Grade 6

May I Just Say

I ate the cupcakes
That were sitting
Perfectly on the chair

And which
You were most obviously
Saving for dessert

Greatest apologies
They were so sweet
And so very good
Lucy Juedemann, Grade 4

War Is Peace in the Making

For there to be peace
There must be war
Like a wildfire
It must burn everything
Before green shoots up again
Every side has their version of peace
That is why they war
For there to be peace
There must be war
We have our peace
Because we have fought our wars
Alex Martin, Grade 6

Smiles Are a Contagious Disease

Smiles are a contagious disease
They spread easily like jelly
With one glance you caught the disease
Smiles are a contagious disease
You never know when you will catch it
This disease will start to grow inside of you
It will build up until you explode with joy!
The smiles are everywhere now!
Smiles are a contagious disease
A good disease
A great disease
Ella Grant, Grade 6

My Mind

My mind is a world of imagination
with shapes all around you
and many colors in the darkness
Mind is a world of imagination
with many things unexplored
and words you never heard of before
Mind is a world of imagination
with things that go hi and bye
and ask if you have the time
Mind is a world of imagination
that is special for you and you only
because of who you are
Jessica Ornelas, Grade 6

Moving On

I move on to the next thing
As my toes get sore from walking
I forget everything in the past
And I move on
The sun so bright
Making my eyes so weak
While it makes the plant stronger
And I move on
My room with so much from the past
That it all floats around me
I wiggle myself out of here
And I move on...
Wendy Morales Gonzalez, Grade 6

Unique

It's not bad to be different
Everyone is unique
People are special in their own ways
What's inside matters the most
Everyone is unique
Believe in yourself
What's inside matters the most
Don't be afraid to stand out
Believe in yourself
People are special in their own ways
Don't be afraid to stand out
It's not bad to be different
Megan Wu, Grade 6

Hold on to Your Future

Hold on to your future
Even if you are hurt
Hold on to your life
Even if you do poorly at times
Hold on to the right path
Even if you make a few turns
Hold on to your loved ones
Even if you fight
Hold on to your belongings
Even when they are gone
Vinata Kondragunta, Grade 6

What to Do if You Lived in the Ocean

Play with the dolphins.
Avoid being eaten by a shark.
Feed the hungry fish.
Swim away from the waves.
Don't make a killer whale angry.
Save people who drown in the sea.
Don't get caught in fishing nets.
zzz ... sleep safe and sound in the ocean.
Yum, yum, yum! Find your food by yourself.
Don't harm the rainbow fish.
Stare at the shore with your friends in the sea
Angela Huang, Grade 4

My Hair

I love my hair
It is so fair
I put it up and down
And all around

It is straight
I sometimes have a complaint
My hair is wavy
But sometimes it gets crazy

In the morning my hair is a mess
And I try to make it my best
As you know I really do
Care about my hair
Victoria Reilley, Grade 6

Unicorns

I love unicorns jumping on rainbows,
While their silky pink mane flows.
I never want to let her go,
If she follows me home, I'm so delighted,
My mom, however will not be excited!
We will go to games and play,
Until the end of the bright day.
The floor she sleeps on all night long,
And I will sing her the best sweet song.
She will let me get on her back and fly,
Into the shiny, starry night sky.
We will travel the whole world wide,
Over the moon and stars we will glide,
What a fantastic, joyful ride!
Parmdeep Ghataora, Grade 5

The River

It's like a river
beautiful flowing and sweet
The river sees you
Mackenzie Juliette, Grade 6

My Emotions

I thought you understood
how I was feeling, but no
I was wrong, really wrong.

I feel broken, lost, depressed, and sad
Confused, tired of everything, and unhappy.
Why can't people be happy?
Why do bad things happen?
Why is life so hard?
WHY?

If I could be a butterfly
I would fly away and go on out to the world
and never come back;
I would be free.

I feel locked in a dark, dark cave
where I can't get out;
I'm trapped.

Sometimes I just feel really down;
I don't know anymore,
but I know that I'll be okay
as long as I don't give up and move on
because life goes on.
Elizabeth Lopez, Grade 6

Beautiful Secrets

The beauty of a secret
And the promise not to tell
The beauty of a new grown sunflower
And the reassurance that it'll grow well

The beauty of a stage
On opening night
The beauty of everything
Lies in plain sight.

I've told you a secret;
You've promised not to tell
The love I feel for this world
Makes my heart swell

And if I told you my feelings
Would you think me crazed?
For the joy I feel right now
Would make you amazed

Tell me a secret
I would never tell
The love I feel for you
Makes my heart swell.
Eva-Marie Jones, Grade 6

Mine Craft

As I grab my controller, I start the game,
I walk by animals I soon shall tame.
I build a base, I call it my domain,
I honestly hope it will sustain!
I lumber over to my bed,
Then my screen becomes red.
It gave 2 options, title screen or respawn,
Then I yelled, "COME ON!"
As I Was mining wood I saw a cave,
It was deep, dark and black, but I was feeling brave.
As I go deeper and deeper,
I start to hear zombies and creepers.
I press a random button and then I fall,
I was mad because of the time I used after all.

Ethan Horne, Grade 5

Outer Space

There is no single place like Outer Space.
That is why it caused the Space Race.
Venus is an upside-down wall going round and round.
No-one knows the size of the whole Cosmos.
Neutron Stars are rapidly rotating Pulsars.
Calisto is the most cratered moon we know.
Matter cubed then squared equals energy that's theory.
All forces have opposite but equivalent.
Coronal mass ejection mess with sense of direction.
The Universe is wide from side to side.
Quasars are far beyond the most distant stars.
Blazers are really blazingly blindingly brilliantly bright Quasars.
No-one knows everything about the whole cosmos.
That why Space is my most favorite place.

Calvin Fritts, Grade 5

My Two Bad Cats

From the shelter we saved two kittens young,
Sweet at first but weren't quite right.
They were soft of fur but rough of tongue,
But little did we know they liked to bite.
One was a bit of a black coated brat,
He came with a snotty nose that glistened.
Dad gets mad when he gets into this and that,
It would be much better if he listened.
The other is the oddest cat you will see,
Tortoise color and oh so curious.
Late at night she turns on and watch's TV,
Waking dad making him furious.
Despite all the things they've done,
Our family's hearts they've won.

Orlando Hess-Tharpe, Grade 5

Siberian Tiger

He is an amazing and fascinating tiger.
He is as fast as a race car and has the reflexes of a ninja.
He loves to play action video games, read thrilling books, and
watch YouTube on his phone and computer.

Blaine Fitzgerald, Grade 6

The Wonderful School

The school I go to is the best.
I like it here because I don't stress.
I have lots of very good friends.
We take care of each other to the day ends.
This school does a lot of exciting things.
Like the chorus goes on stage to sing.
There are clubs like Beta and FCA.
There are a lot of choices every day.
like having fabulist foods to eat.
They have a lot of good sweets.
Lunch is always full of new treats.
I like recess it is the very best.
Because I have worked hard and need a rest.
Boo! Yah! this is the best place for success.

Colby Smart, Grade 5

Lexi's Lovely Laundry Machine

Laundry Day!
Oh no I must get away!

We'll help you get away.
Lexi's Lovely Laundry Machine
Will surely make your day.
Get laundry out of the way!
I guarantee you'll get good service.
Program it and your laundry's in its drawer.
You can even name it something
Crazy, we'll make sure.

Enjoy Lexi's Lovely Laundry Machine.
For laundry will stay in its drawer.

Alexandra Francisco, Grade 4

Life Is an Airplane Flight

Life is an airplane flight.
The earaches and crowded seats
            might
            bring
            you
            down,
    but you have to realize,
that is not all it has to offer.

As you get higher, higher, and higher, the views only get better.

When you finally land,
you reflect on when your wheels first left the ground,
and something amazing started.

Quentin Pileggi, Grade 6

I Give Thanks For

I give thanks for…
my caring mom…she takes care of me,
my helpful dad…he helps me with my math homework,
my fun brother…he plays sports with me.

Sebastian Nicholson, Grade 4

Wind

The wind soars through the sky, helping its friends the birds fly as it gives them piggybacks. It
races airplanes, in and out of the clouds stretching it's invisible talons over the finish line. Wind stampedes across the ocean,
shoving forward the slow waves into roaring currents. At
night it slugs through the air softly, singing it's lonely song about how no one can see it.

As soon as dawn lights the horizon wielding its fiery torch, wind bounds out on the grass,
cheerfully bouncing and blowing with all its might onto warm and sleepy animals and watching
them scramble back into their beds shivering as it barrels backward laughing.

It ric-rockets out of the leaf blower, blowing leaves into piles during its autumn time duty.
During playtime, wind stealthily creeps up on people and swirls around them, whipping at their
faces, stinging their eyes with its invisible stinger, creeping up their sleeves, pant legs, and down their shirts, tickling their spines,
and wrapping its icy body around them like freezing cold sheets.

When wind gets tired, it sleepily drifts across the sky watching children play and tumble, as it
turns to a warm breeze, catching the children when they trip and soon, the wind drifts off into a cozy slumber.

Olivia D. Doiron, Grade 6

I Am

I am a boy who enjoys video games.
I wonder what power ups there are.
I hear the jumping noise, the music, the sound of enemies being defeated, the cries of creatures.
I want to beat the level, bosses, and get a record time.
I am a boy who enjoys video games.
I pretend that I am the main character in the game.
I feel excited, addicted to it, frustrated, relieved, happy, and shocked by some things.
I touch the controller and buttons.
I worry that I will not succeed or get an effect.
I am a boy who enjoys video games.
I understand how every character thinks and feels.
I say that I can beat the bosses.
I dream of beating the game.
I hope that the game is not way too hard either.
I am a boy who enjoys video games.

Christopher Duncan, Grade 5

The Alligator in the Sawgrass

Sawgrass rustles through the Cerulean water like razors,
The Forlorn lighthouse is worn away as its Gumbo-Limbo and Cypress frame wears way to the sands of time,
The Alligator Snapper sits motionless like a rock on the lake bed.
An old, grey bearded hunter, with his rifle, feels no remorse for law breaking,
A whip-poor-will sends its calls through the marsh to crackle until dawn.
Dawn. The Sun returns to work as the Guiding light of the Earth.
Hundreds of Egrets, Herons, Ibises, and Spoonbills raise their eggs at the Rookery,
The Alligator starts its daily routine as it grabs a moss-green bass in its menacing jaw,
The Marsh is abound with the sounds of the A.M. as the tourists sweep in.
The Careless tourist throws a water bottle into a pile of reeds,
The Rare Sienna-brown Florida Panther hides in the Oak hammock.
The fish hide from the Anhinga and the Tourists,
The ducks go for crumbs, thrown off the pier by the hordes of tourists.
The park closes and the marsh goes back to its natural state of wilderness, as the Gator in the Sawgrass comes back.

Tyler J. Baldwin, Grade 6

Fall

I feel the cool air on my face
The multicolored leaves fall near me
A hungry bird searches for food
The bare trees stand over me
Busy ants go up and down their hill
The scent of mint lingers in the air
When I look up I see a clear sky
Bugs are crawling on the slow growing plants
The blissful silence is beautiful
When I feel the tree the bark is rough
When I step on the leaves,
they crunch under my feet
Birds are talking to each other
God's creation is amazing as far as we can see.

Denson Pollard, Grade 5

All Things Pink!

I happen to love all things pink,
Poodles and post-its and yummy fruit drinks!
Teapots and lip gloss and flowers galore,
But don't stop there, there's still so much more!
From plastic pink toys in the grocery store aisle,
To all of my clothes in a massive pink pile!
The curtains and bed sheets I have are pink too.
When my birthday comes around, you'll know what to do!
Flamingos and piglets float in my mind,
Pink is the best invention of mankind!
They say it's for babies but they're oh-so-wrong,
Because in my heart, pink will live long!
It's a pink eraser that saves you during a test,
That's just because pink is the best!

Inica Kotasthane, Grade 6

Lake Bowen

You can fish,
Like it's your only wish.
Everyone jump in the lake,
But I can't guarantee there won't be a snake!
I love Lake Bowen so much!
Don't step on a stick, crunch, crunch, crunch.
Oh the fish go munch, munch, munch all day,
When all we want to do is play.
Oh please, please don't frown,
It's your turn to tube, next time around.
You think you're so cool, since you have saltwater in your veins,
Me, I have freshwater in my soul that I cannot contain.
You can see, I just belong here,
I guess, it's just my kind of atmosphere!

Chloe Moyers, Grade 5

I Give Thanks For

I give thanks for…
my loving mom…she takes care of me,
my awesome dad…he coaches me in basketball,
my funny brother…he plays tricks on me.

Dominic Ward, Grade 4

Soccer

Soccer is my favorite game,
No other sport is the same.
The only time you use your hands,
Are if you're throwing in and,
When you are a goalie you can.
Offense is my favorite place,
Against their defense, face to face,
You shoot the ball and, BOOM!, you score,
And that's what you were hoping for,
I also love playing in goal,
You between the two poles.
They shoot, you catch, and your hands seal,
Boom! you punt it down the field,
The ball's a bullet, and with a thud you've won!

Pierce Koreniuk, Grade 5

Football

Football is my favorite sport,
You can play it even if you're short.
If you get tackled that's okay,
Get back up and continue to play.
There are many positions in the game,
Great players get to the Hall of Fame.
The best part is the Super Bowl,
"Boom" through the uprights for a field goal.
You might throw a Hail Mary,
Or catch it and be legendary.
Down the field for a touchdown,
Or punt it off with a frown.
The game of football is really great,
There is nothing in it to hate.

Jackson Reel, Grade 5

Snowboarding

Snowboarding just fills me with glee.
We get a pass to go for free!
It takes skill to go down the big hill.
It is so cold you can't feel the chill.
Personally I think wiping out is fun.
Races are tough when you run.
We go to Utah to use the boards.
Just boarding itself is its own reward.
"Swoosh" pealed, and exited, amazed.
The mountain is like a doughnut with glaze.
If the snow is artificial it has a price.
The blinding snow is cold as ice.
I know how to stay warm in the cold.
To board you really have to be bold.

Benjamin Ashby, Grade 5

I Give Thanks For

I give thanks for…
my lovely mother…she takes care of us,
my funny dad…he makes me laugh,
my helpful brother…he helps me when I need it.

Asin Sajan, Grade 4

Change

Do you listen? Do you care? What's it like over there? What did I do to make you leave?
Or was it just your feeling growing inside of me?

Even though your words cut deeper than my soul, they pry me open with a hole.
Don't you know? I've cried myself to sleep at night. I waste my time thinking of you.

But what do you mean to me? Every time you look at me, it's like my heart shatters into a million pieces. I trusted you. But you didn't tell me the truth. I know I've got some flaws. I know that you don't care. And sometimes change is for the better. For me and you, just know that I care.

Isabella Shin, Grade 5

The Memories on the Walls

I stood there, staring at the walls that brought back memories of times at malls and school halls.
The memories were sketched with pencils, pictures, and pens.
The best memories were the ones with friends.
I would look at the walls every day that made me wonder of how fast I grew old.
Many times I would grow cold.
So staring at the walls helped my stress of days to come.
It also showed me how foolish I was and dumb.
As I came out of my staring at night, I would lay in my bed, staring at the light.
I would fall into a deep sleep that reminded me of all the memories that I would keep.

Kierstin Rowles, Grade 6

I'm From

I'm from the winning catch to get the 6 points for your team to win the game.
I'm from the half court shot to wow the crowd.
I'm from the legs to run the 2 miles.
I'm from being in the roaring crowd.
I'm from the plane ride to the tropical resort.
I'm from the million dollar run 100 yards down the field to score.
I'm from the catch to get me in the hall of fame.

When life gives you lemons make orange juice and leave the world wondering how you did it!

Shawn Updegraff, Grade 6

The Coaster at Six Flags

One week in summer, I went to New Jersey, a state that is home to the tallest roller coaster on Earth.
My Dad and I went on a ride, 456 feet in the sky.
It is called Kingda Ka; the logo is a tiger that has big paws.
We got in line though it was long; we were already thinking what could go wrong.
We got in the ride; the seats were not too wide.
It started, in the car, we saw the acceleration track was far.
My stomach turned to mush, I knew somebody was about to push the launch button.
It launched, it went up the hill, and I prayed the supports would stay very still.
In a flash, it was over; I knew my friends owed me lots of cash.

Christian Garcia, Grade 6

Winter's Arrival

Fall is here and it feels like just yesterday he was a sapling.
The time has come to let go of all of his leafy friends.

He says goodbye as he watches his friends fly away in the early morning draft.
Soon he will have bare branches and the family of robins will move out of the nest that they built in him.
He now waits for winter to come and go and the arrival of spring to come.
Then his leaves will grow back one by one.

Tylor Carroll, Grade 5

Vast Vanderbilt Boulevard

My neighborhood is filled with cars racing and
twisting and turning to where they need to be.

My neighborhood is a home to millions of kids
dashing to Byron Lake Park on their bikes like a
swarm of bees on a hot summer day.

My neighborhood is lucky enough to have an
immense speedy double decker train coming
down the tracks. Choo! Choo!

And it is famished for more wonderful people to
move into Oakdale.

And it is beautiful day and night as the
marvelous shining moon looks like it will fall
right in your backyard.

Giovanni LaSala, Grade 6

The Weird Planet

When I woke up on the icy and hard ground—
I peered at the sky and I saw different colors in it.
I knew that it wasn't sunrise because of the starry skies
And I didn't see the shiny yellow light.

After I saw the gorgeous skies
I looked at my surroundings
And they were barren.
There weren't any buildings in sight,
And there was just the rocky ground and the skies
That surrounded me.

After I stared at my surroundings,
I realized that I wasn't on planet Earth,
Because it was untouched by water,
And my surroundings were stars of different colors and rocks.

Mia Cisewski, Grade 5

Snowboarding

I grabbed my blue snowboard, helmet, and goggles ready to go,
Looking down Turnpike Hill one of the biggest hills in
Medway, Maine.
I looked at my cousin in her hot pink sled,
Her cheeks were like two cherry tomatoes.
My mom said, "Ready, set, go!"
I leaned forward and so did my cousin.
So we were off and ready to go,
I hit a bump and did a front flip.
My snowboard went flying,
As I flew on my back and rolled down the hill,
Then I sat up yelling, "I'm okay!"
As everyone was dashing down the hill to check on me,
We all laughed with fear,
Then after we went to Nan's house to drink hot cocoa.

Gabrielle Brackett, Grade 6

Diamonds at Night

The hues of the sky transform into blackness,
Leaving not a streak of color, only darkness.

Glistening stars flicker and wink,
I stare into space, wonder and think.

The silvery moon casts a magic of its own,
From miles away, resembles a precious gemstone.

Comforting glow throughout the night,
Breathtaking and worth-capturing sight!

Majestic, Mysterious, Magical
Moon.

Somaya Tahir, Grade 5

My Maddox

The one I love is the one that I want to
spend my whole life with. He is/was
the one I love. His name is
Maddox. He never got mad
at me, when I took his
hat. We always
hugged
every day. I
wish I'd never left him.
And he got very red when
we hugged and talked. He's so cute.
You will know if a boy likes you when they turn
red!!!!
xoxoxoxo

Maya McMullen, Grade 6

Winter Fun

Warm, cozy fireplace,
With amazing, delicious, yummy cocoa,
When it is really cold out,
You know Santa is coming!
Jingle! Jingle!
Comforting relaxing music.
Play! Play! Play!
Let's go see the snowflakes!
When it's snowing,
We should do a snowball fight and make bases.
By dawn, we are covered in snow,
From head to toe.
We warm up by the blazing fireplace.
Winter is amazing!

Erica Preston, Grade 4

I Give Thanks For

I give thanks for…
my loving mom…she gives me presents,
my funny grandma…she buys me anything that I want,
my awesome friend…he takes me everywhere he goes.

Tre'von O'Neal, Grade 4

Ode to Pancakes

Oh pancakes
Your crispy bronze edges
Scream delicious to my face
Oh pancakes
You're like the harmony to my beautiful name

Oh pancakes
When you're paired
With that yellow melted butter,
You're like duet singers
Going to the Grammies.

Oh pancakes
You start out as a pale liquid
And turn to a soft brown,
Exactly when you hit the frying pan.

Ahhh!!!
You bring saliva to my mouth.
Oh pancakes
You mean the whole world to my tongue!
Olivia Barbosa, Grade 5

The Story Her Eyes Hold

Who is that lady standing right there?
I quickly notice her eyes and hair.

Her eyes were sad, but told a story,
About her and a deep blue sea.

She was standing there on a ship one night,
When the "Boom!" of thunder gave her a fright.
The "Zap!" of lightning and the "Crash!" of the ship,
Made her next a quivering lip.
The sight of the ship falling into the sea,
Would have been enough to scare me!

Falling, falling. Down, down,
Made her miss her little old town.

Yet somehow she was here today.
I'm not sure how, all I can say is hooray!

I'm just glad I wasn't there!
All off that would have given me more than a scare!
Marissa Love, Grade 6

Fall

I wore a warm jacket, scarf, boots, hat, gloves, and a sweater,
The wind blows through my hair with a small chill,
When I rake the leaves it's like the waves of the ocean,
They keep getting bigger and bigger as the time goes by,
The wind sings like the howls of wolves,
When the moon and stars come out,
They look like a shining crystal lagoon.
Eden Witham, Grade 5

Soury Lemonade

A breezy summer day, oh how perfect,
A glass of ice cold soury lemonade would taste.
I set up a soury lemonade stand. Many people will love that!
Oh, so soury my lemonade is!
Many speedy cars pass by, will they stop?
A big neighborhood means tons of soury business.
That thought made me think of my empty pool.
I made tons of soury lemonade and filled up my pool,
Many people came for my wonderful soury lemonade,
When they all saw my soury lemonade pool,
They screamed, "Let's all jump in!!"
Splash! Splash! What fun!
Diving and swimming in soury lemonade.
Soon my pool was filed with neighbors!
In an instant they all drank my soury lemonade all up!
I guess it is time to make more,
For tomorrow and tomorrow!
Michael Perez, Grade 4

Never Back Down!

Never back down, always stick to the ground
stay true to yourself be you and only you
Never back down stick to the ground!

Do what you want not what someone else wants for you
follow your dreams and reach for your goals
never give up keep on trying

Never back down stick to the ground
life is a journey you may follow
Live life like there's no tomorrow!

Never give up but,
always give in and never quit!

Never back down stick to the ground!
Love you and only you!
Brianna Gonzalez-Sullivan, Grade 6

Snow Day

Snow as white as fluffy clouds.
Beautiful Christmas lights,
Through out the night.
The cold weather breeze in my hair.
The nice warm fire in my face,
And a sweet cup of hot cocoa in my hand.
In the morning,
I can make snow angels in the snow,
And make gingerbread houses.
Its so much fun.
I see the wonderful decorations in the morning.
I look outside and I see snow on the ground.
So grab your coats and your mittens,
Because it's a snow day!
Hip-hip-hurray!
Jeremy Kerr, Grade 4

I Am

I am a fun fashionista
I wonder what the world will be like when I grow up
I hear the sound of my friends' laughter
I see a coral reef with lots of bright and colorful fish
I want to be a professional softball player
I am a fun fashionista

I pretend when I acted in Goldilocks and the three bears
I feel the fluffy fur of my cats
I touch a smooth, round softball
I cry when I chop onions
I am a fun fashionista

I understand how to take care of horses
I say that a girl can do anything
I try to play every sport that I can
I hope to get better at all sports
I am a fun fashionista

Caitlin Kilroy, Grade 5

Blue

Blue is the water in a far blue sea, as salty as can be.
Blue is blueberries, round and juicy in the spring.
Blue is cool like a mint on a clear winter day.
Blue is cold when a snowflake hits your mouth.
Blue is fresh, as if it is ripe to drink.
Blue is cold like it's winter.
Blue is moist after it rains.
Blue is shiny, like a diamond reflecting the sun.
Blue is a sad feeling you get when you are teased.
Blue is the sky on a nice summer day.
Blue is one of the colors that we salute to.
Blue is a diamond that shines like a star in the dark.
Blue is a puddle from melted ice.
Blue is the sound of the waterfall in the Amazon forest.
Blue is the sound of rain hitting the windows Tip! Tap! Splash!
Blue is a wet feeling in the cold water.
Blue is a drop of water from a cold rain storm.
Blue is smooth and wet.

Micah Williamson, Grade 4

My Legs

My legs help me do gymnastics
My legs help me ride my bike
My legs help my ride my scooter
My legs help me dance
My legs help me run as fast as I can
My legs help me chase my neighbors

My legs help me play man-hunt
My legs help me play sports
My legs help me ride my friends Segway
My legs help me give piggy-back rides to my cousins
My legs help me go anywhere I want
My legs help me be the best runner ever

Giuliana Gorgone, Grade 6

Storm

Boom, crack, smash, bash
Debris and trees fly by in a flash,
These are the calls of the storm.

Creatures run, creatures hide,
The storm shows no sign to subside,
The storm grows stronger, no signs of weak,
There goes another lightning streak.

Rain comes down, pelts with pain,
Next comes the forest of sleet so elite,
Last brought rain once again, caused floods,
Pain to farmers and their buds.

The world seems to fall, as the storm destroys all,
But then comes out a light that's never been seen,
The sun, then a rainbow
The world has become once again keen

James Duffy, Grade 6

Autumn

September
Says to kids it's time for school.
It sucks in the summer warmth,
Picks leaves off one by one.
Spreads coolness everywhere,
Tells wild animals to hibernate.
October
Spreads candy to house to house,
Pulls pumpkins out of the earth,
Paints the leaves orange and yellow,
Decorates houses when no one is looking,
Carves pumpkins and puts them down on each step.
November
Spreads first frost on grass,
Hunts turkeys for Thanksgiving,
Grows evergreen trees everywhere,
Turns puddles into ice,
Blocks the sun's warmth.

Sean Connor, Grade 4

Swimming

Jumping in, making a big splash,
Weaving around so I don't crash!
Swimming is such a great blast,
My arms and legs moving fast.
Butterfly, Backstroke, Breaststroke, and more,
Some people might think it is a chore.
Splish, splash, whoosh, kaboom,
the sounds of the pool seem to bloom.
The team meets up before the meet
"Come on guys we must defeat!"
kicking my feet, splash, splash, splash, splash,
I zoom down the lane in a flash!
That night we won the tournament, it was great to represent!

Makenna Carothers, Grade 5

Christmas

C hoirs
H onest
R espectful
I ntroduce
S ing-a-long
T errific
M emories
A mazing
S uper

yet the best part of Christmas
is spending time with your FAMILY.

Jesus Guerrero, Grade 4

Summer

Summer freedom, up all night
Pools, fools, long plane flights
Flying kites in the light
Floating boats out of sight
Beaches, waves, some huge, some calm
Surfers hanging ten
Fireworks in the night
Go boom, boom, bang
Flip flops on the sand;
Go flip, flop, flip, flop
Fool's gold with glittering lights
Summer is such a delight

Mary Russo, Grade 6

Memories Far Away

A day in December
A night I can't remember;
Memories far away.

We built a snowman
And went inside
To think about the day.

We drank hot chocolate
A sweet confection;
With affection
We drink away.

Jade Pegus, Grade 5

Gray

I'm not brave but I'm not scared.
I don't know what to choose.
I'm not nice but I'm not mean.
I don't know what to choose.
I'm not old but I'm not new.
I don't know what to choose
I'm not black but I'm not white.
I'm gray.
I'm gray.
I'm gray.

Lauren Irwin, Grade 4

Black

I am the color of darkness and despair
And I sneak around when no one is there

As I slither through the night
I can bring forward no light

For I am hiding behind your door
Waiting for you to start to snore

I'm awake when you're asleep
I slink around like a creep

If you want to know when I'll stop
I never will, I'm a locust eating its crop

I am black

Evan Tefft, Grade 6

Gray

Gray is the cat
Who sleeps on your bed
Who licks your face every bright morning
Who thanks you for the food
The cat — who got what it wanted —
Is now
Gone.

Gray is the fog
Of the early dew-dropped day
Thick, mixed with uncertainty
Covering the land
Showing you the way
The fog, with great pride,
Leads you astray...
Like the cat

Maggie Lowden, Grade 6

The Art That I Do

The art that I do
the feelings that I feel
come together as one or it's not one at all
they find the spirit, they find the love
all at once, all above
as they come together
they find their form as they press
down on the blank

It's not a lie it's a find of what's inside
that you have to hide
it does what it wants
it gets what it gets as long as it's true to you
if you have to hide
the truth is in here
just a blank paper it has appeared.

Alexa Murphy, Grade 4

I Don't Understand

I don't understand
    Why people don't talk to me
    Why the world is so cruel
    Why people argue
But most of all
    Why there are wars
    Why there's terrorism all around
    Why there is suicide
    Why there are guns
What I understand most is
    Why God made me
    Why my parents love me
    Why I got to school
    Why I have to love myself

Tamara Sanchez, Grade 6

I Don't Understand

I don't understand...
    Why people lose lives
    Why people lie to people
    Why there are bullies
But most of all...
    Why more people turn
    Why people don't do homework
    Why people don't listen
    Why people are not thankful
What I understand most is...
    Why we learn
    Why we grow
    Why plants grow
    Why we go to school

Henry Hernandez, Grade 6

I Don't Understand

I don't understand...
    Why cats and dogs are colorblind
    Why dogs run away
    Why people move away
But most of all...
    Why people argue over stupid stuff
    Why there are wars
    Why there are stars
    Why there are words
What I understand most is...
    Why the sun goes down
    Why there are sounds
    Why birds chirp
    Why there is money

Dylan Martinez, Grade 6

Leaves

The harsh winds bluster around
    Gloomy, golden leaves falling
The duration of life span is ending
Brown, naked, eerie branches found.

Adam Mazurkiewicz, Grade 6

Zany Karshick Street

My neighborhood is enchanted
with an abundance of cardinals chirping joyful tunes
and doing high flying acrobatics in the blue sky.

My neighborhood is full of an immense noise
from cars zooming by my house.
Vroom! Honk!

My neighborhood is a scary place to be during Halloween
with haunting ghosts and scaring kids
pacifying each other with candy

And it is snowball fights in the flat glimmering powdery snow
on a winter day with cheerful snowmen and laughing friends

And it is a happy place with joyful kids
that makes me glad to call this place my home.
Joseph Fazzingo, Grade 6

Gray

A woman dressed in white
    has since been betrayed
Though her thoughts may confuse
    they do not go astray
For her fellow in black is such a mysterious array
Of good and bad
    right and wrong
        so close but far away
The couple, so peacefully evil, quite a strange puree
Though their differences are quite strong
    their relationship never strays
That may cause confusion to others
    but don't worry — their love will never decay
For the black of the night
    and the white of the day
Of mysteries and confusing display
Clad in gray
Jillian Shaw, Grade 6

Adventure

Seeking the time of your life
To come out of your shell and have fun
To take risks or chances
To yell as loud as you can
And to be comfortable with the world around you
To listen to the birds
Or watch the sun set
When you've made it to the top of the mountain
To let excitement and happiness fill you
Your heart pounding out of your chest
Taking pictures of the glorious sun
Slowly going down
To hide
Behind the mountain
This — is adventure!
Kaylee Suchocki, Grade 6

My Thumbs

I'm glad I have opposable thumbs.
The things they can do make me want to hum.

I like to be able to hold lots of things,
Like chocolate, or cookies, or bells that go ding.

Without my thumbs I couldn't play games,
Like *Minecraft*, where there are wolves to tame.

There would be no drinking from a mug,
Or giving someone a proper hug.

I wouldn't be able to hold a pen,
Or write about a bear's rainbow den.

That is why my thumbs you see,
Are the very best part of me.
Ally LoPresti, Grade 6

The Virtue of Music

While dressing in the back of the stage wings
I heard my friend saying her play lines
I went to where I emerge and sing
I sang my piece without a hint of whine

My music soared to family and friends
To enemies and allies just the same
To bring disliking to its rightful end
And so we all did join in life's great game

Oh may we all find peace, joy, hope, and love
From the source of music, which is open to all
Be cunning as serpents, yes, but gentle as doves
And may we all bring peace but bravely stand tall.

Oh God, you sent your dear beloved Son
We'll obey your commandments till life's done.
Catherine Graham, Grade 6

War Is a Grave Yard

war is a graveyard,
not everyone survives.
war is a graveyard,
the unlucky families might cry.
war is a graveyard,
there's a lot of dead bodies.
war is a graveyard,
everyone hopes to go home.
war is a graveyard,
some come home
but not the same.
after seeing the graveyard,
fallen allies and friends.
when you come home,
you will never want to see the graveyard again.
Jamir Harris, Grade 6

My Family Culture
My family culture is fun.
We all love the food.
We all love to see each other.
This is our family culture.
Our family culture is love.
We all see beautiful things in one another.
This is our family culture.
When they are setting up something,
All the kids help.
This is our family culture.
Kenadia Rozier, Grade 6

My Amazing Teacher Ms. Schiff
She is as bright as a star
She is as caring as a care bear
She is as pretty as a rose
She is as sweet as candy
She is as joyful as a summer day
She is as funny as a monkey
She is as tall as a tree
She is nice as a flower
She is as talented as a dolphin
She is as colorful as a parrot
Gabrielle Eaton, Grade 4

My Friend
She is nice
She is pretty
She is sweet
She is a crisp air breeze
She is yay
She is a sunny day
She is sweet
She is nice
She is pretty
She is candy
Gina Mooney, Grade 4

Hopscotch
On the one
Past the two
Across the three
Upon the four
Towards the five
Aboard the six
Among the seven
Away from the eight
Amid the nine
Across the ten!
Luke Mitchell, Grade 5

My Dad
My dad can build stuff
He fixes things really well
He inspires me.
Ronald Jones, Grade 4

I Am
I am a boy who likes playing soccer.
I wonder where I'm going to play.
I hear my friends yelling to pass the ball to them so they can score a goal.
I see the ball moving back and forth to friends.
I want to make a goal without my friends taking the ball.
I am a boy who likes playing soccer.

I pretend that I am an Olympic soccer player.
I feel the soccer ball hitting my shins and me falling on the ground.
I touch the soccer ball octagon pattern.
I worry that I'm going to fall and break a bone.
I am a boy who likes playing soccer.

I understand that I can get better at soccer.
I say kick me the ball.
I dream of a goal without passing.
I try to make a goal.
I hope to play in the Olympics with kids my age.
I am a boy who likes playing soccer.
Alec Castle, Grade 5

I Am
I am a girl who enjoys doing gymnastics
I wonder when I'll join gymnastics class
I hear my sister cheering me on as I turn a cartwheel landed in a front split
I see the wet grass and hope I won't slip
I want to do a front handspring, but I'm a little afraid
I am a girl who enjoys doing gymnastics

I pretend that I'm a famous gymnast on stage
I feel happy that I do gymnastics, because it is such a healthy sport
I touch my pink hand grips
I worry that I won't try a front handspring
I am a girl who enjoys doing gymnastics

I understand I need to stretch before gymnastics
I say I can do it
I dream that I'm a gymnastics star
I try some more gymnastics tricks
I hope that one day I will become a gymnastics star
I am a girl who enjoys doing gymnastics
Sonia Johnson, Grade 5

Orange
Are the leaves crinkling beneath your boots?
Is the rising flame in the fireplace?
Is the smell of Nana's homemade pumpkin bread coming out of the oven?
Are the monarch's wings so smooth and delicate?
Is the fresh, crunchy carrot plucked right out of the ground?
Is the calm fall breeze whispering in tree's branches?
Is the slipper salamander trying to wiggle off my hands?
Is the gooey and salty caramel melting in my mouth?
Is the bounding tiger trying to catch its prey?
Is the tangerine with a powerful citrus smell making my mouth water?
Maddie Daniel, Grade 6

Acting 101

In my mind I think of you,
you're the thing that makes me true.
Not unicorns, princes, or even my smarts,
my true love is acting not any other arts.
I tried dancing, singing, playing a tune,
in all those things I felt like a baboon!
No one understands exactly what I do,
not improv, monologues, silly stuff too.
Imagination is the key when you're with me,
you can be anything you want to be.
Face expressions, stage directions, even crew,
everything, anything it's all up to you.
All this advice is really true,
acting is everything you need to be you.

Sydney Threatt, Grade 5

Perfect

My mind is blank,
not knowing what to write
The clock is ticking away,
Ticking and tocking all day long

Will it ever stop?
Will it ever end?
Seconds make minutes and minutes make hours
It goes on and on

All I need is a little spark
that'll make me burst into flames
All I need is that perfect little idea
for that perfect little poem

Pranavi Doodala, Grade 5

My Best Friend

When we're together we will win.
Of course we will cause we're like twins.
We stick together just like glue.
It's always fun when it's me and you.
We get together and we play.
When we do, it makes my day.
We make weird sounds like "phew" and "pow,"
It makes everyone say "wow!"
We always have such good luck.
And when I fall you pick me up.
Amiyah is my best friend's name.
In my book you're hall of fame!
You are like my family,
I just want to sing with glee!

Emily Cantrell, Grade 5

I Give Thanks For

I give thanks for…
my fun mom…she plays with me,
my helpful dad…he helps me with my math homework,
my funny brother…he makes me laugh.

Jorge Malo-Fasani, Grade 4

In the Streets of St. Augustine

It was a cold afternoon in the historic place.
The students explored every edge, every face.
As they walked down the street,
The howling of the wind seemed discreet.
What they used to read in a book,
Now came to life!
It amazed them with just one look.
But from jail cells to the Fountain of Youth,
The fourth graders must come to face the truth.
That their St. Augustine field trip has ended.

Tiffany Zalewski, Grade 6

Autumn Is Red

Red is autumn leaves gently falling to the ground and a
big juicy apple waiting to be eaten.
Autumn breezes gently blowing while a child eats a big
crunchy apple.
Warm sun being absorbed by all living things while
children crunch in the crisp leaves.
The smooth air of fall outside, but inside yummy
smelling things are baking in the oven.
A juicy apple sitting on a branch in the orchard while
a spectacular sun is setting.

Alex Bonenfant, Grade 6

Cold Morning

I woke up this morning with freezing toes
I also had a really cold nose
I turned the TV on and put on a robe
I knew winter was coming cause it was so cold
I got a boggin and put it on my head
I pulled up the covers and laid in my bed
I put on my jacket and pulled up the hood
I turned on the heat almost as high as I could
I went to the welcome mat and opened the door
I was scared it wouldn't be warm anymore.

Cody Justus, Grade 6

Freedom

F reedom is awesome.
R ights are our patriotic "rock and roll"
E ducation has helped us flourish as an American goal
E veryone has learned to use it,
D ifferently in our America, because
O utstanding history has blossomed greatly to help us
M ake the most out of it, so try to be an important role.

Aaliya Ibrahim, Grade 4

A Wonderful Spring

The dew drops from the just fallen rain
The rain tapping on the roof top
The chocolaty Easter candy in my mouth
The spring breeze brushing across my face
The beautiful scent of the vibrant flowers in my yard
This is going to be a great spring.

Mattingly Reaven, Grade 4

Ode to Ice

Oh how I love to look at a clear, shiny piece of ice.
I love how you sparkle in the sunlight,
as if you're a crystal.
Most kids need toys to be entertained,
but all I need is you ice.
I hate to think about how one of these days
you could fall into the wrong hands,
and melt.
So I figure, may as well spoil you for as long as I can
I run inside, and right away
know exactly what to do.
I'll give you a special treatment
you'll never forget,
a lemonade bath.
As I dip you in,
I see the smile on your face.
Now it's summer,
and you might melt,
but I will always remember you
even when you're a puddle.
I hope you will remember me.

Jordan Summerfield, Grade 5

The Job

Red went bravely over to Orange,
Ready to go to work.
Cautiously they both went over,
The border to yellow.
Yellow was happy to go,
And on they went to Green's.
Green, the health nut, brought out fruit to share,
And over they went to blue.
Free skies and waters was Blue's realm.
Everyone here? No wait!
On to purple next.
The wisest of the wise,
Purple held great power,
Because without her,
The job could,
Not be done.
The group is gathered,
The clouds are gone.
Out is Mr. Sun,
Now everyone is ready for the
Rainbow!!!

Kaitlyn Clougherty, Grade 6

What If

What if Florida got hit by a tornado
I would watch to see if it was coming my way
What if Florida got hit by a tsunami
I would climb a building and see if it could find me
What if Florida got hit by a hurricane
I would leave that state
What would you do?

Haylen Van Tassell, Grade 4

Black

Black has long sharp claws like knives on the T-Rex fossil
It is a tall black lamp post, like a stick with a light,
A girl's long, black hair flowing in the wind,
The tall muscular man in the shadows looking so mysterious,
The big black backpack on the kids

Black is the soft, warm, black fur on the cuddly black dog,
The rough black skin of the Mosasaurus,
The smooth, round, ball-like big blackberry
The rotten bumpy banana skin,

It is the taste of black, burnt chicken,
The black cooked marshmallow, toasted by the fire,
The chocolatey goodness of black M&Ms,

Black is the smell of ashes from a burning fire,
The smoke from the factory's smoke tower,
The disgusting smell from a black trash bag,
And it is the beautiful smell from the black perfume bottle

Black is the rattling from the black rattlesnake,
The growl from the black bear.

Anthony Massey, Grade 4

Being a Wide Receiver

When I'm on the field, I get to my spot,
Man, today is so hot.
I run up the field, awaiting my pass,
I hope it really isn't too fast.

When I see the ball coming to me,
I try to shake off the very tough D.
I set my feet and jump up in the sky,
Sometimes it feels like I can fly.

I extend my arms and make a great catch,
I feel like a dog playing fetch.
I get past defense by dodging and spinning,
I score a touchdown and my team goes on winning.

I spike the ball straight down to the ground,
I feel that I am Hall of Fame bound.
As the fans see me celebrate they scream "HOORAY!"
I heard that I was the Player of the Day.

But the other team was feeling bad,
So I told them what a good game they had.

Luke Pietrzak, Grade 6

Grandpa

Oh papa I wish I would've met you.
I bet you were real nice.
I know you would have took me fishing every day.
Gaga my grandma told me stories about you.
One day I will met you.

Mitchell Sheffield, Grade 4

A Winter Wonderland

The air grows chill as cool flakes float down from the sky.
The clouds are gray and the wind dances through the air.
White snow blankets the grass like a wool sweater.
I stick out my tongue and twirl around the icy grass.
A carrot-nosed snowman looks at me with a friendly smile of coal.
I look around at the neighbors shoveling snow in layers of coats.
Red and green wreaths dangle from doors along the street.
Snowballs whiz through the air and snow angels dot the ground.
Colorful lights illuminate all of the houses across the neighborhood.
I am truly in a winter wonderland.

Arti Singh, Grade 6

The Most Thankful Day of the Year

Taking a glint at the Thanksgiving parade while we
devour mouth watering food
Forks and knives scratching against the plate
as we cut the beautiful turkey
The door handle as we enter the Thanksgiving house
The pumpkin pie I took the time to
make on the table
Several dinner rolls going in my mouth
Thanksgiving is so great!

Aubrey Stutmann, Grade 4

A Poem

A poem does not have to be lengthy,
It does not have to rhyme,
And it does not have to be funny or serious
It comes straight out of your mind

It could be about cars, Mars, a guitar,
And even a straight line
A poem does not have to be specific like this one you're reading
In this very moment in time

Patrick Williams, Grade 6

Christmas

On Christmas Eve there is no fright
Showing off colors so brilliantly bright
On the tree that stands before me
It is tall and great with glory
Wake up in the morning with presents all around
I grab some cookies and some tea
And sit by a Christmas tree
Wake up in the morning with presents all around
Pine needles falling down...

Layla Maloney-Yodlowsky, Grade 5

Phoebe

P ainting and drawing is very fun
H aving fun with my friend
O r singing in the car and cheerleading inside or out
E ven maybe collecting more dogs right now, I have 28
B est at being myself
E very day I'm happy and cheerful

Phoebe Rodrigues, Grade 5

Fall

Leaves are green in spring,
But in fall brown comes along.
The wind is cold,
But the fireplace is as warm,
As the hot cocoa is in my cup.
The breeze comes along,
So put away the summer clothes,
And get ready for fall!
Summer is gone, but fall comes along for three months.
Get your delicious hot cocoa.
It is yummy in my tummy!
It's time for fall!
Now it's cool but will soon be time for winter.
We have a long time to enjoy fall now.
It's almost time for Halloween, and for costume.
After that it's Thanksgiving.
Then it's time to say goodbye to fall,
And say hello to winter.

Julianna Taylor, Grade 4

I Am

I am a softball player playing first base.
I wonder if I am any good.
I hear the screaming of the parents on the bleachers,
They are so excited because we won.
I see the ball soar and land on the field.
I want to win this game so badly. I love to win.
I am a softball player playing first base.
I pretend that I am playing in the Olympics.
I feel confident when I am up to bat. I want to hit well.
I touch the ball's red seams.
I worry that the fast softball will hit me very hard.
I am a softball player playing first base.
I understand the rules of a softball game.
I say a lot of cheers.
I dream that I will become professional.
I try my best to succeed.
I hope to beat and dominate the team we are playing.
I am a softball player playing first base.

Emily Cronin, Grade 5

Winter

December is opening presents in front of crackling flames,
And Santa flying in the depths of night.
Angels singing carols in gorgeous voices,
And candles in the windows while gentle snow flies softly down
January is dark, cold nights,
And lots of snow, snow, snow and wind that blow, blow, blows.
Sleds shredding snow on their way down the hill,
And slipping and sliding on ice.
It is igloos full of kids, too.
February is a hint of relief but not enough,
And grey clouds of snow that never stop coming.
Too much snow, not enough wood.
The worst part is that we have no more hot cocoa!

Evelyn Chaney, Grade 4

Nature's Relaxation

I sat on the warm, soft sand
Where the golden sunlight was the strongest
Where the breeze played with my hair
The waves crashed
And rolled along the shore
Barely touching my toes
Sand dunes stretched themselves,
Higher and higher
Creating hilly landscape farther up the beach
A lighthouse rose from the forest on the cliff
Shining its light to warn fishermen of danger
In the fog that lay up ahead
Sails from boats poked at the sky
As they hurried along the ocean
Foam rose with the waves
And the green plants that thrive in the salty water
Swayed between the waves
Shells in the sand glistened,
It is truly nature's relaxation…

Erasmea Harding, Grade 6

It's Fall

I know it's fall when
Kids tall, small, round, or skinny
Wear long sleeves,
Gloves and coats.

I know it's fall when
Summer disappears
And the warm water
Becomes freezing cold.

I know it's fall when
Trees, tall and spikey,
Lose leaves, golden brown,
Float down onto the ground.

I know it's fall when
Friends gather together around the fire
And slurp hot chocolate with mini marshmallows
Enjoying fall.

Carson Vasser, Grade 6

The Little Cricket

I saw a little cricket at school in the hall
It was jumping around like a little bouncy ball
Be careful little cricket, watch where you go,
or you'll get stepped on, Oh no!
I saw a little cricket at school in the books
It was chirping so loud, the librarian had a mean look
Be careful little cricket, or she'll find your nook!
I saw a little cricket at school during lunch
It was hopping around a big bowl of punch
I went over to get some, when suddenly I heard a loud crunch!
Eww, poor little cricket, now I've lost my appetite to munch!

Chloe Hall, Grade 5

Fall Is Finally Here!

Wearing bathing suits for swimming
Turns into wearing
Long sleeves and sweatpants for cold autumn days
Inhaling the amazing wood burning fires
While raking an immense pile of leaves
The beautiful leaves falling off the tree
Were like a colorful rainbow in the sky
Listening to the crinkling of the leaves
Under your feet while walking
Jack-o-lanterns scream with light
To whoever passes by them
Delicious and sweet candy apples baking
In the oven for Thanksgiving
People waiting for their Thanksgiving repast are
Famished nomads with no food or water
Pumpkin guts are slimy, wet, long but
The outside is smooth
Brilliant colors of autumn
Red, yellow, orange
Beautiful crystal frost on the grass
While you play outside with your friends

Emma Kate Carew, Grade 6

Baseball

Baseball is so fun
You play in the sun you throw, hit, run
And when you pitch your arm must be stronger than anyone
When you hit a dinger
You do a bat flinger
You jog around the base with a smile on your face
When you touch home plate
Your team will celebrate
When you rob a homer that team gets mad
And starts throwing their caps,
And they realize our team is not trash
When you get the sign
To steal second base
You race to the base when the ball crosses the plate
You slide and a dust cloud is all over the place
And when you look at the
Ump he says you're safe
If the ball gets by be ready to fly to the next base
When you steal home base
You will need some speed
For this is the winning run your team will need

Evan Roche and Frank Kula, Grade 5

It's Spring

The flowers are growing strong
Birds sing their songs
It's spring
What a great day, to see them all play
Making nests for the young, who will born soon under the sun
When they are strong
We can again hear their song

Julissa Torres, Grade 6

Same

Same is a weird word
Alike?
Perhaps
Similar?
No
Friendship?
Yeah!
Friendship means common
Common means alike
Alike means similar
Similar means same
You know?
Same isn't a weird word after all
It's good, refreshing, nice
And it's a symbol
Of love and friendship!

Ryan Allen, Grade 6

Beautiful Diamond

Oh
The
Diamond
How small
Yet so valuable
How smooth and
sparkly I want one
Hidden in the rocks only
For some people to find it
Discovered only sometimes
So pretty everyone wants
Some of it, it is found
In certain rings
It's a beautiful
Diamond
Ring!

Lakyn Bailey, Grade 6

Life Is a Bottle of Friendship

Life is a bottle of friendship,
that is always full,
Life is a bottle of friendship,
that cannot be replaced,
Sometimes the bottle gets knocked over,
and out spill a few,
Or sometimes they can be gone
in an instant,
like a leaf in a fall breeze,
But even though they sometimes go,
Your bottle will always be full
Life is a bottle of friendship
that is always full
Life is a bottle of friendship,
Even when there is only,
a drop left.

Charly Beasley, Grade 6

Confidence

Trusting, believing,
Braving the storm.
Confidence is powerful
And peaceful.

Priceless, timeless,
Loveless, powerless.
Believe in yourself!
Confidence is soothing
And reassuring.

Beauty, greatness,
Reliability, popularity.
Confidence helps you through it all.

Wonderful, ugly,
Pretty, ragged.
Confidence convinces you to be brave.

Eleanor Kloss, Grade 6

Be

Be false or be true.
Be nothing or be you.
Be bright or be blue.
Win all or just lose.

Be strong or crumble.
Speak out or mumble.
Be confident or humble.
Lead the pack or stumble.

Do well or do worse than you should.
Do more or do less than you could.

Be anything you want to be,
Because after all, it's not up to me.

Rise up, fall down, but always pull through,
Because after all, it's all up to you.

Kelsey Hertz, Grade 5

I Love to Sing

I love singing
it's all I do
I love to sing
with you
I love singing with friends
I love singing
I would sing until the end
I love singing
It's my favorite hobby
Sing on a plane or in a lobby
I love singing a whole lot.
Even if I get sad
I would never stop.

Sakura Pettway, Grade 4

The Elephant

The elephant
He parades through the Savanna
Arrogantly showing all
His triumphant call
Mimicking the sound
Of the harmonious horn
The elephant
Reaching high
To get some grub
Or crouching low
Choosing a shrub
Weighing a ton or more
If on a scale
The numbers would soar
The elephant
A gentle giant of nature
Wouldn't hurt a miniscule mouse

Pierce Hand, Grade 6

New Year's Eve

Feel the cold morning air as I wake up
The floor is freezing as I step on it
I creep down the cold steps and grab a cup
I sit down on the couch and start to knit

I stand up and walk to the ice window
I look out and see white snow falling down
I walk out the door and see no shadow
I stand there and look out and see a town

The town is aglow with laughter and joy!
I can hear the sweet singing loud and clear
I see the children playing with their toys
I can hardly wait until the new year!

The ball is set and ready for dropping!
This year will be a fun one that's shocking!

Ansley Mossburg, Grade 5

Hispanic People

H ard working and confident people
I nspiring and bold people
S trong, supportive, and honest people
P eaceful, patient, and unique people
A wesome people
N ice, loving, and jolly people
I ntelligent and respectful people
C olorful and creative people

P ositive and truthful
E qual
O utgoing and open minded
P roud to be Hispanic
L oving
E nthusiastic, encouraging, and eager.

Grace Leiva, Grade 4

A Day at the Beach with No Thoughts to Think About

I stroll the boardwalk.
My mind so empty.
No thoughts to think about.
The hot sun burning my skin.
Still no thoughts to think about.
Action happening around me.
But still no thoughts to think about.
I head home finally something to
think about.
I think about my day at the beach
waiting until I go again.

Aqsa Khawaja, Grade 4

Fall, Sweet Breeze and the Colorful Leaves

Fall, sweet breeze,
every color, not just green.
Fall, sweet breeze,
makes you want to dance and sing.
Then there's the colorful, colorful leaves.
Watch them blow in the breezes.
There is yellow, red, orange, and green.
All the colorful, colorful leaves,
you rake them up into a pile,
then you jump into it.
And you will go wild.

Shaniyah Williams, Grade 6

Yellow

Yellow, the color of the bright hot summer sun
The taste of a ripe fresh yellow banana tastes great in the morning
Can you hear the buzzing of the yellow jacket in your ear?
I feel the static of the yellow balloon in my hair
The smell of the beautiful wild sunflower patch
Can you see the yellow bus going to school?
The sweet yellow corn grown on the farm tastes amazing in the
summer
There is always a yellow duck quacking in my pond
The soft baby chicklet's fur feels very soft on my cheek
A yellow lemon smells as sour as it tastes

Tyler Donaghy, Grade 6

Maze in the Mind

Our minds are always full of mazes that should end, but can't
Our minds are always full of ideas and creativity
Our minds are always filled with obstacles that block creativity
Sometimes come back to the same idea again
That's what makes our mind a maze
When we get stuck somewhere or don't know
Which way to turn
Our minds might start to fill up with obstacles
But these obstacles just make your ideas and creativity brighter
Our minds are full of mazes, that I don't want to
End...

Ashley Rice, Grade 6

Freedom Isn't Free

Freedom isn't free
for those who lost their lives,
for those who got hurt,
for the ones that got home safe, but lost friends,
and for those who never healed.

Freedom isn't free
for many families,
for those not knowing,
for those who wait every day,
for those who are scared every day.

Freedom isn't free
for those who don't forget,
for those who wake up screaming,
for those who are scarred for life,
for those who never saw their families again.

Freedom isn't free
for those who were killed,
for those who were tortured,
for those who starved to death,
for those who served proudly.

Freedom Isn't Free

Michael Tubbs, Grade 6

Hunger

I feel a rumbling,
an earthquake;
inside of me.

The groaning,
and mumbling
of my stomach
overpowers me.

I feel like passing out,
the hunger is too much;
but then...

A simmering plate of food
is pushed in front of me.

I feel relief;
I bite in...

I feel the wonderful food fall down my throat,
and
the wine trickling into my mouth.
My stomach sighs contentedly,
and all is good
once more.

Abie Russ-Fishbane, Grade 5

The Nature in Life

The tree has a beautiful leaf.
The roots are creeping.
The dirt giggled.
The leaves plopped on the ground.
The trees danced as the wind blew.
The ants marched up the tree.
The squirrels picked acorns one by one.
The roots are whispering shhhhhhhhhhhh.
The wind is whistling though the air.
The branches look like bird claws.
The sun is burning the crispy trees.
The trees have colorful leaves.

Isabella DelSesto, Grade 4

My Eyes

Big, big, big, blue eyes
To look all around at the flies
I see beautiful flowers
When we have rain showers
My eyes show me where to walk
When I look to talk
I use my eyes to read a book
Or they even help me cook
They shine so bright
During the night
I see scary bees
I look up to see trees

Savanah Diaz, Grade 6

Sounds of the Forest

The forest is dark
Night has fallen
Foxes nearby bark
The bees take a break from the pollen
Wolves creep out from dens
Fish jump out of the water
The sparrow calls to its friends
A black bear saunters
The forest is dark
Night is wising
The forest is filled with hoots and barks
The sun is rising

Chloe Allensworth, Grade 6

Winter

Winter winter it's freezing.
Cold outside.
The snowflakes are gently falling,
And the wind is blowing softly.
Christmas lights are bright green and red.
White snow and ice are everywhere,
Candy candy fun to eat,
Can't you see!
So what I'm trying to say is I,
Love winter!

Maria Cantoli, Grade 4

Eyes

My eyes let me see
The beautiful world around me,
Where would I go?
Who would I be?

My eyes let me see
The beautiful colors around me,
Like orange, blue, yellow,
And purple, green, and ruby

My eyes let me see
The beautiful things around me
It would be like a sad song,
If my eyes did not see.

Katelyn Valvo, Grade 6

My Hands

My hands are great
My hands are tough
They could help move a crate
They help me when it's rough

My hands throw a football
They help me when I'm on the field
They help me shoot a basketball
After the game we all kneeled

They help me catch a ball
They help me swing a bat
They help me make a call
They help me clean my mat

Daniel Burkhardt, Grade 6

My Feet

I love my feet,
They take me everywhere I go,
And with every passing year
They grow and grow and grow.

When someone comes and tickles me,
My heart steps up its beat,
I go and give a loud giggle,
And I'm knocked off my seat.

When I'm getting bored at school,
Or feeling teary and down,
I can always look at my feet,
Every time without a frown.

Erin Finnerty, Grade 6

Viper

Viper sits in tree
waiting to silently strike
fast as lighting, bang

Thomas Livingstone, Grade 6

Life Around Us All

Life around us all
Some of us short
And some of us tall
With little leaves
Who have little green veins
Just like us
We even have parades
Celebrating great things
Having amazing meanings
Remember life around you
The trees
And the wet moist dew
And since they are there for us
We should be there for them too
This great world around us all
Around us ALL
Because,
There is life around us all

Alyssa Webber, Grade 4

Raging Storm

A raging storm…
The wind whistled beyond
My tiny cocoon
Lightning made a glorious
Burst of light bleed through
My crooked blinds.

A raging storm…
Thunder boomed with
Power and excitement
The moon barely illuminated
The heavy blanket of clouds.

A raging storm…
Trees twisted and turned
Holding on for life
Dogs howled with the fierce wind
The storm raged on and on…

Haley Demirdog, Grade 6

Bottle of Tears

A bottle of tears
That made love blind
A bottle of tears
That broke my mind
A bottle of tears
That broke my heart
A bottle of tears
That shattered my fight
A bottle of tears
that lost my light.
I had thought my
heart had taken
flight

Chloe Schmitt, Grade 6

I Am

I am honest and respectful.
I wonder how the Earth spins.
I hear thunder.
I see a tree.
I want to become a scientist.
I am honest and respectful.

I pretend I am a morning chef.
I feel the grass.
I touch the ground.
I worry about getting people upset.
I cry about getting hurt.
I am honest and respectful.

I understand how gravity works.
I say that everything happens with reasoning.
I dream that no bad things will happen in my life.
I hope I get more pets.
I am honest and respectful.

James Traverso, Grade 5

I Am

I am athletic and kind.
I wonder when the Eagles will win the Super Bowl.
I hear people screaming.
I see thousands of people cheering for two teams.
I want to become a football player.
I am athletic and kind.

I pretend I am a superstar.
I feel a baseball in my hand.
I touch a controller to play a game.
I worry about losing.
I cry about getting hurt.
I am athletic and kind.

I understand my family and friends.
I tell jokes to my friends.
I dream about being in the NFL.
I hope that I will do something good every day.
I am athletic and kind.

Alex Pak, Grade 5

The Blue Sky

Sky, sky, sky,
Maybe it rains,
Maybe it cries.
I wonder some days,
Why it is so happy.
I think to myself,
Skies are sad, too.
Rain, snow, hail, shine,
Now it is time to go outside.
Playing outside is the best thing to do,
Maybe you don't think so, but I certainly do.

Alyssa Stanley, Grade 6

Ballet

I hear the piano begin to play.
I start the combination; I love ballet.
Leg turned out, a perfect fifth,
My teacher says I have a wonderful gift.

Standing at the barre, I hold myself high.
My arm lengthens, reaching for the sky.
Toes pointed, my leg extends,
I come back for a plie, and my leg bends.

Tendus are next, my foot brushes the floor.
It comes out pointed, I point it even more.
I prepare for a turn, make my turning leg straight,
I do it so well, I get to demonstrate.

Jumps are last, a perfect one I can do,
My teacher is proud, I am too.
The music is ending; I land one last time,
This class is the best I've done in a lifetime.

Mary Connelly, Grade 6

Orange Cactus

Out in a desert is an orange cactus,
It's spikes are far more tactless
than any other sharp cactus thorns,
and will survive any storms.

The orange cactus can survive without water,
it can survive temperatures hotter
than a whopping 10,000 degrees,
people even call it the tough tree!

I have no idea how sharp it is,
but scientists say its thorns are 12 inches!
However one day, a tornado came along.
It actually ripped it out of the ground — where it belonged!

A sightseer saw that cactus fly into the ocean,
there was just so much shocked emotion!
100 feet deep it might not survive,
it absolutely, definitely will not thrive.

James Patrick Brown, Grade 4

Thanksgiving

Thanksgiving is when you spend time with your family,
Having so many brilliant decorations up.
Amazing colors are everywhere,
Making the perfectly cooked turkey with your family.
Wind blowing in your hair, having the best year.
Placing all the excellent and yummy food on the table,
Then saying what you are thankful for.
When the meal is all done taking a slow walk.
Then when we are done we go back to the house,
And celebrate my birthday.
Then we pray, what an amazing night.

Miranda Volmar, Grade 4

Wicked Awesome Shore Drive

My neighborhood is glorious walks by the
ingenious flowing river that lead into a
glimmering ocean that is as immense as the Pacific.

My neighborhood is the squealing of the
neighbors as they dash around their font
yard zoom, zoom, slamming into each other,
"Tag you're it!"

My neighborhood is the squeak of the
creeping bridge screaming as you take your
daring steps, one foot in front of the other.

And it is the whistling of the blue birds
and the sun smiling down at you.

And it is the trees swaying in the breezy
wind at night that puts you to bed.

Amanda Hamze, Grade 6

On This Quiet Night

The cool, salty breeze races by
The grass dances in the wind
As I make a path to follow
The blue and purple butterfly
Fluttering by.
As I make my way to the glistening water
I glare into the sunset
As it dips into the ocean.
As the darkness takes over
The shimmering stars glisten
Then the light in the lighthouse ignites
It beams across the waves.
Behind the waves
The trees hide miles away
You can see them shivering as the wind passes by.
Suddenly two birds soar across the waves into the sky.
I hear a toad groan
On this once quiet night.

Rylie McCormick, Grade 6

Fall

Tender and tasty, the turkey is ready
Everyone there can't wait to eat
Sometimes the food can't be beat
All the family keeps the rhythm steady

The fall leaves are falling down
Almost everyone gasps in joy
All the girls, even the boys
Leaves this pretty can stop a frown.
The decorations are very neat
The jack o lanterns and pumpkins are a sight
Let's hope they don't give a fright
Candy is given on every street.

Brooke Bonnett, Grade 6

It's About

It's not about chicken it's about turkey and
Warm rays of sun shining down
Traveling out of state and having a blast

It's about laughing and having a great time
Playing football and arguing about touchdowns
Getting dirty and having bruises

It's about spending time with aunts and uncles
Saying thanks and eating pumpkin pie
Mashed potatoes and green beans

It's what I love

Chris Semel, Grade 5

Amazing Sunset

I gaze at the orange, pink, and blue sunset.
A mix of salt and fresh air enters my nose as I breathe in.
While strolling through the grass that pokes and tickles my legs,
I notice a small lighthouse.
The walkway to the beautifully painted
white and green lighthouse is so close,
I can almost touch it.
My hair dances as a cool breeze tickles my face,
leaving goosebumps on my arms.
The sound of waves crashing along the shore and
seagulls squawking amplifies as I walk closer to the sea.
The sky is getting darker.
I lie down on the cold and smooth sandy shore.

Jered Chavez, Grade 6

Invitation Just for You!!!

There is a surprise party
to celebrate the birthday of Marty
He is turning six
An entertainer will be there to show his bag of tricks
It will be in Disneyland
We will eat while listening to a famous band
The party will start at ten
Get an R.S.V.P from Mr. Ben
And if you want free transportation with us
We will be riding in a bus
If you have any questions
and you want to call, please do
And guess who we are inviting? YOU!!!

Razelle Temana, Grade 6

My Thanksgiving

Rushing around the house I savor the dessert we made
In the car listen to my mother lecture me about not
squashing the dessert
When we enter I detect the perfume of the turkey cooking
After I notice the football game is on
I enjoy the way the mashed potatoes tickle your tongue
As we exit I wonder how long until next Thanksgiving.

Olivia Cammon, Grade 4

The Color Blue

It's omnipresent
High and low, this color is content
The sky and the sea it represents

Home to the fish in ocean foam
Home to the birds who freely roam

Sky to soaring
Sea to swimming
Self-rule to roaming
Sadness to sobbing

The victory of war
The color near the shore
The shade above where there are clouds and more
The tear of a child from their core

Celebration, action
Heaven, amen
Darkness, deepness
Sorrow, misery
The color blue...

Matthew Naumann, Grade 6

Snap!

In the jungle...
I see a long dark path waiting...
Waiting...Waiting...
For a kid like me to walk through
In the jungle
I hear a twig snap
My head spins
All I see is one long dark path...
Waiting...Waiting...
For a kid like me to walk through in the jungle
I feel a shadow linger over me
As I take my last steps out of the jungle.

The cold winter blows my hair awry
My dark brown eyes glisten when
The bright yellow ball of fire shines my way
It lasts a moment...
Shadows fill the sky again...
The cold breeze comes...
The ball of fire is no more...
As the long dark path
Appears once again.

Raven Aliberto, Grade 6

Thanksgiving

Thank you for all my mouth can taste

The rich, juicy cranberries whipped up and ready in a warm bowl
Chips and dip ready, out on the table, an appetizer for our
famished Thanksgiving guests
The tasty turkey bathes in the pan with its friends corn and gravy

Thank you for all my ears can hear

The timer buzzing is music to my ears
Listening to the Thanksgiving Day parade
marching band trumpeting down the NYC streets
My family enjoying their Thanksgiving repast
while cheering for the New York Giants

Thank you for all my eyes can see

Turkeys take time to tenderize in the toasty oven
Dishes clatter, glasses clink, as dad thumps
The turkey on the table
Plump pumpkins sitting next to cornucopias
smiling at eager Thanksgiving guests

Ann O'Connor, Grade 6

Where to Go

He moved past the people with their ears as
Cold as ice
Zooming and curling in the sunrise
Some people didn't know what it was
All they knew was that it was fearless to do anything
And was willing to hurt anyone in sight

He moved slowly trying to find humans
Didn't matter if they're short or tall
Or big or small he just needed to
Freeze someone.

The bitter cold frost coming in
And out
Swirling and swirling all about
Where to go he didn't know
Up or down, left or right that's
His fight

One day he's strong and confident
The next day shaky and scared
Where to go he'll never know.

Justine Finnegan, Grade 6

Love

Love is in the air.
For someone to care.
We all show this affection.
It's when two people have a special connection.
They love each other with no doubt. That's what love is all about.

Faith Brown, Grade 4

Sports

I love sports.
Sports are my everything.
If there were no sports, what would I be doing now.
But I play football and I play outside linebacker and it's awesome.
But I used to play defensive back of tackle. They were both cool.

Camrin Dandridge, Grade 4

Holidays, Holidays, and More Holidays

I've got my eye on a haunting, horrifying Halloween,
With all the creepy crazy costumes around
With all the crackling candy wrappers aground,
It will be the super spectacular scene.

A holiday that is a totally terrific Thanksgiving,
With a lot of totally terrific turkey,
With all of our family together, we will be very perky
When everything is ready to eat it will be very relieving.

My birthday is on the twentieth of outrageous outstanding October,
I hope I will get some perfect precious presents
there will be some excellent big events,
When the clock chimes 12 a.m. it will be sadly over.
Jaime Aubuchon, Grade 6

Midnight Lego

When I went to sleep,
my Lego started to weep.
They wanted me to play with them,
so I jumped out of bed on a whim.

When I sat down at my table,
I made sure all of the pieces were stable.
There is Batman, here is the cave,
I started to build Jason Todd's grave.

After playing for hours
I built one last tower.
My eyes started to close
so I jumped into bed right when the sun rose.
Andrew Francis, Grade 6

A Day to Remember

The sun was almost gone.
It was starting to thunder.
The water was glistening as
The grass rustled...
The lighthouse shined and flickered
Minute by minute
Hour by hour.
It started to pour down rain.
The lighthouse door rattled as the lightning streaked across the sky.
Finally it started to rain.
Soon the rain ended.
People ran and jumped and played,
As the sun shined
As night fell and the misty rain reappeared.
Kaylie Caruso, Grade 6

Northwest African Cheetah

Dominic Stadvec
He is a Northwest African Cheetah.
He is as fast as a wolf running in the night.
He likes playing games, watching TV, and shooting the basketballs.
Dominic Stadvec, Grade 6

Where I'm From

I am from red, white, and the USA,
The home of the free
And the brave.

I am from basketball
Where the ball flies around the court
And the point guards dribble down the court.

I am from Tarpon Springs Middle School
Where everyone learns something new
And where all people of all ages are always happy.

I am from Florida, the sunshine state
Where the sun shines brightly
And the beaches are endless.

I am from a family
Where everyone loves each other
And they would do anything to help one another.
Raymond Zagorianos, Grade 6

Passing by Stars in the Dark of Space

This space out here I thought I knew,
This darkness lets me glide right through,
The blinding light of stars in dark,
No, not the space I thought I knew.

A shooting star makes a perfect arch,
Around a star that pierces dark,
This peacefulness surrounds me here,
As I tremble with remark.

I keep on going, full of wondrous fear,
Of what I might see or find out here,
All of this space that's left to explore,
I'm just wondering if I'm alone out here.

This space is not empty, there's much to explore,
All of these questions leave me just wanting more,
I'm baffled by life itself as you can see,
I'm just wondering what's out here for me.
Shannon Swain, Grade 6

Love That Book

Love that book
Like a cat loves to purr
I said I love that book like a cat loves to purr
Love to read it in the night
Love to call out Man, I love this book!
Don't want to stop reading it, like a kid doesn't want to stop playing
And read it like there's no tomorrow
I said read it like there's no tomorrow
And never want to let it go, like a baby with its binkey
Don't want to let anyone else read it when I'm done
When I read it, it makes me happy
Guineviere Keeler, Grade 5

Leaves Are Falling

Driveway barely able to be seen,
Leaves are falling in red, yellow, and green.

Raking leaves to and fro,
Thinking soon we'll be getting snow.

O'er time they fall again,
Now the raking will soon begin.

Leaves are falling on my yard,
Raking all these leaves is very hard.

Swimming, swimming in the lake,
Oh please, do I have to rake?

Raking leaves to and fro,
Thinking soon we'll be getting snow.
Kaeli Waldstein, Grade 6

Ode to Gymnastics

Oh gymnastics
I feel chalk on the high bar
The wind whipping across my face
The thumps of my feet hitting the mat

Oh gymnastics
Muscles burning like fire
Sweat trickling down my body
The ripped skin
On the palms of my hands.

Oh gymnastics
Hard yet great
Never boring
Whenever I'm not there
I wish I were.
Noah Clifford, Grade 5

Heaven and Hell

Heaven

Where the supreme gods and goddesses live
It is like a floating fluffy cloud
No living thing could fly past the border
Heaven and the gods play a part of earth
Epic light sparkles upon the palace
Radiation makes the palace affluent

Hell

Where bloody devils and undead live
Screams and cries fill in the underworld
Flames eat the dead body and last forever
It is like a torture chamber with darkness
Punishing and torturing the criminal
Henry Chen, Grade 6

Ode to CC

Fur like gold
Yellowy perfect
Baby tiger
Shiny eyes that glow-in-the-dark

Beautiful stripes
Speedy as a jaguar
Human climber
Midnight lollipop thief

Always hungry
Runs at the sound of the can
Drinks from the sink
Who's afraid of water?

Playful in her own way
Bites me all the time
Homework destroyer
Hissed at by sister cats

Brave and bold
Sleeping tight
Keeping me company
Soft and strong
Cameron Lampl, Grade 5

Nature

What would life be like,
without that lovely soul?
Without that warmth and happiness,
which enchants me to adore.

It is a thought worth pondering
but would it ever happen?
Maybe it will and maybe it won't,
but what if it does?

Would there be life?
Plants, animals, humans
Where would we be?
Are we going to disappear?

Would that small, golden drop,
of hope and future;
be extinguished with depression?
Its all a mystery!

Waiting to be unraveled,
waiting to be known,
waiting to be alive,
and not alone.
Keertana Yalamanchili, Grade 6

Nature and Life

Each simple moment
an animal lives
is a line of a poem.
It writes and it gives
to our world made of time,
words, love, and breath.

The first line is birth.
The last line is death.

It's not sad.
It's just nature
at work with her pen,
writing poems and lives
again
and
again.
Sammuel Costa, Grade 4

Just a Normal Day

To start my day, I stretch out on my bed.
Then I wake up and look in the mirror,
I see what my Uncle says, knucklehead!
I look at the window it is all a blur.

I hear footsteps in the kitchen, oh boy!
I know not to go so I get anxious,
they called me in and I was filled with joy.
We go to mom's car she says "bye" to us.

I run to my room pulling drawers open,
trying to decide what to wear this day.
I was putting on my favorite lotion,
I sprayed my hair with thing, hairspray.

I am as busy as a bumble bee,
I am ready for this day, come at me!
Mikayla Grogan, Grade 5

Siblings

With siblings you can never tell
If something might or not go well

Sometimes you like them
And they too in return
Other times you feel like
Your alliance made a turn

They might seem like a sour pickle
Then turn into a billion nickels

But no matter what they are
They'll always be there
And no matter what happens
You will still really care
Natalie Pan, Grade 5

Friend Catastrophe

My friends are really mean to me,
When I call them, they never stop to see,
They act like they know everything,
And won't listen if I talk or even sing!

I really wish that they'd be a bit nicer,
And not scold me for no reason, whatsoever!
They make me feel rage, like a fire,
And are so fierce, almost like a tiger!

They give everyone a second try in games or dance,
But for me? Not a chance!
They break all the rules and when I break one,
That's it, it's over, I'm done!

When they hurt me, they never apologize,
And ignore my calls and also my cries,
I meet them at school every single day,
But, they're still my friends, so I guess they're okay.

Diya Dinesh, Grade 6

Owl, Oh Owl!

Owl, oh owl!
In the hollow tree,
We see you in the sky
With your beady little eyes

Your fluffy little feathers
We admire very much
You are so beautiful,
Wise, and sensible

Owl, oh owl!
What an honor it must be
So sneaky and sly
We like the way that you fly

The way you follow us
Everywhere we go,
Twisting your head left and right
You see us clearly in the night

Ashly Guaman and Camila Maza, Grade 4

Winter Night

Sparkling snowflakes shimmer
as they linger in the crisp wintry air,
moonlight pouring through,
creating shadows beneath massive evergreens.

Fire flickers in a blaze of color
through frozen frosted windows.
Glistening snowflakes fill my fur-lined boots,
making my feet freeze as cold as ice.
I shiver as I wade through the powdery flakes
towards the blazing fire.

Jessica Li, Grade 5

Once I Had a Snowball

Once I had a snowball, I threw it to a friend,
  who caught it in the air and threw it back again.
Once I had a snowball, I kept him as a pet,
  he rolled down the stairs and made my bed wet.
Once I had a snowball, I used it to make a snowman,
  and away he never ran.
Once I had a snowball, I kicked it like a ball,
  my play was wonderful, right into the goal it falls.
Once I had a snowball, I taught it how to cook,
  it made pizza cream cake, the recipe is too hard for me to make.
Once I had a snowball that was so proud,
  it did so many things despite it being so round.
It made so many memories now it has to melt,
  for now it is spring and the heat is too hot to be felt.

Sanjula Chitty, Grade 6

Joy Is the Greatest

Joy is a great gift
Don't get me wrong.
One's heart it can lift
Into happiness and song.

You can share it with everyone,
Your neighbors, your friends;
By giving joy
Instead of any passing trends.

Spreading joy
Is very easy.
I hoped you learned something,
So don't become teasy.

Dario Scully, Grade 5

Summer

Every year the warm air touches me,
I look at the blue waves coming from the sea.
The air that is cold begins to flee,
The fireworks are shot off and they show their beauty.

Every day the days are longer,
Plants will become green and even stronger.
The sun shines so bright its blinding the eye,
As it sits like a glowing red ball in the sky.

The air is so hot and sticky and it's hard to move around,
I jump in the pool to cool myself down.
But, soon it will be the end of summer,
And school is around the corner and makes that a severe bummer.

Zachary McFaden, Grade 6

Gage

G reat at splitting wood
A nnoyed by my brother
G ym is my favorite subject
E xcited to go hunting, camping, and fishing

Gage Hale, Grade 5

Football

White, stripes.
Thrown, caught, ran.
Always in the air.
Rollable, kickable, catchable.
Brown, hard.
Football
Antez Starks, Grade 4

My Family

Do you know why I feel so blessed?
Because my family is the best.
I love my family.
They always care for me.
They are by my side every day,
I am lucky, don't you agree?
Nathan Pidgeon, Grade 4

Family

F unny
A lways there for you
M ore caring than anyone
I mportant
L oving
Y our best friend
Ahmed Al-Judai, Grade 4

Jaslyn

J olly during Christmas
A wesome at Math
S mart when I do work
L ove cute things
Y ellow is my favorite color
N ice to people
Jaslyn Cortez, Grade 4

Mmmmm

I have eaten all
the ice cream cake
out of the freezer
that you were probably
saving for your birthday
but it was super delicious and creamy
Morgan Rogers, Grade 6

Autumn

A ll the leaves are gorgeous
U nbelievable beauty
T ime for Halloween
U GG boot season
M any colors
N ice weather
Taylor Bryant, Grade 6

Where I'm From

I am from warm blankets,
from Windex Cleaner and picture frames.
I am from the dog barking, the washing machine running, and the Beatles' music.
I am from the rosebush
my grandfather and I planted,
the red petals glistening.
I am from Christmas puzzles and sleeping in,
from Mel and Jaree and George.
I am from the last minute cleanups around the house
and always overpacking our luggage,
from "Stop fighting or I'm taking you to jail!" and "Don't bring worms inside!"
I'm from going to church on Sundays
and praying every night before bed.
I'm from North Carolina, Oklahoma, and Canada,
grilled cheese and watermelon.
From the time we drove nine hours to Disney World,
the arguments about the radio,
and the way my mother regretted not booking a flight instead.
I am from the photos on the computer upstairs,
the memories they hold,
the moments that they grasp and never let go of.
Katie Todd, Grade 6

The Place I'm From

I'm from a town of stone that no one owns,
where kids laugh and play all day.
I'm from a corner reading as quiet as a mouse
I'm from a place that always feels like home.
Even when I'm alone.
I'm from a school of bears
where everyone cares.
I am from a locker strong and true which won't open until the code is through.
I'm from nature tall and fair
and cool wind that blows through the air.
I am from the ocean big and strong. It's body stretching for miles long.
I am from a house with no other children at all.
Then come two more both loud and rambunctious sometimes they are quite proud.
I am from a game of feet and cleat where all everything comes down to the second.
I am from rocks reaching high to the sky.
Why they are there no one knows why.
I am from lightning striking the air,
As if it has no care.
I am from a family tree that is still growing strong as I learn the way.
I am from me and others, who came before
I am me and me is my poem that I now own.
Annelise McGee, Grade 5

A Trip to the Beach

The salt water tickles me this early afternoon.
The sun beats down on the distant sailboat with red and white stripes.
Seagulls feed on fish from the mouth of the ocean.
The waves crash at the shore causing water bubbles and sand to mix.
Children play at the shore happily, making sand castles, hills, and holes.
Sea turtles come to shore laying their eggs and back to the depths they go.
What a trip to the beach!
Jeffrey Mustalir, Grade 6

Summer

S ound of frogs croaking
U nder the waterfall
M aking mud holes
M ore day light
E at popsicles
R unning through cornfields
Clayburn Addair, Grade 6

Rose

Blood red rose
I'm grateful for it
I think I should pick it
And plus, it has beautiful "leaves"
Ow, why does it hurt so much
Maybe it was the thorns and not the leaves
Emma Savage, Grade 4

Thanksgiving

I see my family
I smell turkey
People are talking
I taste ham
I hug my family
Thanksgiving
Mia Bella Comi, Grade 6

Thanksgiving

I see family and friends.
I see delicious food.
I hear people talking.
I taste sweet potato pie.
I hug my family.
Thanksgiving
Makenzie Brooks, Grade 6

Grani

Strong, great
Shooting, running, fighting
Change, personality, proud, weakness
Fearing, running, crying
Terrified, scared
Coward
Diondra Homer, Grade 6

My Family

F un when we're together
A wesome to be around
M emories made for sharing
I nteresting and creative
L oud in the house
Y oung at heart
Gia Masci, Grade 4

Silver

Silver is the rising mist in the early dawn.
Silver is the snow settling on the trees
Silver is the color of love encircling you finger.
Silver is the smell of bare minerals exposed to the air.
Silver is the sound of slamming of iron in a forge.
Silver is the stars on a dark, peaceful night.
Silver is the taste of raindrops on a maple leaf.
Silver is a finely wrought chain resting on a slender collarbone.
Silver is the rough edge hewn from the earth.
Silver is the glowing lake in a full moon.
Silver is the smooth feel of a polished vase sitting primly on a tabletop.
Silver is the peeling bark of a gray birch.
Silver is the smoking ashes left after an angry fire.
Silver is the cascading waterfall and a running stream.
Silver is the stormy clouds in a thunderstorm.
Silver is icy breath billowing out.
Silver is a reflective puddle on a rainy day.
Amanda Fulton, Grade 6

It's About Writing

It's about creating a world that is completely your own
Pencil and paper are your sidekicks
Creating word by word…

It's about new ideas popping out of nowhere
Jotting down notes
Thinking hard

It's about filling pages up with wonder and mysteries
Taking readers to another dimension
A place where anything is possible

It's about typing up a copy to send to a publisher
Holding your breath
Waiting for a response

It's about messy copies, pleased fans, and bringing your world to life by words.
Julia Zhang, Grade 5

Thank You…

Thank you for all my eyes can see…
Turkeys as big as beach balls line the shelves of grocery stores.
Family friends dressed up in their best apparel.
My aunts and uncles roasting and toasting away in the bustling kitchen.

Thank you for all my tongue can taste…
Creamy, canned cranberry sauce covers my plate that is
chockfull of crusty cornbread and tasty, tender turkey.
Moist apple pie warms my wet mouth.
Exquisite repast my family has made together.

Thank you for all my skin can feel…
The once fluffy, comfy coat room is now an icy dull closet.
My aunt's wooly coat immersing me in cozy warmth.
My relatives are an immense sea of people dousing me with farewell hugs.
Hannorah Ragusa, Grade 6

Sophia

It means smart, loving, and kind
It is like a calm ocean
It is like boating
It is the memory of my mother
Who taught me kindness and honesty
When she goes places with me
My name is Sophia
It means amazing things
Sophia Peacock, Grade 4

Makynna

It means friendly, outdoorsy, trustworthy
It is like a forest first thing in the morning
It is like going to the beach
It is the memory of my brother
Who taught me to ride a bike
When he rode his bike
My name is Makynna
It means champion
Makynna Bryan, Grade 4

Exciting

Like when Christmas comes…
Like on your birthday…
Like when you're going on vacation…
Like when you get an "A"…
Like when you win a game…
Like on Halloween…

You are excited!
Matthew Motichka, Grade 6

Me

I wish I could fly
Like a bird
And I dream of myself
I am AMAZING
I used to be cool
But now I am AMAZING
I seem to have blown your mind!
But I'm really chill.
Justin Hopkins, Grade 6

My Angel

I have an angel by my side
Which tells me to follow my dreams
When once in pain I loudly cried
It says, "Do not scream!"
If full of sadness I wear my sadness crown
It says, "Cheer up do not frown."
When once I wished to get a fish
It said, "The fish might drown!"
Sophia Ruiz de Vivar Iddon, Grade 5

Haunted Halloween

Spooky spirits running all around,
The night is cold and they are expecting you.
Be careful because they might startle you by saying boo,
    they will scare you because they have nothing better to do.
You think you are safe in your house, but suddenly you hear a sound.

Frightened, you run quickly upstairs,
you realize it was just the trick-or-treaters fooling around,
You feel like someone's watching you and again you hear the sound,
    You can hear it echoing all around,
You can't see anyone but you know someone's there.

You start trembling when you hear a scream,
the phone rings and you pick it up.
Someone tells you to beware and you hear a knock,
Petrified, you slowly open the door, but you wake up,
    it was only just a dream.
Mariah Villalta, Grade 6

Where I'm From

I am from trophies
from footballs and shoulder pads
I am from the big brown house
smelling like candles
I am from the daisies

I'm from Thanksgiving football and a funny family
from Lori and Carol
I'm from dirt biking and joking around and from playing outside.

I'm from "Be good in school" and "Have fun"
and "Rock-a-bye baby"
I'm from trips to Orlando
I'm from Stonington and Ireland
steak and hot dogs
from William falling down the bowling alley lane and bruising his back,
family pictures in the safe in the closet
Ben French, Grade 5

Martha Graham

Martha was born May 11th in 1894
A simple baby, yet later in life she would become much more
She became an instructor at a music school
The melodies and dances she choreographed were modern and cool
She was the first dancer to perform at the White House
When she danced, the colossal theatre was a madhouse
She extinguished traditional steps of ballet
And received highest civilian ward of the USA
Her first dances were deft on bare stage with just costumes and lights
She traveled around the world as a cultural ambassador, while she saw the sights
The purpose of her dance was to bring an increasing awareness of life
Eric Hawkins was her husband, and she was the wife
Her final performance was *Time of Snow* in 1969
She kindled an audience for over 70 years which is a long time
As you can see Martha Graham had a long time to shine
Layla Reilly, Grade 4

My Day in Nature

When I am outside, I never want to go back in
Some people ask me why
Well here is my answer
When I am outside I hear peaceful sounds
Like when the birds sing their majestic song
And when the wind breezes through my face
I could see a bug munching on a leaf and
Brown acorns from a gray squirrel
I feel the smooth leaves like a small smooth feather
There are so many kinds of beautiful flowers
Above me I see trees looping over me
And so many colorful leaves on the ground
I love nature and nature is beautiful.

Raquel Guillen, Grade 5

A Different Life

Where would it be…
by the beach.
waking up to the sounds
of the relaxing waves hitting the shore.

At the end of the day
listen to the calming waves lull you to sleep.
I can imagine the sun setting on the horizon…

Every day is different
when you are living a life
beside the sea.

Maria Duharte, Grade 6

The Storm

Roaring winds escort me to my throne
Cold drops fall as I shake my mane
The sun does not rule the skies alone
Though when I leave, it will be the same.
My thunderous growl echoes in the sky
Rattles on the mountainside
And bounces to where the villages lie.
Through cracks my paws slide
Spreading a ruthless chill
No matter what, I will get there, valley or hill.
I am a cold and damp swarm.
I am a lion, a storm.

Lindsey Newman, Grade 5

A Friend Is…

A friend is not a bully
A friend is confident in you
A friend is there when you need
A friend is good at telling jokes
A friend is someone who cares about you
A friend is helping you through and through
A friend is always ready to comfort you
A friend is helping you up when you fall
A friend is Gianna!

Monica Coller, Grade 4

Silent Night

A cold silent night lies beneath the moon,
Full moon brightening the night.
Shuffling leaves through the cold elastic wind,
No one to be seen, but me.
I walked through the lighten night,
Suddenly there was a whistle, no a howl.
I stopped in my tracks to listen to the beautiful sound,
It was getting closer, running through the leaves.
I was scared, frightened even,
Then It was pitch black.

Caroline Cranford, Grade 6

Jason

Athletic, greedy, and funny
Son of Everton and Sonia
Who loves family, basketball, and chicken
Who feels sad about the fact that Wilt Chamberlain died
Who gives respect, focus and patience to the game of basketball
Who fears danger, drugs, and alcohol
Who'd like to see Stephen Curry
Who dreams of being a 6'3 NBA all star
Student of Clover St. School
Grant

Jason Grant, Grade 4

My Grandfather

I miss my grandfather, with all my might.
Sometimes he is with me, when I sleep at night.
I was there when he died,
I remembered, because everyone but me cried.
It was on Halloween when he passed,
A couple of months after my mom and dad got married.
A part of everyone he carried.
I know he is still with me,
Everywhere I go.
This for sure I know.

Paris Aryonna Brown, Grade 6

Freedom

F reedom means respect,
R emember if you want to be treated equally,
E veryone has the freedom to gain,
E xcellent leaders, citizens, and educators of our country
D efine freedom in many ways, so that we
O bey the rules and
M ake ourselves patriotically free.

Ahmad Elkasaby, Grade 4

Dogs

Dogs are fun pets.
I think they are the best.
They might annoy you when they bark,
but who cares, have fun and take them to the dog park.
Stay in the sun and have some fun all day long.
Don't even worry about your dad and mom.

Sy'Niah Stokes, Grade 4

Nature

When you go outside do
You just breath happily? Shouldn't
that feel like nature when you exercise
You breathe in as if it was like nature

When you just look at the trees and how
Animals are living in Mother Nature
Don't you just get that felling that
You're going to be happy.

Jesus Williams, Grade 6

Fall

In the fall the leaves are falling
On the ground
It is time for Halloween
To get a pumpkin or go to a corn maze
It is fall
It is cool dry air, it is time for school
It is time for football, and apple cider.
Friends family all together
Having fun in the fall

Noah Kraft, Grade 4

Baseball

Red and white flies by,
A tiny blur thrown around.
A serious game,
Not silly at all.
Amazing game so true.
If the ball is strongly hit with a bat,
It can soar into the sky so blue.
I love it too,
It can even be a dream to wish for too.

Eddie Borysenko, Grade 4

A Kiss of Death

The strength.
The speed.
The venom of a
Black Momba.
Enough strength to crush bones.
Enough speed to chase down a jungle rat.
Enough venom to kill 17 men in one strike
The Black Momba
has a kiss of death

Caleb Hill, Grade 6

Fall

Squirrels rustling the leaves
Leaves crumbling under my feet
Bees passing by
The sun shimmering through the leaves
Leaves falling on me
Squirrels climbing trees
Leaf blower

Brett Littel, Grade 5

When I Am...

When I am tired, I am as a sluggish business man at dawn
hearing the alarm clock ring saying just let me sleep.

When I am melancholy, I am like an old returned doll
sitting on the shelf waiting for someone to buy me.

When I am irked, I am as a shark on Robert Moses
beach no one wants to go near me.

When I am jubilant, I am like a bride figuring out that
she is getting married jumping here and there.

When I am adventurous, I am like a sailor in the middle of the ocean
checking out where he is and if he sees land.

When I am afraid, I am like a mouse hearing the scratching of the cats nails
coming closer and closer.

Danielle Roppelt, Grade 6

Fall

Oh, wonderful fall!
The cute costumes for Halloween,
And the awesome festivals.
Also, lovely decorations and trick-or-treat.
Later at night the spooky scary,
Halloween movies come on tv.
They're my favorite movies of all.
The best part for me is the roof down on my car.
We party with loud music.
Then we drive to the scary houses for Halloween,
And we get lots, lots, and lots of yummy candy.
The best part of Halloween is the enormous pumpkins,
And taking out slimy seeds too.
Some cool stuff about Halloween is that I can do pranks,
So what I'll be doing this Halloween is scary prank eyes in the bushes.
I also love to make Jack-o-lanterns,
And that's why I love fall, thank you.

Jenna Ali, Grade 4

Ready for Halloween

Costumes and costumes, which will I be?
A witch, a mummy, or maybe a pumpkin.
A goddess, a bat, or Rumple Stilskin.
I finally found my costume and transformed into me.

I'm ready for Halloween and I have everything I need.
I have my costume and bag don't you see.
Can we go now, hurry up, don't tell me you need to pee.
I remembered what I forgot and I remembered to get Mrs. Sneed.

I'm out with my friends trick or treating.
One is a bee, another a tree, and last is me.
Can't wait to get candy don't you see.
Finished trick or treating and I'm going to get a sugar rush because of candy eating.

Ethan Lam, Grade 6

Football

Football
Hard, working
Throwing, running, kicking
Very hard hitting game.
Jump, spin, side step.
Hot, cold,
Football
Matthias Calhoun, Grade 4

Basketball

Basketball
Fun, sporty
Dribbling, running, taking
Players, bench, fouls, shots
Drinking, stealing, fouling
Excitement, sweaty
Huskies
Nakissa Burleigh, Grade 6

Tests

You wake up in the morning
and realize
You have the PSSA
You run to your backpack
and zoom out the door
like a cheetah
to take that test
Joe Abbruzzesi, Grade 5

I Am

B rave
E ager
T hankful
A wesome
N osey
I ntelligent
A wesome
Betania Perez-Temaj, Grade 4

Smile

I see it
I see it I do
I see a smile
Oh what a beautiful smile
A smile full of joy and light
A smile so big and bright
Oh, yes it's true, that smile belongs to you
Grace Keesler, Grade 5

Dream

Dancing my heart out
Thinking I am full of life not death
All my energy goes to my heart
And spinning like a tornado
Makes me think life is a dream
Avery Flanigan, Grade 5

Pumpkin Spice

I know it's Halloween when I hear children's feet slapping the ground,
running to collect more candy that keeps them up all night.

I know it's Halloween when I can finally open the windows,
and I can feel the wind rush to my face, while hearing the birds sing their soothing songs.

I know it's Halloween when the leaves start to turn
yellow, orange, and red, oh, so heavenly.

I know it's Halloween when at night
I can feel the shiver crawl down my back when thinking of spirits in the dark night sky.

I know it's Halloween when the smell, oh yes, the smell
of pumpkin pie and vanilla candles linger in the air.

I know it's Halloween when people start sticking Styrofoam skeletons
in the ground and fake spider webs on every tree.

I know it's Halloween when I feel the rush of trying to find as much candy as I can
before my parents ruin all of my fun.

I know it's Halloween when I have the best time of my life!
Katelyn Richards, Grade 6

Door Opener

There are two doors in front of you
the one with heartbreak…and happiness at the end
the one with happiness …and heartbreak at the end
Which one do you open…which one do you peek into
It's all your choice…they are your doors
millions of doors are still…still being made
this is your door…this is your choice
choose carefully…and choose now.
You walk into a door…you don't know which one
you are blindfolded…like every human being

And your heart breaks.
IT'S HEARTBREAK TO HAPPINESS.
Satisfied?
No.
Sad?
Yes.
But that's because of the heartbreak…you don't know your feelings anymore,
You're overcome with heartbreak

And then your life breaks
And it's happiness now.

Amelia Posner-Hess, Grade 6

Summer Time

Summer is the best time, summer is the most fun of all,
So many things happen in summer like fishing and swishing the ball in the goal.
I eat delicious cheese, and see bees and fleas.
Also we eat potatoes and tomatoes while we enjoy a warm summer breeze.
Summer is amazing! I can't forget the theme of my summer song out of my head.
Napthali Mullings, Grade 4

Time Will Run Out

Playing soccer and basketball,
it doesn't seem like much at all.
But in the end, those few hours spent
will be worth much more than 10,000,000 cents.

Time is such a valuable thing,
it's short like a piece of string.
Don't waste your time like everyone else.
It will be great, see for yourself.

Go to the fair and have a blast,
that moment in time won't last.
So have fun and do whatever you want,
your time will run out if you don't.
Savannah Burns, Grade 6

American Love

Under the sun, a Nation proud
Hear our bravery, strong and loud.
Fifty States that are bonded by love,
Soaring free on the wings of a dove.

The eagle defends us, with valor, so strong,
To keep us from evil, and right all the wrong.
Unity binds us, guarding the Earth,
Eternally fighting the darkening curse.

With hope in our hearts, we search for the light,
Protecting the world from the shadowing night.
Infinite Liberty and Justice stand tall
May our Land of the Free never crumble and fall.
Connor Adams, Grade 5

Fall

Leaves fall red in crimson piles
It becomes darker by the minute
You grab your jacket and decide to take a visit
Children start to play, their faces lit up with smiles.

Summer has past, today it is fall
May hues fill the sky
Beautiful views from up high
I see beautiful flowers, I hear autumn's call.

Halloween has started to come around
Temperatures drop effectively
Trees get chopped down aggressively
Animals are all over the hunting ground.
Yaphet Tedla, Grade 6

Owls

Owls, owls, in the night, flying under stars so bright.
Big eyes looking, wings full of might, mouse nearby,
they put up a fight, both owl and mouse but in the end,
the owl won. The owl full of might.
Ocean Unger, Grade 4

War*

The sun rises
Bringing hope for a new day
A new life…
Once there was
Destruction as far as the eye can see
Houses crumbled and boats in the harbor destroyed
But happiness fills my chest now
We have defeated the enemy
I can now return home to my little boy and girl
Who look up to me
With those big happy eyes
I hope they find inspiration
In destruction and debris
Just like me
As I look up into the hope filled blazing sun
Whose orange rays have set the ground
On fire with color
I find my inspiration to get back up and serve my country.
Riley Mills, Grade 6
*Written from the perspective of a soldier

Someday

Someday...
Someday I will play the violin
Someday I will get hired for a job
Someday I will be a father
Someday I will be famous
Someday I will be in an orchestra
Someday I will get married
Someday I will master multiplication
Someday I will get straight As
Someday I will get As in math
Someday I will get my own computer
Someday I will be in an all county orchestra concert
Someday I will become a doctor
Someday I will be in college
Someday I will get a master's degree
Someday I will be noticed
Someday I will get my own TV
Someday I will get through summer break
Someday...
Elian Oliver, Grade 6

Isaiah

Isaiah
Smart, talented and an expert
Son of Dezaree and Nathan
Who loves animals and catching fireflies
Who feels happy when weekends come
Who gives hugs and kisses to my mom and dad
Who fears bad dreams and bears
Who'd like to see Jamaica and Costa Rica
Who dreams of going skiing
A student of Clover Street School
Sperry
Isaiah Sperry, Grade 4

The Bully

On a good day my grades where taking flight,
Then some kid walked up wanting to fight,
I thought to myself, he is only half my height.

He said I will give you a bruise,
He thought I was going to lose.
But there was no way, I was amused!

I thought up a plan,
To say you're the man,
It might not be right,
But he will feel bright.

I told him that,
And he said you're fat,
The teacher called him over
And that was that.

If you get in a fight,
You know it's not right.
Your ego will be a pile of rubble.
Even worse you'll get in lots of trouble.

Sam Rhodes, Grade 6

The Puzzle of Peace

Earth is like a puzzle.
We citizens are the puzzle pieces,
And peace is the glue.
In order for us to form a work of art,
We need peace.

Earth is scared about becoming a planet like Mars.
No one there, barren, empty.
But peace is joyful, smiling, happy, confident.
And we puzzle pieces feel scattered.
I wonder if we, as pieces, will ever be connected?
Perhaps, patience, participation, planning, pleading,
These are all words coming from the puzzle pieces,
Waiting for a miracle to happen.

It may take three years, five years, or even ten years,
But if we stay patient and keep on trying,
We will always be a step away from our work of art.
And when the time comes,
There you have it,
A Masterful Puzzle of Peace.

Chloe Park, Grade 5

Christmas Is Red and Green

Christmas is Red and Green
It tastes like nuts out of the nutcracker
It sounds like joy coming from every mouth
It smells like a good candle my wonderful grandma puts out.
It looks like people with a smile on their face and opening presents.
It makes me feel HAPPY!

Ali Boyle, Grade 4

Ocean Storm

The water lapped at my feet
My toes wiggling in the soft sand beneath
The salty ocean smell, lingered about
As the thunder gave a menacing shout

The gray waters receded once more
Taking in more sand than the wave before
The dark clouds above, advanced upon the sky
In an inevitable chase, as the thunder howled a cry

The first rain drops, fell from the heavens
Plopping down by the dozens and dozens
I held out my hand to the blessing from above
As the thunder erupted a scream; A scream defying love

I turned and ran, ran as fast as the winds
On my face, snug in place, lay the slightest of a grin
The sand was hard, hard and cold
Just then, the thunder, bellowed one final roar

Sagar Gupta, Grade 6

Good Times

The table
Filled with laughter
Good times and
Amazing memories.

The table
Full of smells
Warm food
Amazing tastes.

The table
With cousins, aunts, and uncles
Grandparents, dads, and moms
All sharing amazing memories together.

The table
Familiar faces laughing and singing
Especially the laughter and playful screams of children
The table — a place where I feel at home.

Abigail Kikta, Grade 6

Halloween Night

I walk out my door and this is what I see.
Witches riding on their brooms and looking back at me.
Black cats come out to be seen.
Bats fly around me looking so mean.
Monsters and ghouls come out to frighten up the night.
Suddenly I notice a light, so bright.
Is it what I think it is?
It is the sun?
I'm so glad that all these monsters will be gone.
I hope they are banished and never seen again.
These scary creatures are nobody's friends.

Keyur Patel, Grade 4

Lion vs Lamb

Lion
Majestic, proud
Roaring, snarling, prowling
Sahara, zoo, farm, Greenland
Bleating, leaping, grazing
Meek, gentle
Lamb
Hannah Green, Grade 6

Bow Meow

Cat
Small, gray
Hurting, scratching, stalking
Streets, homes, backyards, parks
Barking, running, licking
Big, brown
Dog
Jennifer Dominguez, Grade 6

Cats

Cat
Fun, playful
Purring, sleeping, running
Food, naps, toys, fur
Eating, pouncing, biting
Hairy, cute
Lion
Nathan McLaughlin, Grade 5

Fun in the South

My trip to Chile was very fun,
I got to see everyone!
I had the chance to see and play,
With the cousins I love every day.
Together we were buds at times,
And now I'm very proud to say,
I traveled to Chile and loved the stay!
Sofia Arriagada, Grade 6

Summer and Winter

Summer
Hot, sunny
Fishing, swimming, sunbathing
Beach, sun, snow, hail
Skiing, ice skating, freezing
Cold, icy
Winter
Sydney Dudash, Grade 5

Summer

Summer
relaxation
playing in the water
full of laughter and family
happy
Nicole Rangel Capelle, Grade 5

The Relaxing Peaceful Autumn Season

Splashing and swimming in the clear pools turn into,
jumping in three feet deep crunchy leaf piles
Closing the refreshing pools
And setting up the horrific undead zombie decorations for Halloween
Baseball fields empty out and football stadiums fill up as fast as
the salty waves crashing on the beach
My T-shirts, swimming trunks, and tank tops
go to wait in the closet till next summer
Then my warm furry winter clothes jump out to protect me from the freezing wind
As school starts,
Families have time to bake crusty sweet apple pie and prepare for a
humongous Thanksgiving dinner
On Halloween children dress up in spooky costumes,
Then fill their candy bags the same way a squirrel packs his acorns
The ground is covered with colorful leaves,
Like an artist who had just painted a new masterpiece
As kids snack on Halloween candy, families await an immense repast in November
Busy as bees families order gifts for Christmas and prepare the tree
As the leaves wither away, a clear white sheet of snow covers the land...
Welcome winter!
Christopher Budhwa, Grade 6

Spooky Halloween

I know it's Halloween when…
Ghosts and goblins, spooks galore, scary witches at your door,
Jack-O-Lanterns smiling bright, wishing you a frightful night.

I know it's Halloween when…
Kids scream and shout bursting my ear drums
as I run from the scary monsters in the haunted house.

I know it's Halloween when…
There's a spider at my window, a monster at my door, the
Jack-O-Lantern at my table keeps on smiling more and more,
there's a ghost who haunts my bedroom, a goblin whose face is green,
they used to be my family until they dressed for Halloween.

I know it's Halloween when…
Witches screech with all their might, as they brew potions
All Halloween night.

I know it's Halloween…
Black cats meow, and pumpkins are lit, may luck be yours on Halloween.
Kaliope Patatoukos, Grade 6

My Dog Jojo

My dog Jojo is black and tan and I am her biggest fan.
We keep her hair long in the winter so she will not shiver.
She doesn't like to go out in the rain because she thinks it's a pain.
She's not big but tough and likes to play rough.
She barks like she's tall but doesn't know she's small.
She wants to chase cats although she's the size of a big rat.
Her favorite thing is to eat. She will bark until she gets a treat.
She likes to sleep on the bed and sometimes up by my head.
Jojo is my friend and my buddy. I wouldn't trade her for any amount of money.
Cody Chartier, Grade 6

Football

Playing football is a loud blast,
To play you have to be pretty fast.
Crash, is the sound it usually makes,
Playing football is worth what it takes.
In your pads it's really hot,
Try not to hit your team's mascot.
When you're playing football the crowd will roar,
The cheering keeps it from being a bore.
The cheerleaders keep it peppy,
The players are all "bicepy."
When you're playing you have to score,
To win you have to do more.
When you play you have to win,
One day I hope to win the Heisman!

Tyce Hill, Grade 5

My Furry Friend

My furry friend Belle is small and sweet,
When I look at her, my heart skips a beat.
She has the curliest, softest fur,
There's never been a dog quite like her.
Crash! When I hear she is in trouble,
I will be there on the double.
I give her a worried quick glance,
Her sorry eyes put me in a trance.
I can't believe all the tricks she can do,
She won't even chew on your best shoe.
But she will shake hands, sit and fetch,
As far as pets go, Belle is a catch.
My little dog is so gentle and kind,
She's my best friend, and always on my mind.

Anslee E Johnson, Grade 5

God Is…

God is my keeper,
He is my redeemer.
He will keep me safe through the night,
He's like a diamond that shines so bright.
God has given me a good family,
God has always been the key.
We learn more about him on Sunday,
He has paid the price no one will ever pay.
He loves me truly,
So we shall never act cruelly.
Satan makes you do things you're not supposed to do,
God will lend you a hand and help you through.
He died to save our lives,
For his kingdom we should strive!

Emma Kate Beheler, Grade 5

I Give Thanks For

I give thanks for…
my lovable mom…she keeps me safe,
my awesome dad…he buys me what I want,
my younger brother…he plays with me.

Ethan Horruitiner, Grade 4

Scaring People

Haunting somebody night by night,
Some people will get a fright.
Scaring people is a blast,
Jumping out really fast.
Some look up stories on phones,
While others chatter like broken bones.
Jumping scared like a kangaroo,
Some give a very loud, "Boo-Hoo."
Some sound effects may be boom! and bang!,
While others may be screech! and clang!
Jumping for joy, you got your first scare,
You did it, because you accepted their dare.
Scaring people is a blast,
Until they scare you back at last.

Mason Collins, Grade 5

Swimming

All you swimmers take your mark!
I better get ready so I can start.
Swimming breaststroke is super easy,
Swimming butterfly makes me queasy!
Goggles on my head to protect my eyes,
If I dive without them I would look like I cried!
Splash, my eyes hurt like crazy,
I probably look a little hazy!
When I finish I look fine,
Like a man on fire I'm feeling divine!
I had just won the challenging race,
Boom, they disqualified me and I'm pale as paste!
I practice so hard until I ache,
I won my race right and I need a break!

Garrett Watson, Grade 5

Basketball Star

Shooting, shooting with the ball,
Please, I beg don't hit the wall!
All the players are dribbling,
The fans also start nibbling,
This game involves some blocking,
Players mostly be smack talking.
When you are shooting, use the backboard,
This is a key to a way to score.
Plus this is a fun sport,
To block and run down the court.
It is amazing when they do a dunk,
Like when Griffin jumped over a car and the trunk!
It is fun to play a basketball game,
Just get to the ball, dribble, look, and aim!

Brendan Young, Grade 5

I Give Thanks For

I give thanks for…
my lovely mom…she takes care of me,
my awesome dad…he takes me places,
my funny dog…who makes me smile when I come home.

Sophia Watsky, Grade 4

Daybreak

Creeping up the hills
And spilling shades of orange
Across the sky
Is the sun
Who is making its journey
To the top of the clouds
Warmth settling over our shoulders
For now.

And as the day moves on
It will begin to glare
Angrily at the creatures below
At a buzzing heat
Bringing sweat to our foreheads
Then eventually cooling off
To let the moon take over.

The next morning
It will begin climbing
And ascend to the top
To begin the day
With a fresh start.
Emily Roberts, Grade 4

I Am a Stallion

I am a stallion,
for I love to run.
Merrily trotting
under the sun.

I am a stallion,
free and wild.
I love to whinny,
just like a child.

But then I get caught,
And am no longer wild.
I am taught
to pull a wagon.
like an oxen

Although I don't like it,
I can still run.
Acting like a child,
under the sun.

I am still a stallion.
Angelina Xu, Grade 4

Art

The garden looked like artwork,
On the bright summer day,
When I saw shadows on the path,
I ran down to talk to them,
And started to play.
Ryan Kedanis, Grade 5

What Video Games Mean to Me

Video games are so much fun.
Video games are for everyone to play.
But sometimes, you just want to be done.
But we can make a game called Horses Hay.

Moms, Dads, and Brothers can play,
Sisters, Aunts, and Uncles too.
Everyone can play so come today.
We will make a video game crew.

Since 1985, they've become a big hit,
from Super Nintendo to Wii U it's grown.
If you don't get one, you will have a fit.
Then you will feel all alone.

But until then, keep them in your heart,
for you shall always do your part
Jayce Walker, Grade 5

Shopping Fever

Shopping with bags full on my arm
I love shopping at the mall
When I shop, there is no harm
I shop for things both big and small

At the mall it sure is loud
There's way too many people here
I wonder why there is such a great crowd
But of course, I do not fear

There are so many people I know
I'm in just about every store
The bright colored walls, sure make it glow
I'll be there so long my feet will get sore

When I'm shopping, I buy a lot
Then I go to the parking lot.
Erin Miller, Grade 5

That Sweet Cat of Mine

My cat is lazy and fat—
Eating this and that…
That sweet cat of mine!

He is orange and furry
And never in a hurry.
That sweet cat of mine!

Overweight and plump —
Sitting on his rump.
That sweet cat of mine!

Eating everything in view.
Making the lizards shoo.
That sweet cat of mine!
Stephen Crum, Grade 5

My Eyes

I love my eyes,
They help me see skies

My eyes are blue,
Maybe like a shoe

My vision lacks,
So I need contacts

My eyes are light,
But also very bright

My eyes are like an ocean,
Always in motion

I love my eyes,
Yes, I love my eyes
Rosalie DeDonato, Grade 6

Space Flight

The rocket is soaring, soaring so high.
The astronaut is smiling so, so bright.
It is so beautiful, flying so high.
The rocket is soaring, as high as a kite

The ship has made it, so high into space.
It feels like we're moving, so very slow.
The astronaut has a smile on his face.
He doesn't want to fall, right down below.

He starts to spin, around and around fast.
He might throw up, let us hope he don't!
He feels as he is having a big blast.
He starts to feel very, very sick but he won't!

It's time to return to the Earth, so sad.
But the astronaut is a little glad.
Aaron Sprouse, Grade 5

Red

The color of death
Surrounds me
Lounging leaves
Lethal lava
Burning
Appealing apples
All of it
Taunting me
Bravely, I keep going
But I can feel the vicious vibe
Of death
Staring
With his red eyes
But, I refuse
To look
Sujay Shah, Grade 6

How Doth the Little Cub

How doth the little cub
Make her fur shine,
And to comb it out on wood,
And then to see her dine,
Oh it looks so good!

How sad she looks,
She looks very bad,
She hides in the nook,
And snuggles up her dad.
Caroline Swenson, Grade 5

My Love

Oh my love
How I love you
Every day of my life
After a safe day
You are always there
With your arms open
And a cute smile
And I love you so much
Thanks for everything you have done
Thank you with all my heart
Diana Carbonell, Grade 6

Bunny

Fluffy as Cotton
Fuzzy as a Spike Ball
Happy like a child's smile
Popping like popcorn
Good as a marshmallow
Warm like a fireplace
White like snow
Blue like the ocean
Colorful like flowers
FAST as the years go by
Eddie Vega, Grade 5

When I Get There

The angels sing songs
Filled with love and joy
Hoping you will hear them
And thy hate will be no more
They sit by the cross
Waiting for you to join
They see you coming closer
Tears stream down your face
They say its okay
You're now in the right place
Kenna LeBaron, Grade 6

Siamese Cats

Siamese cats are smart
Their colors are brown and white
They are from Thailand.
Kevin Guilfoyle, Grade 4

I Am

I am a girl who is an artist.
I wonder if I will get better.
I hear the pencil screeching up against the paper, while I draw a picture for my mom.
I see a good future ahead of me in art.
I want to win an award for best artist in the world.
I am a girl who is an artist.

I pretend that I am in an art show.
I feel like a great artist who takes pride in her work, amazing work.
I touch my pencil to draw.
I worry that I will not make enough money to survive.
I am a girl who is an artist.

I understand how to do a shadow technique.
I say that practice makes perfection.
I dream to have an art show.
I try to achieve my goals.
I hope that I will be a famous artist in Paris.
I am a girl who is an artist.
Maya Kaplun, Grade 5

I Am

I am a girl who likes playing soccer
I wonder if we won or lost
I hear the referee blowing the whistle, my teammates calling for a pass and saying I'm open
I see my teammates scoring goals and winning the game
I want a soccer trophy and a golden medal for a reward

I am a girl who likes playing soccer
I pretend that I'm playing for the FIFA soccer
I feel nervous that we'll lose, and excited that I might score a goal
I touch the moving soccer ball gently
I worry that I won't get past the goalie and score

I am a girl who likes playing soccer
I understand the game of soccer and offense
I say I'm open please pass
I dream that I'll play professional soccer
I try to score a goal
I hope that I will be in the FIFA soccer championship
I am a girl who likes playing soccer
Claire Carroll, Grade 5

Where I'm From

I am from piano, from iPad and Legos.
I am from the candles.
I am from the Oak Tree, the Dogwood.
I am from celebrating birthdays and fun, from Mac and Dad and Mom.
I am from the activities and relaxation.
From "Behave" and "Listen."
I am from Veterinarian.
I am from Lexington, Oreo pie, hot dogs.
From the beach, the Broadway at the Beach, and the golf cart rides.
I am from home.
Ella Timberlake, Grade 6

The Chalkboard

Every day they wrote on me,
with white chalk for all to see.
Math, assignments, lessons, and more,
don't scratch me, it will make your ears sore.

Then one day there was a new board in here,
it was white with markers that sometimes smear.
To this day I remember his face,
as I realized he was taking my place.

Then as I began to frown,
a child almost knocked him down.
And as the white board almost shattered,
I realized this fight hadn't mattered.

Dana Mackin, Grade 6

Halloween Horror

Creeping crackling cracking candy wrappers
Creamy crisp coated chocolate bars
Cool creative costumes from Mars
There are kids dressed as rappers

Halloween is always held in the fall
My brother goes to a haunted house
My mother keeps finding a mouse
The candy comes from people big and small

Eerie echoing sounds through the night
Hey, Jake is a piece of American cheese
Can I have some candy please?
My Halloween was amazing, my candy tastes just right

Jassmyn Nesmith, Grade 6

The Life of a Teddy Bear

I was sitting on shelf in a store,
and guess what, it was a real bore.
A kid came over and said with glee,
"Mommy, can I take him home with me?"

The mother said, "Yes, of course dear."
She reached up and said, "Here."
We were in the car going for a drive,
we looked out the window and arrived at five.

We got out of the car and went inside.
now I know this is where I reside.
I was taken upstairs in the arms of my new friend,
this is where we will play and laugh until the end.

Lauren O'Brien, Grade 6

Waterfall

The water flows fast and steady
Without a fault to be seen
No thoughts flow around me as I glide through the water
Waterfall

Lily Kenner, Grade 6

The Beautiful Forest

The sun was glowing over the forest
The roots look like fingers
The dirt giggled
The acorns fell on the ground
The roots stretched a mile
When I jumped over it I thought it was going to touch me
The branches tickled the ground
The acorns went plopped on the ground
The tall trees almost touched the beautiful sky
The leaves are dancing in the trees
The roots are blocking the path
The leaves were swinging down onto the ground
There were a lot of twigs on the ground
What a beautiful forest

Marisa Joseph, Grade 4

The Night's Light

The lighthouse...
Beams bright as the sun strong and still,
the wind roars, the water tickles.
Zoom! Birds fly in unison.

The lighthouse...
guides ships back home, blinking in the distance.
Silent and priceless,
In the day pointless, at night necessary.

The lighthouse...
Tall with spectacular views,
Birds rest at the peak,
Finally the lighthouse is not alone.

Angie Bardales, Grade 6

Eddie Spaghetti

Eddie, Eddie, how are you?
My friendly dog I got from a rescue.
You came to our family ready to greet,
Oh how I loved you at our first meet.
You love to bark at the door,
And leave all your fur on the floor!
You get to sleep all day at home,
And when I come home I give you a bone.
I brush you, feed you, and take you for a walk.
And in return you watch over me like a hawk.
Your name might be Eddie.
But we love to call you Spaghetti.
Oh Spaghetti, Spaghetti I love you so much.
Nothing can take you away from this crazy Duffey bunch.

Brady Duffey, Grade 5

Rubber Ducky

Rubber rubber ducky, how I love you,
When I take my bath, your squeaking makes it not a none,
When my mom comes in to say I'm done,
I say I'll remember our day of fun.

Evan DeArment, Grade 6

King of the Creek

New rod, new reel. Let's try it out
Bait up and hope to hook up
Bad luck, lost gear
Brother catching fish left and right
Not a bite for me in sight
Long wait, stolen bait. Sun glare, hard to bare

Cast it out. Another wait
Then, zzzzzzzzz zzzzzzzzzzz. Drag screaming!
Pole bending and bending
Heart hammering, people yelling
Have to zone it out to land the fish
The water boils, get my first look
Bigger than expected
Pump and reel. Pump and reel
Get the net!
Too heavy to get over the pier
Need grandpa's help to land my fish

Wow, a great birthday present!
My biggest fish ever
Over 15 pounds and over 40 inches
The mighty blue catfish, the King of the Creek!

David Lask, Grade 6

Why I Love Parks

I like the park it's fun to be,
first the slide as I glide and
then the swings as we please, we have fun as time goes by.

The day goes by
so much fun
it gets colder as the
sun goes down.

When it gets dark
we hear a bark
and then we say
good bye to the park
and leave the park.

Anvitha Varakantam, Grade 6

House of Horror

When I came up to the front door
I shivered
I knew this was going to be a rough journey.
I put one foot in then the next
I knew I was in danger
This was all a dare from two friends of mine.
I knew if I didn't no one would doubt me.
I'm all the way in and once again I shiver
When I heard voices and screams that's when I
knew this was my death wish.
You think I'm alive but now I've become
the voices in the house.

Brayden Southerland, Grade 6

Light

Light is here,
Light is there.
Light is pretty much
Everywhere!

In a classroom,
Outside,
Even in the moon!

But the light I am talking about
Has not been recorded.
Don't worry, from one person to another,
This light has been transported.

Please, I'm begging you,
Let this light in you burst!
But in order for this to be done,
You must be kind, first.

Making a difference when being kind can be hard
And extremely tough, too.
To make it easier, treat others they way you'd want them
To do unto you.

Sapna Stanley, Grade 5

Fall

A plethora of scents hit my nose,
my feet are cold down to my toes.
I turn the stove on; with the tea kettle on top,
allergies kick in; I get a cough drop.

The tea kettle whistles,
announcing its dismissal.
I get my favorite mug,
pour the tea and get all snug.

I open the window and smell the crisp autumn air,
it's so soothing I sink down in my chair.
As I see the colorful leaves sprawl,
I know without a question, it's fall.

Katerina Zick, Grade 6

Life Is a Battle

Life is a battle,
forever unfolding.
Life is a battle,
forever in dismay.
Life is a battle,
forever letting all its secrets out.
Life is a battle,
never truly won.
Life is a battle,
sewn together with the love and hatred of the world.
Life is a battle,
always causing grieving.

Shiloh Eberhardt, Grade 6

Christmas

C hrist was born
H appy times
R eindeer fly
I ncredible food
S itting around the Christmas tree
T he tree is lit up brightly
M emories made
A ll gather around the fire
S inging Christmas carols

Breanna Dotson, Grade 6

My Pitbull

My dog is gray,
his eyes are blue.
He likes to play and eat a lot, too.
He is big and likes to chase me around.
If I fall,
he licks my face,
when I fall about.
Javier is a red nosed pitbull.

Josue Soto, Grade 6

Splash!

Splash!
I jump in the pool
Splash!
Don't I look so cool?
Splash!
Why bother to go to school?
Splash!
When you can jump in a pool!

Ketturah John, Grade 5

School Days

Get on the bus
Unpack your stuff
Do some snacking
Then lunch
Minutes later
Recess!
Soon math and reading
Day ends!

Kyle Alt, Grade 4

Pet

My dog Snowflake
Is very cool.
He can dig holes
Under the fence.
He can run fast.
He can jump high.
He will listen to me,
And he will not attack anybody.

Christopher Quick, Grade 6

I Am

I am a girl who likes playing outside.
I wonder if my sister will play.
I hear the birds singing in the tree and my two dogs barking at my neighbor's dog.
I see my friends playing in the yard with me.
I want to make it to the very top of the tree.
I am a girl who likes playing outside.

I pretend I am flying I'm like the birds.
I feel scared when I am playing outside in the dark with my friends.
I touch the small wiggle worm.
I worry that I am going to get locked outside.
I am a girl who likes playing outside.

I understand how to play outside in my yard.
I say it is beautiful today.
I dream of red and blue birds.
I try my best to play.
I hope I can climb to the top of the tree.
I am a girl who likes playing outside.

Ashley Brookshire, Grade 5

I Am

I am a girl who likes Warwick gymnastics
I wonder if I can do flips
I hear lots of coaches yelling at students to do back handsprings on tumble tracks and floor
I see students doing full turns into the soft pit
I want to be able to do front handsprings into the pit
I am a girl who likes Warwick gymnastics

I pretend I can do anything I think of
I feel very nervous at Warwick gymnastics, I barely talk at gymnastics
I touch the smooth helpful chalk
I worry that I will break something on the rough bars
I am a girl who likes Warwick gymnastics

I understand how to do pullovers on bars
I say barely anything at gymnastics
I dream of being on a team
I try to do my best
I hope I will be able to do flips on beam
I am a girl who likes Warwick gymnastics

Emma Boulanger, Grade 5

Yellow

Yellow is the color of the bright school bus on its way to school
Yellow is bees pollinating the bright sunflowers
Yellow is the smell of fresh lemons being cut for refreshing lemonade
Yellow smells of freshly baked pancakes
Yellow tastes of corn on the cob at a summer cook out
Yellow the taste of warm and soft cake in celebration of a birthday
Yellow the sound of the sun exploding into a new day
Yellow sounds of baby ducklings quacking in search for food
Yellow feels like a bee stinging
Yellow feels of a sticky honeycomb, sweetness

Sierra Kimball, Grade 6

Montauk

Earth's horizon as far as you can see,
Warm sun, clear skies, an ocean breeze,
Sandy beaches and hiking trails, bonfires and sunsets,
Cruises under the moonlit sails,
The lighthouse where the island bends,
This is Montauk — The End.

Giuliana Caliendo, Grade 4

Christmas

Ahh the snow that glitters like the light on my Christmas tree.
Fire crackling.
The sweet scent of new cookies coming out of the oven.
Chocolate melting in my mouth.
I let the silky ribbon slip through my hand.
Could anything be better?

Aine Kolpa, Grade 4

Shooting Star

I looked up at the stars shining bright,
And the moon shined down on me.
I asked for a sign that life is good,
A shooting star appeared to me.
And now I know that God is great,
and my guardian angel is watching over me.

Matthew Skalamera, Grade 4

Thanks to All

Beautiful scent of the turkey
The whistling wind
Amazing set up of the table
Delicious taste of the mashed potatoes
The super greasy turkey resting on the dining room table
Giving thanks to all on this wonderful Thanksgiving

Dazer van Leeuwen, Grade 4

My Momma

How much I love my momma,
I love my momma,
Because she loves me.
I love my momma,
Because she give me the things that I need.
I love my momma, because she takes good care of me.

Jakaylah Boykin, Grade 6

It's Turkey Day

The smell of that delicious turkey
The taste of the stuffing was music to my ears
The sound of the drums at the football parade
Turkey cooking in the oven
Soft touch of the mashed potatoes in my mouth
I can't wait to get my paws on that food

Shane Corcoran, Grade 4

The Best Thanksgiving

Turkey cooking in the oven
The microwave beeps when the corn is done
Smoke rising out of the turkey
Cranberry sauce makes my mouth water
Catching the football in my hands
Thanksgiving is now over but we still have next year

Scarlett Brookes, Grade 4

Excitement

Excitement is winning a golf match.
Excitement smells like the ocean air.
Excitement tastes like freshly made chocolate chip cookies.
Excitement sounds like the golf ball hitting the bottom of the cup.
Excitement feels like summer vacation.
Excitement lives in me.

Thomas Mayernik, Grade 6

Luxurious Longboat Key

Longboat Key is fun!
My family and I were all beach bums.
We had sand in our hair and did not care.
We were relaxing by the pool,
and rejoicing because we were not at school!
It was the perfect way to end summer!

Sarah Mccluskey, Grade 6

Joy

Joy is like fresh air on a cool autumn day
It smells like new scented candles
It tastes like a warm cup of steaming hot soup
It sounds like waves crashing along the shoreline
It feels like a cozy, soft blanket
It lives in the warmth of my heart

Kyra Hayden, Grade 6

Thanksgiving Celebrations

A turkey goes in the oven
My family pulls into the driveway
Mouthwatering gravy sizzles in the pot
The mashed potatoes excite my mouth for more
I hug my family before they leave
Thanksgiving is over but next year will come

Grace Peters, Grade 4

Thanksgiving Day

As I enter the house, chatter rises
I creak up the stairs until I enter the living room
The smell of food was so strong I couldn't bear it
I put the first mouth watering piece of turkey into my mouth
This Thanksgiving was like no other
The best Thanksgiving I bet.

Ivan Gomez, Grade 4

Crystal the Casual Comic Fan

Crystal went to the comic store,
Her friends thought it was quite a bore.
Then a nerd came by,
He thought he was fly.
But the girls just showed him the door.
Michelle Salas, Grade 6

Dino Dinner

Dinosaurs
Giant, mean
Stomping, roaring, eating
Smiling as they eat you
Carnivores
Zach Tucker, Grade 6

Oranges

Orange
Sour, juicy
Lick, bite, eat
An orange is very orange!
Fruit
Dillon Morales, Grade 4

Tomato Sauce

Tomato sauce
Delicious, spicy
Eating, slurping, dripping
Fresh from the pot, hot!
Red gravy
AJ Mathes, Grade 4

Ice Cream

Ice Cream
Cold, refreshing
Spooning, tasting, decorating
Mix for 30 seconds enjoy!
Sundae
Grant Stewart, Grade 4

Cars

Cars
Fast, smelly
Drive, honk, spin
They race better than people!
Automobiles
TJ Yanarella, Grade 4

Parrots

Parrots
Cute, soft
Hanging, squawking, swooping
Flying feathers to cuddle with!
Birds
Kayleigh Levecchia, Grade 4

Andrew Curtin

Born on April 22nd and was born to wealth,
But during the Civil War, he had very bad health,
For his second term, he beat Gorge Woodward,
Followed his grand dad's foot prints, and went into politics,
He became governor of Pennsylvania in 1861,
Being governor wasn't very fun, he was governor during the Civil War,
And he was close friends with the man who said "Four Score,"
He moved to Russia for a few years, leaving his family shedding tears,
His dad was an iron foundry owner, and ran it until his life was over,
He helped to extinguish the colossal war, to never be seen again no more,
When he came back he smelled musty, and you have to admit very dusty,
With the war in cinders, he came back without pointing fingers,
The war still gorged a permanent mark, and could come back with just a single spark,
He lived a long life of 74, and died the same place he was born.
Andrew Simmonds, Grade 5

Halloween

Halloween
Spooky, dark, mysterious, orange
Sibling of Christmas and Valentine's Day.
Lover of Pranks, Candy, and Kids.
Who feels
Lonely in Winter, excited in October, and Sad in Spring.
Who fears
Apples given out instead of Candy,
Kids not allowed to eat Candy, and being different than other Holidays.
Who Would like to see
More kids having Fun, Friends sorting treats together, and Frightful Costumes
Resident of Spine Chilling Lane
Halloween
Maggie Liu, Grade 5

The Forest Party

In this forest there are red, yellow and orange leaves
Trees, rocks and animals party in these parts
The roots were as long as gigantic stretched mozzarella sticks
The leaves swayed side to side slowly to the ground
Plunk, plunk, the pine cones plunged in the lake
The sky illuminated with the sun
The path was as narrow as the garden snake in grandma's yard
The squirrels were as happy has eight kids on Christmas going to Disney
Billy broke branches off the tree
At night the bats broke through the sky
Num, num, I ate a sandwich in a second
The sun broke through the darkness and shined on the great lakes as it made a rainbow
Luca Mallari, Grade 4

You Are

You are a house of cards waiting to fall down.
You are a tower; when life gets too hard you fall.
You are a fragile vase; when you fall and break your friends will put you back together.
You are a bottle of emotions; when you get shaken up you explode.
You are a system so complex no one can figure you out.
You are a music note and there are no others like you.
You are a cow wandering through the field of life.
Parker Foster, Grade 6

Colors Change

Rusty metal used to be metallic and gray
What used to shine off of it was the sun's rays
It was nice and clean
Until it got wet
That's when people began to fret

If you leave your bike out in bad weather
Your bike definitely won't look any better
In fact it will become a really dark brown
And you won't be able to ride it around

Its chains will fall off
And so will the paint
Nobody will like it and neither will you
All of this is very true

So this is how metal things change
Of course there are many other ways
This is just one that changes its color
But it's also the one that makes me shudder

Josiah Chu, Grade 6

Soil

Solitarily laying in wait for a future of blank
    emptiness, the beginning, end, everything
No future in my most far-fetched fantasies

Occasionally, probing plants greet me by digging into me
    like power drills
They thank me for providing free food
My one true friend

Quiet as a drop of water sliding down a window pane
Immobile, illiterate, unwanted
Dark
    Dank
        Deprived
            Dead
Time squandered
Every year the same thing
Forgotten, lost forever
The eternal void
My life

Liam May, Grade 5

My Hands

I love my hands because I do so much with them
I can play video games with them
I use my phone with them
I love my hands because I do so much with them

I love my hands because they're useful
I throw a basketball with them
I can catch a football with them
I love my hands because they're useful

I love my hands because they're strong
I write with them
I punch the punching bag with them
I love my hands because they're strong

I love my hands because they help me
I do push-ups with them
I hold a drink with them
I hold a book with them
I love my hands because they help me

Joseph Collins, Grade 6

Still Standing

I feel useless, clueless.
Don't want anything to do with it.
Can't complain because it's gonna happen over and over.
Sometimes I just wanna go in the corner
And cry
I wish a nice boy would come and wipe it
From my eye.
And say, "It gonna be all right." And
Hold my hand for the rest of the day.
When I go home, I pray
Wishing for better days
And go to sleep and wake up
And start the day, knowing I'm the topic on everybody's mind.
I keep walking till I'm at my class.
Watching those mean girls stare at me, talk about me.
I think to myself,
"They wanna be me."
But at the end of the day,
I hold my head up and put a smile on my face.
Because I'm still standing.

Kare Cash, Grade 6

The Cat in the Window

The cat in the window sees everything
It sees the sun rise and set
The cat in the window watches all the cars go by
It watches the corn grow and the birds fly by

The cat in the window is a sight
That sits there every day and night
It sees all the traffic and all the planes
The cat in the window sits like a statue and sees everything

Colin Fulmer, Grade 4

Hope Awaits

Love heals the heart and soul
While happiness stays as joyful as can be
Wishes giggle as they fly up to the sky
So sky whispers back,
"Go to the stars and tell them what you hope for"
The wishes follow his orders and the stars explained,
"Go to the kids that wished you, and make it come true!"
So the little wishes go to each house to make a dream come true
And as they do it, hope awaits those wishes

Camille Donovan, Grade 4

October
October is the month of fear
It includes Halloween.
Pumpkins ghosts, goblins and more.
When you go to the haunted house
Some might say give me a tour!

Although all days in October aren't scary,
This month includes Halloween.
When children dress up and go
Door to door saying trick or treat.
Oh, all the costumes that can vary!

October, October the month I adore
You're one of the months that can give so much more.
From the most beautiful fall days
To the most scariest fall nights
October can spread the lights.
Allison Nkansah, Grade 6

The World Is Full of Evil
This world, Planet Earth, is full of evil
It's because of how they're raised usually
Evil is known as sin from the devil
Evil people treat others brutally

One evil group is based off their beliefs
They will do anything their gods need em'
So to stay safe, we need the Army's chief
They give others very little freedom

Some countries are so mean to their soldiers
They make them go on suicide missions
They will behead people from the shoulders
They put prisoners in bad conditions

The world is covered in evil and war
I just wish that the world could agree more
Alex Cothran, Grade 5

Black
An evil presence poured into the room
Giving an eerie chill of doom
Lurking around every corner
The scent of death, a saddened mourner
The room went dark with a deafening screech
With this, everyone lost their speech
The lights returned with a crack
All cowered in fear at the man draped in black
The man walked straight through the wall
The guests screamed, then started to fall
Down, down, down, they go
To their death...
They encountered the final blow
From deep down, out came a hiss
They fell into the black abyss
Anthony DeNoon, Grade 6

A Wonderful Wonderland
I know it is fall when...
Rosy cheeks fill the streets
Rakes collect
Gigantic piles
Of colorful leaves.

I know it is fall when...
The aroma of pumpkin pie fills the kitchen
And the smell of cooked turkey
Enters the grand dining room.

I know it is fall when...
Ducks and pelicans soar
Through the grey sky,
Leaving the sky bland
With no flavor.

I know it is fall when...
Children place snug, warm scarfs around their necks
Keeping them warm against the cool night air,
And put fluffy decorative mittens
One by one on their
Soon to be frigid hands.
Ellie McCreary, Grade 6

My Eyes
My eyes are blue like the ocean
They give me the ability to see emotions
When I wake up, I see the sun
In my dreams I have the most fun

I love the way my eyelashes are long
They never block my vision so I don't go wrong
If I didn't have my eyes I wouldn't survive
They show me where to arrive

Lessons are learned all from sight
They show me how to write
When it's night they close
When I have dreams I can see a rose
Makayla Gonzalez, Grade 6

Feeling Nature
OPEN YOUR EYES,
look at the glistening beauty around you.
OPEN YOUR MIND,
think of all the colorful gifts being given to you.
OPEN YOUR HEART,
think of what you give nature.
OPEN YOUR HANDS,
you're free, nothing is holding you back.
Go out there, enjoy what nature has to offer,
mountains, valleys, oceans, hills, trees, flowers,
Enjoy, and make the world a better place
by doing your part.
Habiba Khirie, Grade 5

Something I Know for Sure

My path twists and turns and nothing is certain,
Almost nothing gets through the wall
that blocks my attempts to find my future
and see who I truly am.

In the present and the past,
I fail and failed so many times.
People say that there will be many more victories,
but maybe they lie,
For how can they be so certain of something they do not see?

I barely know anything
in the vast amount of knowledge of this world.
I have barely any right to judge this world.

Yet I judge it as beautiful and amazing.
I judge it as harsh and cold.
I judge it as mean and abandoning.
I judge it as mysterious and interesting.

And I have perfect right to judge it,
Because I am different.
I smile, laugh, cry, and shout like you,
But I could be anybody.

This is the one thing I know for sure.

Mahima Muddu, Grade 5

Things to Do in Autumn

Spring into a pile of rustic red leaves,
crisp and warm against your skin.

Sip the cool, sweet cider, from freshly picked apples
that are soft and sun baked, with shining crimson skin,
and smoothly slip into your hand.

Wear the soft, ruby red sweater with small creamy colored
buttons that fiercely fights the wind, a wool shield.

Carve bright orange pumpkins filled with gooey pulp.
Later cook and spice the seeds, that melt in your mouth

Whistle along with the sulking trees, who whine in the wind,
ripping the oaks' bitter cold arms and roughly tugging
at their leaves.

Whip the pumpkin into a pie and
embrace the wafting fragrance.

Climb the stiff, green pine — the sticky sap on bumpy brown bark
shines on your hands — get to the perfect branch and
look out at a blazing red sunset.

Feel the weather change, snow softly falling.
Close the doors of autumn with a smile.

Hannah Rosenberg, Grade 4

Winter

Cold December winds, cuddle up for Christmas
Having fun rides on a sled or snow board
The shine of an angel on top of a tree
Opening presents in front of a fire
Waiting for Santa's footsteps on the rooftop
Wanting to hear Santa's sleigh jingle and jangle

Having a January snowball fight in the cold howling wind
As animals cuddle and hibernate in a den
Your nose is runny as you play in the snow
Having a fun sled ride with your brother or sister
As icicles form around your house
Sitting by the fiery flames and warmth

Hear the roar of a snow blower in the cold February snow
Snowflakes falling left and right
Red and pink for Valentine's
Winter is awesome, can't you see?

McKenzie Korenkiewicz, Grade 4

Light

The one thing that is unstoppable
The one thing that is your savior
The enemies of shadows
Once it starts within you the breeze will calm you down
But once it's gone
Get ready for a nightmare.

You can't see
Or feel the breeze
A monster on every corner
Every step into the unknown
Controls you until you can't comeback
Overcome it
Or disappears with it.

Once your back in the light
Don't attempt going back in the shadows
Or you'll be forever within its grasp.

Gabriel Cruz, Grade 6

School

I don't like school.
I'm taught how to divide,
But I'm not taught how to do my taxes.
I've never been taught how to get a job.
But I do get to dissect a frog.
But as long as I know what 8456/9056 x 263 is,
I'm all good.
If I know where my heart is,
I'm successful,
But no, that's wrong.
Almost all things I'm taught are unimportant.
And to think,
I'm writing this poem for a good education.

Alyssa McKenzie, Grade 6

Touchdown

With the ball,
Down the field,
To the 50,
Toward the 10,
Over the goal line,
For a touchdown.
Brock Burres, Grade 5

My Dad

M y dad is a survivor
Y ells at my sister a lot

D oes everything with me
A lways helpful
D oes funny voices
Angel Cote, Grade 5

Soccer

S occer is so much fun to play
O n the field
C an I score the ball
C an I pass to help score
E veryone can play soccer
R unning is something you do a lot
Hannah Federico, Grade 5

Thanksgiving

I see my family
Okay food
I hear the tv
Turkey on the table
Hug people
Thanksgiving
Thomas Clark, Grade 6

Summer

S ound of birds chirping
U nder the waterfall
M idday mud fights
M idnight water fights
E xplore the forest
R ustling in the leaves
Logan Bailey, Grade 6

Joyful

J esus in your heart
O nly you can take your joy away
Y ou can give joy to others too
F or joy is what makes you happy each day
U nbelievable glows on your face
L oving and caring for the people around
Abriana Brown, Grade 6

The Privilege of Freedom

Freedom is a right that lets you determine who you want to be.
Freedom is a gift that always means so much to me.
It sparks a meaning that makes me want to spread my wings and fly.
And even in the darkest times, its glory will never die.
Day and night, our flag waves back and forth, glistening in pride.
Like a light bulb, freedom ignites the passion and bravery of our hearts from the inside.
Because of our freedom, every day, I feel overflowed with joy.
And knowing this assures me of all the girls and boys.
Yet it disheartens me when I think of those who aren't enriched like we are.
The thought of not possessing the freedom is really bizarre.
But one day, we will make a difference that can fix all that.
In fact, all of us can, both Republican and Democrat.
And in the meaning of freedom, one thing is true:
America is the home of all especially me and you.
Matthew Hayes, Grade 6

Tattered and Broken

The dog lies there on my bed
Tattered and broken
A desk curls up snug in a corner
And never in a million years will it be clean

Tattered and broken
I will never forsake him
And never in a million years will it be clean
The only noticeable object is a picture when I was three, smiling as wide as a river

I will never forsake him
A desk curls up snug in a corner
The only noticeable object is a picture when I was three, smiling as wide as a river
The dog lies there on my bed
Julia Sherman, Grade 6

Bold and Bodacious Ben

Athletic, friendly, and hilarious
Who enjoys playing the forward position in soccer.
Who is able to score goals in soccer.
Who wonders what he will do as a job when he grows up.
Who feels good when cruising around on his nickel board with friends.
Who fears moving heights, like roller coasters.
Who cares about his brother, mom, dad, dog and friends.
Who dreams of making the high school soccer team when he's in 9th grade.
Ben Weiner-Goldsmith, Grade 5

Winter Whining

I'm not going to sleep
Mom tells me "No way!"
She tells me, "You may play when I tell you that you may."
"But we got to sleep for all winter, so why can't we sleigh today?"
"It's getting cold," Mom says
And I say, "What happens if we starve one day?"
Mom says, "It's all right. We have a lot of honey and berries," and sends me to bed
Tucks me in my cave saying, "Good night."
"Sleep tight."
"Don't let the frostbite bite."
Sarah Koh, Grade 4

Rosa Parks

Go to the back of the bus, Rosa Parks, go to the back and stay
No, I won't; I think that's unfair and I'm just too tired today.

But everyone knows the rules, Rosa Parks everyone knows if you're black
You can't eat at white restaurants and on buses, you sit in the back

So now it's time to move, Rosa Parks No, I'm not moving at all
I've got a voice and I'm going to use it and thousands will hear the call.

We're coming to sit with you, Rosa Parks, People black and white did say
We're coming to change America and bring equality here to stay.

And so the train of heroes passed Lewis Clarke, Mary Ann Cary and MLK
They all helped stop slavery in America to this very day.

And although slavery has stopped in America, Russia, Pakistan and China
Don't understand that slavery is wrong and imprison innocent people and think that they do no wrong.

We need to teach them, to make them understand
That slavery is bad, a terrible thing to withstand.
Let's tell them it's awful let's tell them it's bad
To hurt other people to make them feel sad.

Let's all join the fight to stop the cruel system
And we'll succeed, I know
One day there will be peace and the world will ripple with freedom.

Swecha Agarwal, Grade 5

Fall in Georgia

I know it's fall when…
Leaves are bursting with red, oranges, brown, and yellow
and flutter like dancers to the ground
When bushes are bare and serve no place for hiding animals
And flowers' colors begin to fade and the petals start to wither.

I know it's fall when…
Rabbit's fur start transforming fluffy and grey
And squirrels gather acorns for winter
When the bird chirps grow weary and faint
And the bears prepare for a long slumber.

I know it's fall when…
The running water in the river grows cold
The drizzling rain feels like falling ice
The lake has a thin layer of frost skimming the surface
And icicles begin to crystalize on the roof trim of my log cabin.

I know it's fall when…
The fire is crackling and roaring softly under the mantle
When the cold of the night bites my toes because they aren't covered by my thick flannel blanket.
And when I bring back my retired sweatshirt to keep me warm while I sit by the fire stroking my dog.

I know it's fall in Georgia once all of these fanciful experiences have occurred.

Summer Major, Grade 6

Ode to a Chairlift

Oh, chairlift
What can I say?

You carry me up
The mountain
Every winter day
You speed up the mountain
Like a cheetah on a track

You're taller
Than my house
Higher than
Mount Everest!

And as long as
The ocean spreads
You bring me
Up and down

Ode to you chairlift
So I don't have to
Walk up this mountain

But I forgot you were there
So I walked up the
Mountain instead
Maya Aylesworth, Grade 5

American Soldier

He walks right to the platform
He heads straight for the plane
He looks back at his family
And he can sense the pain

Into their eyes he looks
Their souls as open books
They are so sad to see their dad
For only one last time

He heads straight into battle
The gunshots like a rattle
He looks down at the ground
His friend now he has found

Then as he tries to save his friend
A bullet soars straight towards his head
He know he will not get to save
For this will be his bloody grave

Yet even though he now is gone
His memory lives on and on
In his children when the play
You can see it day to day

He would live on from deep within
Jessica Shipp, Grade 6

My Great Dog

I have one dog! How about you?
Boom! He is huge and really likes shoes.
I used to have two, and now I'm blue.
We might get another dog to be very new!
No matter how young, no matter how old,
I will find a dog to be big and bold!
My dog and I have very much fun,
We laugh and play and love to run.
I taught him tricks and he did none,
At night he snuggles and likes to hug.
In the morning he pushes and tugs,
No matter how cold he keeps me snug.
His name is Boomer, proud and strong,
Boomer loves me and I'm not wrong!
Abigail Robertson, Grade 5

My Dog

My dog is smart, his name is Scruffy,
He is cute, but not very fluffy.
When he gets a toy, he tears it up,
Even though he is no longer a pup.
My dog is spoiled and very greedy,
When it comes to running he's very speedy.
When I am at the table to eat,
He waits for food below my feet.
My dog likes to play in the backyard,
To get him back in is very hard.
He needs his blanket to go to bed,
When I hold him he can't help but shed.
He's the sweetest dog I've ever known,
With him I will never be alone!
Olivia Ireland, Grade 5

My Partner in Crime

Kara, is my sister my friend,
Our Laughter and Giggles never end!
She is pretty like a flower,
We are together till' last hour!
She and I have long blonde hair,
Golden, Silky, Blowing in the air.
Kara is so very tall indeed,
To her I am a tumbleweed!
She is my partner in crime,
Sleepovers never have bedtimes!
We are glued together always,
As so we will be for all days!
She is my friend through and through,
To this day, that is still true!
Sarah Reilly McMahon, Grade 5

Heroes

The wall of heroes
Stood tall in the night
With the heroes' graves put there
In the spring
Danny McAndrews, Grade 5

My Hair

My hair is fluffy like a cloud
It's smooth like the fur on a bunny
It makes me not look bald
My hair is long

My hair is as brown as a football
My hair is cozy like a dog
My hair is soft
It's on my head

My hair is wavy like the ocean
It's long like a neck on a giraffe
My hair grows fast
It makes me who I am
Matthew Aglietti, Grade 6

My Hair!

My hair is long
It has ends that are blonde
My hair is like a song
I love my hair from Earth and beyond

My hair is curly, it's also strong
It's like the colors bond
I will have my hair forever long
It has ripples like a pond

My hair will never be short
To me my hair is a magic wand
It will never be bought
Of my hair, I will always be fond
Serena Dhande, Grade 6

My Ears

I love my ears
They help me hear
When in doubt
They get me out

I love my ears
In the morning I hear the birds call
I also hear the acorns fall
I even hear all the tall giraffes

I hear the sound of the ocean breeze
And the jingles of my keys
Also the beautiful forest trees
I love my ears
Nicholas Orphanos, Grade 6

The Evening Beach

Cool ocean breeze blows
The ocean licks up the shore
The Sun slowly sinks
Haley Simpson, Grade 6

Winter to Spring

It started as one, then it grew to more
The ground turned into a white blanket.
It was only white, not green like before.
Soon the snow covered my little anklet.

I walked outside into the freezing cold.
My whole body shuts down from the bad freeze.
Soon I wake up to something to behold.
I look all around and feel a warm breeze.

It is springtime now, with many flowers.
I have slept through the whole winter.
I get up to see if I have powers.
I walk into a room, to the center.

I am in my house, in my little room.
I have no idea what happened, then boom!

Tanner Jones, Grade 5

Where I'm From

I'm from dirt from the baseball fields.
I'm from the new Nike shoe smell
I'm from the fingerprints on the video games.
I'm from the exhaust smell from dirt bikes.
I'm from getting hit in the face with a soccer ball
I'm from the snow days to the hot days in Cape Cod
I'm from the winning streak to the smell of defeat.
I'm from the sweat from mountain biking.
I'm from the basement smell of growing up.
I am from my brat sisters.
I'm from chlorine from the pool in paradise.
I'm from the bedtime stories.
I'm from the paper cuts from homework.
I'm from my first times in my childhood.
I'm from the pine needles on the Christmas tree.
I'm from the grease on the pizza.
I'm from injuries that got me into the hospital.

Payton Neale, Grade 5

Silence

You can talk but it will not answer
You can listen but it will not speak
It may bring you into a phase of quiet and peace
Or it may frighten you
And if it does
You will start pulling words out from the depths of your throat
And as they roll off of your tongue and into existence
It hides
And when you have come to a halt
It will appear and greet you as an old friend
'Til the end
Because it is there when you are silently grieving
It is there when no sound has the wanting to emit itself
It is there
It is silence

Josephine Kinlan, Grade 6

Fledgling

Swimming in an elliptical well
Coiled like a little bell
I feel toasty and warm
I feel safe
I feel sound
I sleep all day round

My eyes are closed
But
I see my bones grow
I see my blood flow
I still feel safe
I still feel sound
But
I don't want to be here all year round

My eyes are still closed
But
I have whirl wind of energy
I feel strong like a bull to explore the new world
With beak like a hammer
I break open strong walls of my elliptical cage
I am a fledgling on a fresh page

Samir Batheja, Grade 5

Wide with Wonder

A little girl, always looking up,
Up at the big girls high on the beam,
Up with eyes wide with wonder,
Wanting, wishing to be just like them.
But soon that girl, not so little anymore,
Found herself high on the beam,
Performing skills she had seen from below.
And in the very spot she had stood so long ago,
A little girl was staring up at her,
Up with eyes wide with wonder,
Wanting, wishing to be just like her.
The big girl, once the little girl,
Now wonders something new,
Has she become the one whom others look up to?

Kristi Yu, Grade 6

Eyes

I use my eyes to see
Contacts go in my eyes so I can see the world
I see colors and people
I love my eyes because they let me see
My eyes get tired
I close my eyes when I go to sleep
Dark circles around them.
I stare at things with my eyes
My eyes are black inside when I blink
I put mascara on my eyes
My eyes are brown
I love my eyes

Natalie Malatino, Grade 6

Where I'm From

I am from Glasses, from Windex and Glass Clorox
I am from the peanut butter chocolate cookies that my Nana bakes.
(They taste sweet and gooey)
I am from the big oak,
and tall graceful dandelions in the front yard.
I am from the July 4th cousin cookout
and brown hair, from Roma, and Tony, and Lisa.
I am from being neat, and being late.
From famous opera singers,
and the heart that stopped beating.
I am from going to church for Sunday school and morning worship.
I'm from Thomasville, from pasta and pizza.
From the stone my Nana passed,
and the staples that were put in grandaddy's back,
and the empty chair at the dinner table.
I am from the photo album in the cabinet.
Some I never got to meet,
with old torn pictures,
and some moments shared.
They are close to my heart,
and are very dear to me.

Morgan Adams, Grade 6

What Is Orange

Orange is leaves turning colors as the days grow cold.
Orange is pumpkin festivals with lots of sights and things to do.
Orange sounds like jack-o-lanterns crackling
on Halloween night.
Orange sounds like flames sparking in the fire place.
Orange smells like oranges as they are being
squeezed into scrumptious orange juice.
Orange smells like maple leaves as they change
into orange and get ready to give off maple sugar.
Orange tastes like pumpkin pie that is
still warm as if it is just out of the oven.
Orange tastes like clementines, with their sweet tangy taste.
Orange feels like smooth orange peels
as they slip off like clothes.
Orange feels like soft leaves brushing against
my face like a paint brush as they drift down from above.
Orange is marigolds swaying in the wind.
Orange is autumn with all the pumpkins
and color changing leaves.
And lastly orange is orange.
No doubt about that!

Alexa Wyborney, Grade 6

Someday

Someday...
Someday I will see my dad
Someday I will go to the army
Someday I will have a family
Someday I will be honored
Someday I will become a general
Someday I will become a grandmother
Someday I will be a strong fighter
Someday I will make a life in another place
Someday I will see my kids marry
Someday I will live a life that I was going to live
Someday I will be a true hero
Someday I will be the honor of my family
Someday I will be happy in another country
Someday I will be the new generation
Someday I will be a new leader
Someday I will enjoy my life
Someday I will finish my work
Someday I will rest
Someday I will see my family again
Someday...

Michelle Hernandez Ramirez, Grade 6

Too Much

I try to think and sort it out,
But it's no use.
It's not clear, no light can penetrate through.

It's not functioning, I can't control it,
It's too much.
My eyes swim with fog,
I am partially blind.

It's too much, my brain protests,
My shoulders ache from carrying the weight.
My heart tears apart from time I wasted.

I close my eyes, measured breath,
It stays there still.
I think there's no hope,
I am feeling futile.

It's too much, my mouth screams,
I collapse, crying.
I lay there, trembling; it's too much.

Jennifer Lee, Grade 6

Terrific Winter

The fluffy white is dropping from the sky,
And kids are playing and building happy snowmen.
It is Christmas and kids are dancing and singing,
It's a fun day today!
People are drinking warm yummy hot cocoa,
By the cozy campfire!
What a perfect winter!

Isabella Halvorsen, Grade 4

Neil Armstrong

Went on an escapade to the moon
This journey could have been a blunder or full of doom
In July he started his strenuous quest
Wanted to be the first one to set foot there and be the best
Born on August 5th
Died on August 25th
Being in space is what he relished

Karan Patel, Grade 5

I Am

I am a kid who runs a lot.
I wonder if I'll come in first.
I hear my teammates cheering, my coach yelling, feet pounding on the ground, and people panting quickly.
I see my teammates and coach at the finish.
I want to come in 1st, 2nd at the finish line.

I am a kid who runs a lot.
I pretend that I have come in first place.
I feel my muscles burning from running and sweat running down my forehead.
I touch my green water bottle.
I worry I won't come in first every time.
I am a kid who runs a lot.

I understand that I'm not the best runner.
I say that I'm really tired.
I dream I'm the best runner.
I try to do my best.
I hope I come in first, second or third.
I am a kid who runs a lot.

Logan D'Arezzo, Grade 5

I Am

I am a boy who likes board games
I wonder what my opponent will do
I hear the soft scratch of the pawn moving across the board for my opponents checkmate victory
I see my opponent thinking about his next strategic move
I want my opponent not to realize their queen is in danger
I am a boy who likes board games

I pretend that a little war is taking place
I feel the little pawn beneath my fingers getting ready to move for victory
I touch the small chess piece
I worry my opponent will make a move for victory
I am a boy who likes board games

I understand players can lose games
I say good luck, good game
I dream I'll become a chess master
I try to do my best
I am a boy who likes board games

Dakotah Saddow, Grade 5

Where I'm From

I am from trains,
From Glade and Febreeze.
I am from a bacon smell on Sunday Mornings.
I am from daisies, the tulips.
I am from eating together and going to church, from Sutton and Jake and K.B.
I am from the thoughtfulness of others and respect.
From don't lie and get good grades.
I am from everyone should be treated equally.
Treat everyone like you want to be treated.
I'm from Charlotte N.C, Scotland and Ireland, leftovers and chicken.
From the rules of golf, the last name change when entered America, and the army.
I am from the 25 scrap books in my grandparents' house filled with pictures from my family's past.

Henry Scott, Grade 6

Baseball!

B ANG is the sound of a good baseball hit
A n amazing home run flies over the fence
S print around the bases and try not to get out
E veryone can play this great game
B OO goes the Pittsburgh fans when the other team throws to first
A 's have a switch player on their team
L os Angeles has two great teams
L ou Gehrig was an amazing 1st baseman

Connor Anderson, Grade 4

Christmas

Christmas day will soon be here
It's a holiday we hold so dear
Friends and family come to play
We make cookies all day
A ginger house is in front of our presents too
A Merry Christmas
to all of you

Kelin Leyva, Grade 5

Wonderful Winter

Cold breezes, warm snow boots, cozy jackets,
And terrific, wonderful snow!
Winter, winter, winter, wonderful winter!
Winter is cold and fun too!
Hanging out in snow making angels with
Friends and family.
Wonderful, awesome winter!

Alyssa Kellyghan, Grade 4

Freedom

F reedom is very important,
R ights are what you need
E ducation might help you gain more freedom in
E very way possible to succeed
D escribe it any way you want because
O utstanding rights are all you need
M ainly for becoming a great role model, the land of the free.

Omar Mahmud, Grade 4

Freedom

F inding freedom is awesome
R emember your rights as a citizen of the United Sates because,
E very citizen is part of the land of the free
E ducated people make our history.
D ifferences are appreciated but need to
O utgrow intensely.
M ake the most of your freedom count, because you are its liberty.

Yasmin Hassouni, Grade 4

I Give Thanks For

I give thanks for…
my lovely mom…she helps me with my homework,
my awesome…dad he plays basketball with me,
my little brother…he lets me play with his gecko.

Jayson Rodriguez, Grade 4

Autumn Peace

I open one eye
stars blink through silver curtains
wisps of clouds play peek-a-boo with the moon
I breathe, in and out
and peacefully, I stand

I tiptoe into the hallway
everyone is sleeping
I hear soft breathing
I breathe, in and out,
and peacefully, I walk

I arrive in the kitchen
the dishes are stacked in the sink
everything is still,
I open the door and cross the threshold
I breathe, in and out
and peacefully, I leave

I move through the forest
crickets sing their night song, an owl hoots
I breathe deeply, in and out
and peacefully, I stay

Alexander Sayette, Grade 5

My Mouth

My favorite body part is on my face
With it I can shout words that can be heard from the south
I can also whistle, whisper and stick out my tongue
You guessed it, it's my mouth

This part makes the dentist tell you to open wide
Your mouth can also help you chew your food
Your mouth can swallow your favorite drinks
It can be water, milk and even soda too

Your mouth contains very special things too
It contains your pearly white teeth
I'm pretty sure I made my point
And how the mouth is so unique

Jason LoSchiavo, Grade 6

What to Do if You're a Chipdactyl*

Fight for peace.
Glide in the wind.
Explore the world.
Learn about the true nature of everything in the world.
Find all the little blue eggs in a scavenger hunt.
Beat everyone to breakfast to claim the first and best egg sandwich.
Race along the wet, muddy, and stone-covered ground.
Fly around a tricky obstacle course with a lot of very tall trees.
Play Monopoly on the little green and blue board.
Win the big chipdactyl-of-the-year trophy.

*A chipdactyl is a cross between a chipmunk and a pterodactyl.

Max Mills-Wren, Grade 4

Thanksgiving

Thanksgiving
Happy, joyful
Praying, eating, thanking
Play lots of games
Holiday
Nia Thornton, Grade 6

Time

Time zooms by so very fast
You forget what day it is
It feels like if time is faster than light
You think it has been 12 minutes
When really it's been an hour
Luca Gentile, Grade 6

Frightening Frogs Come Free

There once was a girl with some frogs,
She never left them in their logs.
They escaped their cage,
The girl had some rage.
All were lost and eaten by dogs.
Mia Ehly, Grade 6

Scary Smart Siamese

There once was a scary fat cat,
Who wore a large and tall red hat.
He sat there quiet,
He's on a diet.
He was slightly afraid of rats.
Lucas Ferreira, Grade 6

Magical Dog

There once was a Golden Shepherd,
Who always caught the early bird.
He did sweet magic,
And learned a cool trick.
Where he learned to catch his song bird.
Leonel Montalvan, Grade 6

Jesus' Return

Trumpets are blowing
I think I know what it is
Jesus has come back
I am floating towards the sky
So are the Christians around me.
Vaughn Foster, Grade 5

Football

Football
Messy, easy
Running, tackling, catching
Defensive end, tight end, and kicker
Sport
Andre Wilkes, Grade 6

In November

In November, the world around me is changing and my senses come alive.
I see the leaves gently swaying with the wind, on the branches.
I smell the fire burning in the warm fireplace while I snuggle in my bed.
I taste a freshly baked turkey with some warm apple cider on a cold day.
I feel the chilly whirling wind brushing against my face.
I hear the howling wind and the chirping birds while they chat to each other.
I just can't get enough of all the special things November brings!
Madeline Paik, Grade 4

Life

Life is seen in the stars.
It needs faith to complete the constellation
but its story will keep us going.
Even though the big problems may seem impossible to be faced alone,
together even the smallest star
can form a bright hero
who can slay the mightiest dragon.
Logan Wilbur, Grade 6

Freedom

F eeling freedom is glorious,
R emember the less fortunate who do not have it.
E veryone deserves the right to have freedom, whether they are timid or courteous
E ach person is special in their own way and should fit.
D on't you think this is true?
O bviously, it states this right in the Constitution.
M ake sure to remember your rights, because they are part of our history solution.
Hufsa Husain, Grade 4

Freedom

F reedom, freedom, make it fair!
R ights help you become constitutionally free.
E arth wants people to gain more freedom
E verywhere,
D ifferent cultures just want a piece of our freedom tree.
O ver and over again, your freedom tree continues to grow, so let us pull together and
M ake freedom stand tall, for you and me.
Alisha Ibrahim, Grade 4

Turkey Day Celebration

The sound of the turkey cooking is music to my ears
The sight of the table being set is bringing happy thoughts to my mind
The taste of the stuffing is going to be awesome
The smell of the feast is bringing memories back from past Thanksgivings
I can already feel the warm food on my tongue
Happy Thanksgiving all!
Evan Drobish, Grade 4

BeautiFall

Golden sunlight shining through trees.
Silence occasionally broken by a hum of a bug or a chirp by a bird.
Squirrels and chipmunks uncompromisingly stealing each other's food.
Bushes shining like emeralds.
Leaves falling like confetti.
As the sun comes down the moon comes up showing fall's silvery beauty.
William Yi, Grade 5

Talking to Nature

Sun, shine
Sun shines on the moon and earth
To let us see his beautiful light

Moon, dream
Moon dreams with the sleeping children
Not knowing the sun compliments her craters

Stars, watch
Watch the planets go round and round
And one day be like one of them

Earth, listen
Earth listens to the conversation in the clouds
She sits and slowly changes
Gabrielle Donovan, Grade 4

Me

Yes, that's me
Look and you'll see
My hair is black like a black cat
My eyes are brown like dirty dirt
My arms are chubby like a full bottle of water
My hands are soft like a squish soft marshmallow
My heart beats loudly like a drum being played
I'm here to be supportive and fun
I'll never be mean to my best friend
My friends are there for me to the end of life
I live to make world peace
I hope in the future for flying cars
I dream arguments will never happen in life.
It's all clear as can be.
That's positively, absolutely me.
Jayla Carson, Grade 4

Down by the Sea

White waves wash away loose sand
Salty air welcomes you into the depths of the unknown
Small seashells are replenished with every crash
Seagulls caw into the distance, filling the quiet
Crystal clear water revealing a glimpse of the ocean floor
The tips of beach grass sway with the soft breeze
A pail and shovel sit alone, partially buried in sand
The bright blue sky stares down, no clouds in sight
A small sailboat far away is the only sign of human life,
But animals beneath the surface dance
Small fish dart and chase throughout the shallows
Dolphins leap and dive out near the horizon
Everything is in perfect harmony
Out of nowhere a rustle breaks the rhythm
A young girl slowly approaches humbled by the scene.
Marissa Gianvito, Grade 6

Turkey in the Oven

The wonderful turkey in the oven.
The potatoes boiling on the stove.
The turkey coming out of the oven made my nose crinkle.
The mouth watering taste of the potatoes filled my mouth.
The nice smooth table cloth filled my hands with joy.
I hope it is like this next year!
Killian Yombor, Grade 4

A Thanksgiving Birthday Celebration

The bright wrapping paper with red bows on top
The laughing and cheering as the presents go around
The zesty lemon bars that melt on your tongue
Warm hugs from my relatives as we say goodbye for the evening
The big birthday cake smells like pink frosting
I love my birthday especially this one
Grace Siersma, Grade 4

Grandparents Are...

The delicious smell of the best food ever!
Smiles and joy at Christmas.
The relaxation of a spa.
A fun day at the park.
Laughter erupting during a fun board game.
Gorgeous flowers blooming in the yard.
Devon Pomeroy, Grade 6

Thanksgiving

The brilliant table set up
Every one talking to each other
The luscious mouthwatering turkey scent in the air
The palatable turkey sliding down my throat
I grasp the metal utensils tightly in my hand
That's how my amazing Thanksgiving will be
Connor Bourdon, Grade 4

The Great Feast

Thanksgiving Day dinner bell rang
Crisp leather brown turkey sitting on the stove
Warm grease on the sweaty turkey fills the air
Delicious mashed potatoes dancing on my tongue
Juicy bone and meat arriving at the tip of my mouth
I am thankful for Thanksgiving.
Aaron Gardner, Grade 4

Time to Give Thanks

I love when family walk in the door in the cold
The laughter of family at the dining table
the big fat turkey in the oven roasting
I love how the hot apple pie lays on my tongue
I love the hot steam on my bare face
Happy Thanksgiving!!!
Jayden Lesser, Grade 4

My Eyes

My eyes help me see
They help me see what is out there
Without my eyes I wouldn't see the tree
It's thrilling what my eyes could do

Without my eyes it would be black
I like to see what my eyes could do
I wouldn't be able to put my candy in the sack
What would I do without my eyes

My eyes make me stronger
My eyes are everything
It will never be a wonder
Because these are my eyes

These are my eyes
I never knew how much my eyes could help me do what I love to do
What a surprise
I love my eyes

Natalie D'Agostino, Grade 6

The Birth of Earth

The rumbling rocks try to recede
But my pull is too strong.
I try to be hospitable,
A home for lovely lingering life.

But I am covered with volcanoes,
Spewing lava every day.
It is like an endless flood of misery,
But finally, after eons of waiting,
Trees grow and oxygen is created.
Oceans, mountains, and flat lands make way
Piles and patches of plants sprout up.
It is like a man wanting a home but gets a kingdom instead.
The feeling is amazing.

Suddenly, creatures pop out everywhere
Cute, cuddly creatures wander my surface.
It is like everything bad in the universe, has turned good.
Finally, I am hospitable.

Ali Ahmad, Grade 5

The Best Thanksgiving in the World

The waves of steam coming from the delicious, warm
pumpkin pie makes Biscuit run into the kitchen.
I bite into creamy, warm mashed potatoes.
I add a hint of gravy.
Then, the turkey comes out.
It was hot, almost burning my hand. I did not care.
I bit into it. It was the best turkey ever.
Ding! The pumpkin pie Biscuit smelled is ready.
When I get my slice I add vanilla ice cream and whipped cream.
When I finish I play with my cousins.
Now this was the best Thanksgiving in the world.

Sydney Kaltman, Grade 4

My Friends

My best friend Elmerl
Is like an Angel to me
My other best friend Dante
Is like a lifesaver to me
My other best friend Christian
Is like a helper to me
My last best friend is Yobani,
He is very nice and kind to me.
All of the friends I have are nice to me and
I do know one thing, they are all good hearted.

Carlos Jimenez, Grade 4

The Pretty Forest

The roots blocked the path
While the sun glazed into the forest
All day and night
When the roots tickled the dirt
They giggled from miles away
When they giggled
Into a forest
Just like this one.
When the branch goes off the tree
While the squirrel chased its acorn.

Maxwell Sampson, Grade 4

In the Woods

In the woods
There's a deep dark never-ending tunnel before me.
Animals roam,
Bugs creep and crawl,
And little girls are screaming.
Day breaks
And the screaming turns to laughter,
The animals are playing together in a pond nearby,
And the bugs hide away in a hollow log.
The woods aren't that scary anymore…

Kaitlyn Ackley, Grade 6

Surprise Spider

I am a banana spider black as a widow
I am hidden in bananas and I can jump out when I want
I am the most poisonest spider that help me but not prey
I can cut open bananas and cover it up
I can surprise prey
I am a banana spider

Xzavier Melendez, Grade 5

Birds

Twirling and whirling by windows
There is a pinch gone in a blink
Speeding and squawking when a cat comes around
Eating great gifts of food
Bustling to build nests
'Gathering delicious worms for their babies' supper
Trying to survive in the harsh world

Shelley Kozdra, Grade 4

Something Great

The roots are as long as the Nile,
The acorns, clinking on the branches as they fall.
The roots were tickling the ground.
I love the sight as much as chicken.
I love chicken…
The roots look like claws, scratching the ground.
The trees are so tall they could go up to space!
The sun is shining up the surroundings.
Nothing here but nature, but it is still beautiful.
I see many different things, all in the same place.
All of this makes me think,
About all the other secrets we don't see.
Behind these trees, could be something great.
But we don't know
What comes next.
In this beautiful world.
Something better or something worse?
We don't know.
But we can find out
If we just turn around.

Dylan Gardner, Grade 4

My Sister Meg

My sister, we used to hang out
on summer days with gusts of wind.
Those were the days. I loved those days.
Now my sister is sixteen, and I am eleven.
Now we are older. We watch movies, and do activities.
And I still love it. It reminds me of those days.
And I can't wait
for more wonderful days to come.
My sister, her name is Meg,
she is sixteen and always elated.
But she is kind of bossy.
She has freckles, and brown hair and emerald eyes.
She is artistic, and visual.
She is also smart and kind and sweet.
She is older than me.
She is a teenager.
When she is happy, she is elated.
When she is mad, she is furious.
But that doesn't matter,
Because I love my sister.

Julia Autry, Grade 6

Little Frog*

How doth the little frog
Never ever stop his little hop?
And in the water he is on his log
And loves to clean his house with his little mop.
How neatly he washes the river bank
Then he plays with his friends
He now is cleaning his tank
When he goes to sleep his story ends.

Mackenzie Price, Grade 5
*Inspired by Lewis Carroll

Costume Party

Every single day,
I look around,
And I see a costume party.
It's a grandiose costume party,
With the people dressed as "cool,"
People dressed as "rebellious,"
People dressed as many other people alike.
But,
There are very few people,
Who come dressed as themselves,
They are the real spectacle of the party,
Nobody understands the people who don't put on a costume,
So everybody mocks it,
"Not normal,"
"Weird,"
"Ugly,"
If that is their opinion,
That they are ugly, or weird,
Then the reason for the costume party,
Is to look normal.
Define normal.

Lauren Potak, Grade 6

The Ball

Boom, smack goes the ball
I cannot stop myself to see it at all
I go to see what's going on around the block
Then somebody hits a good knock

I ask them if I can join in
They say yes, so I grab a uniform out of the bin
Now I'm up to bat feeling a tingle go down my spine
The pitcher winds up and throws the ball in a fast straight line

I try my hardest to hit that ball
I do hit the ball; it goes really high and then starts to fall
As it soars over the fence, I run the bases
Watching all those smiling, happy faces

Now I feel like I'm playing under the lights
With the pro's deep deep into the night
It's the ninth inning tied one to one
But the boom, smack goes the ball

So again I hit the ball right past the home run fence wall

Jimmy Dougherty, Grade 4

Stitchy

S titchy likes to sleep
T akes naps anywhere
I nsults the dog as much as he can
T reats he likes to eat are birds
C ats are what he likes to hang out with
H e is my cat and I'm as happy as can be
Y ou can hear him purr when I stroke his back

Jason York, Grade 6

Friends

Friends are like supports holding you up.
Filling you with lots of hope
so you don't want to mope.

Making sure you're always all right
making sure you're not locked up tight.
They make you feel light as a feather,
no matter the weather.

Sometimes nobody can set you free,
But a best friend that fills you with glee.
You might not have a lot,
But just one friend will make you happy with
What you're got.

Kaiya Pelkey, Grade 4

Christmas!

Christmas is right around the corner.
I am so excited!
All the magnificent presents piled high.
I love Christmas because of the cold air,
And the cheerful spirit.
All the cozy, warm blankets,
Make me happy.
The hot scrumptious drinks are wonderful too,
Like hot, yummy coffee and amazing tasty cocoa.
I love the Christmas tree because,
It smells excellent and looks incredibly beautiful.
I also enjoy decorating the house,
And making it seem magical!
That's why I love Christmas.

Ashley Lirette, Grade 4

When I'm Reading

When I'm reading it takes me away,
It takes me somewhere far across the bay.
It lets my imagination run free,
And the only character in the book is me.

Reading is fun because books can be fake or real,
And it can also change the way you feel.
Sometimes books cause a commotion inside your mind,
And while reading others, peace you may find.

I carry books with me wherever I go,
In my bookcase, backpack, bedroom — my books run the show.
Reading will always be a hobby for me,
Because it always makes me show my glee.

La'leya Thomas, Grade 4

I Give Thanks For

I give thanks for
my loving mom...she takes care of us,
my amazing dad...he continues to be my friend,
my awesome dog...he protects my sister and I.

Jalen Storch, Grade 4

Summer Paradise

Waiting for a summer breeze for vacation
Or for a great wave to go surfing
With the beautiful blue waves
Or would you rather go for a ride on your horse?
By the way
There is no school no work and
No waking up
Every amazing morning
The beautiful blue skies
And the delicate green leaves
Call for me to play
Would you like to walk on a hot beach
And enjoy the summer breeze?

Zaynah Mohammad, Grade 4

When the First Snow Hits

A piece of sparkling snow quickly hits the ground,
Then two, and three, what can it be?
It's the fun of winter joy!
Over me is a tree,
And I see yummy cookies on a plate,
People are singing jingles today.
Bright lights are shining on my face,
Warming my heart.
Families are all together,
Huddled together by the cozy fireplace.
I'm so happy to say,
Yay! Hurray!
It's Christmas day!

Mia Dominguez, Grade 4

Blue

I am very blue
just like you
you think this country
is free
but this is a lie
because we have to go to school
and learn nothing more than we know

Now I am gray
because parents say
go to school all day
and my favorite friends say
schools is the baddest of the bad to our brains

Ritvik Shah, Grade 6

Patriotic

America, the land of freedom.
Many people from all nationalities gather to celebrate.
Electing their own president.
Remember our fallen family and friends.
Independence and having a right to vote.
Celebrate with laughter and joy, your freedom.
And never forget our 9/11 heroes.

Esmeralda Cartagena, Grade 6

Where I'm From

I am from football, from Alienware, and Dota 2.
I am from the smell of my dog, Arden.
I am from the table flowers, and the woods in my yard.
I am from fooseball games, and being small, from Robert, and Christian, and Langefeld.
I am from the bright, and the strategic.
From you will do great things, and I love you.
I am from Jesus Christ.
I am from North Carolina and Germany, and my mom's hamburgers, and my mom's spaghetti.
From the time when one of my ancestors came from Germany to America,
and the time I flew my first plane, and competitive video games.
I am from the attic with all my family's priceless pictures.

Daniel Langefeld, Grade 6

The Peace of Equanimity

I am from the place in the world that I call home
   used to be completely made of stone.
I am from a place that I call my second home
   revolves around something unique but unknown,
I am from the second place that I say is elegant and classy
   even though it used to be just grassy.
I am from that place as the years passed and went on
   it grew with more beauty and class then a thought possibility do not make it undergo.
I am from a place as the heart grew as it started to dance after it grew with maturity that was unspeakable of the kind before,
I am from that place that had ever existed in a lifetime that grew with pass down memories that were unsupported
   that made their life through the unnoted.

Morgan Browning, Grade 5

Merry Christmas

Hearing the Christmas bells makes me feel swell.
They go ring-a-ling and then start to swing.
Christmas trees so big and tall with many decorations and so many different creations.
Going outside makes you feel so jolly with smells of fresh mint and the sight of bright holly.
Then the great old St. Nick zooming through the sky with eight amazing reindeers to help him fly high.
It's Christmas day, the preparation is done. It's time to sit back and have a day full of fun.
You can open up the presents that Santa brings, while the jingle bells once again start to ring.
You could get a PS4 or a toy tiger that likes to roar.
At around lunch time you can visit family, and tell them about your morning fun and eat ginger bread cookies until the day is
done.

Daniel Horowitz, Grade 5

The Best Thanksgiving

Gazing at the shining television watching the humongous
Thanksgiving parade in the big city
The people crowd and yell at the parade and they watch the people pass by on the rocky street
The scent of the big, beautiful, turkey sizzling in the burning oven
Mouth watering turkey and the mashed potatoes making my taste buds tingle
The football smacks into my hand and run down the living room
Have a Happy Thanksgiving.

Katelyn Walter, Grade 4

Summer Night

Summer is here as the tree watches the bountiful sun set. The air is as boiling as the hot desert heat.
The tree watches the sun go down and the crickets trill. "It is a beautiful summer night," said the worn out tree.
She started to close her eyes for the first time in summer.
As she goes to sleep the whole world went quiet. No whistling wind and no crickets chirping, all was quiet and all was sleeping.

Lea Mascio, Grade 5

Fishing

I fish so much I love it so dearly
I grab my rod and tackle box and go
I hate it when it is rainy and dreary
I catch five I stop to watch the lake flow

When I start feeling jerks I get happy
But when my line snaps I get very sad
When I start reeling it in I get shocked
When I finally catch one I am glad

When I have enough fish I go to rest
When I don't have enough I stay and fish
After I go and rest I feel my best
I catch all these fish to put in a dish

I love to get bass when I go and fish
But I also love to catch big catfish
Ryan Gibson, Grade 5

One Window

One window is all I need
to see what is going on
in the world
to be connected to the inner world
to see what I am
by looking at kids
and other people

One window is all I need
to see the rain come down

One window is all I need
to see who is outside my home

One window is all I need
to make sure kids are safe
and to see all the adventures before me
Jumarrion Melvin, Grade 6

Jaileen

I love myself.
I love myself to death.
I don't care what everyone thinks.
It's not their body.
I feel so good about what I wear.
People think different about me.
I don't care what they think.
I know their just trying to bully me.
People don't like my hair but I don't care.
That's their opinion
I really love myself.
I was born to be nice and sweet.
But sometime people get on my nerves.
I love my style, I love my hair.
Hi my name is Jaileen and this is my life.
Jaileen Deleon, Grade 4

My Demon*

I have a demon in my hat.
He tells me what to do.
I wanted to eat tacos
but he said to me,
"No, you must eat your vegetables."
Which I didn't like.
So then I wanted to go outside,
I wanted to ride my bike.
He said I must walk.
I wanted to play with markers,
he said, "No, you must use chalk."
Cooper Fickes, Grade 5
*Inspired by Lewis Carroll

Sun

A holder of light
A symbol of a new day
Burning, sparking, flaming
The sun dances on a stage of sky
An ancient wonder
A delicate sphere
Glowing, Smiling, Sizzling
The sun plays among the clouds
An eternal firefly
A hundred summers twisted into one
Shimmering, Laughing, Illuminating
The sun sings for an audience of the world
Hannah Noble, Grade 6

Being a Tree

The tree shall not move
But his branches are
Light
They move with the
Wind
When fall comes
He has to say
Good-bye
To his leaves
But in spring he says
Hello, again
With flowers in his hands
Vincent Cassells, Grade 6

Love Is a Gem

Love is a gem.
That many want but few get.
Love is a gem.
That shines in the dark of night.
Love is a gem.
Sought after by every soul.
Love is a gem.
Priceless as a man's life.
Love is a gem.
That many want but few get.
Isaiah Bradner, Grade 6

Me

I want to be me
I want to be free
Let my wings out and fly
But you're dragging me back
I am caged once more
I will set myself free
And find the key
I won't ever fret
Maybe cry a little bit
And this is the true me
Don't let anybody drag you down
Because this is your real self
A burst of emotion
From happy to sad
All trapped inside
A monotone face
Some don't want to be seen
Some don't want friends
Both are not me
I'm in control
Show my true colors
Vanessa Chen, Grade 6

Sun

Rising from silent slumber
Waking the bluebirds
Shining bright
Watching the world
From high above
Joyful light
Slowly sailing west
For my sleep
While my friend
Rises from her slumber
To paint her canvas black
Till I rise again
Waking in the east
Longing for a new life
Forevermore cycle
I grow tired of
Waking, rising
Sleeping, shining
Watching the world
From high above
Forevermore cycle
Bella Fournier, Grade 5

Seasons

Fall
Windy, cool
Refreshing, playing, cooling
Leaves, color, flower, sports
Watering, growing, raining
Hot, rainy
Spring
Malachi Toman-Daniels, Grade 5

My Feet

My feet.
My feet help me walk.
They bring me places so I can talk.
My feet bring me everywhere.

My feet.
They bring me out of the heat.
They walk on the street.
My feet bring me everywhere.

My feet.
They can run in a track meet.
They bring me around the room to make it neat.
My feet bring me everywhere.

Kaitlin Biggin, Grade 6

Winter

The night is cold, I am inside,
Under warm blankets I love to hide.
When morning comes I run and see,
My frosted window shows snow covered trees,

I go to get my scarf, gloves and hat.
As I pick up the snow I lightly pat,
Soon a snowman starts to appear,
And shows the season of winter is here.

Not long after that, I came inside,
Drinking hot chocolate, while sitting at the fire side.
Winter is my favorite season of all,
Because it is when lovely snowflakes fall.

Maraya Bailey-Cohen, Grade 6

Green

A struggling plant,
Under the winter frost,
Fighting the cold,
Trying to survive.
Others like him died and decayed.
All seemed lost.
Hope was almost gone,
Suddenly,
A surge of warmth and a beam of light shone through the snow.
Quickly hope nested back,
And growth,
And life.
The plant had turned into a beautiful rose,
Spring has come.

Samuel Scalzo, Grade 6

I Give Thanks For

I give thanks for…
my loving mom…she takes care of me,
my helpful stepdad…he helps me with my homework,
my playful brother…he plays with me.

Brandon Kim, Grade 4

Atlanta Braves Baseball

I love to play baseball when the spring calls
I hope I will play in the major league
When spring comes around I start playing ball
I hope I will not get picked off by greed

I hope to be able to play first base
I will practice daily with what I got
I always lay my baseball in a case
I don't strike out but hit homeruns a lot

So now I will have to prove myself
I will overcome any obstacle
Soon I will hang my trophy on a shelf
And I will never go in a circle

I will play for the Atlanta Braves
I'll keep strong until I play for the Braves

Justin McCraw, Grade 5

I Love Fall!

It's turning cold,
Brilliant colors everywhere!
It's fall!
What do you know!
Colors, leaves, and pumpkin patches.
Plus some mouthwatering hot cocoa.
A cold breeze and Halloween.
Shouting trick-or-treat!
Lots of love from family.
And a huge Thanksgiving feast!
Crunch! Crunch! Jumping into a pile of fun and colorful leaves!
Costumes, raking around the school,
Yummy pumpkin pie topped with whipped cream.
Such fun times!
Well, fall is over the colors are gone.
Next fall will come back.
With more family and fun!

Ava Patrick, Grade 4

Monster Legends

Some people say computer games are lame.
But to me they're full of action,
It doesn't matter what others claim.
Playing makes me feel like I'm in another dimension.
Anything can happen when I play.
In Monster Legends, there's a lot to explore.
There are many different types of monsters and beasts.
You could buy some gems from the online store,
That provide for the monster's feasts.
Almost everything is possible in this world.
But don't play too long on the computer my friends,
Your parents will surely get mad.
Because games aren't as important as schoolwork,
And if you don't do that schoolwork,
Your grades will definitely be bad.

Cristian Pepe, Grade 4

Teachers

You push your students
to do and to work their best.
You make everything precise and never
blunt. You make things exciting and
not boring like I'm falling asleep.
Thank You

You are so nice and friendly
like a very peaceful dog. I like
Mrs. Hoehlein's slimy but cute frog in the classroom.
I can even hear it croak when I work! I like Ms. Cushman's
long, blonde hair. It is very striking in the light.
Thank You

Thank you for taking your time with us to really
understand if something seems confusing to us.
Both of you teach
writing, science, social studies, math,
and reading.
Thank You!

Isabelle Moran, Grade 5

I Am

I am a daughter and a friend.
I wonder what animals want to say when they make a sound.
I hear the sound of the birds chirping.
I see the trees swaying through the window.
I want the days to go slower in the summer.
I am a daughter and a friend.

I pretend I am a poet writing this poem !
I feel happy when I get to see my friends.
I touch the freezing water as the tide comes in on the sandy beach.
I worry when I am late for school.
I cry when I get hurt.
I am a daughter and a friend.

I understand that school is the best place to learn!
I say that one should always try to learn new things.
I dream about being an engineer.
I try to bring up creative ideas in my mind.
I hope that I will find out why water is clear.
I am a daughter and a friend.

Anika Keshri, Grade 5

Yemili

Yemili:
creative, playful, loving
lover of pandas, kittens, and puppies
who is able to love dogs and able to get into a good collage
who feels happy when I see my family happy
who wonders if the zombie apocalypse might come
who fears poisonous spiders and poisonous snakes
who would like to go to Hawaii with my family and friends
who dreams to be a dog lover and help endangered animals

Yemili Velasquez, Grade 4

Spectrum

Red is the color of blood and hate
It ends the same as a fish and bait
Leaving you in a very bad state

Orange is a mix of yellow and red
It can mean booby-traps, with treasure ahead
Leaving you rich, or leaving you dead

Yellow is the color of smiles and joy
It's like a small dog with a brand new toy
Or two happy parents, cradling their new boy

Green represents our Mother Earth's land
Of course, not the color of its smooth, soft sand
It's the color of the plants in their fertile farmland

Blue is the color of a great big sea
It represents things being free
Like a sitting seed, growing into a tree

Purple is the color of royalty
Back in the day it was rare to see
So if you bought it you'd be filled with glee

Now as for my poem, this is the end
As all of the colors slowly descend
To you

Bear Bottonari, Grade 6

Ode to Money

Crisp, green money, with your power galore.
You are one of the few,
who can grant most wishes.

You wear the monuments of the ages,
You carry your scent through the centuries.
I save you, protect you,
And I know you do the same back.

Money, you're as green
as the plains, as smooth as silk.
You sit there relaxing, acting all cool.
Yet, as you do nothing, you do everything, effortlessly!

My dearest, the best, the thing that does all.
The base, the fulcrum, the pivot,
the balance point of life.
A thing of great beauty,
used wisely by some.

Money, when you are used right,
there is no denying
that you are the highest on the chain,
the supporter, and most importantly,
the loved, as I love you MONEY!

Jake Cahn, Grade 5

Summer
Summer
growls in
with clouds and
sunny days

It blows away
the cold
and brings in
the warmth
then leaps away
Esfetania Rocha, Grade 6

My College Dream
My college dream,
A never ending thing.

Dreaming of college makes me feel so free,
And with good skills I'll get a degree.
Having this dream is still a fantasy,
Going to college will be my reality.

My dream is my future view,
And dreaming of college gives me a clue.
Casey Taylor, Grade 4

My Cousin Jordan Oliva
She is as fast as a leopard
She is as nice as a flower
She is as sweet as candy
She is as caring as a care bear
She is as strong as an elephant
She is as soft as a blanket
She is good at drawing as an artist
She is as funny as a clown
She is as good at singing as Taylor Swift
She is as beautiful as a rose
Tristen Allen, Grade 4

Kiersten
She is as funny as a hyena
She is as tall as an elephant
She is as smart as a horse
She is as extremely awesome as an eagle
She is as beautiful as a peacock
She is as kind as a dog
She is as talented as a monkey
She is as sneaky as a fox
She is as quiet as a mouse
She is as fast as a cheetah
Jordan Adams, Grade 4

Seeds
Gray, small, and fluffy
Giving life to its own kind
Just about to burst
Sophia Cotrotsios, Grade 5

School
School time is here, I'm so excited.
I can't wait to meet my teacher.
I'm so delighted. Couldn't wait to tell my friends what I did this summer,
and if they tell me what they did, I hope it won't be a bummer.
I love school. I love it the best.
Until you have to take a test.
I love everybody in my school.
We might take a field trip to the pool.
The food is so good, and lovely so much.
That if I touch the chocolate I might get the chocolate touch.
My friends are so friendly.
That's why I go to this school.
I love it so much.
I love it.
I love it.
I love it.
Na'ila Noble, Grade 4

Blue
I love the smell of blue-scented markers and blue paint
I love the sound of the waves splashing onto the shore of the beach,
The feel of the warm sand on my feet, and the taste of a cold ice cream cone.
I love splashing in the waves and jumping back onto the shore.
I love to watch the clouds go by all over the blue sky
And surfing on my blue and green surf board through big blue waves,
Walking on the hot and sandy boardwalk to play fun games,
And the taste of blue snow cones near all the shade.
I love the feel of the blue snow cone melting in my mouth
And the feel of melting snow flakes on my tongue.
I love the taste of cold, melting snow,
And rolling down the big, cold, snowy hills on my blue and green sled
With my mom pulling me in the front and my dad in the back
While I lie back and watch the big blue sky and all of the clouds
And then I crash! Into a big pile of snow.
I love the feel of cold snowflakes when they melt in my hand.
John Bradley, Grade 4

Thanksgiving
Thank you for all my eyes can see…
Immense tables could go around the world with splendid, diversity of repasts.
Friends, and family fill your house as a concert that is sold out.
When autumn leaves are falling and Thanksgiving time
is near it warms the heart of those you hold so dear.

Thank you for all my tongue can taste…
Scrumptious, warm apple pie the family brings every year
Hot cocoa soothes my throat as I gulp it clean
Superb mashed potatoes manipulating my taste buds.

Thank you for all my ears can hear…
Ding! Savory turkey, packed with splendid
stuffing and hickory ham on the side
Time to be together, turkey, talk, and tangy weather
Goodbye, goodbye, see you next year keep warm for the winter.
Shanel Franco, Grade 6

Peaceful Places

Peaceful waters,
Where swans stay
They go to bed at night
And wake up to greet the day

Peaceful trees
Where owls hoot
They fly so much
They don't step foot

Peaceful world
Full of nature
All the same
With different feature
Madryn Hanser, Grade 4

Beautiful Forest

The forest is so very pretty,
I'd rather be there than in the city!
I love to smell the sweet flowers,
Smelling them for hours and hours.
I hear lovely, chirping birds,
Saying long gibberish words!
I see the bellowing trees overhead,
"Hello" they would've said;
But that's only if they could talk,
Or read or jump or play or walk!
So now you all very well know,
About the beautiful forest so.
And go every morning and every night,
Away to the forests, light.
Kashvi Ramani, Grade 4

Cute Little Puppies

Cute little puppies are all I see,
Brown ones, white ones all around me.
Friendly, playful little creatures,
Spotted, blue eyes, and other features.

Cute little puppies make me so happy,
Because they are part of the family.
Petting their soft, fluffy fur,
Making sweet sounds like a cat's purr.

Cute little puppies greet me from school,
Happy to see me, that's so cool!
Cute little puppies can be your friend.
Love them and care for them until the end.
Jasmine Rosario, Grade 4

Forever Letting Go

Tightly holding on,
Don't know how to say goodbye,
Feel like you are here,
I will hold you in my heart.
Virginia Bresler, Grade 6

Purple

I walk with panache,
with power and strength.
I'm royal and rich:
quintessential.
I take risks; I am free.
Once I was sad,
but courage and heart,
worked together to free.

I came to power
and was fierce as a lion.
I roared, and they became quite diffident.
Making it quite hard to be taken seriously,
the risks were premeditated,
albeit articulated,
I am thirsty for power,
for all that I want.
I am purple,
most royally charged.
Erin Payne, Grade 6

My Teeth

Oh my teeth,
My pearly whites
They always stand out
Like a star in the night

All braced up
Colors sparkling and vibrant
And man, oh man
Are they extremely reliant

They allow me to chew and smile
Every single day
I can grind them when I'm nervous
It takes the pain away

And one more thing
That makes them worth even more
They show all of my treasured emotions
And let them take off and soar
Jacqueline Paduano, Grade 6

Ryan/Ingalls

Ryan
I am athletic, strong, awesome, cool
My family is caring, loving, nice, awesome
I love basketball
I need a pool
I give anything
I fear nothing
I want to be a cop
I would like to see snow
I wonder if I could do a back flip
Ingalls
Ryan Ingalls, Grade 5

Hello Fall, Hello

Orange, black, brown, yellow green,
Those are all the wonderful colors I see!
Pumpkin carving, pumpkin picking!
Amazing crunchy apples!
What is that I smell?
Pumpkin spice,
No! Pumpkin pie!
No! Candy! No! Apple pie!
Yummy hot delicious cocoa.
The hot, cozy fireplace calms me down.
I snuggle up with my warm fuzzy blanket.
I see the bright blue sky,
With puffy, fluffy clouds!
The wind howls like a million wolves.
I have never been so ecstatic in my life!
This shows how excited I get,
When I get to say hello fall, hello!
Martina Nemia, Grade 4

Fluffy Sheep

Across the field or fluffy plain
They walk or bumble
Their bodies so fat
With fluff, head to toe
They bumble along, so soft and so quiet
It happened so swift and happened so light
A sheep is just fluff
So furry, so fluffy
A sheep's life is nothing but cotton
It's just a big herd, but nothing forgotten
Centuries of walking and still no success
A destination miles from reach
But, there is still hope on this earthly plain
It never gets old, just trotting and trotting
We reached it, we reached the old shrine
Years of just walking, but we never sighed
A sheep's life is cotton, but also destiny
Michael Brown, Grade 4

Gold

Gold is the fiercest shade
More beautiful than ruby or sapphire
Gold is the stench of bold decisions
Getting out of your shell
Gold is a feast of gold-plated food
A meal fit for Midas
Gold is cold polished bricks
Eye catching and full or worth
Gold is ringing bells
The loud sound gliding through the air
Gold is wet autumn leaves
The sweet rain's scent gliding off the leaves
Gold is the buzz of a honeycomb
Holding a delicious treat
making your fingers stick
Haley Maka, Grade 6

It's Time

Tickety tock tickety tock
Watching the clock
Tickety tock
Waiting and waiting…

Tickety tock tickety tock
Time is slow and painful
Tickety tock
The rain now cries like angels!

Tickety tock tickety tock
Heart is beating like a drum
Tickety tock
Oh, time can be lots of fun!

Tickety tock tickety tock
The time has now gone dark
Tickety tock
When will this just end!

Tickety tock tickety tock
Now I slowly give in
BEEP! BEEP!
Now the clock has stopped.
Michael Petrie, Grade 6

What I Love to Do

It's about...
Toes pointed
Legs straight
Twirling

It's about...
Getting dressed up
Lots of attention
Shining lights

It's about...
Lots of rows
People clapping
Roses

It's about...
Long days
Long nights
Practice

It's about...
Elegant costumes
Hairspray fumes
Pretty tutus
Ava Pellegrino, Grade 5

Fishing Is too Cool

When I go fishing I go with my dad
I am a multi-species angler.
I am not the best but I am not bad
When I'm fishing I let out my anger.

Me and my friends play football together
I play with my friends during recess time.
I love cold and cloudy type weather
This is difficult when you have to rhyme.

I have never been saltwater fishing
I would absolutely love to go there.
I doubt I will go but I am wishing
I am worried I will mess up my hair.

I'm always bored good thing I like fishing
When I'm fishing I am always itching.
Thomas Lee, Grade 5

Love Alabama Football

Alabama is awesome at football
And all I have to say is roll tide
If they lose it feels like I'm in a brawl
But most of the time I am satisfied

Alabama is better than everyone
They can crush whoever they want to beat
They explode off the line like a cannon
Alabama is a wall of concrete

Alabama is great at everything
We like to defeat our enemy
Watching them win is very tickling
The teams we play can get very angry

Alabama is the team to root for
Alabama does and will always soar
Brett Parker, Grade 5

If You Are the Sun

If you are the sun
    give the roses sunlight
Let there be sunlight
    so the children can play
Hide behind the tall
    buildings so it's not so hot
Make the violets bloom
Shine brightly
Smile while you shine
Hide behind the puffy
    big clouds
Make people warm
Dry the muddy puddles
Let everyone have
    fun in the sun
Claire Park, Grade 4

My Bike

Every single sunny day,
I hop on my bike and ride away.
Up and down my small little street,
Feeling like an Olympic athlete.
Going up and down that hill,
What a rush what a thrill.
Pedaling as fast as I can,
The wind feeling like a strong fan.
When I brake my tires squeal,
It's hard to believe that sound is real.
Passing my neighbor's dog,
Riding through my friend's mud bog.
But at the end of the day,
I can say that I rode my bike away.
Coleman Roberts, Grade 5

Battle Field Four

My mom makes me do my chore,
Before I play Battle Field Four.
If you are not good at the game,
Do not even feel ashamed.
It's a game for only one,
But you can still have fun.
If your friend comes to play,
You can take turns anyway.
In the game you can climb walls,
But make sure you just don't fall.
If you secretly steal a tank,
Try not to make a single clank.
If you earn enough tickets to win the game,
You can add your name to the Hall of Fame.
Shaydon Hinson, Grade 5

My Love for Books

When I read I go away,
To a place with knowledge every day.
Sometimes I read before bed,
Sometimes I read to fill my head.
You see me reading all around,
Where I read there is no sound.
Without a book I will Freak out,
I'll start running all about.
When I read I am feeling fine,
I'll read every single line.
I read a very vast variety of books,
You will see if you look.
Books are like different worlds you see,
If you tried it you would agree.
Lucas Gaines, Grade 5

Fall

Fall trees
Colors everywhere
Bursting from trees around me
"Oh, I love fall so!"
Adrian Schilling, Grade 5

The Sky Is the Limit

The sky is the limit,
You can do anything,
The sky is the limit,
Reach for the stars,
The sky is the limit,
Play in the clouds,
The sky is the limit,
Jump over the moon,
The sky is the limit,
Do what you do
The sky is the limit.
Charlotte Elliott, Grade 4

Love Is a Battlefield

Love is a battlefield
Filled with bullets whizzing past you
Occasionally hitting you
Not very hard though
Just enough to hurt
If one hits you
Don't give up
You will win soon enough
I say once again
Love is a battlefield
Never give up
Walter Webber, Grade 6

Life Is a Massive Clock

Life is a massive clock
always ticking away,
Life is a massive clock
that will work without batteries,
Life is a massive clock
that will not be too fast,
Life is a massive clock
that will not be too slow,
Life is a massive clock
that will stop some day,
Life is a massive clock
William Jarrett, Grade 6

My Friend Clark

My friend Clark is gray and blue.
My friend Clark is especially true.

My friend Clark has great big fin.
My friend Clark has a sharp toothy grin.

My friend Clark now has to flee.
My friend Clark is heading out to sea.

I will miss my good friend Clark.
My friend Clark is a great big shark!
Jerry Taylor, Grade 4

Moving as One

The music plays I listen closely,
I don't know why I feel so ghostly.
I feel as if my feet are off the floor,
I'm dancing like I never have before.

I take a step to my right,
The music's playing and I feel so light.
I escape into my own little world,
I leap, jump, and even twirl.

The lights turn off the curtain closes,
Next I am given a bunch of roses.
The dance is now done,
Moving as one.
Sophia DiFolco, Grade 6

Smile!

Everywhere I go I try to smile,
People say they like my style.
It is something that I always do,
I do it to help the people feeling blue.

I try to smile even when I'm mad,
My grin is biggest when I'm really glad.
People can see me from a mile,
You're never fully dressed without a smile.

People see me and they smile,
I can tell they'll do it for a while.
When I go to any place,
I see people smile and it lights up my face.
Jacqueline Nicolaus, Grade 6

My Hair!

My hair makes me me.
It makes me feel free.
My hair blows in the breeze.
It is so full of ease.

My hair makes me me.
It will never make me flee.
My hair flows like a stream.
It makes me want to beam.

My hair makes me me.
It shows who I want to be.
It is the color of a lamb.
My hair makes me what I am.
Kimberly Westenberg, Grade 6

Soccer

I love the green fields
Playing soccer in green grass
Looking at the ball
Max Winstead, Grade 4

My Arms

I love to use my arms
I love them every day
I use them when I dance
I use them when I play

I love them when I walk
I love them when I run
I use my arms to pitch
I use my arms for fun

I love my arms when I eat
I use my arms to say,
Thank You for helping me,
I love them every day.
Gabriella Gigante, Grade 6

My Eyes

My eyes are my light
They shine so bright
My eyes help me see
When I dance

They help me when I'm sad
Then they make me feel glad
My eyes truly help me
So I can prance

My eyes are very cool
They help me see the pool
They light up my face with glee
I can wow a crowd with one glance
Ariana Paduano, Grade 6

House of Secrets

House of secrets
House of lies
House of threats
and house of spies

House of sickness
House of hate
House of spite
and house of gates

House of bedlam,
far and wide
House of secrets
House of lies
Jeffrey Wooters, Grade 6

The Shadows

Shadows stalking prey,
Below the weeds around them,
Waiting to strike them.
Ian Bliss, Grade 6

Christmas Day

I'm so excited for Christmas.
It is my favorite holiday of the year.
I love giving my family presents.
That's when I spread the Christmas cheer.

I love the ringing bells.
People play them so nice.
For my Christmas dinner I want
my turkey and rice.

I set up cookies and milk for Santa.
And mom says, "It's getting late."
No need to wait up for Santa.
When he comes, he'll eat the cookies on the plate.

That Christmas morning
I woke up to see.
The cookies were gone
and there were presents under the tree.

Theodore Clayton, Grade 4

I Am

I am a girl who loves to dance
I wonder if I will ever be famous
I hear my dance teacher clapping to beat so we get the rhythm
I see kids dancing in the dance room with me
I hope to be flexible like the older girls are

I am a girl who loves to dance
I pretend I'm dancing with people watching me
I feel I know all the moves in my very, very fun dance
I touch my very fluffy tutu
I worry I will fall off the stage and get hurt

I am a girl who loves to dance
I understand I will not be the best dancer
I say never give up dreams
I dream of dancing with the Rockettes
I try my best when dancing
I hope I will be dancing all around the world someday
I am a girl who loves to dance

Abigail Fratus, Grade 5

Love Myself

L ife is a current, so let it take you along
O ver all my experience, I know
V oice…inner voice, let it shine
E ven though it may be scary, do it

M y life and your life achieving goals every second
Y ou are beautiful no matter what people say
S ave your life by loving
E njoy what you have not what you don't
L ove the life that was made for you
F or you, for life spread the word.

Kaylie Tennant, Grade 4

Christmas Coming Along

Christmas is coming along,
I could hear friendly footsteps on my roof.
Bearing presents for under my tree.
Feeling the cozy fireplace in my house,
Ornaments jingling again,
And snowflakes dropping by,
Stocking and filling the stockings up,
I could feel a cold breeze come by,
I can hear a Merry Christmas out of my window,
Christmas is coming along!

Sofia Leon Portela, Grade 4

How to Have a Wonderful Christmas!

Placing cookies for Santa on Christmas Eve.
Then you wake up on Christmas morning.
And seeing all of the wonderful presents,
They're all stacked one by one by the tree.
Amazingly most of them are for you!
Then you look out the window.
And there's snow falling gently from the sky,
You sit by the warm coy fire.
While drinking some outstanding hot cocoa,
What a perfect Christmas.

Andres Torres, Grade 4

My Ally

Ally
Loud and Hairy
Who belongs to Eddie
Who loves walking, barking, and eating
Who experienced love, joy, and fun
Who fears loud noises, strangers, and trumpets
Who accomplished bringing playfulness into the family
Who feeds on dog food, bugs, and tree bark
Who lives in his doghouse, living room, and outside
Who belongs to the class of wolves

Jamie Wheeler, Grade 6

Freedom

F reedom you are important to me, with
R espect I truly remember my duties.
E ach and every day
E veryone deserves the equality of this life.
D etermined citizens and I unite together for
O ptimistic goals to celebrate our freedom,
M ostly, because we are the land of the free.

Fouad Abdulghani, Grade 4

Dads

Dads are nice.
Dads are our teachers of hunting, fishing, and sports.
Dads help us.
They make us feel better when we are depressed or sad.
They are joyful and happy.
They are our dads.

Nick Albertini, Grade 4

Dark and Stormy Night

It was a dark and stormy night,
Dark clouds covered the night sky even
Even though there was a bright moon
Dimly lit outside.
The thunder boomed repeatedly,
As the lightning scattered across the night sky.
Palm trees bent to and fro,
The howling wind grew stronger and stronger.
The night was filled with darkness,
This Halloween night.

Daisy Vartabedian, Grade 6

Wintry Weather — The Days of December

The days are short
The nights are long
Cold December winds begin to sing their song
Lights, strung upon the tree
Shining brightly for all to see
The frost so Icy cold
Tells a promise that's foretold
The snow wraps the ground in a blanket of white
We are all filled with joy this holiday night.
Merry Christmas!

Mia Meccia, Grade 5

Gold

GOLD is the sun.
GOLD is first place.
It makes me think of the GOLDEN sand on the beach.
It's shiny and sparkly like the stars.
GOLD is me laying in a patch of GOLDEN sunflowers.
GOLD is rare.
It's on my mom's GOLDEN earrings.
GOLD is joy.
GOLD is the sunset.
GOLD is a winner.

Averi Miller, Grade 4

Flowers

When spring comes around,
The flowers start to grow without making a sound,
The flowers are dark at night,
They sparkle with dew at morning's light,
Soon the flowers will be high and tall,
And will spread joy to one and all.

Dora Chen, Grade 4

Frosty Fall

The tree's leaves dive to the frosty field.
She was disappointed that her companions will leave her,
But they will come back after winter.
The tree will have to keep the supply of water and food
Because she can't get that in the winter.
She will be bare, cold, and will want her winter coat.
The tree will have to last the cold until spring.

Emily Charleston, Grade 5

Christmas

The snow came down softly
During the chilly night
The smell of the hot coca and the warm cookies
Filling the cold air
Watching Christmas movies and singing

The next day snow on top of cars and driveways
Parents hoping their kids don't come late
Kids playing in snow and building snowmen
Celebrating the birth of Jesus Christ
Around the Christmas tree
Opening presents and sharing the joy
That is the true meaning of Christmas

Yanelyse Cruz, Grade 6

Curiosity

Of course you say "Curiosity killed the cat"
Is just a silly old idiom

Well,
I say it's a TRUE fact!

My award-winning
Breathtaking
Shiny looking
Golden Retriever

Killed the neighbor's cat
Curiosity was his name

Sarah Swope, Grade 4

Gymnastics

With a leap and tumble, flip and cartwheel
Jump and spin in the air you can hear and feel
The crowd cheers you on with delightfulness
You are happy the crowd is satisfied with happiness

Looking at the crowd you feel a great sensation
Stretching gracefully brings much pride to you
Arms floating through thin air, landing happily
Jumping like a wave in a big ocean you can feel the wind

With a bliss smile you run for your medal
Once again you have made it smile
Gymnastics is never ordinary

Aishani Sreejith Komath, Grade 4

Best Birthday Ever

Wrapped presents in a pile
Scents of sizzling chicken in the oven
The delicious taste of the chocolate iced cake
Feeling that giant drop of wax from the candle
Chatter of everyone saying goodbye
It was the best birthday ever.
No one can ever beat it.

Luke Kleiven, Grade 4

Indiana Jones

"Kapow!" Indiana Jones is cracking his whip,
He takes lots of mysterious trips.
Thrown in a pit as black as the night,
Snakes hiss and bite and give him a fright.
He finds lots of good artifacts,
He always stays on the right tracks.
The bad guys always chase after him,
He never loses his life or limbs.
The actor's name is Harrison Ford,
He never leaves me or my family bored.
He is also Han Solo in Star Wars,
He always travels very far.
I have watched the movies of them all,
He will always stand so very tall.

Andrew Schmidt, Grade 5

Piano

You can learn to play any song,
It can be short or very long.
The notes can go across the page,
If you're good enough you can play on stage.
You are never too young to start,
Beethoven started by listening to his heart.
They'll say, "Practice makes perfect." all day,
"I know that it is true!" I'll say.
Never give up or you will forget,
How to play songs, that will make you fret.
"BONG!" Goes the piano when you hit the wrong key,
It's just what happens when you play care-free.
The piano can play a beautiful tune,
In front of the crowd at my recital in June.

Reagan Moore, Grade 5

My Eyes Were Opened

I once was blind but now I see
God will never stop loving me.
I once was deaf to the call of God,
Now I hear and I am awed.
I once lost hope now it's newly regained
God's kingdom will very soon reign
I once was still
I have now regained will
A savior has come
And our sins are done.
We have been forgiven,
Thank God for the blessings we've been given.
I used to take things for granted
Now I know my life is enchanted.

Kamryn Natale, Grade 4

Moon

M arvelous, magical, milky pearl shining
O ver the sweet white blossoms of moon-flowers
O ver the silent ocean
N ight, Night, Night

Felicia Taly, Grade 5

A Dreamer, a Believer, an Inspiration

If you think he was ordinary, you are mistaken.
As a child, he found a clever way to feed his favorite chicken.
He loved to play with toys that move,
And pull the strings to make them groove.
In New York, he became an established puppeteer,
As Macy's Wondertown window shoppers would cheer.
One year, as the Thanksgiving Holiday came close,
He thought of the immigrant workers who were morose.
He imagined a lively parade that had
Gigantic floats that made people glad.
He dreamed, he believed, and inspired by a childhood marionette,
He made the headline of the New York Times Gazette.
Even though Tony Sarg died in 1942,
The Macy's parades still live on and so might you.

Soraya Remaili, Grade 5

Red

Red is … the hotness of the fire that burns big and bright.
The juicy apple you bite into.
The color of love, as warm as a hug.
It's the color of the leaves in the fall.
It's the warm lifeguard sweatshirt you wear.
The strawberry you eat.
It's the anger inside you.
The first color of the rainbow.
The one true brown that's the lightest of all.
The sweet smell of roses in spring.
The bright red scarf you wear.
The cardinals that sing a delightful song.
The red car starting its engine.
The smell of a cherry blossom candle.

Skyla Hannon, Grade 6

My Hand

My hand is cool
My hand is neat
My hand is a special treat
It helps me do the things I like

Drawing, video games, and holding handles on a bike
Without a hand, I couldn't write
Or pull the covers over at night
I couldn't go on the bars and swing

I basically couldn't do anything
And so I say
My hands help me every day
Especially at school

Olivia Cristadoro, Grade 6

I Give Thanks For

I give thanks for…
my awesome mom…she takes me places,
my cool dad…he plays with me,
my best friend…she makes me laugh when I'm sad.

Isabella Rodriguez, Grade 4

It's About Thanksgiving
It's about
Giving
Sharing
Being thankful

It's about
The turkey
Stuffed stomachs
Lasting forever

It's about Thursday night football
Staying up late
Hoping your team wins

It's about
Going to your relatives' houses
Playing outside
Having fun

It's about the time for giving!
Dimitrios Angelakos, Grade 5

Our World
Our world, tis to thee
It's more than what one person can see,
With wars raging over the years,
And winning battle cheers.
A war is more than thee,
For as far as you can see,
As if George Washington was here,
He'd say "Oh, the war is near!"
As for Betsy Ross,
She made the American flag,
It was oh so beautiful,
It did not lag or drag.
As for Benjamin Franklin,
He was smart and cool,
He made a lot of inventions,
But did not bring them to school!
Don't forget Martin Luther King Jr.
He had a famous speech,
It was called "The Dream,"
And he gives his heart to each.
Jonathan Kong, Grade 5

Christmas
C ookies
H oliday
R ed
I ncredible
S anta
T ree
M istletoe
A wesome
S now
Jenni Juan, Grade 4

Life Is a Highway
life is a highway
it's very long
sometimes it's my way
most times it's wrong
with twists and turns
it's a little rough
but I huff and puff
even when it's tough
it is long
but I don't stop
it leads me wrong
I still don't stop
life is a highway
Quentin Haupt, Grade 6

Winter Fun
The cold wind breeze,
Blows through me.
Making ice sculptures with snow.
Playing snowball fights in winter.
Winter is the best.
You get to have yummy, hot cocoa.
What fun building snowmen.
Kids having fun.
Snow angels happy as can be.
Watching holiday movies,
Going on amazing trips,
With your family.
Winter is marvelous!
Julianna Clark, Grade 4

Spring Day
Spring!
Spring!
Spring!
The beautiful flower with pollen in them!
While we're Easter egg hunting,
I love spring's beautiful early sun,
Beating on us.
I love spring,
It is so amazing spending time,
With my family
"Egg!"
"Look I found an egg!"
I can't wait to see what's inside!
Giada Giovanetti, Grade 4

Ninja Mask
I am a mask
Black as a bat
I'm part of the shadows
No one can see me coming
I fight crime in style
I am never seen
I am a mask
Ethan Hodge, Grade 4

The Planets Will All Say "Hi"
When the moon slowly comes to an end,
He'll say he's been a very good friend,
Said that he shall help the sun,
To make us all have so much fun!

So when dawn breaks into a day,
They help us not to go astray,
We can't find any hint of Mars,
So when you look up, just look at the stars.

Then Uranus shows his planks,
If nobody tells a single lie,
When someone explains all their thanks,
The planets will all say 'Hi.'
Nika Pourmohammad, Grade 5

Dancing
Hip Hop, Jazz, and ballet too,
Any kind of dancing is what I do.
Dancing is fun and very cool,
You can even dance in the pool.
You can pounce, jump up and down,
And you can even twist around.
Costumes are cool and very fun,
They are beautiful in the sun.
Clogging, Acro, Lyrical too,
Making noises with our shoes.
It is like playing on a cloud,
Competitions are very loud.
Clogging makes a very big, "Pow!"
Dancing makes me say wow.
Adisyn Thornton, Grade 5

The Sweetest Sister
Sarah, the sister I never had,
When I am with her she makes me glad.
Sarah is really loyal and cool,
Sarah helps me with my math in school.
We have fun when we are together,
We will be best friends forever.
Sarah is as pretty as a bird,
She is really smart is what I've heard.
Sometimes we are nasty and lazy,
Sometimes we are happy and crazy.
Sarah is a pretty daffodil,
She is better than a dollar bill.
When we both met it was meant to be,
Sarah and I never disagree.
Kara McGowen, Grade 5

I Give Thanks For
I give thanks for...
my loving mom...she takes care of me,
my cool dad...he makes me laugh,
my playful dog...he plays with me.
Valery Arias, Grade 4

My Sister

We may not be sisters by birth
But somewhere deep down within me
I feel like I've known you forever

You're my angelic sister
Held close to my heart
We were friends by God's choice
But sisters by our own
You're so pure, you're so true, you're so beautiful

You're my true sister forever
True friends are by your side through it all
True friends are there
To catch you when you fall
True friends give your life a happy lift
True friends are a most precious gift

You're a friend, my companion
When you come for tea
You listen to my problems
And sort them out for me
With happiness and smiles, with pain and tears
I know you'll be there throughout the years
I love you a lot, best friend

Kimberly Olan, Grade 6

Witches Broom

a witches broom is full of fright
dashing through the starry night
meeting clouds and darkness delight
leaving marks in the night that shone bright

giving potions a little touch
they say a broom is never too much
brooms are assistants
they never help too much

putting darkness in a deeper spot
it is not just an old mop
nothing can stop them
not even a cop

they have a good job
and easy to keep
no wonder it is not just a mop
and they never go to sleep

once it has lost all its magic and fun
it's time to retire and be done
and say good bye
but the memory is not a surprise.

Emily DeRenzo, Grade 4

My Grandmother's Flower Pot

Granny's flower pot,
Thrown on the ground,
All because of the man,
Who dressed in black and threw it at her

I look at it closely,
Looking at the red stains on the shattered pot,
Wondering if Granny was now in Heaven,
Smiling down at me

But the pot is so empty and still, no plant grows,
Except one that is,
A small, yellow dandelion that just sprouted,
Shining bright yellow like the sun

It's so strange,
That the flower is the only thing alive,
In the pot,
That was my Granny's

A grin climbs up my face,
Not because of Granny or the pot,
But because of the dandelion that still stands tall
And represents a new life and that I'm not alone

Jimmy Lee, Grade 5

War

The brook chuckles,
The bluebirds sing a song.
The wind dances
And the duck paddles along.

Oblivious they are.
Oh! How I wish I were too.
But, alas, I cannot.
Just like you.

War,
The horrid word rings in my ear.
For I am scarred to never forget.
Forget what happened here.

War,
When too many look into Death's eye.
The last thing they will ever see.
To leave many in despair, to cry.

The day it robbed me of sight,
It left me to suffer, to ask why.
Though, I cannot see,
I will always remember what it has done to me.

Laura Ospina, Grade 6

My Legs

I really truly love my legs
They help me every single day
They are like little pegs
That you play within a board game

I can run, walk, jump, and play
In every activity I participate in
You can run and frolic on your way
It's really fun to play with my legs

Sports, I actually could not play
Without my legs I would be really upset
I couldn't play anything in January, July, or even May
This is why I love my legs

Zoe Galanoudis, Grade 6

My Arms

I love my arms and they love me
My arms are growing and I am too
Without my arms, I would be sad
Without my arms, I would be mad

Without them I couldn't play a lot of sports
I couldn't do hockey, baseball, or karate
Without my arms, I couldn't hit the ball
Without my arms, I couldn't make the call

I can help my dad out with much more pride
Helping my mom and sister is easy too
Without my arms, I couldn't help out
Without my arms, I would have to shout

Nicholas Cipriano, Grade 6

Brown

You don't know I'm here
At least you don't notice me
Without me you would fall apart
Don't let me go
For if you do then your world will dissolve
I'm strong
You can rely on me
For all these years I've held you up
So why now are you letting me go?
You cover me with all the things you think are important
But really it's me
Please
Please
Don't let me go

Sofia Putorti, Grade 6

I Give Thanks For

I give thanks for…
my loving mom…she takes care of me when I'm sick,
my nice dad…he takes me places,
my helpful sister…she helps me with my projects.

Levy Kinlock, Grade 4

Thanksgiving

Leaves changing from green to red,
I love the tasty pumpkin bread.
Thanksgiving dinner is on its way,
The turkey waits for me on a tray.

We watch the parade every year,
When the floats come we always cheer.
When we all get together we have a great time,
It's always fun when it's time to dine.

I can't wait for my whipped cream treat,
The pumpkin pie tastes so sweet.
It's always fun when it's time to eat,
Last year's is going to be hard to beat.

Alaina Cain, Grade 6

I Love My Hands

My hands are my favorite body part
They push around a shopping cart
I love drawing with my hands
I love my hands

I use my hands to eat
I text with my hands
Cookies are waiting for my hands to touch them
My hands make me happy

My hands are silly
They are my best friends
I play sports with my friends
I love my hands

Samantha Blitz, Grade 6

Colors of Christmas

The colors of Christmas that come in my head,
Are gold, green, white, and red.
Rudolph's red nose glows through the night,
Leading Santa's sleigh out of sight.

Not one white snowflake is like another,
They are all different from each other.
Green trees covered with a blanket of snow,
Look beautiful when they glisten and glow.

The golden star on the top of the tree,
Shining bright for everyone to see.
The colors of Christmas are in the air.
Can you see them everywhere?

Elizabeth Belcastro, Grade 6

I Give Thanks For

I give thanks for…
my caring mom…she takes care of us,
my helpful dad…he helps me with my chores,
my funny sister…she tickles me until I laugh.

Neena Binoy, Grade 4

That Time of Year

On a calm, winter morning when I looked out my door,
There was a blanket of white covering the grassy floor,
The feelings inside me all filled up with glee,
As I scanned every bush, shrub and tree

It's that time of year when you hang up your stockings,
And when your boots go "ccrruunncchh" as you're walking,
And when all the girls and boys who celebrate Hanukkah
Light the eight candles shining on the menorah

On the night of December that all of us love,
When with family and friends and the stars up above,
When you wait to hear the sleigh bells all ringing,
A night of joy, happiness, dancing and singing

When it's time to drift away,
To that wonderland that you don't see during the day,
Waiting for him to come,
To see what awaits you in the morning,
The presents of fun

It's that time of year that we've all been waiting for,
When the blanket of white covers the grassy floor,
When the children are happy cause St. Nick has come,
But soon, we all wait because that time of year is done.

Mallory Schuster, Grade 6

The Beach

It's about fun and games till the day is done
Fires burning
Glow sticks glowing

It's about jeep rides
Sand dunes
Jumping into the waves

It's about laughing and playing
Having a good time
Late nights

It's about crabs pinching your toes
Boogie boarding
Surfing the waves

It's about climbing on the jetties
Jumping from rock to rock
Catching fish

It's about eating hoagies
Drinking soda
Eating hot dogs and burgers fresh off the grill

It's about what I love!!!

Kendall Knox, Grade 5

The Best Day

Watching cars pass one by one,
I grow impatient as time goes on.
Watching palm trees stand high and tall,
It's still summer in the fall.
The breeze is cool and the sun is warm,
We're so close I start to squirm.
We finally arrive and fun is happening everywhere.
A day at the beach is the best day ever.

Adrian Leon, Grade 6

Anastasia Island

The place I went to is Anastasia Island.
It was so beautiful it was blinding.
Anastasia Island is in St. Augustine.
The beach was so beautiful at night.
I was camping at Anastasia.
I think mosquitoes were not a problem at Anastasia.
You can camp, swim, and even relax.
I think you will have fun there.

Thomas McFadden, Grade 6

Up in the Mountains

Colorado is the best!
Because it's so fresh.
It has mountains tall.
Where you can see it all!
You can run and play all day.
Just to be in the sun and have fun all day long!
You can see mountain lions and deer.
The air is so clear!

Zoe Loerzel, Grade 6

A Kiss of Love and Two Locking Lips!

A kiss of two locking lips an unbreakable chain.
A kiss that can always ease the pain.
As the love is as warm as a snug cabin on a cold winter's night.
As a love so bright it shall scare away the night.
Until the dawn we will fight the fight.
To keep our love warm and tight.
As a crimson colored sun battles the moon.
Our love will never end anytime soon.

Charlotte Niblett, Grade 6

War Is a Dark Night Sky

War is a dark night sky,
    a worldwide occurrence that blinds us in darkness
Stars twinkling like the eyes of the wounded,
    saying their goodbyes before they fizzle out.
But black fades to navy and then to robin's egg.
The moon goes into hiding, shoulders slumped, ashamed.
Reminding us that all bad lightens up,
    maybe not forever, but just long enough.

Lily Doebler, Grade 6

Outsider

Am I beautiful or ugly?
Do people like me or hate me?
It makes no sense how
People treat me
Because how black I am and
Clothes I wear.
I'm an outsider, but that's okay.
I am different
But I'm beautiful different.
Karmen Kelly, Grade 6

Christmas

C hrist is born
H ear the angels sing
R emember He died
I love Christ
S adness came
T reasure his love
M y Jesus
A wesome God
S ome amazing story
Audrey Duty, Grade 6

Christmas

C hrist is born
H eavy presents
R oof tops are busy with reindeer
I n the lane snow is glistening
S now everywhere
T oo much food
M any presents
A lot of them are mine
S anta came to my house
Tyler Casey, Grade 6

Christmas

C heerful for God
H appiest day of the year
R emember the love
I love the tree and stockings
S anta is coming
T oo much food
M any gifts
A mazing people
S ome awesome times
Hannah Belcher, Grade 6

Narwhals

I am a Narwhal
I'm gray as a storm cloud
I swim fast
I am strong at hunting prey
I can swim and hunt
I can flip and jump
I am a Narwhal.
Shawna Quain, Grade 4

Footsteps

Footsteps!!! e'er I shall follow,
Economics and the reason,
Business and the vision,
You have done it and I will do it too
The snow is deep,
Your footprints are marked,
As they are, I will step

Then when there was a rather dark day,
A blizzard strikes covering the path of that you had laid those years ago
Your strength smiles, endurance thrives,

Oh the snow, Oh the snow,

Stepping o'er the pile
Creating my own path
Learning new things
And making my own mark

I have done it, I have made it
I have decided I can't follow your footsteps, no more
It's been a great journey, I can't wait for more
It's now time to start making my own footsteps in the snow.
Oh Father,
What a journey you have taken me through.
Vivan Gupta, Grade 5

The Storm

Waking up to a gust of wind racing against my window
Shivering as I walk outside
As I step off my patio and onto the green grass
A dull gray cloud appeared over me
When I looked down all I can hear is the sound of bullets smashing against the pavement
Frightened at what was going to come next

As I started heading back to my door
All I can hear was the sound of the sky shake and rumble
Then I knew that the race has begun
I tried to run the speed of a cheetah
But I was not nearly as close

I finally got inside
As I slammed the door shut
Lightning came my way
I ran into the living room

I pick up the phone
The power was soon out
I sat on the couch
Under a blanket
Trying to keep calm
The storm was soon out

Olivia Almodovar, Grade 6

I Can't Write a Poem Today

I can't write a poem today because...
A alien is in my house with his blaster
I was scared he would hurt me,
But he made my house a disaster

He had a scary face.
He chased me and I had an untied lace.
He broke the fridge and then the table.
His big ship had a label.

Now a cow and a sheep is in my house.
Run run little little mouse
Over the table I leap.
Please don't hurt me alien, bleep bleep bleep.

Finally I am alone,
But I hear a little tone.
I open the door and see,
the alien is behind me

Mike Muyobisnay Morocho, Grade 4

The Night

Lights flicker, shadows dance.
Night has arrived,
And his sister, the day
Says goodbye.
In the distance, a coyote howls
There is a sound of rabbits
Scampering away in response.
The stars,
Just risen
Above everything
Give off a small
But strong amount of light.
The wind swirls around the trees, breathing deeply.
There are robins and bluebirds
Flying away, all in the
Very quiet
Presence
Of
Night.

Larissa Samson, Grade 4

Spider Bite

Spider bite, spider bite, bitter and cold.
This bite will sting at least that's what I was told.
It will happen to everyone, big and small.
But this is not the spider bite you think it is.

A spider bite is fierce, dreadful, and it will always hurt.
It's the mean voice, it's the unwelcome feeling,
but to some, it's loss, the loss of family members.

The spider bite is sorrow, grief, anger,
stress, strife, and pain,
and it will always leave a mark.
To many, it could be a bad grade
to losing a very important thing...
or person.

Spider bite, spider bite, bitter and cold.
But this feeling can be turned around,
and this I wasn't told.

Jolissa Ramsland-Basirico, Grade 6

Thanksgiving Dinner

When the Halloween pumpkins are gone,
And the leaves have all fallen to the ground,
When the air has turned windy and cold,
Then Thanksgiving will soon be around.

Thoughts of the family all feasting together,
Pleasant pictures of past times appear,
To dwell in each heart and each mind,
Thanksgiving is here now nothing to worry.

The kitchen has amazing smells,
The dining room looks so fine,
Decorations of turkeys on the wall,
And now we are ready to dine.

First the napkins are placed at our laps,
Then the prayer for the meal to be so holy,
Then we stuff the delicious food in our tummies,
And we hope it will all digest!!!

Aidan Shea-Katz, Grade 4

Madison/Rossignol

Madison
I am shy, quiet, cheerful, sweet
My family is loving, loyal, thankful, honest
I love my two nephews Daman and Jaxson
I need to read all the books that I can
I give my mom big bear hugs when she is sad
I fear spiders and being alone
I would like to be a teacher when I grow up
I would like to see Paris and England when I grow up
I wonder what the future will be like
Rossignol

Madison Rossignol, Grade 6

Anna/Avery

Anna
I am childish, caring, silly, eager
My family is funny, awesome, weird, kind
I love my dog Abbie Sue
I need my friends
I give help to those who need it
I fear death
I would like to be a musician
I would like to see peace throughout the world
I wonder how technology works
Avery

Anna Avery, Grade 6

The Game
People yelling
Flags waving
Snacks crunching
Feet banging
People slurping
Some singing
People gasping
People catching
Mouths drooping
Mascot shooting shirts
Angel Avendano, Grade 6

My Pet
I get off the bus,
She comes to me.
And I pick her up,
And hug her.
Then I wash her,
Then I feed my pet Casie.
And sometimes,
She gets on my everlasting nerves,
With her barking.
But I still love her very much!
Teonne Jinkins, Grade 6

The Thing in the Night
A raccoon in my house
its quiet as a mouse
A raccoon can be black and white
It's hard to see in the night
I walked slowly towards this thing
I don't know what it will bring
I turned the light on so I can see
I'm still wondering what it will be
It's not a raccoon so I took a breathe
This cat scared me half to death
Lillianna Diaz, Grade 4

My Heart
My sweet mom
I see you every day
Oh how I love to hug you
When there's a stressful day

You are there with me
And have a smile every time I get home

Thank you for being there
Thank you with all my heart
Nya Heyward, Grade 6

Aunt Luchi
Aunt Luchi is nice
With her green eyes, and sweet voice
She inspires me.
Alex Deffer, Grade 4

Thanksgiving at My Aunt's
I walk through the door and everyone is talking and laughing
The mouthwatering scent of the turkey and mashed potatoes is in the air
I can't wait to eat the best turkey you could ever have
But I had to wait for everyone to sit down
I glanced at my Aunt who was sitting across from me
I picked up my silverware and grabbed a wing of the turkey and started to eat
What was your Thanksgiving like?
Brian Crossan, Grade 4

Thanksgiving
I see parents cooking food to eat
I smell turkey, chicken, bread, and meat sitting on the table ready to be eaten.
I hear people chatting at the table eating their food
I taste food we eat selected on the table
I touch the electronics sitting on the couch and food
Thanksgiving
Aaron Burthe, Grade 6

Farewell
The tree says farewell to the leaves passing by.
He smells the pumpkin pie in the oven.
As autumn comes to a stand, the tree realizes how lovely its leaves are.
It was cloudy like a storm was about to hit.
The wind was as quick as lightning, the gust also pulled down more leaves.
It was as cold as winter. Well, it is almost here.
Liberty Tremblay, Grade 5

Imagination
Imagination is like running through the flower fields of your dreams
It smells like glittery fairy dust
It tastes like Mad Hatters' piping hot tea
It sounds like a princess singing from her tower
It feels like jumping over the moon
It lives in my warmest dreams
Sophia Bere, Grade 6

Happiness
Happiness is a family holiday gathering
It smells like hot chocolate on Christmas morning
It tastes like roasted marshmallows over a fire pit
It sounds like the roar of the crowd when you win your championship game
It feels like a fuzzy blanket on your cheek
It lives in my heart all of the time
Brian Billig, Grade 6

Imagination
Imagination is like a million different, wonderful thoughts in your head.
It smells like a bunch of scrumptious homemade cookies right out of the oven.
It tastes like a delicious ice cream dessert.
It sounds like a million beautiful choirs of angels singing in your ear.
It feels like a relaxing daydream.
It lives in the creative minds of everyone's beautiful bodies.
Daryl Boich, Grade 6

Starry Starry Night

The starry night is all mine for now
Whenever I look at the sky I see me
I have so much intelligent somehow
Growing to be so anciently old me

I see the gorgeous stars smiling at me
The white moon dazzling how brightly glows
The shimmer is very pretty to see
The calming breeze is like my radio

The sky I like to watch and see the moon
I will fly to the sky in a rocket
Up, Up and away I will soar so soon
I want to build an electric socket

One day I will decide for my own good
For I am still learning about childhood.

Kayelee Nations, Grade 5

Christmas Eve

On a blustery cold Christmas Eve,
Families are snug around the warm, cozy fire.
Sharing memories and stories.
All covered in soft blankets,
There they lay.
What pretty lights twinkling around the house.
What do I see?
Is that a Christmas snowman?
They decided to go ice skating!
"Oh boy oh boy oh boy" the children excitedly yelled.
After skating for hours, it was time for a yummy cup of hot cocoa.
I hope we can do this another Christmas Eve again.
Then time for some scrumptious s'mores but when
The children were done they pleaded "more more more"

"Oh what a great day of what a great day,"
The children said.

Arianna Richards, Grade 4

Rain

I pour down, windy and numbing.
My rain is rushing high.
The wild drivers are splashing on the streets.
They're slipping, sliding, falling everywhere.
I drop.
My rain is harder, faster, colder.
Lightning and thunder booming at my wake.
My washing, wild waves are at war.
I fall on the cold concrete.
I stop.
The flood recedes.
The light shines through.
The sky is clear and shining.
I go, with a storm at my side.
I leave.

Leela Kaul Tickoo, Grade 5

I Am

I am a basketball player
I wonder if I will make it into the NBA
I hear the sound of a basketball bouncing on a gym floor
I see a basketball hoop
I am a basketball player

I pretend that I am in the NBA
I feel a basketball in my hands
I worry about my friends and family
I cry when people cry
I am a basketball player

I understand that things don't go my way that much
I say don't give up
I dream about amazing things like basketball
I try my best so I can succeed
I hope I grow up to be an athlete
I am Colin Libby

Colin Libby, Grade 6

Brown

Like the trunk and roots, brown is sturdy and stable
From predators a tree protects
Birds in their nests
The squirrel that lives inside
With its acorns from the harsh winters it hides

Brown stays in the background and does not seek attention
Strong and organized, the color of protection
Brown is everywhere, yet unobtrusive
Appears in the fall, replacing bright colors, orange and red

If for home you are longing
Brown will give you a sense of belonging
Practical, sensible
Brown is approachable and inviting

Materialistic, secure, natural
Brown

Phoebe Chen, Grade 6

What I Am Good At

I am good at being a brother and a son
At least that's what my Mom says

I am good at drawing and riding bikes and petting my cat
Also what my Mom says

I am good at eating my vegetables, pizza, and Mac and cheese
Also what my Mom says

I am good at fishing and running and driving my Dad's excavator
Also what my Mom says

But what I'm really good at is Math

Zakary Klees, Grade 4

Nature

It crawls, it growls, it scurries and screeches
It flows in the water of rivers and creeks
It sparkles and booms, and lights up the moon
Nature is what it is

It grows out of the ground, and falls from the sky
It can sometimes even fly
On the wings of a bird, in a flock or a herd
Nature is what it is

Or at night when the stars shine bright
It hoots, howls, and sings
Because here is its chance, its very chance, to be many, many things

Brooke Ledda, Grade 6

Home Sweet Home

You may not know,
but home has much meaning to it.
It's the best place to relax,
whether big or small.
Home is perfect in every way.
Does not have to be decorated,
because love will embellish it.
To not realize the value of home,
is to not be blessed with it.
A building is made of bricks and mud,
but a home stands on love, care, and respect.
Cherish it, value it, love it.
Home Sweet Home.

Hooran Awan, Grade 5

Mothers

What makes a mother stand out from all others?
Well, one is selfless and kind
Strong in heart and mind
Who will raise you up when you fall
Come rushing over when you call
Sing a lullaby in the middle of the night
Console you and hold you tight
She will dry all of your tears
Calm all your worst fears
Protect you till the very end
Even be an understanding best friend
Wanting for you the very best
A true mother can stand prouder than the rest

Amber Choi, Grade 6

Heartbreak

When I dream of you,
My heart is full of pain.
Every day I long to see your face.
Without you around my heart seems like an empty glass;
I cry thinking of you, knowing that I can't go back.
Where can I find another love like you?
Knowing that you and I are through.

Joshua Atkinson, Grade 6

Sinking into Christmas Excitement

Wonderful long, cool walks,
Deep in the snow.
I can tell Christmas is near,
And as we cheer, we can hear,
"Ho ho ho," loud and clear.
Have you heard at night the wind sing,
Bright and strong?
Well maybe you were asleep.
"Wake up, wake up,"
You old brilliant slug!
It's Christmas Eve!
Your presents are ready.
Go check out what incredible things you received!
After that, let's go down to the factory,
Where it's always happy,
And then bake a few yummy gingerbread men!

Tess Kruger, Grade 4

Fridge

The depth of the fridge we're afraid to know
The two month old spaghetti growing hair
It's a nice little place were germs grow
Along with grapes and a pear
The buttermilk is curdled and chunky
The lettuce is slimy along with the spam
Old cheddar cheese smells moldy and funky
And a spore lined jar that might be jam

Duke's one year old mayo has died
There's cornbread in tinfoil from New Year's Day
Along with the play dough that dried
That crawled up the sides about to escape

A half eaten egg and a key lime pie
Not hungry anymore, shut the door, bye

Andrew Thompson-Gregory, Grade 5

Trees and Leaves

I think of leaves as ripe red apples
I see these leaves from inside a chapel
I think of leaves as bright stars
I see the leaves going so far
I think of leaves as nice juicy oranges
That just got tipped in some wet porridge
The trees are as brown as creamy chocolate melted
I think this tree just got belted
Falling falling down on the ground
It just made a sound on the ground
Whirling and swirling flying around
All the way down, down, down
The ground is damp just like a swamp
Then my boots go stomp, stomp, stomp
One thing left it's a clover
Now it's time for Fall to be over

CJ Korowicki, Grade 4

Patriotic

American of red, white, and blue.
I love these colors, it is so true.
My brother loves Yemen,
I have no clue,
But I love America,
The red, white, and blue.
Dawood Alhobishi, Grade 6

Easter

Easter is blue.
Easter tastes like candy.
It sounds like birds chirping.
Easter smells like flowers.
It looks like dyed eggs.
Easter makes me brighten up!
Brandon Litzinger, Grade 4

Christmas

Kids opening their Christmas presents
Grandmas baking Christmas cookies
Families talking after a long time
The snowflakes coming from the sky
Snowballs while we have a snowball fight
Christmas
Jaylene Tineo, Grade 4

As Time Goes

As time goes we get older
No one lives forever
As time goes we think back
About all the great times
As time goes you become wiser
Enjoy life as you can
Matthew Nozick, Grade 6

Apology

I ate your pound cake
that you were going to
eat with cold milk

Forgive me, it was
so warm
Estefani Alvarez, Grade 6

Swim, Swim, Swim

My mom, brother, friends, and I,
On the Fourth of July,
It was sandy,
And rocky.
Oh the old Key West,
It was the best.
Kaitlyn Lowe, Grade 6

Soccer

Super spectacular soccer is superbly fun
The exciting amazingly awesomely game is heart pounding
The equally excellent half are well rounding
See cool players swiftly speeding down the field running!

The most popular passionate played sport in the world
Most people favor this fascinating game
It has ever evolving exquisite fame
The compelling competitive uneasiness in the air swirled

Millions of fans roaring cheering and chanting for their teams
The player steps up and shoots a magnificent and score
The game is over and fans want more
Just because the game is done, the curious creative fans think of more games to come.
Matthew Taylor, Grade 6

Halloween

Tonight is the night when spirits roam
You might hear the crying of various ghosts
You may catch a glimpse of a shadow near a post
Will you survive this day with dead souls as you go home?

You turn to find a horrifying face
You start crying for help, but nobody comes to your aid
You begin to calm down but part of you remains afraid
Then you realize it was just your friend in a creative creepy costume so you start to embrace.

Trick-or-treat, trick-or-treat
Give us candy, give us cake,
Give us something good to take
Please be quick and give us something good to eat.
Nicole Rivera, Grade 6

Love Defined

Love comes from the heart.
It rises and rises like the vines of roses.
It might even feel like fire.
You feel love when you see the person you like.
When you suddenly feel like having a dance with her.
When you see her delicate eyes just staring in the crowd.

Love is feeling like you could fall on your knees for that one person.
Then, suddenly, comes that special moment when it's all about the person you love,
And then you feel like kissing her.
Suddenly, you both kiss.
You feel that nothing is going to stop you.
And the only thing that matters
Is that one person whom you are in love with.
Jacquelin Corona Hernandez, Grade 6

Vicious Lion

He is a powerful lion.
He is as fierce as a vengeful hunter.
He likes eating snacks, traveling to Universal Studios, and swimming in the pool.
Elyas Fresse, Grade 6

The Mind Is a Maze

The mind is its own universe.
Starting with nothing.
Growing into infinity.
So large something new is always coming.
The mind is a maze.
Twists and turns,
that never cease to amaze.
Each turn is never the same.
For, the mind is a maze, that will never be the same.
Just take a moment to gaze upon this universal maze.
But don't let it drive you insane.

Simon Denton, Grade 6

Mind of Wonder

You ask yourself do you have a mind of wonder
A mind full of stories untold
A mind that makes its own hardship
A mind most people don't take it as it is
A mind that never stops thinking and dreaming
A mind that can make anything better or worse
A mind full of hidden secrets, secrets that never be told
A mind that can easily tell what someone is feeling
A mind that knows it will be something great some day
So I'll ask you again do you have a mind of wonder

Joshua Miles Barling, Grade 6

Red

Red is the color of joy and hope,
And shiny apples in the fall.
The sound of red is a crackling bonfire,
And the "crunch" of leaves beneath your feet.
Red is the smell of tart apples in an orchard,
And new cherry blossoms in the spring.
Red is the sweet taste of caramel,
And luscious strawberries perfectly ripe.
The touch of red is smooth and sharp,
Like ivy coiled up on tree bark.

Maddy McFee, Grade 6

Freedom

F reedom is what we have,
R adiant religions describe us as a nation,
E verywhere there must be freedom,
E ach person has the right to express their voice.
D ifferent citizens are all united as the same.
O ur home of the free is where
M any people want to be.

Haiqa Niazi, Grade 4

Winter

Winter is fun when you find somebody.
They love, have sun, and have a wonderful time.
It's the most wonderful, loving year.
When you just believe and care,
Thank your love for this time of year.

Enacoret Parziale, Grade 4

My Emotions

When I am tired, I am as exhausted as a runner who lost
stamina in the first mile of a dreadful 10 mile race

When I am sad, I am like a poor puppy getting put
into his uncomfortable cage

When I am annoyed, I am as enraged as my dad
when the New York Mets give up a run to lose the game

When I am calm, I am like a prairie dog laying in a beautiful
field of wheat swaying in the wind

When I am scared, I am as frightened as a little boy going
through the gateway haunted house

When I am lonely, I am like a stuffed animal sitting on a bed
waiting for my owner to come back from vacation

Evan Mistler, Grade 6

America the Beautiful

From sea to shining sea, America
So beautiful may you forever be
How glorious you stand, America
The beautiful, the homeland of the free

Oh beautiful for her sacrifices
May her symbols of democracy wave
For the past has shown her sacrifices
Our America shall stand tall and brave

For when America calls to duty
She answers a battle cry of freedom
When her heroes return from their duty
Their enemies fear because we beat em'

Throughout her years of much sorrow and pain
The home of the free and the brave remain

Will Cothran, Grade 5

Snow Day

One very cold winter day,
School has been canceled for a snow day.
I've been out of school for two or three weeks,
Kids hit me with snowballs,
Then I trip like I'm weak.
The fireplace is warm and cozy,
With lots of space.
When I get tired I go to sleep,
Christmas came in just a sweep.
Presents under the huge Christmas tree,
And all of us got only two or three.
I thought it was all an enormous dream,
And I was calm as waves on a calm stream.
Today was a very good day,
It was also a marvelous snow day.

Nicholas Blandford, Grade 4

My Pet
I have a pet,
his name is Chico.
He is intelligent.
We did not buy him,
he came to us,
because he got abandoned.
At first, we called him Solovino.
I liked him.
My dad taught him
how to sit, jump, and stand.
Then about 9 weeks later
we bought 3 more dogs.
Two are pitbulls,
Rocky and the other is Tigre.
The last one,
we adopted him,
and his name is Max.
He's a labor dog.
I like Chico the most,
our first pet.
Aaron Regino, Grade 6

One Window Please
One window is all I need
To see the fears that I once had
To see the dreams I have already had
To be lost in love
For a touch of freedom
To meet my destiny
To have my closest friend near me
To be special
To reveal the true me
To be able to see the changes in life
To see all the animals being cared for
To see myself as a vet
To see all the children creating new things
To see new inventions every day
To make people jealous
To be noticed
To imagine the impossible
To be in the present, past, and future
To look at how beautiful the future is
And to see the light of life
Cali Drake, Grade 6

Rice
My hair is nice
I smell like spice
All around the little mice
As I cook rice

In my hair I found rice
What to do with my mice
Oh Lord my rice is nice
Have to have a little spice
Zoray Walker, Grade 5

Autumn Leaves
Autumn leaves
stick to my clothing
as I take another dive
into the leaf pile.

Autumn leaves
crunch beneath my feet
scurrying away as I kick them.
The trees are bare, the leaves beside them
Making no motion.

Autumn leaves
Maple, ginkgo, willow,
orange, red, brown,
weave down the sides of the trees.
Tsehaynesh Rigotti, Grade 5

The Sea
Waves crashing on the shore,
Children playing and splashing galore
The sea's majestic force,
More treacherous than an obstacle course
Tides surging and ebbing,
Fisherman nearby, picking up netting,
As the evening sun, sparkling and shining
Above, is setting
A force like no other,
Majestic and filled with wonder
Deep, deep down in the depth of thee,
Creatures swim constantly free
The sea,
Thou should respect thee
The sea, oh the sea, beautiful, we can all see
Skylar Campbell, Grade 6

I Love School
I love school.
Cause I am a fool.
I have fun in all my classes.
I like running in gym.
I meet new people every day.
I see new faces,
Cause new students move in.
I like to make friends,
So I can play.
I like my new teachers,
In the 6th grade.
They're fun,
And they are sometimes boring,
And they keep me snoring!
While they tell their stories.
Rodrigo Ciriaco Soriano, Grade 6

Ode to Inventors
Ode to inventors
those who create
those who innovate
those who think outside the box.
Ode to inventors
told they can't do it
called crazy
been shot down
but still believe.
Ode to inventors
work hard to make it
through thick and thin
ignore the haters.
Ode to inventors
they made it
blockbusters
successful
top-sellers
all because they believed.
Aisha Nabali, Grade 5

Sweater Weather!
I know it's fall when…
People wear sweaters,
All bundled up,
Walking in the city.

I know it's fall when…
Kids play in leaf piles,
The leaves stained red, orange, and yellow,
Flutter down from the sky.

I know it's fall when…
The trees full of color,
Sprayed with autumn,
Wave in the wind.

I know it's fall when…
Families gather outside in their coats,
Eating, chatting, and playing in their yards,
Enjoying the newly arrived season…
Alyna Williams, Grade 6

Snow! Please Don't Go!
Oh snow, oh snow
I can see you in the sky
Very bright with a lot of white

Oh snow, oh snow
Frozen ice that bites my nose
I wish I had enough clothes!

Oh snow, oh snow
Come play with me and stay
And hopefully, you won't melt away!
Anna Julia Candida, Grade 4

I Am

I am a dancer and a horse rider
I wonder if there will be flying cars
I hear my dog bark
I want more fish
I am a dancer and a horse rider

I pretend to dance on a stage when I'm in my room
I feel sad when people die
I touch soft fur
I worry about my friends and family
I cry when animals die
I am a dancer and horse rider

I understand that bad things happen
I say proudly that I believe in God
I dream about unicorns
I try to do good on math tests
I am dancer and a horse rider

Jaden Miracle Grubb, Grade 4

Whimsical Washington Avenue

My neighborhood is a humming bird whistling lullabies
to her babies and immense tulips ready to burst out a
lovely poem and juicy ripe apples dangling from
a lime green tree saying, "Take me away."

My neighborhood is like a breathtaking butterfly that
broke into a spontaneous song.

My neighborhood is a Christmas miracle while you're
dancing around the smoking fire pit and peering out of a
window observing joy and you see a stunning sight of a starry night.

And its so divine at Thanksgiving dinner gazing and
drooling at the scrumptious, enormous turkey doused in
gravy saying, "Just do it!"

Whimsical Washington Avenue is a marvelous place but
it can irk me sometimes.

Ava Angela Boldi, Grade 6

Orange

Orange is the brilliant show of light at every sunrise and sunset.
Orange is like the leaves of a colorful autumn tree.
Orange is like the crunch of someone eating a good carrot.
Orange is the sound of a bright and tasty orange being sliced.
Orange is like the feel of a ripe juicy orange.
Orange is like touching a slimy salamander.
Orange is the scent of a delicious clementine.
Orange is the smell of a fresh fruit smoothie.
Orange tastes like just-squeezed orange juice.
Orange tastes like sweet sorbet.

Aidan Leary, Grade 6

Black

In the dark of night,
You're shivering with fright.
Heart beating oh so fast,
Finally the light comes at last.
Justice and peace overrule evil,
As depression slips away like a tiny black weevil.
When purity and death mix,
Grey comes out with a whole bag of tricks.
Confused, not sure where it came,
Wherever it is, grey wants to play his game.
This game is not very fun,
But more or less of a destructive one.
White will go first, then black, then white again,
For a game of chess is going on, where the loser will likely strain.
White moves a pawn, and then black's knight takes the pawn,
But white had planned that, so white's queen took the fawn.
Convoluted and evil, black had planned that too,
So then black took the queen, leaving white unsure what to do.
Black ends up winning this sick and cruel game,
And white is thrown in a room, with nothing but a flame.

Lucas Pash, Grade 6

I Am

I am a girl who likes doing gymnastics.
I wonder what we will practice today.
I hear the bars jiggling, the trampoline's springs moving,
People dismounting off the balance beam and landing.
I see people bouncing on the trampoline, flipping on bars.
I want to learn a lot of things.
I am a girl who likes doing gymnastics.

I pretend that I can do anything I imagined.
I feel my heart pumping in my chest from doing flips on the bars.
I touch the mat with grace.
I worry that I will not be able to do anything.
I am a girl who likes doing gymnastics.

I understand that I will not be able to do everything.
I say I can do it.
I dream to be on a team.
I try to do anything possible.
I hope I will be one of the best at gymnastics.
I am a girl who likes doing gymnastics.

Lauren Boulanger, Grade 5

Mr. Shark

How doth the small shark
Use its wide jaws
To bite into Noah's ark
And it makes its own laws?

With all of its gray flesh
How happy it grins,
And the fish it eats is fresh.
It is amazing the way it uses its fins.

Matthew Hagen, Grade 5

Family

My family is fun and wonderful.
They are my heart and soul.
I really care for my family.
I love them so much.
I love when my mom and my sister do my hair.
I am about to have another sister.
She is going to be the best thing that ever happened to me.
I love my family and my family loves me.
They mean the world to me.

Amari Epps, Grade 4

My Eyes

Big eyes, big brown eyes
Looking at the sky, watching butterflies
Flowers, flowers pretty flowers looking up at rain showers
Majestically tall towers
My eyes shine bright
Oh at night in the light
Looking up at the sun so much fun!
My eyes weigh a ton
Big eyes, big brown eyes

Marcella Flaherty, Grade 6

Dreams

I lay down in front of my stove and
I imagine everything that a dreamer would see.
I pay attention to the light and dark
They connect with me.
I go fast but then slow
I feel the warm air crawling on my neck
and my dog rests his head on my chest.
I bet he is dreaming, too
but I daydream!

Emerson Kelly, Grade 4

Popham Beach

If you listen closely you can hear the ocean waves
from here.
The summer breeze feels good on my hair and
especially my hot sunburned skin.
My sandy, wet feet were ready to get back in the
water again, and so was my beat up board.
The burning sun went behind the clouds for a second
then came back out and shined down on the sparking water.
Life was good in my home at Popham Beach

Olivia Whitehouse, Grade 6

My Heart

You have no idea how my heart fills for you.
You are prettier than roses.
One day I hope I will be on my knees asking for your hand.
When you dance, it's like a flower in the wind.
It's as if fire strikes me when I see you sad.
It hurts me when I see tears in your eyes.
I just want to hold you in my arms and kiss you.

Landon Dudley, Grade 6

Don't Be Afraid

They treat us like a hockey puck zooming around.
They threaten us so they can get away with it.
Our pain is their pleasure.
Bullies don't deserve pleasure.
Not until they stop.
They bully to be "cool."
At least they think they're cool.
We shouldn't let them manipulate us.
We aren't air planes.
They think we're afraid to tell the adult.
Let's prove them wrong.
Tell an adult.
The bully's threat is fake.
They're just trying to deceive you.
They think you're the oaf, yet the bully is.
Do something about it.
Don't be afraid.

Sarah Houghtalen, Grade 6

I Always Have to Listen

"Honey."
   "Yes, Mom?"
      "Get your brother."
         I always have to listen.
   "Honey."
"Yes, Mom?"
"Clean your room."
I always have to listen
"Honey."
   "What, Mom?"
      "Go get the mail."
         "Okay, can I stop listening—this is outrageous."
"HONEY!"
(Mom, I don't want to help you)
"But I was going to say, Dad got you a pool."
   "I don't care Mom—wait, WHAT?"
      "Yeah."

Isabelle Laliberte, Grade 4

Blue

Blue is the color of the glorious sky when I look up.
When I smell Blue, I think of the blue scented pencils in my house.
Blue is the taste of the tasty blueberries in my backyard.
Blue is the feeling of the river under a bridge.
Blue is the sound of shiny blue books dropping on the floor.
When I smell Blue I think of the color of the soggy blue oceans.
Blue is blue paints on my table at school.
Blue is the feeling of horrible blue hair.
Blue is the sound of glass shattering on the floor.
Blue is the color of the whales jumping up and down.
When I smell Blue I think of blue tasty lollipops in my lunch.
Blue is the taste of the amazing blue ices.
Blue is the sound of people punching blue backpacks.
Blue is the color of blue seals swimming.
Blue is the color of my face when I get stressed out.

Tyler Kyriakos, Grade 4

A Girl's Best Friend

Sweet not shy, the apple of my eye,
My pooch is one I can't deny.
Crack! I hear she broke the vase,
But how could I get mad at that face?
With fur of brown that grows so long,
In winter she stays nice and strong.
Woof! She barks, loud and proud,
Across the fence, other dogs bow.
At night she sleeps inside her bed,
With her blanket tight and nicely spread.
Aww! We say as she's cuddled at night,
The room might be dark, but her love is so bright.
I would be empty, without her by my side,
My dog, Maya, is my love and pride.

Arissa Katemba, Grade 5

My Feet

My feet can let me go from place to place
Feet can wear socks and shoes
You can put on nail polish
Also they can wear many types of socks

They can let you stand up
Feet can let you run from place to place
Feet in the morning and at night
First comes the left then comes the right foot

Feet can be slow and quick
Feet can come in big or small
They can be wet or dry
These are high and low feet

Victoria Classi, Grade 6

Storms

Storms can be big and they can be small,
Sometimes they can be louder than a wolf's call.

The wind blows fast,
Much harder than the last.

Lightning strikes the sky,
Don't you even wonder why?

Storms can be snow, hail or rain,
All of them together is three times the pain.

When I see a storm I say hello,
When you see a storm you say oh no.

Hannah Myers, Grade 6

I Give Thanks For

I give thanks for...
My loving Mommy, she makes me feel loved,
My amazing Daddy, he is the best,
My big Brother, he is always there for me.

Lilly Rose Swann, Grade 4

Baseball

The game is about to begin,
The big question is who will win?
I get to my position which is first base,
The opponent hits and sprints to my place.

My teammate throws the ball to me,
I make the catch and it is out number three.
They call my name; it's my turn to bat,
The crowd cheers and begins to clap.

The pitcher winds and throws a fastball,
I get ready to swing as I stand tall.
The ball hits off my bat and soars towards the sun,
The fans go wild, I hit a homerun.

Cameron Glance, Grade 6

My Favorite Sport

Football is the game I play,
When you win, you will say, "YAY!"
The defense has a mean, strong glare,
When the quarterback throws the ball in the air.
If you're tired, you say a prayer,
That the clock will soon start to blare.
Your score just better be at the top,
Because if it's not, you will need a pop.
You wear protective pads like helmets,
So when you put them on, you're set.
In the play, you dare not daydream,
Because you will let down your team.
If you get tackled and you fall,
You just better hold on to the ball!

Steven Sparks, Grade 5

Football Greats

I see the quarterback standing tall,
Looking down field and chunking the ball.
From the strong arm of Rodger Staubach
To the mighty power of a J.J. Watt sack.
Michael Irvin down field for a "Hail Mary,"
Can always be very scary!
Observe the bursting speed of Bo,
And Barry Sanders the touchdown hero.
ACL tears are so very mean,
Sometimes as mean as Big Joe Green!
All of these players are good at the game,
Now they're rocking in the Hall of Fame!
In pro football, to be a king,
You have to come home with a Super Bowl ring!

Gabriel Blanton, Grade 5

I Give Thanks For

I give thanks for...
my loving mom...she respects everyone,
my fun dad...he takes me places,
my active dog...she's always there to play with me.

Allyson Valdez, Grade 4

Christmas

C hrist is born
H oliday
R eindeer on the roof
I ncredible time with family
S inging Christmas carols
T rees all lit
M aking delicious snow cream
A ll presents under the tree
S parkling wrapping paper.
Kyleigh Cook, Grade 6

How the Moon Glows

How the moon glows
is by the sun.
The moon reflects the sun's light
from below during the night.
So beautiful at night
and wonderful to see.
So shining and bright
you can drive in the night.
A way of light to read by the river.
Annja Russell, Grade 6

Beautiful

B eauty lasts forever
E very day it shines brightly
A n amazing smile
U ntil the end of time
T alented
I ncredibly fearless
F aithful
U nbelievably nice
L ooks like an angel in disguise
Wade Vance, Grade 6

Who Could Judge?

They be mean to me
They sing about me
In a really bad way.
They hate what I wear.
I'm like a stick
In the forest.
Nowhere to play.
I'm tall as I can be
They might just call me tree.
Dionne Ellis, Grade 6

Fall

Chubby squirrels gathering acorns
Leaves turning different colors
Leaves falling everywhere
Twigs on the ground
Leaf piles everywhere
Dying flowers
Chipmunks scurrying across the ground
Sergio Santiago, Grade 5

An Ocean of Imagination

Imagination, you can think of anything.
You can think of so much you could call it an ocean of imagination.
You can think of cars, sandy beaches, your dream house, so many things.
An ocean of imagination it's like your own little world.
It's where I go in math class, science, and social studies.
An ocean of imagination,
if you don't have an imagination you wouldn't be able to do much.
It's like the waves of an ocean, the water goes up and comes down just like your imagination
Imagination, you can think of anything.
Jason Simmons, Grade 6

Welcome to New York City

The people walk the streets as the taxis honk and beep,
I love the hustle and bustle all through the city.
As we pass the sign of the green girl and Glinda the good,
We see all the people walking as fast as they could.
As my aunt, sister, mom, and I see the show,
We say New York City is the place to go.
When we leave the wonderful NYC we say thank you, New York, you were wonderful to me.
When I come back to this amazing place, I can't wait to say welcome to New York.
Gracey Waterman, Grade 6

The Amazing Amanda

Generous, creative, energetic.
Who enjoys swimming on the Rutgers team.
Who is able to play classical music on the violin.
Who feels happiest when she's traveling in national parks.
Who wonders about what college she'll go to and what she'll study.
Who fears poisonous spiders even though she's never been bit by one.
Who cares about her mom, dad, and brother.
Who dreams of going to Harvard University.
Amanda Sun, Grade 5

Summer's Day

The sun sparkles like the ocean's water reflecting off the light.
The branches sway with the wind, and he is hoping to himself that his limbs don't break.
The squirrel scampers through the flimsy limbs of the tree looking for acorns.
The grass dances all around the tree waiting for its next rain.
All of the other trees are like giants compared to him.
He is getting ready for fall, excited for the pretty leaves.
The air is getting cooler for fall to settle in.
He can't wait to watch the kids jump into his leaves that have floated down.
Tanner McKim, Grade 5

Life

Life is life.
From the pile of dusty books sitting on the couch to my journal, lying on the table.
To the cars on the rack to my picture of Lolo.
Day to night.
My first step to my first picture.
As time passes so do people.
But there is one place they remain forever.
In my heart.
Ella Navarro, Grade 4

Fall

I feel the fierce wind blowing through my hair
Blowing it back, forth, and everywhere
I smell the fresh cider, juice and tea
The gigantic platter of delicious turkey
I can hear the chatter in the work room
Of difficult times and successful times too
But most of all in my heart
I feel the pounding love of family, food, and a wonderful holiday!

Samantha Heaver, Grade 6

It's Me!

It's me, the girl who likes to talk
It's me, with my own taste in fashion
It's me, the girl who loves to make new friends
It's me, remember I'm in fourth grade now
It's me, and I'm changing, growing
It's me, this nice, weird girl
It's me, with some tricks up my sleeve
It's me, remember this unique and talented girl!

Tianna Morris, Grade 4

Lacrosse

L ove the game.
A game of fun and pain.
C areful of the ball and where it is.
R un with the ball and avoid getting checked.
O f course winning is still the best.
S o fun when you score a goal.
S uper.
E xtraordinarily fun.

Peyton Smith, Grade 5

My Name

It doesn't really have a meaning, it's just my name
My name isn't unique not that easy to remember
But it's what my parents chose for me when I was born.
My name sounds like a book,
Waiting to be read, interesting to read and figure out.
My name is my own, one of a kind like me.
I keep it for myself,
Because it is my own.

Kendyll Cassel, Grade 6

New School

This year was difficult because I changed schools,
I thought I was going to act like a fool.
This school is cool and I love it,
I don't hate it one bit.
My classroom is upstairs and it is shared by two teachers,
My classroom has a lot of cool features.
I had a rough time changing from a school that I knew,
But the teachers and the students are very cool.

Aidan Gonzalez, Grade 6

A Summer Vacation

We are on the way to the hot summer beach,
To feel the hot sand between our toes.
When we get there I am going to lay out in the blazing sun.
My mom said I could go swimming,
In the terrific cool refreshing water.
My Dad is at home having a cookout,
He said he did not want to come, but it is fine.
I will have fun on my summer vacation.

Jana Hanson, Grade 4

I Am Venicia

Caring, friendly, and thoughtful
Who enjoys playing with her friends, and drawing.
Who is able to play waltzes on the piano.
Who feels happiest when she's with her friends.
Who wonders what she'll get on her next birthday.
Who fears failing a test, and bugs biting her.
Who cares about her family and friends.
Who dreams of learning more songs on the piano.

Venicia Wong, Grade 5

Life Is a Tree

Life is a tree,
it has bare branches and brown leaves,
but it also has
flowers and green leaves.
It may have dead branches, but those dead
branches fall away to new ones.
Because what really counts are the new branches
reaching for the sky.

Ella Tran Izenour, Grade 6

When I'm Reading

When I'm reading, the book takes me away.
It takes me to a magical land oh so far away.
In this land I'm a character.
I do awesome things —
I ride horses faster than light.
I ride fire breathing dragons through the night.
I fight like a pride of lions protecting my friends.
And sooner or later my journey comes to an end.

Colton Carpenter, Grade 4

Coffee

The coffee grounds black as pitch
Are filled with an ebony charcoal
The cream and sugar plunge in majestically
The concoction swerves to brown velvet
In a few ticks of the clock
The coffee
Magically
Dematerializes

Supraja Sudarsan, Grade 5

Possibility

I am surrounded by love
I am lovable

I am surrounded by joy
I am joyful

I am surrounded by fear
I am fearful

I am surrounded by beauty
I am beautiful

I am surrounded by care
I am caring

I am surrounded by passion
I am passionate

I am surrounded by knowledge
I am knowledgeable

I am surrounded by possibilities
I learn anything and everything is possible

I know that I am everything possible
Kendall Abruzzese, Grade 6

It's About My Disney Cruise

It's about a week of dessert
Ice cream falling
Drinks calling

It's about being with family
Aunts, uncles,
Kids and grownups

It's about fun and joy
Waterslides when night falls
Ping Pong and basketball

It's about Disney characters
Minnie and Mickey
Donald and Daisy

It's about being on the sea
water flying
you sighing

It's about Disney movies
The one and only Cinderella
Mary Poppins and her umbrella

It's about my favorite vacation ever!
Madeleine Day, Grade 5

My Dog Brownie

My dog stays quiet in his dog house
He waits for his dry crunchy food
When he gets up he sees a mouse
But he is stuck like he is glued

When we play he always barks
We have to keep him on a leash
When he scratches us he leaves a mark
He loves when he gets unleashed

When we put him up he whines
He has a roof over his head
After words he seems to shine
He has a very small but soft bed

I love my dog Brownie very much
When I pet him, he is soft to touch
LeAnna Carithers, Grade 5

The World's Lovelist Cat

Meow, meow says my shiny cat
Glistening in the moonlight
No one even dares to tell him scat
On how he is a beautiful sight

Oh this cat is such a beaut'
He is so quiet as he will roam
It seems as if someone put him on mute
He will roam till at last he arrives home

I wonder if he likes to be alone?
That's okay because I do too
But I just wish his face was shone
At least that is what I want him to do

On how my cat is so beautiful
And as he walks, he is so graceful
Kennedy Mills, Grade 5

Mom

My mom is very pretty
She once brought home a kitty
I will always love her!

She always keeps me happy —
When I am very snappy.
I will always love her.

She always makes me smile
When I haven't in a while
I will always love her!

Sometimes when she's gone
She will always call at dawn
I will always love her!
Austyn Sofo, Grade 5

Jeremiah Gilbert-Eldridge

I was feeling sad
Laying down on my bed
Keep my feelings away
Crying almost every day
Put my feelings in a safe
I looking some type of way
Thought I was dead pretty much every day
Please just listen to what I'm try'na say
They was running their mouth
Every single day
But that stops today
Can't take no more
They slammed me against the door
Saying that I was poor.
Jeremiah Gilbert-Eldridge, Grade 6

Fall

As the leaves fall off the tree,
slowly as could be.

While the air gets colder,
and the trees grow older.

Chimney smoke throughout the air,
as it slowly spreads a glare.

Children in bed trying to sleep,
while not hearing even a single peep.

You can hear the wind rushing by,
with the beautiful night sky.
Kristin Russell, Grade 6

The Night of the Storm

It was a dark and stormy night.
I stared out of my window,
To watch big luminous clouds.
Thunder erupted from them,
To strike the wet, musky ground.
The air felt cool upon my face,
The moon shone brightly in the sky.
A tree almost came up,
From its wet, muddy grave.
A tornado came up from the ground,
A gale so strong and harsh.
It tore up the puffy clouds,
And turned the sky dark...
Ethan Beggs, Grade 6

Lonely, Little, Left Out Duck

There once was a small rubber duck
Who's owners bought him for a buck
He was put away
Until one fine day
He was brought out to his great luck
Adrianna Scafiro, Grade 6

I Am

I am from Buddy, the big blue teddy bear
From Legos and my old blanket
I am from big living room/big open
I am from the tree I climb on as a monkey
The tree was wide, big and fun
I am from Nanny's house for Christmas
From Nanny and Uncle Gary and the Christmas tree
I am from the dad who is a hunter
From the mom who is a coffee drinker
From let me rephrase that and get'r done
I am from kindness, honesty, being nice to people
From not lying to people
I am from Lancaster, PA, turkey and pizza
From the mom's dad who died in a plane crash
Old blue teddy bear, old blanket and Nike Jordans
From the Nike outlet
I am from Black Ops 2

Joseph Morgan Kirchgessner, Grade 6

Eyes

Eyes you help me to see
And sit on my face so beautifully

You look like the pretty blue sky
And just make me want to fly

You tear when I'm sad
And bulge wide when I'm glad

You blink so softly in the silent night
And even when you're hurt, you always put up a fight

Eyes, oh eyes you are my favorite body part
You are like a piece of art

Oh I just love my eyes
Like everyone loves pies

Rachel Chillemi, Grade 6

Orange

Scream, scream, it's Halloween,
Get great treats, or find great ticks.
Caution as you walk out, orange lurks about.

The jack o' lantern stares at you,
Its flickering eyes watching, waiting for your wrong move.
Take cover! The headless horseman is coming.

You are not scared, for great rewards come from great risks.
You clash against the man,
He strikes back,
As quick as a flash, you blow out the candle in the pumpkin head.
He drops dead.

The horse explodes into candy and oranges,
At last orange has given joy to the world,
With great risks, has come great reward.

Daniel Wang, Grade 6

What's in the Ocean?

Dolphin pods swimming and playing gleefully
By beds of coral and schools of fish,
Sharks lurking in the blue waters stalking their next meal,
Crabs skittering on the ocean floor pinching the water
With those big claws of theirs.
Deep below the ocean's surface unknown monster fish
Awaiting to be found,
Long strings of seaweed waving around as schools of fish storm past.
Rocks, thrown around, landing with a thud,
Layers and layers of salt building up the ocean floor,
Humpback whales singing their beautiful songs,
Oysters, the guardians of the glistening pearl, sitting on the
Golden sand,
Sea lions gliding swiftly and gracefully through the water
Darting around, full of joy.
Now at the end of the day, all the ocean creatures and critters
Turning home, awaiting another day.

Kira Dunn, Grade 6

Blossoms in the Moonlight

The blossom tree stands by itself in the moonlight
Nothing else but voluminous hills, birds, and lakes
Gentle breezes blow by, swaying branches
Pink blossoms have been blown away
Floating in the dark blue sky, in the moonlight
Many feral birds start flying with them
Starting to shroud the blossom tree, taking flowers
Making an array of blossoms in their nests
Now doing a poise in their nests, boasting
Wily they are, using the pretty flowers
Other blossoms, now near the lake
The gentle breeze, finally leaving, settled them there
Drifting down northeast in the water
The village at the end, it has a surprise
As the repercussion of it was not so well

Michelle Liang, Grade 6

A Lonely Valentine

Crying her eyes out on this sad, depressing day,
for the one she had loved, has drifted away.
The voluminous sorrow that she feels inside,
as she sees him loving someone else on Valentine's.
Her life was deranged,
her only true love treated her like a stranger.
She shrouds her face when he walks by,
trying so hard not to cry.
She is a wellspring of anger and sadness,
as she couldn't repress it or feel any happiness.
Her love had left her without a goodbye,
not even giving her a reason why.
So, she sat down,
crying her eyes out on this sad, depressing day,
for the one she STILL loves, has drifted away.

Elaine Droxler, Grade 6

Kindness

Kindness is like God.
It is always there for you.
It smells like warm cookies.
It tastes like victory.
It sounds like laughing.
It feels like warm water.
It lives when we're nice.
Brandon Schwartz, Grade 6

Summer and Winter

hot,
blazing, sunny,
swimming, fishing, playing
vacation, barbecue, hot cocoa, Christmas,
skating, snowing, sledding,
cold, freezing,
ice.
Noe Salazar, Grade 5

To a Marvelous Place!

As I stroll down the woody walk,
The sun burns it up.
Sea and sand as far as I can see.
Gulls in the air,
The wind in my hair.
As I make my journey,
To a marvelous place!
Caroline Rickard, Grade 6

A Friend Is…

A friend is helpful.
A friend is nice to you.
A friend is friendly.
A friend is believing in you.
A friend is giving you luck.
A friend is like a $1,000.00 bill.
A friend is Ben, Tom, Aidan and T.J.!
Donald Blanco, Grade 4

A Peaceful Day

The sun setting above the beach,
Water rushing back and forth.
Sailboats waiting,
Wind puffing.
A lonely bucket missing its owner,
Plants drinking from the salty waters.
What a peaceful day!
Ariel Pogorzelski, Grade 6

God

Our Heavenly Father —
He is always with us.
In all times, good and bad
To show us the right path in life
Undying love and forgiveness.
Ty Taylor, Grade 5

Broken Beyond Repair

I was the most beautiful piece of China in the drawer,
Covered in light pink and purple fuchsia flowers with paisley designs,
Covered in petals that overlapped and underlapped,
And pollen so detailed you could almost smell it.
I was always clean and shiny,
For I was daily cleaned and polished,
Sitting on my throne while all of the other China collected dust.

But I fell to the floor,
And with a single bang, I cracked into a million bits.
The pieces of me were swept up and thrown out,
Just like the leftover food from earlier that day.
As if I was never their prized possession,
Like all of it never happened,
Like the good times never existed,
Like I was always in the trash can.

I can never go back to the good old days,
When I was so admired and cared for.
Once as beautiful as all of the cosmos combined,
As worthless as a losing lottery ticket,
I will always be a Humpty Dumpty,
Broken beyond repair.

Julia Manolios, Grade 5

Where I'm From

I am from my mom telling me to erase any bad things from the past
From exotic tuxedo clad birds swimming into my dreams
From my sister's feelings woven into her gorgeous artwork
I am from the delicious scent that reaches my nostrils
As my mother cooks her tasty chicken

I am from the weekly stench of horse poop and the thrill of taking
off the ground with my equine friend
I am from Beatles and Buddy Holly posters littering my bedroom
From books flooding my room
From my family, who bring me a sense of security and love

I am from teleporting into the past, present, and future
From the lines of a single book
I am from the magical realm of triangular hats and
Spells waiting to be unearthed by the flick of a wand
From the pounding hoof beats of my four legged companion as we canter across the stars

I am from brushes awaiting my brothers command as
He transforms a plain white shoe into a masterpiece from the soft, sponge like texture of clay
Moments away from being sculpted into the secrets locked away in my mind
I am from talk of bees grazing on freshly mowed grass
From a mystical world where tripods grow on pinecone trees
Elizabeth Sokolova, Grade 5

The Beach

The sand roasts my feet
The water glistens like diamonds
The sun scorched my skin

Benjamin Frady, Grade 6

Trip Around the World

My trip around the world
Started out so great
But I'm very sad to say
I had an unfortunate fate

Mean old Lady Liberty
That's where it all began
When I fell right out
Of her nasty copper hand

I traveled to the Eiffel Tower
Hoping for a change
But I fell right of the balcony
I suppose it's nothing strange

I went to see Big Ben
"TICK-TOCK, TICK-TOCK"
That's now all I can hear
Since I got stuck on the clock

Now I'm in the hospital
Feeling quite depressed
(I just found out my medical bill)
And now I'm very stressed!!!
Autumn Beard, Grade 5

Thanksgiving

The Autumn leaves are falling
Thanksgiving must come soon,
   The final Thursday of this month,
We'll feast on heavenly foods.

   The day is now approaching,
Filling up our dreams,
   We must rehearse our prayers,
Until they're said with ease.

   The turkey has arrived
With only days to spare,
   Our house within is such a rush,
Where to look, where must I stare?

   The smell has risen far away
From where all is prepared
   Scents meander through the house
The meal we will have shared

   The time we've been awaiting
Families to gather 'round
   Peace and love upon the table
No peep, nor slightest sound.
Étienne Strandberg-Houzé, Grade 5

Smiles Are Never-Ending Rainbows

Smiles are never-ending rainbows,
that are filled with joy.

Smiles are rainbows,
that can be mixed with tears.

Smiles are rainbows,
that can hide regret.

Smiles are rainbows,
that anyone can have.

Smiles are rainbows,
that can show true love.

Smiles are rainbows,
that show passion

Smiles are never-ending rainbows,
that are filled with joy.
John Hatch, Grade 6

I Am

I am a football player
I wonder if I am going to get tackled
I hear a whistle on the football field
I see a football
I want to win the game
I am a football player

I pretend to play zombies
I feel a tackle
I touch a football
I worry if we are going to win the game
I cried when I broke my leg
I am a football player

I understand if we lose
I say it is okay if we lose
I dream to be in the NFL
I try my best
I hope to win
I am a football player
Rob Lyons, Grade 6

Mom

Mom is such a special word.
The loveliest I've ever heard.
A toast to you,
Above all the rest.
You're so special,
You are the best.
I love your cooking,
And also you.
And I know you love me too.
Shamaia Robinson, Grade 6

Stag

You, stand tall,
You, stand strong,
You, are brave,
You, are a stag.

You, gallop past me,
faster than the speed of light.
You, can do anything,
You, are a stag.

You, see the enemy,
You, do not back away,
You, stay calm,
You, are a stag.

I, stand tall,
I, stand strong,
I, am brave,
I, (am a stag).

I, see the enemy,
I, do not back away,
I, stay calm,
I, (am a stag).
Kevin Kurti, Grade 5

The Beauty of Optimism

I watch the slaves tend to the farm,
   my father forces them.
But they don't care how hot it is,
   or ravel of their hem.

They work and work and never stop,
   sweat running down their face.
But they just keep on working hard,
   and keep a steady pace.

When they are finally all done,
   they come inside to eat.
They're given inedible slop,
   with grits white as a sheet.

The slaves are always worshipping,
   hoping for better lives.
They try to be optimistic,
   but pain cuts deep as knives.

I hope my father knows he's wrong,
   and sets those poor slaves free.
They deserve a better life,
   but they know hope is key.
Kendall Simmons, Grade 6

House of Pain

House of pain
no one knows
what happens
behind this door.
House of pain prepare
for what's behind this
door. House of pain once
you enter you can't ignore. House
of pain I don't think you
should shut the door. House
of pain he'll be
right there at
the door. House of
pain you better run while
you can. House of pain
time's up it's too late.
House of pain
I wish you
the best of luck
House of pain
RIP is just enough
Rah'Tia Wheat, Grade 6

Leaves

Leaves falling and tumbling off the trees,
Down the hills
Swept up into a pile with other debris
The wind spills
Brand new coats
With two long sleeves,
Running and jumping
In the leaves
Laughing and playing
Singing songs
The leaves blowing about
And joining along
Children shouting
And getting rowdy,
The day turns cold
Becoming cloudy
Before long
It's dark and raining
"Come inside, no complaining!"
The end of another fall day
The truck comes to sweep the leaves away.
Freya Anderson, Grade 6

Sports Are Fun for Everyone

Basketball, baseball, and football too;
They will all fit you.
So pick one good and pick one fun;
You can even pick to run.
Join a team; it will be awesome,
And the last thing is
There's many sports to pick from.
James Civitano, Grade 4

Baseball Blues

Missing the third strike I sing the blues
The guiltiness is kicking in
Walking off the field I sing the blues
Oh it would be nice to win
Taking off my batting gloves and helmet
They say, "Good job!" but I just grin

My hands sing the blues
Blisters hurt so bad
My hands sing the blues
All I am is just plain old mad
I can't explain the pain
It makes me so sad

My feet sing the blues
From standing so long
Oh my feet sing the blues
Was my stance wrong
I just don't get it
I felt so strong
And I'll keep singing the blues
Until I get a hit
Ryan Perry, Grade 4

Remember

I remember time long ago,
When I played time stopped,
I was always ready to go,
Whenever I was happy, I did a little hop,

That time still lives on,
Though it has not been long,
That time still lives on.

In me, in you,
That time still lives on.
We've all changed,
Over the years — very,
Time changes,
Loved ones lost,
Not love.

Legacies made,
Promises kept,
Days going by without a thought.

That time still lives on
Alison Samudio, Grade 6

My Puppy, Jax

My puppy is funnier than a clown
he feels like silk
he sounds like a pig
he smells like a dog
I love him with all my heart and soul.
Brennan Stallings, Grade 4

Nature

Tree, please stand tall
And give off shade for me
Flower, grow strong and proud
And have nothing to fear
Mountain, let the sun glisten
Over your rocky hills
Sea, wash along our memories of the past
Snow, sparkle through the ups
And downs of life
Moon, shine on the present
Clouds, lead us to our future
Sun, give us laughter
And life

And together we can make this world
A better place
For you and me
Sierra Wilcox, Grade 4

Love Is a Raging River

Love is like a raging river
Always changing direction

Love is sometimes nasty
like a really bad infection

Love isn't always true
but if it isn't, it is when you say I do!

Love is really special
and heartwarming a sight to see

Sometimes love stings like
a tiny angry bee.

Love is like a raging river
always changing direction
Scottie Johnson, Grade 6

Survive

A little boat
washes ashore
broken and tattered
the deserted island, dark,
how will I survive
create a fire
find young coconuts
make a shelter
signal a plane
those were all
the thoughts that
ran through my
head as my
little broken down boat
floated ashore.
Caroline Harper, Grade 6

Our Trip to Cozumel

On a clear sunny morning our white cruise ship slowly glided on the blue waters and docked in Cozumel.
Everyone briskly walked with excitement down the ramp to find their tour bus.
Anxious to explore the culture of the Mexicans the tourists boarded their buses with no fuss.
The talkative and endearing tour guide named Maria explained the history and customs of Cozumel in her broken English
including why the Mexican flag was red, white and green.
We rode in the noisy bus to a cultural center on the Island where we ate chicken tamales so fresh they smelled like wheat.
Most of the tourists in our group bought T-shirts and other souvenirs but for my friend I bought a sweet treat.
After a few hours we boarded the noisy bus and returned to our ship — boy was my trip worth the money.

David Penaylillo, Grade 6

Siblings

When I broke my wrist, I depended on Jose.
When I was scared of the dark, my brother would read me a story.
When I would give up, Jose would keep cheering me on.
When my brother broke his elbow, he depended on me.
When he needed help, he would call me.
When he would be sad, I would cheer him up.
We would change each other's worlds.
That's until things changed. We got a new brother and sister that depended on us as older siblings.

Flora Reducindo, Grade 6

Thanksgiving

The turkey goes in the oven and mashed potatoes are being stirred,
the table is set and candles are lit with light
The oven beeps and leaves crinkle while we run inside to take the potatoes out
Turkey melts in my mouth and cake is so sweet and luscious
Grandma's hug feels full of love as she walks through the door with a fluffy blanket all for me
Sweet potatoes with marshmallows come out with a great scent of sweetness once they are served
Have a great Thanksgiving!

Samantha Deyo, Grade 4

To Learn Your Loved One Is Lost

I think of before this war, when your happy heart would soar.
But think how much it must cost, to learn your loved one is lost.
Then you received the letter one day, which broke your heart and swept the pieces away.
But think how much it must cost, to learn your loved one is lost.
And now you just sit and watch the waves get tossed.
But think how much it must cost, to learn your loved one is lost.
And now, too easy to accost, you can say only: But think how much it must cost, to learn your loved one is lost.

Isabel Wallacavage, Grade 6

Fall Is Upon Us

As the tree prepares for winter he says goodbye to his friends the leaves. With the wind blowing the tree always feels a swish of gust.
He almost feels like he was swept away by a tornado. He always looks at the children jumping in a big pile of leaves as if they were
on a trampoline for the first time. He wants to jump with them, but he can't because trees aren't humans. With the harsh cold on
it's way, the tree always sees workers getting their plow trucks ready for another cold season. Every time the tree gets hit by wind he
feels like ocean waves are taking him to a nearby island. Most of all, the tree knows it's time to hibernate. One time each year he
opens up his eyes in the fall to see people putting up Christmas decorations and the first thing that comes to his mind is children
opening up their presents on Christmas day.

Trenten DeSchuiteneer, Grade 5

Megalania

He is a fascinating ancient learner.
He is as smart as a dictionary in a super computer.
He likes reading encyclopedia books; loves to learn new things, and experiencing what life has to offer.

Kristopher Gil, Grade 6

I Apologize

Please give me a chance to explain
There must be something wrong with my brain
I'm really sorry, I truly care
What I did was completely unfair
Just don't know what I was thinking
With all this shame, I feel like sinking
I know you're very, very mad
What I did was super bad
I did not mean the words I said
Don't know what got in my head
Please forgive me, on my knees
Please forgive me, oh please, oh please

Wendy Torres Barahona, Grade 6

Where I'm From

I am from ice cream and dirt bikes and dune buggies.
I am from video games and hot, hot days.
I am from the wooded brush and the prickers next to my house.

I am from opening presents under the Christmas tree
I am from Greek blood.
I am from Avanti's Pizza and More.
I am from awesomeness and Transformers.

I am from mosquito bites to poison ivy.
I am from turkey on Thanksgiving,
I am from my awesome and kind family.

Christos Tsiakiris, Grade 5

Dino, My Dog

Dino
Barker, eater, walker
Who belongs to Lucia
Who loves to eat and bark
Who feels lonely when everybody leaves home,
Excited, and strange around people he doesn't know
Who fears doors when people knock, getting hit, and loud noises
Who has accomplished being a great family member
Who feeds on what his family gives him
Who lives in a bed and chair
Who belongs to the class of mammals
Canis Familiaris

Isaac Herrera, Grade 6

Legos

I was made to be fun
And can easily be undone
Build me up high
Until I touch the sky
Red, yellow, green and blue
Some pieces are old, while some are brand new.
Here are some things to build if able ...
A shop, a house, a smile, a stable.
I hope you've had a nice time!
Now, come on over and build something fine!

Clara Mae Scott, Grade 5

Majestic Matthews Road

My neighborhood is like a race track
with all of the speeding cars that
instantaneously bolt down the busy
Matthews Road.

My neighborhood at night is so starry,
when I am observing the constellations, I
feel like I am up there in the immense solar system.

My neighborhood is filled with a plethora
of chirping blue jays whistling their beautiful songs.

And it is the sound of the whistle on the
soccer field that makes me feel amazing inside.

And at night it is the sound of the
whistling a car makes when it drives by.

Grayson Hill, Grade 6

Green

I bounce and bring joy
To every girl and boy
Although I am just a cover
I sway gracefully among others
The epitome of nature is obviously me
And sometimes I whisper to you with a breeze
While other times I wish to be you
I sit on many trees
But become envious with ease
I have an omnipresent disease
Once the weeds attack
You wouldn't dare come back
I will sicken you with my contamination
You won't want to have a celebration
The disgust, the envy, the hatred
I'm not so mellow
Once you mix the blue and yellow

Emma Pribanic, Grade 6

Nothing

I sit there
Ready to write
I have an idea in mind
But when I pick up my pencil
It all disappears, all my thoughts
I had them, then I lost them
Like they weren't even there in the first place
And my mind has nothing to give
Just like my paper
Thoughts racing through my head about what I'm going to write
And what my teacher will say when I show up to school tomorrow
With a blank sheet of paper
All I can hear is the clock ticking as if it's trying to intimidate me
I try to think harder
Nothing

Lindsey Healey, Grade 4

When I Am…

When I am weary, I am as moody as a student
who got a 52 on their math test

When I am gloomy, I am like a lonely cow,
left behind on the mundane farm

When I am irked, I am as frustrated as a soccer player,
who hasn't scored a goal in weeks

When I am ecstatic, I am like a teacher waiting for
their new students to arrive on the first day of school

When I am creative, I am as famished for new ideas
as a dog waiting for food after a long day

When I am adventurous, I am like a cruise ship
sailing around the whole world

Melissa Giordano, Grade 6

The Oak Tree

A great oak tree stands there so broad and tall
With leaf colors of orange and yellow
In the enchantment of beautiful fall
The bright colors are brilliant and mellow

The great oak tree's leaves are so full and bold
The breeze starts to pull on their lively leaves
As the air gets more frigid, chilled, and cold
The vivid tree looses its leafy sleeves

The colorful tree is now dull and brown
As snow starts to land on the tree's brown bark
The tree's leaves are now on the snowy ground
As the day slowly turns to frigid dusk

As the days get warmer and more lively
The oak tree's grow back green and brightly

Olivia Cothran, Grade 5

Winter's Dream

As the feathers start to grow and the leaves start to fall,
autumn is here, and ready to leave.
Soon winter can come right on in.
Winter will zooooom as fast as it can to be there on time,
fall is now dying while it lasts soon it will be all but sand,
as the cold weather starts rolling in.
The trees old leaves start flying off into the distance
as the wind catches them like the firemen's trampoline.
Off the leaves go into the distance as the tree looks and says,
"I wish them good luck" as they can start a new life.
As the weather gets colder and colder,
the tree starts to get sleepy and starts getting sleepier and sleepier
and ends so sleepy that's when it finally happened.
It's in its final leap stage THE DEEP SLEEP and when it wakes,
it starts all over again.

Alex Vansen, Grade 5

Sweet Silver Bells

I see the sweet bells swing
I hear their music ring
Within every shake they become louder
They make me think of sweet dew on a flower
Their music lathers you with joy
In Christmas they sing, "Little Drummer Boy"
Ring-a-ling-ling
Such sweet music they bring
Ding-ding-ding
Christmas songs they sing
Carolers use them to complete a song
With sweet, silver bells, you could never go wrong

Ella Richmond, Grade 5

Free Topic Dilemmas

Hmmm…What to write about?

I could write about water, earth, even soil,
Or the about the milk that's about to spoil.
Dragons, gorgons, gods galore,
Rainbows, cupcakes, what's some more?
Witches, wardrobes, lions so fierce,
With claws like steel just ready to pierce.
Mummies, zombies, 3-headed dogs,
Harry Potter and chocolate frogs.
What's more interesting is that I'm almost done,
Wow, that was easy and kind of fun!!!

Anna Liu, Grade 6

My Eyes

Eyes, I'll always use them.
When I rise,
At the break of dawn
I'll open them as I yawn.
My eyes,
I use them to see,
The sky and the trees
Beautiful sunsets and the ocean breeze.
Eyes for seeing my friends and family,
For finding the hoop in basketball
Making the shot, looking at the rim
I have got great eyes and I'm thankful for that.

Victoria Grisanti, Grade 6

Basketball

B ringing the ball down the court
A shot into a hoop will get you points
S creaming from the fans gets the players pumped up
K illing the other team by a lot
E xcitement from the crowd
T ingling feeling in the player's stomach
B all goes up for a shot
A nnoyed if the other team wins
L ots and lots of sweat drips down the players
L ots and lots of pressure if the game is close

Kole Giberson, Grade 5

Kiss of Heaven

A kiss of heaven is like
falling into a bed of roses.

A kiss of heaven is an angel
singing gloria.

A kiss of heaven is snow
falling softly on the ground.

A kiss of heaven is a sweet
sugarplum.

A kiss of heaven is a soft
feather pillow.

A kiss of heaven is warm
hot cocoa in the winter.

A kiss of heaven is a joyful
sun dancing around.
Rylee Manville, Grade 6

The Perplexing Maze

All lost in a treacherous maze
Trying to find my home
I flip, twist, and turn
    Only
      To
        Fall
          Again
           To hard
        Ground
      And agonizing
    Defeat
But I come up again
To continue my journey
The flips, twists, and turns
Lead me to my
Tiny, cramped, but cozy igloo
You have lead me home
Now is the time
For the
Next level.
Leah Bernstein, Grade 5

My Mom

I love my mom,
   as hard as a rock.
She is sweet as a mango.
She goes to hug and hug me so hard.
I love with all my heart.
She's short as a mouse,
   that bounces around.
She's like a butterfly,
   that flies away with the wind.
Kevin Perez, Grade 6

My Hair

My hair is curly, spunky, and thick
My hair is not easy to tame
But not all hair is the same
But my hair is my hair

You may say my hair is crazy and wild
And my hair is different and cool
And gets a little less curly in the pool
But my hair is my hair

I'm not scared to show it off
Or twirl it in the rain
Or even play with it all day
Even when I'm on a train

When I wake up my hair is a nest
I have to brush it all day
And sometimes I want to give it a rest
But we all know my hair is my hair
Julianne Pulizzi, Grade 6

Hunting

I am a hunter
I wonder if a deer is coming
I hear the leaves crackling under my feet
I see a rock out in the middle of the field
I want to shoot

I pretend to shoot a deer
I feel a big tree rubbing on my back
I touch my gun on my lap
I worry if there is a game warden coming
I cry if there is a game warden
I am a hunter

I understand it is hard to get a deer
I say it is fun to see a deer
I dream to shoot a deer
I try not to spook a deer
I hope a deer comes
I am a hunter

Gaven Hale, Grade 6

Me

Sarah
I am foolish, positive, crazy, brave
My family is clumsy, annoying, fun, loving
I love the outdoors
I need food
I give love
I fear my brother
I would like to be a game warden
I like to visit my family
I wonder what the future will be like
Bernardini
Sarah Bernardini, Grade 6

White

Like the feathers of a dove
Complete and pristine
Heading into the distant sky
As they offer comfort and hope

Like the girl that watched them
Distant and isolated
Laying in the hospital room
As death lured her in

Like the boy that stood at her funeral
Formerly innocent and perfect
His slate no longer clean
As his mistake caused a life

Like the judge that stood at court
Plain and neutral
Serving justice all over
As she gave him a new beginning

Like the doves circling back once more
United and pure
Spreading the color on the blank canvas
As they all faded into white
Sophie Chen, Grade 6

My Legs

Oh, my legs,
What fun!
Without my legs,
I wouldn't be able to run!

Oh, my legs,
I use them for sports.
They can be good,
For all kinds of sorts.

Oh, my legs,
I jump for joy!
These are not
Just any toy.

Oh, my legs,
I use them for soccer,
With my legs,
I'm a goal-scoring rocker!

So, be thankful for your legs,
They are always there.
Your legs are great,
They take you everywhere!
Mara Voloder, Grade 6

The Falling Leaves

Leaves from high above,
Colorful and majestic,
Floating in the wind,
Landing on the ground below,
Crunching like a crisp apple.
Abbey Chan, Grade 6

Soft White Clouds

Majestic white clouds,
Entering through the sunlight,
Running through the sky,
Whispering to each other,
A giant field of white clouds.
Danny Lee, Grade 6

Love

There once was a girl named Kim,
Who was madly in love with Tim,
But Tim was a jerk,
And then Kim met Kirk,
And that was the end of Tim.
Abigail Camacho, Grade 5

Icing

Icing
Delicious, sweet
Tasting, smiling, licking
Brilliant colors on my lips!
Frosting
Ayla Bloemker, Grade 4

Icee

Icee
Cold, slushy
Make, slurp, eat
Fun to drink blue ice
Juicee
Armaghaan Hasan, Grade 4

Cotton Candy

Cotton Candy
Turquoise, soft
Fluffy, tasting, melting
Cait and I love it!
Sweet Cloud
Isabelle Sears, Grade 4

Football

Football
Fun, hard
Running, catching, throwing
Love to play with family
My Team
James Durham, Grade 4

The Radio

The radio has been turned on
I forgot anything I'd ever known, just to feel the rhythm

But what if the radio shut off, never to be heard again
The thought makes me shudder

Sitting in utter silence, nothing to drown your thoughts in
Until you remember everything you forgot,
After you turned on that radio

Thoughts come crashing down, like a million pounds of rocks
You can't lift them back up,
You can only hopelessly fall down

What if the world shut down, what if we get stuck in the darkness
What if the radio doesn't turn back on

There are no distractions to hide reality, we cannot hide away
We have to face what is happening, like you must face your thoughts
Who knew that thoughts could be so dangerous

Your hands go numb, a sheet of white spreads across your face
You can't breathe, the air is too thick,
You can't turn away from what you're thinking

Luckily, the radio turns on and the thoughts that you had to bear
Completely clear out of your mind, until you finally settle into bed
With your thoughts
Caileigh Sexton, Grade 6

The Image of Me

I am from flutes whose sound is calming,
Where music fills the empty air, and peaceful melodies calm
The dark harmonies.

I am from friends and family gathering on cold winter nights,
Decorating the tree with jolly ornaments, a wonderful
Brownie aroma fills the house.

I am from a lake where the wind blows silently, where the
Water tickles my toes when I jump in, friends get together
And suddenly it's a family gathering.

I am from Poland where you will find green luscious hills
Great sunsets, wondrous fields with majestic
Sheep dogs, and Grandma's homemade recipes, delicious.

I am from volleyball, when the ball swooshes over the net
Everything feels amazing, sweat on my forehead
Showing I'm working hard. When I spike that ball, it shows my power.

I am from swimming, where exhaustion is the gift of making
First place, I strive for that goal. Trophies are
Given for this joyful occasion, but knowing I did my best is the
Real reward.
Autumn Waks, Grade 6

Whiskers the Cat

He scratches up your face,
He takes up all your space.
He sleeps in the hamper,
And he has a little temper.
If you make him snappy,
He will not be happy.
Do not give him a bath,
Or else you will feel his wrath.
And nobody knows,
That he bites all your toes.
And when he jumps,
It makes a big Thump.
Even though he is as black as a bat,
He is still my cat.
Zachary Johnson, Grade 5

Fishing

I really love to catch some fish,
You can cook and eat them as a dish.
If you join a fishing team,
You must be careful it can be extreme.
If you throw a rod and reel,
It can be a tremendous thrill.
If you go out on a boat,
Cut the engine and just float.
On the end of the line there's a hook,
Be careful to not overlook.
With a rod comes a line,
And it can be tangled fine.
You need to use the right fish bait,
So your catch will be just great!
Palmer Parrish, Grade 5

Books

Reading books get me over the humps,
My favorite though is all the Goosebumps.
I really like all the scary parts,
Most stories have a really good start.
Zap! Good books are everywhere,
I bought them from the store cashier.
I read some books about the atmosphere
I even read books to calm my fears,
I sometimes read books about new ideas.
Reading should just be my career,
I read books about pioneers.
Some books are full of tremendous tales,
Stories I read are never stale,
You can find some cheap at rummage sales.
Gavin Darity, Grade 5

Fishing Day

I threw out the line,
I waited for a fish to bite,
Nothing happened so I reeled it back in,
Then I threw out my line and tried again.
Jerrah Cantrell, Grade 6

Life Is an Open Door

Life is an open door,
Ancient like dinosaur bones,
Full of possibilities,
Made of the unknown.
You make the choice
To enter and find out more,
And when you do you have yet to seek
The vast beauty beyond this door.
It's a world of your own,
You do what you please.
You have your own rules,
Follow them with ease.
Befriend the people,
Make what you choose,
But this is your own room,
Which you'll never lose.
Caroline Musson, Grade 6

Fluffy

I played with Fluffy.
I walked Fluffy.
I talked to Fluffy.
I snuggled him while
Watching movies every
Saturday night.

I slept with Fluffy.
I bathed Fluffy.
I ate with Fluffy.
That is — until my dog Gerald
Ate him by mistake.

But Fluffy the carrot will
Always have a special place
In my heart.
Sam Leibowitz, Grade 5

Fall

I love when the leaves
Down
  Down
    Down to the ground and
They have huge pumpkins this year.
I can't wait for my mom to bake tasty
Apple pie and pumpkin pie.
I asked my mom,
"Is the pumpkin and apple pie ready yet?"
My mom said, "No,
It will be done in 5 minutes."
While waiting, my mom made me
Delicious, yummy hot chocolate.
But when the hot chocolate was ready,
So was the pumpkin pie and apple pie.
This is the best fall ever!!!
Kayla Andreacci, Grade 4

My Dad

I love my dad,
  he loves me.
He's not that bad,
  and he likes to spend time with me.

We love to hunt together,
  we go every Saturday.
But not in bad weather.

He works a lot,
  he works at a hotel.
He loves his job,
  and he's doing well.

I love my dad,
  he loves me.
He's not that bad,
  he spends time with me.
Brandon Moss, Grade 6

For When the Raven Speaks

For when the Raven Speaks —
The fire in the air
Distorts itself past the burn,
The strike of lonely cinders,
Falling past the ashes

For when the Snow Whispers —
A hush amongst the land
The chorus of crickets echoes
Across the white garments
Of lively silence

For when the Tiger Stands —
Regal brilliance shows
The creatures of the forest know
Traverse river, lake, or stream
You'll find no revenge, no wars alone
Just nature's pristine peak.
Madeleine Russell, Grade 6

My Life Is a Tornado

My life is a tornado
Always in motion
My life is a tornado
Busy and fast
A never-ending tornado
Swirling, swirling
My life is a tornado
An unstoppable wind
Trying to find a single friend
My life is a tornado
All over the place
My life is a tornado
Not a disgrace
Luke Whelan, Grade 6

One Night
One night
Silent night
One man still stands awake in the darkness
He is unclear from my window
He isn't making a sound

He walks into someone's house
Slowly, quietly
With a sack swung over his shoulder
That's all I could see from my window

He gets closer and closer
Now he is not there
I hear creaks from the roof
Now I don't see anything from my window

I hear shuffling by the Christmas tree
I see a man outside the
He gets into something
He starts drifting off into the darkness
He yells, "Ho, Ho, Ho Merry Christmas to all and to all a good night."

One night
Silent
I met Santa
Madeline Cohen, Grade 6

Jubjub Wolf*
It was raining full of death the acid rain and the fear trees
People were crying nightmares came to life it was mad
Life was ending right before your eyes people were asking please
Weeping angels killed people just by people blinking it was sad.

Beware the Jubjub wolf my good man
The eyes flaming purple and razor teeth and razor claws
Beware the jabber pig and step away from the 10 eyed fan
And the machine with spiky paws.

And as he thought he stood by the Jubjub wolf
With eyes of death came leaping over the tree of death
And howled as it came near the rolf
that died because it was a meath.

Banana potato! Banana potato! And off with your head
And with the blade slice slice he left it dead with blood
And with its body and head he left the head that was red
The Jubjub wolf was slain he was proud with mlood.

You did you slain the Jubjub wolf how brave of you
Come to my arms my brave little boy, O what joy
Hooray hooray for this little young boy callay callooh
For you and we will celebrate the day for great little Roy.
Adnan Mouzahem, Grade 5
*Inspired by Lewis Carroll

The Dazzling Hamlet of Bohemia
My neighborhood is a place where the
bees are buzzing as they drift through the
glistening tulip gardens.

My neighborhood is the library on a
gorgeous Sunday afternoon, after a
steaming cup of hot tea.

My neighborhood is like the Christmas
tree on New Year's Eve in its leafy green apparel.

And it is the only street that must listen
to the fire houses many oaf alarms crackling

And it is the splendid village that I can
call my home.
Jessica Hendricks-Donato, Grade 6

Where I'm From
I'm from crazy siblings older and young
From the pool I was taught to swim in and I still do today
From the netting on the soccer net to the footprint on the ball
From the climbing tree I grew up climbing
From the raspberry bush growing every year

From the play house growing old today
From the pets that I have to this day
I'm from the snowball fights that never go well
I'm from the stories I create
I'm from the smell of the pine trees
I'm from the cow jumping over the moon
From the stands at the soccer game to playing my own games
I'm from the books that inspire me to write
I'm the language my family made up (Sprench)
That's where I'm from.
Connor Hultgren, Grade 5

A Day at the Beach
A tropical breeze blows through the palms,
The bright shining sun shimmers on the sea,
It lures me to the shore.

My toes touch the sand,
I dash through the hot powdery grains,
The sand soothes my toes.

The rippling waves rush to my feet,
Fish dart through the water like shooting stars,
They swim around my legs and tickle me.

I watch the sun kiss the sea,
The sky turns to a rainbow of colors,
And I wonder, will the fish miss me?
Daniel Listor, Grade 4

Summer

It is summer
When the flowers bloom.
The sun is shining
And people are going on vacation.
It is a good time to go to the beach.
Have some time to spend with your family.
Have some fun when summer is here!
Aidan Zelhof, Grade 4

Ocean's Magic

Splash! Splash! Splash!
O' Ocean, the sun shines bright.
You cool me down
with refreshing, welcoming waves.
I hear your soothing sound.
You calm my mind.
O' Ocean, what a magical creation you are!
Rahmah Chaudhry, Grade 5

Winter vs Summer

Winter
cold, fun
playing, singing, freezing
Santa, Jesus, friends, family
swimming, playing, running
warm, sweaty
summer
Caleb McClung, Grade 5

Summer to Winter

Summer
hot, pool
blazing, heating, swimming
warm, lemonade, chocolate, Christmas
freezing, snowing, skiing
cold, jackets
Winter
Gabe Cabral, Grade 5

Fall

Fall
Windy, cool
Raking, sleeping, exploring
Football, soccer, baseball, Easter
Raining, playing, growing
Warm, sunny
Spring
Bobby Jones, Grade 5

Hidden and Found

Beneath the waves
Where the jewels are hidden
A queen arises
Upon the shore
To claim what she seeks
Michelle Huang, Grade 5

My Dream — The Perfect World

I have a dream.
That one day earth's beauty will be supreme.
My dream has fresh air that hits my face.
No dirty chemicals took any space.
My dream has birds gracefully dancing.
The fish in sparkling ocean were slowly prancing.
This dream has remarkable skies.
The clouds took shape of everything, even pumpkin pies.
The sweet aroma of apples filled the air in my orchard.
It also has a hint of flowers and a sprinkle of Cookies from the courtyard.
The dream has fields of verdant grass with no color but green.
The whole world was invigoratingly clean.
There was no sign of grime.
Everything was pure and prime.
All humans can make this happen.
It's time people should take action.
Then we will do Earth a huge favor.
We will show the true beauty of Mother Nature.
Ansh Doshi, Grade 5

I Am

I am a boy that likes playing basketball
I wonder if I can be awesome
I hear the basketball pounding on the ground and people cheering for me and my friends
I see a coach that helps us play the game
I want to be the leader of the game and middle player
I am a boy that likes playing basketball
I pretend me and friends are good players
I feel good at the end of the game and proud of myself
I touch the basketball's smooth bubbles
I worry that I am going to fall and hurt myself
I am a boy that likes playing basketball
I understand that I am not the best player
I say that I am good
I dream to be the best player
I try really hard at basketball
I hope me and my friends can get better at basketball
I am a boy that likes playing basketball
Austin Denomme, Grade 5

Halloween Time Is Here

I know it's Halloween when I see ghosts hanging in trees,
Scary, frightening, and exciting for children,
One child dresses as a knight and his sister a princess,
Black cats stare with their yellow devil-like eyes.

I know it's Halloween when all kids marvel at the colorful lights,
Above the door are red marks like blood that scare wee ones,
A full moon shines in the sky,
And dark orange-carved pumpkins shine all night.

I know it's Halloween when kids see costumes of ghosts, ghouls, and goblins,
When adults lock all doors at midnight,
Kids are disappointed when Halloween is over,
And all Halloween creatures hide until the following year.
Nickolaos Baris, Grade 6

I Love My Family
Oh family,
I love you!
We do so much together.
We run.
We jump.
We throw softballs.
We catch them too.
Oh do I love you!
Mom takes me places.
Dad buys me stuff.
Sister gives me stuff.
Oh do I love you.
Roses are red,
Violets are blue.
I love my family, do you love yours too?
Alana Chrobak, Grade 4

Sorrow
I sat there in the river
Watching all my sorrows float away
Down the river
Turning the bend

Releasing into the world
Without any warning
And only one word
Why?

My parents always said
To paddle your own canoe
And I finally knew
What it meant
But it was too late
Kaitlyn Siedlecki, Grade 6

Deep in the Night
Blazing hot, the sun.
Shining down, the sun.
Forever burning, the sun.

Shining late, the moon.
White in the sky, the moon.
Marked by many, the moon.

Darkness around, a star.
Speckle of light, a star.
Gleaming with the moon, a star.

All the light,
shining bright,
deep in the night.
Carson T. Katri, Grade 6

Eye
I have two eyes
They help me see
They see things that fly
When they look into a mirror they see me

They can be awful
Oh so bad
I think they are unlawful
And they make me sad

I like my eyes
So cool and hazel
They can see lies
And see water trickle
Collin Slattery, Grade 6

Hair
I love my hair
I really truly do
I swear I love my hair
Without it I'd be blue

I really love my hair
I would trade it for no other type
I swear I love my hair
It's not too long and not too tight

I love my hair so much
When I wake up it looks all crazy
I swear I love my hair
It's all brown and nice and wavy
Makayla Brennan, Grade 6

My Hands
My hands are small
They are tough
They help me move stuff
My hands are amazing

My hands are useful
My hands help me throw a football
They help me use my phone to make a call
My hands help me swing a bat

My hands are smooth
They are strong
They are never wrong
My hands, my hands
Peter Wetter, Grade 6

Whitecaps
Whoosh the whitecaps rolled
As the big boat went right by
With a wake behind
Jalen Smith, Grade 6

Fall
I love fall.
I love the colors of fall.
Red, orange, yellow, and brown.
I love to rake the leaves,
And then jump into them.
The leaves will all go up to the sky,
Then they will fall down to my eyes.
I love to see the wind,
Blow the leaves away.
And I wish I was a leaf,
So I could get blown away.
I love to keep fall leaves,
Because I love the colors.
And when I look at the leaves of fall,
I remember how much fun I had.
Melvin Juarez, Grade 6

Our Lord*
We are the clay
He is the potter
Our Lord made us
God made us wonderful
He made us special
I am his daughter.
He wants me in this world
He made nothing wrong with me
He has something planned for you
And something planned for me
We can do anything
With our God

Thank you Lord for making us unique
Sherralin Nealis, Grade 6
*Based on Isaiah 64:8

New York, New York
Just right above me,
All I can see,
Are buildings around me.
Buildings so high,
That they reach the sky.
Thousands of people and places to go.
Just please don't say no,
And make sure you go!
Sarah Isola, Grade 6

Best Friend
I have a best friend in need,
She likes to read.
She is kind of like me.
I'm not saying who it is yet.
When she gets mad at me, I get upset.
We don't get in a lot of fights,
We watch movies in the night.
I'm not going to whisper, but it is my sister.
Megan Foster, Grade 4

My Hair
Oh, I love my hair
It is everywhere
Thick, long beautiful hair
It is so gorgeous

I can wear it anywhere
Shape it,
Create it, and
Change it

Hair I love so much
So long
Longer than the ground
Oh, I love my hair
Kate Giordano, Grade 6

My Eyes
I love my eyes
Your color is dark brown
Your job is to help me see
You're very pretty

Oh where would I go?
You're football shaped
You're on the very top of my face
You're circled inside

I love my eyes
Your color is dark brown
You're very pretty
Oh where would I go without you?
Emma Cantwell, Grade 6

Eyes
My big eyes are very bright
They show me where to go
Sometimes my eyes are sensitive to light
My eyes can see high, my eyes can see low

At night my eyes go into a doze
In the dark my eyes glow
For pictures my eyes pose
My eyes get cold in the snow

My eyes can see beautiful skies
I need my eyes to see
My eyes love seeing delicious pies
I'm so happy they belong to me
Caitlin Liebegott, Grade 6

Nature
The trees rustling
In the plenty breezy winds,
Leaves willful to fall.
Carson Rider, Grade 6

My Hands
My hands are amazing
They can write anything
I use them to eat
Or wave to someone I meet

My hands are the best
They overpass all the rest
They help me throw a ball
And pick me up when I fall

My hands are so cool
They work hard at school
I use them to clap
Or to open a map

My hands are great
They can open the gate
I can swat a fly
As it zooms through the sky
Daniel Winkler, Grade 6

I Am
I am nice
I wonder why broccoli is green
I hear my brother talking a lot
I see the tv most of the time
I want to see my mom
I am nice

I pretend to be a secret agent
I feel the Xbox controller a lot
I touch the on button
I worry about my parents
I cry when I get hurt
I am nice

I understand a lot
I say funny things
I dream about the future
I hope my parents won't get hurt
I am nice
Caleb Grant, Grade 5

Unseen Levitation
Levitation leaves me wondering every day
And every night
When things seem to fly without force
It brings me joy
Because it is unseen,
Unseen levitation
I ask why is it unseen
My friend said it is just like magic.
I wondered,
I just couldn't get an answer
Until I saw the unseen levitation.
Sophia Kasem, Grade 4

My Hair
I love my hair
It's very wavy
I do not care
If people think it looks crazy

My hair is brown
With blond highlights
My hair is red
You can see it in the night

My hair can be blue
My hair can be green
My hair can be any color
You haven't ever seen
Alexandria Kohn, Grade 6

My Hands
I love my hands,
They are the best,
From scoring goals,
To taking rests

If I didn't have my hands,
We wouldn't be able to write this,
They get me out of situations,
Maybe out of a dark abyss

I love my hands,
They get the job done,
They are the best,
They are my number one
Jake Stella, Grade 6

Pokemon
Pokémon, gotta' catch 'em all,
Some are big and some seem small.
You will trade with people from all over,
Cool! Look I just got a Snover.
You have to fight to get money,
Hey! Look that guy is selling honey.
Crash! Oh no, Team Rocket is here,
I'll have to fight them with no fear.
I fight them with my Jiggly Puff,
After the fight they puffed and huffed.
Well, now it is just getting dark,
Bow! Wow! I hear a Stoutland bark.
We should sleep here to last the night,
See you tomorrow Shh! sleep tight.
Bodey Barwick, Grade 5

Mushrooms
The dangerous thing.
Glowing, haunting, and killing.
These mushrooms shout "death."
Xander Fry, Grade 6

Now

It does not matter who you used to be
It does not matter what you used to do
It does not matter where you've been
It does not matter why you've done what you've done
What matters is now and only now

It does not matter who you plan to be
It does not matter what you plan to do
It does not matter where you plan to go
It does not matter why you do what you plan to do
What matters is now and only now

It matters who you are now
It matters what you do now
It matters where you are now
It matters why you do what you do now
All that matters in now and only now

For we live in the present, not the future nor the past
Dylan Stone, Grade 6

How Do People Effect the Land and Oceans

Yo,
did you know
People hurt earth's land and oceans.
Yo,
Did you know
People hurt the oceans
And it causes commotion
Yo
Did you know
Conserve is a word that you got to know
You better use these resources wisely
Or they got to go
Word!!!
But this ain't all you need to know
You need to learn about the
People, the earth, the land and the ocean you know
So humans STOP!
Get up and walk
Don't just drop that lollipop
Lena Quigley, Grade 5

Winter Fun Time

The very white snow is falling softly from the trees,
And it is Christmas day!
So many presents!
It is awesome.
Mmm, waking up to the delicious smell.
A cup of wonderful hot cocoa.
The taste of the fluffy sweet marshmallows!
Is so hot and so dreamy.
Mmm, makes my tummy sing.
In my comfy pajamas.
Mmm, love that perfect morning!
Rowen Ireland, Grade 4

The Big Big Zoo

Today my wishes and dreams came true,
For today that I was going to the zoo.
As I walked into the zoo I saw some baboons,
Then I saw someone selling balloons.

We saw lots of birds flying around,
And lions and tigers making so much sound.
The grizzly bears were so sleepy and lazy.
And all the others so hyper and crazy.

We walked into the Mouse House where there are lots of mice,
I am always wondering if they like to eat rice.
We feed the sheep a little food,
Some of them weren't in a very good mood.

Lots of snakes were slithering and hissing,
Some animals were running around like something was missing.
At the kids zoo we ended our tour,
Maybe next time we can come and explore some more.
Yifan Guo, Grade 4

My Pet

My pet's name is Frog
He loves sitting on logs
Sometimes we take long walks
But have longer talks

On one fall day, Frog lost his toy
He whined so much "Oh boy! Oh boy!"
I looked around the house I looked everywhere
I did not find it anywhere.

"I hope we find it" I thought to myself,
Looking under and above the shelf
I told Frog that his toy was nowhere to be seen
I told him I even looked in the washing machine.

He went to his bed and quietly sat there
Until I tripped on his toy bear
I quickly picked it up shouting, "Look Frog"
After that he was one happy dog.
Vedant Punit, Grade 4

Alexis/Goodrow

Alexis
I am dependable, kind, honest, responsible, happy
My family is loving, kind, hopeful, busy
I love school
I need more family time
I give presents to my sister
I fear the dark
I would like to be a teacher
I would like to see God
I wonder what I will do in life
Goodrow
Alexis Goodrow, Grade 5

Happy Inside

Every day I go to school and look more and more
Like a fool.
I get pushed and shoved
I am very unloved.
I am broken inside. It's hard to hide
How I am bullied.
But I get good grades
And I find my way
To be happy inside.

Helen Barber, Grade 6

Sunshine

I love the sun and how it shines.
Rain rain go away,
I don't want to see you another day.
Sunshine makes me happy when I'm starting to feel blue.
So sunshine I love you!
You shine so bright,
it's said you have to go at night.
So sunshine good night.

Aryana Taylor, Grade 6

Mind of Illusion

mind of illusion I can't think straight
mind of illusion that's what I hate
mind of illusion I can hear myself think
mind of illusion I'm in my own world
mind of illusion leading me to the wrong place
mind of illusion why are you here
mind of illusion just visions in my head
mind of illusion I can't think straight

Ja'Shanti Calloway, Grade 6

Carleigh

It means friendly, hilarious, sporty
It is like the deep dark ocean
It is eating ice cream on a hot summer day
It is the memory of Kiersten
Who taught me to be trustworthy and creative
When she teaches me to be trustworthy and creative
My name is Carleigh
It means Friendship is magical

Carleigh Scott, Grade 4

Apology

I ate your bag of Takis
that were in the closet;
they had a lot of spices.

You probably were going to eat them for lunch.

I was crying and
drank a bottle of water.

Gary Castro Velasquez, Grade 6

Freedom

F reedom is ours
R espect is a part of it
E veryone wants it
E ffort is needed to obtain freedom
D o not abuse it, because
O utstanding people help others gain freedom
M ostly, for you and me, this is a great ribbon that we cannot untie

Ridwan Ismail, Grade 4

Winter

I love winter because it's cold!
I go to New Jersey to see the amazing snow.
When I'm there, I get presents from Santa.
We make smores sitting around the warm fire.
Snowball fights are totally fun,
And you wear a warm coat.
I enjoy winter!

Kevin Cardona, Grade 4

Caterpillars

Hatches from its egg a tiny larva,
It munches bunches of leaves.
It repeats eating treats and sheds its skin,
And goes to the chrysalis waiting to be reborn
And emerges with wings and learns to fly
And does that more and more.

Noah Bennett, Grade 4

Oh Winter, Oh Winter

I like winter because I like snowball fights,
And hot cocoa makes my tummy smile near the cozy fire.
There aren't any leaves on trees and the snowmen are cold.
The stars are so humongous on a cold winter night.
The Christmas tree is sparkling oh have a nice night, goodbye!
I'll see you next year!

Louis Apolito, Grade 4

Friendship

Friendship is unconditional love
It smells like sweet honey suckles on a vine
It tastes like warm s'mores at a campfire
It sounds like the laughter from each other
It feels like the hugs that you give when you say goodbye
It lives between the moments you share

Aubrey Jumper, Grade 6

The Thanksgiving Turkey

Screaming, laughter, joy coming from every center of the house
On the caramel brown table was a sizzling smoking hot turkey
All the mushy mashed potatoes in my mouth
Sweet sugary maple syrup filled the air
The wind was as crisp as cookies
it was a beautiful, away from the blue, Thanksgiving

Alia Duab, Grade 4

Summer

The summer breeze is blowing,
The cool wind in my hair.
Look at the summer flair!
The sun is shining bright,
The birds are singing tweet, tweet.
The sand is soft,
And the sea is cool and amazing,
All the color around me,
Is popping out!
Tons of outstanding places to go.
School's out, fun is on our path!

Isaac Antoine, Grade 4

Tornado of Names

I am walking down the hall
When someone says "Hey, Toby"
I say hey back, but forgetting his name
I feel like I know him,
but don't know their name
Then I think to myself.
I have a tornado of names.
Then I feel better already,
When I see my two friends.
Knowing they're not lost
In my tornado of names

Toby Hutchison, Grade 6

House of Tears

House of tears
weeks of yelling
years of failing
and days of tragedy
But some houses of good
hours of joy
days of dancing
weeks of smiling
and years of laughter
Not all bad things happen in
houses of tears

Lauryn Roebuck, Grade 6

Born to Be Something

I was born in 2005
I was born to learn
I was born to go to college
I was born to be a woman
I was born to have kids
I was born to be a wife
I was born to live
I was born to have a husband
I was born to be in a family
I was born to get old
I was born to be a sister.

Nilynn Walton, Grade 4

Summer Fun!!

Sitting in the sand,
And the sea comes up.
So you put your hands together,
And you use it like a cup.
You see the water as a kind of motion,
Now you have a sip of the ocean,
You may see a butterfly rest,
Upon a buttercup,
Letting out its drinking straws,
To sip the sweet nectar up.
I wonder if our pepper trees,
Let the bees ever sneeze?
Hot days are for beach days,
I hear the waves,
"Splash splash splash!"
We get to spend time with our family!!

Jada Figueroa, Grade 4

Winter Fun

Amazing cold, sparkly ice,
Shines in the light of sun.
Wear your warm jacket and snow boots.
Make a comical looking snowman.
Do snowball fights,
Make perfect snow angels.
Open huge, glittery presents,
By the warm fireplace.
Drink tasty hot chocolate with your family,
Stand around the Christmas tree,
And sing Christmas songs,
Then the snow melts,
And flowers pop through the ground.
Trees have leaves again,
And animals come out of hibernation.
That is a wonderful cycle.

Alexis Ortisi, Grade 4

Space Trip

get in
the rocket ship.
3 2 1. Blast Off!
Excitement pulses
through my veins
I see earth down
below. Now it is
a speck on the
horizon. The sun
moon, and stars
glitter like the
diamonds in dirt
It is
amazing!
Now we are on
the moon. Awesome!

Emily Miller, Grade 5

Art

Art
Crayons — Used
Canvas' — Piled
Paint — All ready
Artist — Smiles
Imagination — Comes to life
Colored Pencils — They just scribble
Chalk — Dusty in your hand
Paper — Starts to cripple
Tape — Being ripped apart
Fingers — Dirty with the paint
These are most of the things used for art!

June Cumento, Grade 5

Our Love Is Stronger Than a Bull

Our love is strong
We can always have fun
Our love is strong
It's like we're one
Our love is strong
We're always together
Our love is strong
Your skin is softer than a feather
Our love is strong
I love you with all my heart
Our love is strong
That's why we can't depart

Jaeden Robinson, Grade 6

Global Warming

As we are sitting on the couch,
The Polar bears are saying ouch!
It's all because of global warming,
Which is a severe warning.
Don't create fossil fuel,
As that would be really cruel.
It takes place in the North and South Pole,
Let's all take a poll.
We all agree it's bad,
Let us not be glad.
The glaciers are turning into water,
Let us all get smarter.

Ari Kamat, Grade 6

The Mind Is a Maze

The mind is a maze
with ups and downs, lefts and rights
The mind is a maze
with fronts and backs and loop-de-loops
The mind is a maze
with dead ends
The mind is a maze
with a beginning, but no end
The mind is a maze
with ups and downs, lefts and rights

Cameron Quinones-Partain, Grade 6

Jolly Rancher

Jolly Rancher
Terrific, hard
Sucking, tasting, smiling
Sometimes sour, sometimes sweet!
Candy
Zoha Choudhry, Grade 4

Fall

Fall trees are being pushed by the wind.
The birds are chirping.
Animals are finding homes.
The leaves on the trees are falling.
People jumping in leaf piles.
Suzanna Odusote, Grade 5

Trish's Twisted Tiny Wish

There once was a human named Trish,
Who had an impossible wish.
She couldn't converse,
because she was cursed.
So now she just watches her fish.
Areeba Siddiquei, Grade 6

The Bear's Chair

There once was a very old bear,
Who always took care of his chair
He went to the store
And then did his chores
And declared his chair wasn't there!
Ethan Robertson, Grade 5

Icing

Icing
Smooth, delicious
Mixing, spreading, eating
Licking is totally awesome fun!
Sweet!
Benjamin Messenger, Grade 4

Water

Water
Salty, blue
Hide, jump, wave
I like playing in water!
Ocean
Giovanni Marrone, Grade 4

Winter

Winter
Cold, dark
Snowing, freezing, sledding
When darkness starts falling
Season
Elisabet Tapia, Grade 6

Friendly Farm Friends

I woke up ready to leave with the stuff that I need,
I volunteer with no fear at Longstreet Farm that is near.

I jumped in the barn with a smile on my face saying, "I'm here!"
I milked the cows I could show you how, you squeeze their things with a wow.
I feed the horses and the cows while hearing the sounds of meows.

I do the chickens at 1:00 so I keep an eye on the clock,
I feed the sheep and say hello when all of a sudden there comes He Ho,
He, Ho is a hog with lots of flies on his head and is big and has his own bed.

We give the milk from the cows to the pigs who want it now,
The chicken coop has lots of eggs that chickens lay in the day.

I wonder why the horses bite when we are no harm in the day and night,
I have friends who help me too and are nice and know what to do.

I don't care if I have to stay because it's my chance to do more today,
Animals need love and they need me, so I will always be there standing by the tree.
Allison Hamilton, Grade 4

Thanksgiving List

The things I'd like on my thanksgiving list are very much some type of wish
A caring mother and father that loves me so
A warm house that protects me from the snow
Some kindhearted friends that treat me nice
A fireplace that warms my hands from the ice
A delicious turkey for Thanksgiving dinner.
Some healthy treats to keep me thinner
Stuffing and mashed potatoes to top it all off
Now some pumpkin pie to start dessert off.
My caring Aunt Michelle and Uncle Matt
And a very funny turkey hat
A couch, to rest after supper
Please, oh please don't make me suffer
A comfy warm bed for my slumber
Just promise me just no thunder
And after Thanksgiving which was a blast
The next holiday is CHRISTMAS!!!
Now you know what I'm thankful for
Now it's your turn what are you thankful for?
Frankie LoPresti, Grade 6

On the Shore

The heat and humidity hung over the gulf
As the brilliant sunset took over with golden oranges, bright yellows, and delicate pinks
While the sun caressed the sky.
Insects chirped their peaceful melodies
Even though dark odd clouds rolled in.
There's an old lighthouse by the ocean.
It sent glaring marigold beams over the surface of the water.
An Arctic wind flowed about
As the clouds rumbled, rattled, and roared
Chilling my bones.
This beautiful imagery amazed me.
Anna Walker, Grade 6

Air

The air is crisp
The apples, crunchy
It's sweater weather today
And so is tomorrow
The cider is steaming
The apple pie is hot
Autumn is great, even for tots
Sophia Bartoli, Grade 6

Friends

F avorite person
R espect
I mportant
E njoyable
N ice
D ependable
S illy
Randi Richards, Grade 5

Me

I am nice, I am kind, I am sweet.
I can rhyme, I can sing, I can climb.
I can shout, I can scream and rhyme.
I am not nobody else but, ME,
Because everybody is different in the world
and out the world,
But ME.

Kiyanna Thomas, Grade 4

Thanks

I am thankful for
My mom letting me visit
My great grandfather

I have so much thanks
for my mom bringing me to
a fancy hotel
Thor Bello-Wise, Grade 4

Brayden

B est at riding my bike
R uns good
A wesome at playing video games
Y ogurt is favorite food
D o good things
E els are my favorite animal in the water
N ice to people
Brayden Whitehead, Grade 5

Water

Water
Liquid of life
Falling and splashing far
Smooth, sliding like a snake through trees
Hydro
Christian Chiu, Grade 6

Spring

March:
The ice is packed away for next winter.
Spring wears flowers in her hair, waiting for the jackets to come off
March feels wet; morning dew lies on the grass between my toes
March sounds like a little boy jumping in puddles with his black rain boots on
March tastes ripe: Peach juice running down my face

April is elegantly colored with Spring's first flowers
April chirps loudly at my door
April sounds full of water, swaying in the babbling blue brook
April sows seeds, plants pansies, and fills the air with freshness
April feels new: winter is gone; spring is here

Baby bunnies are born in May.
May sounds like people singing for Memorial Day,
Feels like soft fur sliding through my fingers.
May is warm weather, the sun smiling down
May loves birds; they sing and tweet.
Lilly Arthur, Grade 4

Freedom

Every day there was work to be done
Whether it was working under the scorching hot sun or cleaning the house
It was like being stuck on the bottom of a pit surrounded by total darkness
Not being able to do what they want or say what they think
They were all miserable "workers" who never received anything in exchange

When it seemed like all hope was lost a small light was shining
It was a glimmer of hope
Soldiers and leaders who showered slaves with hope
The light was growing brighter with each passing day
Sometimes it would become dim almost falling back into the darkness
It wasn't easy but the light was breaking through the darkness
Giving them a guide to follow and lead them out
They were able to leave the dark pit
Now they were free to do what they wanted
Not being controlled and used
Yet able to have a future
Able to finally have freedom
Sandy Tan, Grade 6

Light

You are light
Streaming through windows,
Awakening the essence that flows on earth,
Restoring life on land and sea

Bursting onto earth
Spreading happiness throughout the galaxy
Reaching the smallest corners and holes
Pampering every bit of the globe

But alas, this cannot last long.
The brightness fades away,
And the glowing ball of light is replaced with a shining sphere of silver.
Asmita Sharma, Grade 5

Red, Yellow and Brown

I know it is fall when
The crusty smell of
Apple pie fills
The autumn air.

I know it is fall when
The trees' branches
Start swaying
With the pace of the wind.

I know it is fall when
The leaves start turning
Different colors
Like red, yellow and brown.

I know it is fall when
The air starts getting
Cold and the warmth
Goes way.
Niki Glynatsis, Grade 6

What Am I Hiding For?

Walking in the hallway
Lockers and backpacks are fill
Trying to fit in and not get caught.
What am I hiding for?

I can't come out,
Something is grabbing me back
The scariness of my soul,
The plain that's going to appear

My features are facing the floor.
Pushing through the crowd.
"Please don't look at me"
I don't want to suffer this pain,

That is not supposed to arise
At me, the single girl.
Who always gets the first sight.
Is this going to last…
Jenny Chen, Grade 6

The Beach

The sand soft like silk,
The water rolling down the shore,
The color of the water,
Sky blue,
It shushed everyone,
Sandcastles tall and strong,
Towels lay down nicely,
Umbrellas sat in the sand for a nice shade,
People of all ages,
Come here for one thing,
Beach.
Eleanor Bloch, Grade 5

Majestic Ocean

It was a dark, windy night
Next to the beautiful wooden lighthouse,
Its beams of light piercing
The everlasting darkness
Like hot spikes through lead.
Clouds are set dark, low, and heavy,
The scent of a storm.
Waves batter the shore line,
Leaving my feet wet and cold,
In the everlasting ocean,
The majestic ocean.
Lucas Bernal, Grade 6

One Little Star

I lift up my weary head
Then my eyes catch something bright
One little star
A tiny flash of light
Surrounded by a vast sea of darkness
One little star
A ray of hope
In the darkness that is the universe
One little star
Although we can't see
How big it really is!
Katy Tayler, Grade 6

George Muller

A terrible boy
A thief a liar
Not even a Christian
Stealing money
Not even a good thought
But one day
Became a Christian
Just by listening
To one story
God came
Straight to his heart
Grace Garvin, Grade 4

Life of the Street

I was skipping in the street
When I heard a cool beat
So I started dancing on my feet
People started coming from all around
It started to look like the ocean deep
They danced and leaped
It was so cool having everyone around
All around town
But soon they all left
And it was quiet and deaf
So I started to skip
Libby Clark, Grade 6

Love My Family

I love, I love
my mom and my dad.
Also my dog and my siblings.
But, let's start to talk
about my parents…
because my mom is a housewife
and a working wife.

She is very caring and loving and lovely!
And my mom is always there,
when my dad is not.
But my dad is a strong loving man
that helps pay the bill sand he is very nice.
And he keeps a roof over our heads
and my dog is nice,
and very protective of our family.
He loves to jump and play with me.
And that is why I love my family.
Miracle Gilmore, Grade 6

This Old Road

As she walks down
This old road
She sings and dances
With the deer
As her hair sways in the wind
And her face glowing
She mounts her Pegasus
And flies off
To pursue her dreams...
A few years later
She walks down
This old road again
Remembering those days
When she sang and danced
With the deer
Then she says her prayers
And falls asleep
Under the shade of the moon.
Alissa Kicklighter, Grade 6

Fall

The leaves are changing,
while I am aging.
The birds are flying south.
The plants are dying,
and I am crying.
It is very cold,
muy frio, muy frio.
I am getting very old.
I'm getting told,
I am very old.
I fear winter is near.
The bears are sleeping,
while I am slowly weeping.
Bianka Gonzalez-Garcia, Grade 6

City of Champions

Pittsburgh is black and gold.
Pittsburgh tastes like a big fat Primanti Bros. Sandwich.
Pittsburgh sounds like the roar of the crowd when we hit a home run, score a goal, or get a touchdown.
Pittsburgh smells like the great scent of Italian food during Little Italy Days in Bloomfield.
Pittsburgh looks like a beautiful sight of the city from Mt. Washington.
Pittsburgh makes me feel passionate!

Tyler Marotta, Grade 4

Long Winter's Nap

Her leaves started to fall down to the ground. She sees her buddy the squirrel gather his nuts because his life depends on it. As his puffy little tail ran across her branch he scurried as fast as lightning.
While she stands waiting, her leaves now have color for a short time. Soon her branches will be covered with snow. But for now she listens for the chirping birds and the rustling leaves as she was whistling.
As the breeze blows around the dancing leaves she is thinking when the soft powdery snow starts to fall, she can't wait for her long winter nap.

Abigail Gilbert, Grade 5

Fantastic Fall Tree

The tree's leaves swirled through the breeze. They danced through the wind like fireflies in the night.
Branches started to shiver on the tree as the leaves blew away. Outside it was starting to get as frigid as winter with a freezing breeze. Frost was starting to appear on the ground and there was dark fog in the morning. She was cheerful when her leaves changed different colors.
She didn't want her leaves to fall off her branches. The tree was as beautiful as the sky in the morning. She will be disappointed when she has to let go of her friends, the leaves. The tree will be bare in the upcoming winter.

Madison Heitz, Grade 5

My Poem, My Home

I'm from the open fields of corn upon the lake, I caught my first bass.
From the sketches I made in the old apple tree.
I'm from the trees and sky and the tears I cry that taste like the salty water of the sea.
I am from the happiness my friends show when they see me.
I am from the animals I see and the joy they bring me to the sadness it brings me when they part from the land.
In the end we end with a beginning my poem, my home.

Kiera Dempsey, Grade 5

Swaying Tree

The tree was shivering on a cold day in the fall. His leaves danced as they lowered to the ground.
A strong breeze pulled his leaves off.
His bare arms swayed like a cobweb. He wasn't ready for winter quite yet.
He looked at his beloved leaves watching them be raked away.
He gazed at all the children. He was sad that a lot of trees around him were green.
He watched the sky get darker faster every night.

Hayden Howes, Grade 5

Poeming

I did my poem today and I am pleased with mine and other's display,
Many stuttered, smuttered, skitted, and smooed, but we all have pride in what we have done and will do.
I may have paused too long or too short, but I am happy, because I didn't snort.
I messed up some, but didn't we all?
I am glad I did it nearly correct at all.

Sara Jordan Caldwell, Grade 5

Thanksgiving!

The sizzle of the turkey getting roasted.
The turkey being brought to the table.
My hand changing the channel to football.
My taste buds enjoying the turkey.
Steam coming from the hot turkey.
And that is the best Thanksgiving ever.
Leo Nikolovski, Grade 4

Spring

S ports season
P raying for the Resurrection of Jesus Christ
R oses and flowers grow and bloom
I t's time of new life
N o sadness, but happiness
G orgeous weather
Santiago Villanueva, Grade 4

Summer

S and in your toes
U nder the shade
M any waves
M uch fun
E veryone is happy
R eally hot
Skyler Bailey, Grade 6

The Ocean Is a House Full of Kids

The ocean is like my house
Sometimes loud and sometimes a mouse
Sometimes we scream sometimes we fight
But sometimes we are brave as a knight
I love my family so dear to me
But sometimes I just need to be free
Quinlan Ayres, Grade 6

Friends

Friends are people who care
They show their kindness then and there
They plan hangouts
And like to eat pizza take out
Friends are people who care
Friends show kindness then and there.
Sophia Hidalgo, Grade 4

Spring

S un shining,
P asture growing,
R ainbows everywhere
I n Immokalee
N othing is better than
G oing on a nice walk!
Jazmin Lara-Vasquez, Grade 4

My Little Baby Sister

My little baby sister,
is the sister I wanted.
I like how she laughs and runs,
and when she cries,
it makes me feel bad.
I take care of her the most.
I also play with her, and make her laugh and smile.
She likes to scratch and bite (a lot).
She exercises more than my family.
Sometimes she wakes up earlier than us.
She likes to go outside to see the animals, to walk or run.
If she's bored, we take her out.
She is almost childish, and likes to play with me,
our little sister, and our little brother.
Now since she walks, we have to take more care of her.
For example, eating pencils, markers, ripping important papers, and drowning.
She didn't feel cold or hot when she was small.
I like how my sister is,
because she is the sister that plays with me,
and makes my angers calm down,
and when I am sad, she makes me happy.
Moises Ramirez, Grade 6

My Window

One window is all I need to see inside of me.
To see myself as I truly am.
To look at the world with new eyes.
To see my true love whom I will spend the rest of my life with.
To see the world change before my eyes.
To make a difference and to see how it effects the world and the people in it.
To grow mentally.
To watch the people who make a difference in the world.
To draw my feelings.
To be inspired.
To lose myself in how I feel.
To see what opportunities lie ahead of me.
To see the world as it is.
To be myself.
To write songs filled with love.
To lose myself in another world.
To be free.
To see what my life beholds.
To change myself.
To better the world.
One window is all I need...

Chloe Edge, Grade 6

The Dancing Tree

The tree is heartbroken as the leaves wash themselves into
A divergent color because he loved the big green leaves.
The sapling cries as the leaves fall to the ground.
As the tree gets colder, he is happy to see the kids still playing and having fun.
The tall beige seedling thinks about when he's going to be cold as ice.
He is ready to hibernate until the spring.
But until then, he is dancing to keep himself warm.

Jacobb Bivens, Grade 5

Riding Bikes

Sometimes simple things are the best, it's true.
Oh, the places bikes can take you.
If you go down a hill, don't fumble.
When you ride, you can hear a rumble.
When you go down hills, go fast.
When you ride, keep it a blast!
Let's continue our fast-paced quest.
When you get tired, take a good rest.
When you are soaring, turn on beats.
Tires and handle bars, annoying seats.
When you wanted to, you could
go gliding through the quiet neighborhood,
Where you can go, bikes can take you there.
Bikes can take you anywhere!

Elijah Jones, Grade 5

Books

Books, oh Books how I love my Books,
I read them all in reading nooks.
Poetry books have really spoken to me,
But my parents like drama, oh how can this be?
I like books much more than plays,
I've only seen two in all of my days.
The sound of pages under my fingers,
The book is closed but the magic lingers.
Pages and pages of Amazing Words,
Like "zip" and "zap" with wonderful verbs.
Shelves full, and books full of wonderful writing,
I read through them all without a lamp's lighting.
My poem is over and watching drama's still wrong,
Just keep reading books and you will stay strong!

Jadyn Sharick, Grade 5

The Season of Winter

The snowy snowflakes are falling down.
The snow makes me laugh and wiggly.
The hot chocolate makes me warm.
The kids play snow fights.
The animals are sleeping in hibernation.
We like to build a snowman.
The kids are having fun.
I like when there is no school.
We like to sled down the mountain.
When we have no school.
We can have so much fun.
I like when the snow sparkles all around the world.
My family and I like having a feast.
With all my best friends ever.

Claudgena Alcime, Grade 4

I Give Thanks For

I give thanks for…
my loving mom…she takes care of me,
my awesome grandma…she gives me treats,
my funny dog…always lays down next to me.

Gabriel Maya, Grade 4

Blue

I am blue
The color of the sky and sea.
I roam about looking to be free.
Hoping for my freedom.

I am blue
The color of sadness.
I feel like crying.
I am a tear falling out of an eye.

I am blue
The color of independence.
I want freedom.
If only I could be free.

I am blue
The color of loneliness.
I feel left out.
I can't make my own decision.

I am blue
I loathe sadness for those who lack freedom.
I am blue

Nitish Sharma, Grade 6

My Arms

Oh arms, you are so strong
Without you, my life would be wrong
I can't swing on the bars without my arms
What would I do without my dear arms

Oh arms, you help me a lot
Without you in basketball I couldn't take a shot
I couldn't dribble the balls without my arms
What would I do without my dear arms

Oh arms, you are so great
Without you, my life would dissipate
I can't bake without my arms
What would I do without my dear arms

Kylie Squires, Grade 6

My Dog

Me and my dog make a great pair.
No better friendship is found anywhere.
We walk, talk, run, and play.
We both have secrets that we keep all day.
We both think and we both can feel.
That's how we know that we are both real.
Everywhere I go, my dog will be there.
He might be very smelly and muddy, but I don't care.
He always listens, even to the smallest command,
That's why I rub him with both my hands.
Even if most of the time I rub you with a glove,
You will always be my friend to stay with and love.

Ryan Henderson, Grade 6

Swimming

Swimming, think about diving off the side of a boat and landing in a colorful rainbow of fish,
corals and water the color of aqua blue.
Grabbing fins, snorkel and a friend or two.
Feeling like you are the most powerful person in the world.
Swimming as though you are weightless, carefree and in swirl.
Come to the Bahamas and you will see.
Water so clear it is hard to believe.
Hog fish, parrot fish, and grouper just to name a few.
This aquarium of sea life is free of me and you.
You are the king of the ocean, swimming with dolphin, stingray and even a shark.
It certainly is a nice place to anchor your boat and park.
Waves sparkle like glass in the sun.
Asking you to jump in and have some more fun.
Swimming is mad for you and for me.
Let's go explore the underworld and you will see.
Life is peaceful and glowing when you want it to be.
Float on the ocean for no added fee.

Patrick Stocker, Grade 6

I Am From

I am from books, from songs, clean laundry, and drama.
All these things are special to me.
I am from my sofa, my food and my yard.
I am from people who came before me and people yet to be.
These are special.
I come from paper, from trees and grass.
From my mom and from dad,
From grandma and grandpa and the other grandma and the grandfather I will never know.
Things are special.
I am from cookies for Santa and math books for Mrs. Gill.
I'm from all the fast food places you will ever know. That's special.
I'm from the salt and pepper, fudge, braces, and glasses. And I will always remember "It's a sin to kill a mockingbird"
That is super special.
I am from the salty spray of the ocean, and the grit beneath my toes. From broken limbs and buds am I.
Those are special.
I am from + and - and ='s. From the American sign language and regular speech.
This… is special.

Bobbie Doherty, Grade 5

Love Is a Diamond in the Rough*

Love is a diamond in the rough,
Being a girl, it is so tough.
I look in the mirror every day,
Thinking, "Will people like me this way?"
I try so hard to be me,
I'm just afraid how people will be.
Do you think they'd really like my hair?
Or, maybe I should find something different to wear.
I'll try to eat healthier to lose some weight,
My friends keep telling me, "This isn't you, it just ain't"
I really do try to like me,
Not someone else I try to be.
Love is a diamond in the rough,
Being a girl, it is so tough.

Bree Musick, Grade 6
*This poem is about liking yourself, and being true to you. Not someone you try to be. Everyone is beautiful.

The Red Bucket

The smell of seawater drifts through the air
My red bucket is on the ground hungry for sand
I find a bunch of hermit crabs racing toward my red bucket
But the ocean isn't going to let that happen
The ocean carries the hermit crabs out to sea
It's time to fill my red bucket with sand
The sand is soft on my feet yet rough on my hands
I stopped filling my red bucket when it is almost full
I hear two seagulls fighting over fish
The cool, gentle breeze makes my hair dance
I look up at the sunset
It is so beautiful
Red, orange, and pink
I glance over to my red bucket
And see a raggedy star on it
The star is yellow and almost brown
A red and white sail appears over the long grass
Someone is calling my name
I pour out all the sand in my red bucket
Pick it up and head for the boat
It's time to leave the beach.
Felicia Peterson, Grade 6

What Was That?!

Was it a monster under my bed?
Or was it an egg cracked on my head?
Could it possibly be?
An alien named McGee!

Where did it come from?
Did it come here for me?
Is it scary or nice?
Will its fingernails be creepy?!!

Is it here to bring a message?
Or is it just a ball of lint
Will it's breath smell like skunk, or will it smell like mint?!!

Maybe it will be cute and furry?
Or probably ugly and scaly!

Now I think I know what it is…
I'm pretty sure I do…
It's not something gross like a frog…
It's just my adorable new dog!!
Avisha Garg, Grade 4

Thanksgiving Day

I wake up happy and excited
I try to find my elf on the shelf
The sounds of the TV in my ear
A little later I smell the turkey my mom and I baked
The delicious stuffing is heaven in my mouth
The hot pan with pumpkin pie excites me
My Thanksgivings are always happy ones
Lauren Clark, Grade 4

Poems

Some poems are good
Some poems are bad
And some poems are very very sad

Some poems are long
Some poems are short
Some poems rhyme while others don't

When I have some time
And don't know what to do
I'll make up a poem or even a few

It could be about love
It could be about hate
It could be about anything in which you can relate

If it turns out bad
Just change some words
It might turn out better, better than ever

Poems can be fun
Poems can be great
And to publish this poem, I really can't wait
Chana Pattashnick, Grade 6

Oh Ocean, Oh Ocean

Oh ocean, oh ocean,
My very old friend,
You were the place I always wanted to be,
Remember all the sand castles you and I built,
You ruined most all of them,
And felt no guilt.

Oh ocean, oh ocean,
My very old friend,
I wanted to come and see you again,
Remember me struggling beneath your waves,
Despite my pleas, you dragged me back,
I fell further and further from the world I knew,
Everything turned perfect black.

Oh ocean, oh ocean,
Then I saw you,
Shimmering in front of me,
You said, "My very old friend,
My very old friend,
At last, at last,
We meet again."
Jillian Nylund, Grade 6

Fall

The beautiful colored leaves falling all around
Colors of brown, red, yellow, and orange fill the ground
The wonderful sound of nature never gets old
For God's beautiful creations are so bold.
Briellie Schuessler, Grade 5

Snow

Snow is white and cold
So blistery and freezing
Falling down on me
Garrett Matney, Grade 6

White Wonder

A beautiful snow
covers the frosty mountains
with a white wonder
Emma Denver, Grade 6

The King

Roar, the king is here.
Breath of fire shows power.
One roar and manes glow.
Tharwat Eltahan, Grade 5

Baseball

Baseball is the best
I like to play second base
Winning takes hard work
Asa Collins, Grade 4

Dripping Rain

Drip drippity drip,
The beautiful sound of rain,
Falling from above.
Simrah Mansoori, Grade 5

Dragons

Mystical dragons
Soaring across the blue sky
Too bad they all died
Ty Dunlap, Grade 5

That Tree

That tree has been there,
Standing for many long years,
How strongly it stands!
Nabil Elidrissi, Grade 5

My Family

Brothers and sisters,
Mom and Dad together, Yay!
Family unite!
Adam Assina, Grade 5

Volcanoes

Volcanoes are cool,
Inside hot, burning lava,
Erupts in ten years.
Emir Hussain, Grade 5

I Am From

I am from my gigantic stuffed animal pile,
from the big dreamy eyed Beanie Boos,
and the collectable Webkinz.

I am from the half brick house with white tall pillars guarding the house.

I am from the crystal clear water of Lake Waukewan inviting us to swim,
the little cabin providing shelter from the storms.

I am from the deep blue boat of our family picnics,
and the delicious Chinese food on Christmas Eve. YUM!

From "You were always so happy when you were younger"
and "Treat others the way you want to be treated"
and "Do your best."

I am from sticking together every single weekend,
and family walks around the neighborhood.

I am from the Pleasanton Hospital in California, Germany, and Greece,
the flakey spanakopita and bratwursts,
and the story of Oma escaping East Germany.

I am from memories that last a lifetime.
Ariana Steinbrueck, Grade 6

Christmas

Yay, December is approaching it is my favorite time of year,
I can't believe Christmas is almost here.
Holiday songs play on the radio,
And before you know it Christmas trees are aglow.
Fudge, cookies, and sausage balls,
They are all so delicious I love them all.
Going to McAdenville looking at the lights,
Walking through the streets taking in all the sights.
Santa at the mall saying "Ho, Ho, Ho."
Ugh, it's off to shop with mom, away we go!
Opening Christmas presents and getting new toys,
Spending time with my family and playing with the boys.
Just remember, Christmas is not about what you get or what it's worth;
The true meaning of Christmas is celebrating Jesus' birth!
Caleb Sturgill, Grade 5

Nature

Rocks and leaves beneath my feet
Trees and sky above my head
A leaf in my hand
The jagged edges of a rock
And not a cloud in the sky
The golden highlights in my hair are so beautiful as they shine in the sun
The sun shines on me through an oak tree's leaves
Leaves fall all around me
The birds chirp so wonderfully
The breeze is just right
The things that you will see and hear if you sit in nature.
Kate Murtagh, Grade 5

Lovely Lafayette Avenue

My neighborhood is irking airplanes zooming
over my house from MacArthur Airport.

My neighborhood is bright red fire trucks
roaring down Lakeland Avenue.

My neighborhood is like a garden when spring rolls in,
there are daisies, roses, and lavender popping out
of every corner of the town.

And it is the immense church, with its elegant colors
and its lights shining brighter than the sun.

And it is the calming sunset tucking you into bed,
the town of Bohemia is a pleasing and splendid place to live.
Abby Molter, Grade 6

Thanksgiving

Thank you for all my ears can hear…
Click! Clank! goes the jingling silverware during dinner
Soft murmurs as we say our prayers before we eat
Roaring laughter after a rib-tickling joke

Thank you for all my nose can smell —
Cinnamon carrots carry colorful scents through the house
An aroma of lovely stuffing in the bustling kitchen
Pretty perfume from all the proper ladies

Thank you for all my tongue can taste…
Buttery mashed potatoes fill my mouth like a Thanksgiving parade
in the immense streets of NYC
Smoky turkey doused in gravy leaves a tangy taste on my tongue
Sweet apple pie is savory sugar in your mouth
Shaun Hill, Grade 6

Escaping the Heat in My Neighborhood

My neighborhood is screaming with magnificent
bees buzzing, kids scoring on BMX bikes, shooting
hoops and football games in back yards.

My neighborhood is silent on the fourth of July then
boom crash fireworks blast into the air like rocket ships.

My neighborhood is kids riding bikes to get freezing
cold Slurpees on desert hot days.

And it's howling in the summer with kids dousing
each other with refreshingly cold water.

And it's the end of the day and the immense display
of fireworks start and the dogs recede into their kennels.
Robert Raymond Dougherty, Grade 6

Thanksgiving Has Come

Thank you for all my eyes can see,
Waiting for colorful floats so anxiously
Golden, perfectly cooked turkey on the table
Beautiful, fiery, apricot and bleached leaves falling to
the ground like a bright snowfall

Thank you for all my nose can smell,
A barrage of scents coming from the kitchen
Fresh morning dew on the grass outside
The aroma of pumpkin pie filling my head with warm thoughts

Thank you for all my mouth can taste,
Tart, sweet flavor from the cranberry sauce
Lovely, appetizing turkey making its way into my mouth
Creamy, flavorful potatoes sitting on my plate ready to be eaten
Madeline Barget, Grade 6

Dog

When I was six I received a four-legged friend
Didn't know about it until that very weekend
I will always love my dog

Even though she gets in trouble for digging holes —
I always blame it on the moles
I will always love my dog

I fill the holes in when I get home —
Sometimes I cover up a gnome
I will always love my dog

We have some of the best times playing ball;
She will always come when I call
I will always love my dog
Katelyn Edwards, Grade 5

Football

I like to play football when it's hot out
I catch a pass and I make it first down
When I made first down my mom gave a shout
I get tackled hard and I hit the ground

I get a good sack on the quarter back
He looks at me and says I will get you
Later someone broke two of there arms, WHACK!
Also I tripped over my own two shoes
People were sad at the end of the game
They were cheering and they got the reward
We had lost to the team, oh what a shame
We still had a good time we just ignored
I told my mom we had a real good time
I'm glad we played in the summertime
Parker Yarbrough, Grade 5

Our Flag

Our flag stands for our freedom,
And we are so proud.
When it waves in the breeze,
It usually draws a crowd.

Its colors are beautiful,
The red, white, and blue.
And when you look up close,
They are so very true.

So today we celebrate our flag,
And this I want to say,
"Our flag waves with honor,
On this special day."
Victoria Martinez, Grade 6

Today

The beauty of the sunset,
Tells us something each day,
That another day has ended
Today.

The beauty of the sunrise,
Tells us this day is here,
That another day is beginning,
Today.

The wind blowing on the face,
Tells us life is a running race,
So, get inspired by the beauty of each day,
Today.

Mohamed Sarr, Grade 5

August Flies By

Oh August, Oh August
You are a special month,
Always shiny and bright
Into the twilight.

August is my birthday month
I can see my day coming
Filled up with joy
Presents and TOYS!

Every August day is warm
So the day has begun,
lets go swim and have some
fun.
Isabella Esteves, Grade 4

Soccer Delight

K yle likes to play soccer and Fifa16
Y es! He made a goal. He
L oves winning games and he keeps his
E yes open when dribbling the soccer ball.
Kyle Conard, Grade 6

Unseen Color

What I had heard, I thought was a lie.
If you had met someone that gave you happiness and love,
It was a blessing from above.
You could then see all the colors of the ground and sky.

I watch as the shadows dance across my face.
With the trees sharp like mountains and leaves bright as day.
The leaves, bright before they turn brown and gray
We all wish fall went at a slower pace.

I reach my hand out, hoping I had become happier sooner.
My hair blowing in front of me.
Now I am happier than I ever could be.
As I look into the distant future.

Norah Philipp, Grade 6

Thunder

Boom, boom, bang, SO loud,
The frightening noise of thunder,
Goosebumps all over.
Zain Rehman, Grade 5

Shining Brightly

Sun is really bright,
Planets rotate around it,
Shining orange-red.
Ahmad Alattaby, Grade 5

Halloween

Halloween,
A time of darkness and fright,
A time to dress up,
And trick-or-treat at night.
Dread and despair is in the night,
While young candy hunters zip their costumes up tight,
Somebody may jump out at you,
As a terrifying scream puts chills up people's spines.
A time of fear,
That happens every year,
We call it Halloween,
At least that's what I hear...

Henry Carroll, Grade 6

Grades K-1-2-3
High Merit Poems

The Sun

The Sun glistens when you look at it.
The Sun sparkles as you move.
The Sun spies on the kids playing.
The Sun bounces from day to night.
The Sun fills the sky with light.
The Sun waits for the winter.
Akash Gobin, Grade 3

Soccer

S port
O ffense
C oach
C orner kick
E xercise
R un
Keanin O'Bryan, Grade 2

Yummy Gingerbread Man

I smell something sweet and spicy.
I smell pumpkin spice cookies.
I smell gingerbread cookies.
I hope I can have a piece.
I ate one and it was super good.
I said yummy out loud.
Jesse Breen, Grade 3

Friends

Silly, respectful
Funny, awesome, cool
A very funny person
Amazing, caring, smart
Caring, fun
Family.
Juelz Walker, Grade 3

Blue

I feel the shimmering water
I see the shimmering diamond
I taste the watery blueberry
I hear a blue mocking bird chirp
I smell a great blueberry pie
Brian Machado, Grade 3

Games

G o fish
A rchery
M inecraft
E lectronic
S imon Says
Jemiah Torres, Grade 2

Cats

They have lots of fur
They like to play with yarn balls
Are really good pets
Cynthia Leech, Grade 3

Between Fall and Winter

Rainbow leaves shoot the ground,
Fall must be here.
    every time I take a step I hear a crunch!
Fall must be here.
Thump! thump! thump! the great oaks start to sleep, and while it sleeps it
drops its siblings so they can sprout,
Fall must be here!

Icy crystals shoot the ground forcing you to find shelter,
Winter must be here!
    a thick blanket of powder covers the ground,
Winter must be here!
Whack! A snowball hits my body, snowball fight!
Winter must be here.
Saijun Rousseau, Grade 3

The Night Saw It All

The sun went down and the moon came up.
Mrs. Smith's classroom saw it all…
The stuffed animals climbed down from the box.
Poet's chair hopped over and joined the stuffed animals.
Computer did the boogie and started up a beat!
The desk and chairs started slow dancing and the magnets did the Macarena.
Promethean did a break dance solo.
Carpet did a flip!
The books all started chatting the cushions had a feast!
Then, they all boogied till…
The very, very, VERY loud alarm rang and put an end to it all.
Sophia Louise Brookswolf, Grade 3

Brown Men

Mmmm! I smell something sweet fill the air.
It reminds me of Christmas.
I sneak into the kitchen and spy a tray full of little brown men in rows.
I pick one up.
He's bumpy and rough.
He has heart shaped buttons and is very hard.
"Crunch!"
I look down and see some left over crumbs on the plate.
I eat some it reminds me of Christmas only weeks away.
It is sweet and yummy and spicy too.
Gingerbread men are a Christmas delight.
Matthew Gagliardi, Grade 3

Winx Club

Winx Club is awesome
The show makes me laugh
The people are funny
I love to watch it because it makes me happy
The people can fly, especially the girls!
They are magical from head to toe
The boys are strong and wear the same uniform
They have tools that are different colors like red, blue, and green
I recommend this to people who like magic, like my teacher Ms. Betances!
A Magical Teacher!
Jarin Rafa, Grade 3

The Mulch Yard

My dad's mulch yard is kind of dusty,
and all the old metal is very rusty.

The pine needles are as sharp as nails,
and that's just one of the things he sells.

When it rains, it's very muddy,
and when I step it feels like putty.

The mulch yard looks like an old barn at night,
and sometimes it gives me a fright.

In fall, he'll rake your leaves,
at Christmas he'll sell you a Christmas tree.
Caleb Lane Brooks, Grade 3

Blue

Blue is the color of the blue Earth.
Blue is the color of the blue sky.
Blue is the color of the blue sea.
Blue is the color of the birds that fly.

Blue is the color of a blue marker.
Blue is the color of the crown.
Blue is the color of the rainbow.
Blue is the color of a frown.

Blue is the color of a blue key.
Blue is the color of a book.
Blue is the color of a blue star.
Blue is the color of a blue book, you take a look.
Shayna Kerns, Grade 3

United States

U nited States you are so special!
N o better nation out there,
I n your name
T o be a token of your
E ducation, freedom, liberty, and fame.
D o not forget that you are important.

S uper America
T each your history
A and name your facts
T ell everyone about your seeds and
E ndless achievements
S ave your name, so you will forever last as the home of the free.
Humna Husain, Grade 3

Thanksgiving

Nice as giving one hundred dollars to your mom.
Respectful as the people that died for us.
Happy like smiling so much that your face hurts,
Fun like jumping off a high cliff.
Love as great as you sacrificing yourself.
Christopher Turcious Benitez, Grade 3

United States

U nited States we are one
N eat nation that treats people fairly with
I mportant history
T omorrow new historical facts to learn about
E veryday lessons and
D ifferent cultures to discover.

S afe services we get
T o make our states feel safer
A nd admirable
T rue people who work hard to
E ducate many foreigners about our
S uper states of America.
Mohamed Elkhoga, Grade 3

Snow

The snow is white,
Kids went out to play,
The kids made a snowmen.
The kids ran to get some carrots
And some raisins.
For their snowmen they used raisins for his smile
And carrots for his nose.
All the children made snowmen.
The snowmen were beautiful.
They told everyone
So that they could come and admire
The best snowmen in town.
Tamia Barnes, Grade 3

Sunset Color

I wanted to paint the sunset,
I mashed every color by hand but could not find it,
A shriek came to me and said,
Tomorrow, wake up and go to the mountain,
and you will find your lovely shade.
I climbed up the mountain in the morning,
I straightened up my paper and started drawing.
I could not find the sunset and dropped the brushes running.
I came back to the mountain in the sunset,
The paint brushes burst into berries,
I crushed them up,
There, I found my color of favorite.
Ella Bao, Kindergarten

Red for Life

Red looks like a shining bright stoplight.
Red tastes like a yummy, crunchy apple.
Red smells like a beautiful rose garden with sweet smelling roses.
Red feels like rage.

Red sounds like a loud fire truck going by.
Red makes me think of a heart standing for love.
Red is a symbol of anger, madness and evil.
Red is the hot heat coming from the sun.
Zamiyah Cochran, Grade 3

Trip to France

Excitedly waiting for the plane
Skies are such a lovely blue
A sudden streak the plane soars down
It looks like a ball of silver
It picks us up we fly overhead

We dash over the milky clouds
I look out the circular window
Lighted streets all over
I grasp firmly onto Mommy
I chew fast huddling with my Daddy
The plane starts to tip forward

We fly down at full speed
Still chewing speedily I close my ears
The landing is rough
Slowing down our speed the plane stops
A sound like the song of the sky

I slowly step out
Cold chill frozen air
Shivering slightly
My Mommy hugs me warmly
I wave goodbye
Evaelle Huor, Grade 3

Hamster and Rat

hamster
cute, soft
eating, loving, caring
rodents, cousins, little, teeth
running, scratching, eating
disgusting, icky
rat
Kylee Mead, Grade 3

April Downfall

Why do droplets of
water pour down in April like
bees swarming out of a broken
hive annoyed and confused?

Where does the water come
from like waves crashing
wildly into a silky, soft, sandy,
slippery, shady, smooth, shore?

What does it do to Earth's
life like when a volcano
eruption destroys innocent
organisms?

When will the answers
come in a simple way like a
summer breeze?
Gus Bova, Grade 3

Black Widow

Black as concrete.
A spider you wouldn't want to meet
Also with a marking of red.
It's probably living under your bed
Strong jaws,
If you see one pause.
This spider is terrible.
It doesn't want to be memorable.
It just wants to thrive
As a spider species still alive.
They are carnivorous
More poisonous
Than a poison dart.
Kerdon Chapman, Grade 3

Stars

Day is gone
Dazzle of night
Stars begin to pop
Skytop cosmos
I gaze up at the stars
Secrets it questions
The moon listens to me
Silence the night
Stars of gold
Brightness
Untold stars
Still out there
Then darkness fills my mind
Logan Yetter, Grade 3

Autumn Time

trees are blowing,
wind is flowing,
for autumn time

cool breeze,
pollen sneeze,
for autumn time

since it's autumn,
time to stay inside,
but you can still
have fun by running
and doing the sock slide
Kaysha Roberts, Grade 3

Fall

Fall is here!
Leaves are falling
and autumn is calling.
Leaves are changing color
and animals come out for supper.
Trees are big, trees are tall,
lets get ready for fall!
Olivia Douglas, Grade 3

White Tail Deer

Brown and white fur and eyes and
Nose as black as night,
Eating fruit blossoms, tree bark, and
Dried grass,
Lynx, bears, hunters, run fast!
Leaping, hopping, darting back and
Forth,
Quietly hiding…tiptoeing through the
Woods, camouflaging in the trees,
Baby deer wobble as they walk for
The first time.
Bella Constantine, Grade 3

Chocolate!

Yummy and sweet, crunchy too
Several kinds of Chocolates
Like white chocolate,
Dark chocolate,
Milk chocolate, and many other kinds
There are many different shapes and sizes
Also lots of
Colors too
It melts in my mouth while I eat it
Chocolates
Are TASTY TASTY all day long!
Lucy Kaupp, Grade 3

Gold

Gold
Mineral that shines
In golden
Rays
Sign of everlasting
Happiness in the light
Of sunrise
As it shines its shiny
Everlasting golden narrow
Rays into the burning
Sun
Kevin Tynebor, Grade 3

Nightmare

Brown eyes closed
Nightmare
I wake up
Crying by the moonlight
Slowly and softly
Wander into my mom's bedroom
In her bed
Huddle closely
Under the golden sheets
I feel scared and sad
We doze back to sleep
Caroline Wilson, Grade 3

United States

U nited States is the best!
N orth America is truly big with
I ncredible states to learn about each day
T omorrow learn more about your history, it is a new day to dig
E ducation is everywhere
D iscover something new from the past because

S tates have a history so very special
T o take pride in their
A merican life
T ake a moment and appreciate
E veryone who is patriotic and nice because
S tates of America you are our home for life.

Ali Chaudhry, Grade 3

United States

U nited together we are one,
N ortheast, Northwest, Southeast, and Southwest
I mportant Americans in all.
T ogether as a team
E ven if you are naturally different
D iscover the loyal citizens that represent us.

S pecial United States citizens
T errific together we are one,
A mazing American history we once built
T o make the United States precious
E qually in every way because our
S acred flag stars are always here to stay.

Hooriya Bagasra, Grade 3

United States

U nited States I love you dearly,
N ew York you are part of my history.
I adore your independence
T o grow
E ach day and
D iscover something new

S o United States please be happy and strong
T o make Americans proud of who they are
A nd gain hope
T o make the United States an
E ndless symbol of our many
S uper constitutional blessings.

Hella Bin Towalah, Grade 3

My Third Grade Teacher

One of the best people that I know!
She teaches from the heart
She makes sure that nobody is left out.
One of my favorite things about her is her humor.
But don't get mistaken!
She is serious too.
She loves teaching and is the best teacher!

Briana Calin, Grade 3

Alexis the Fairy

Alexis the fairy
Sparkling so bright, went out to see the night.
Nelly tucked in her bed tight,
Saw the light, she grabbed her coat,
And zipped it up tight.
She went outside to see
What was flying through the night.
She walked outside and saw the light no more.
So she walked back through the door.
Nelly went back to bed, and slept all night.

Amber Louis, Grade 3

Confused

Adults talk and others laugh,
I'm confused because it's not funny.
Mother teaches me my math,
I'm confused because it won't help me.
Daddy gives me broccoli,
I'm confused because it's not yummy.
I can't buy toys at the toy store,
I'm confused because it's not that much money.
Do people get confused a lot,
Or does it just happen to me?

Kalina Rapoza, Grade 3

Grizzly Bears

I am strong
My teeth sink into my prey
I am an omnivore
I eat greens and meat
I can eat other bears
My nose can detect anything
You can find me in rivers, forests, and tundra.
Try to catch me if you can
My hunting skills are as sharp as can be.

James Sesay, Grade 3

Purple Is Pretty

Purple is… pretty.
Purple smells like… lavender.
Purple looks like… my sparkly backpack.
Purple tastes like… disgusting grape juice.

Purple feels like… a hard, tin pencil case.
Purple sounds like… the closing of a notebook.
Purple is… metallic paper.
Purple is my favorite color.

Akira Aikens, Grade 3

Thanksgiving

Pumpkin pie as sweet as candy.
Feast with a giant turkey.
Loving like soldiers that died for us.
Happy like time spent with my family.
Responsible like a principal running a school

Malcolm Hudson, Grade 3

Vampire Bats

I am small
Wings are so sharp
As they are connected
To makes toes

I love fruits
I am a herbivore
You can find me in caves, forest
As I love to live in trees.
Ahmed Sow, Grade 3

The Change

The petal that makes a rose,
Falls and seems lost;
To rise and open
Come Spring and see again.

I am the petal that makes a rose,
And when I fall all seems lost;
By the blood of love,
Come Spring and see again.
Luciana Ferrante, Grade 2

Santa Claus Is Coming to Town

Snow is white
It snows through the night
Santa comes before the light
Pitter patter hooves on the roof
Santa's magic goes poof
When the dog sees Santa he goes woof
How does he do his magic?
Perhaps it is a trick
Or maybe he's just Old Saint Nick
Ella Emigh, Grade 3

Lions

I live in a pride that's full of lions
I am a carnivore
I like to eat meat
But when I eat
I don't get beat
Sometimes you see me at the zoo
You might see my sharp claws
When I get happy I like to lick
My paws and purr.
Princess Richards, Grade 3

Christmas and Thanksgiving

Christmas
joy, cool
singing, enjoying, playing
cookies, songs, pumpkin, turkey
cooking, tasting, eating
enjoyable, joyful
Thanksgiving
Santino Colon, Grade 3

Pumpkins

Pumpkins
Orange, round
Picking, carving, buying
Decorating pumpkins is fun
Halloween
Aubree DeRose, Grade 1

Dog

Dog
Brown, white
Jumping, eating dog food, playing with me
Shasha loves me.
Shasha
Ines Martinez, Grade 1

Animals

Hedgehogs dig as fast as a mole.
Road runners as fast as a cheetah.
Frogs jump as fast as a kangaroo.
Blue jays fly as fast as an eagle.
Tigers run as fast as a lion.
Emryk Skeen, Grade 3

Play

Play
Sister, friend
Playing, jumping, running
She is one year old
Macie
Leaira Ramos, Grade 1

Ice Cream

Ice cream
Chocolate, vanilla
Eating, licking, scooping
Rainbow and chocolate sprinkles
Summer
Laisha Cruzado, Grade 1

Ruby

R eally likes art
U sually likes sharks
B eing funny
Y earns for more toys
Ruby Welch, Grade 2

My Little Sisters

My little sisters are so sweet
I love them both so much
They make my happy when I'm mad
they make me laugh when I'm sad
Michael Merritt, Grade 1

Flowers

Pretty, lively,
Nectar so sweet.
Oh so lovely,
Colors so neat.
Sun they need
Oxygen and air,
Beautiful flower everywhere.
Erika Linder, Grade 3

Snow

Snow is falling to the ground
Snow is falling all around
Snow is falling on the tree
Snow is falling on me
Snow is falling on the street
Snow is falling to the beat
Oh my, what a treat
Joshua Gamboa, Grade 2

Santa Claus

A man in red,
Delivering presents to you
While you're in bed.
Maybe if you stay up long enough,
You can catch a glimpse of him.
The man in red himself,
Santa Claus!
Victor MacLaughlin, Grade 3

Cat and Tiger

cat
cute, cuddly
running, hissing, playing
whiskers, claws, tails, ears
eating, hunting, protecting
big, dangerous
tiger
Lucas Cintron, Grade 3

Fall

Fall is my least favorite,
It is called Hurricane season.
I do not like hurricanes.
But I like to see the leaves falling,
Full of beautiful colors.
Fall is the season of Thanksgiving
So I thank God for Fall too.
John Paul Forster, Grade 3

My Hero

There was a game called "My Hero."
You could make your player do anything.
He or she could do lots of things
Like play basketball, fly a paper airplane,
Or do lots of performances.
Reginald Ross, Grade 3

A Hot Summer Day

I jumped in the car and off to the beach.
I hoped it wouldn't take two days to reach.
Mom soon started the car,
While I played with my marbles in a jar.
A few hours later it was time for lunch.
And we all ate it with a Munch! Munch! Munch!
"We are almost there," my dad yelled.
We climbed out of the car the sun block I held.
Then I jumped high and rolled in the sand.
Next I jumped in the water as I heard a band.
I played in the water for a while.
That gave me a great smile.
I wanted to build so I got my shovel and pail and I started to dig.
I made my model that looked like a pig.
Soon it was time to go back in the car.
I didn't want to go so far.
After hours of driving we got home at last.
A tiring but wonderful day put me to sleep fast.

Avery Orr, Grade 3

Fall Is Here

Fall is here, you can tell, by the loud ringing school bell.
Hear the leaves and the rustling trees,
changing just like you and me.
Wind breezes past over hills and seas,
like children playing, full of glee.
Students run past hardworking teachers,
as they stomp on crunching, crisp leaves.
Oh what fun that you can have,
in this wonderful, cool Autumn breeze.

Pumpkins, pumpkins round, orange, and fat,
Oops, I think I squashed one when I sat.
Candy corns, marshmallows, treats all that!
A small, black, paper bat I made in class.
Fall is here, enjoy the fun,
eat lots of candy.
Yeah, eat a ton!

Chloe Lin, Grade 3

A Great Day

I woke up in the morning.
I saw a butterfly soaring.
Hot, hot day!
We did not know what to play.
With the sprinkler at the bottom of the slide,
We began our adventure on our ride.
Each trip we bounced down the hill.
Our mother was upset of the muddy thrill.
Hot, hot day! We continued our play.
We rode our bikes to the lake.
Grace found a slithering snake.
We climbed into a boat.
I surely hope it will float.
Hot, hot day! We have exhausted our play.

Julia Chrobak, Grade 3

Horrible Day

Lightning flashing, thunder crashing
Bars of rage a nightmare scream

Temple of anger like a flame
Urchins with silver spikes

A horrible thing in the dark of December
Cold creeps as fire dies, the sky dark and black

Quiet clank of the chains now a silver blade
As bumpy and rough as madness

Black holes spin through space, the color of fear
Lashing, gnashing teeth

Ghost mothers' creak the wicker rockers
Anger as powerful as a hurricane

Slowly, slowly seeping anger, slipping through my body
Like roaring, pouring rain

Carissa Fallon, Grade 3

I Am

I am smart and nice.
I wonder about my real grandma.
I hear my mother loving me.
I see beautiful flowers and a rainbow.
I want a guitar.
I am smart and nice.

I pretend to cook pizza and spaghetti.
I feel happy that I have a mom and dad.
I touch a puppy in the rain forest.
I worry about monsters in my room.
I cry when people are mean to me.
I am smart and nice.

I understand being a kid.
I say I believe my mom will be happy with her life.
I dream that I will see my real grandma.
I hope my mom gets a car.
I am smart and nice.

Liliana Grosso-Pedro, Grade 2

Is It Saturday Today?

Is it Saturday today?
Is it a no school day?
Is the sky grey or
Will the sun yell out "Are you ready to play?"

We are going to the park today!
How about lunch at Subway or
Maybe ice-cream on the way.
It will be a fun filled day,
Yay, it is Saturday today!

Nathan Rollins, Grade 3

Fire with My Cousins

Wood stacked
Surrounded by kindling
A match
A flame
The fire gains
Gold sparks
Flashing in the dark
Crackling noises
A glistening wonder

My cousins gather
Around the fire
We tell everlasting stories
As our laughter bellows
Happiness in the air
We gaze at the fire

Flames die slowly
Flames fade
Cold creeps
As the fire dies
Tatum Andrews, Grade 3

The Animals

Gobble gobble
Wobble wobble
Look at the turkeys go
Look up high
Look down low
Look at those turkeys go
Howl howl
Dowl dowl
Look at the wolf go
Look up high
Look down low
Look at the wolf go
Waddle waddle
Paddle paddle
Look at the penguin go
Look up high
Look down low
Look at the penguin go
Look at the animals go
Caleb Klees, Grade 3

The Fire

Flashing flames
Blood red
Quiet sparks of fire
Flying bye
A temple of heat
Warms my body
The fire glistening and shiny
Lights the night
A magical time
Jacob White, Grade 3

A Halloween Night

Halloween night, a time of fright
The moon up high was very bright.
The decorations all around are scary.
It was so cold my nose red as a cherry.

I went trick or treating with my friends.
The road had many turns and bends.
We visited a haunted house.
Someone there dressed like a mouse.

We walked up to someone's porch,
Where we saw a flickering torch.
We started to jump and scream
So they gave us candy and ice cream.

The next house was also scary.
The woman was dressed like a fairy.
She gave us each a Pixie Stick,
And showed us all a Halloween trick!
Katie Dudkowski, Grade 3

Roller Coaster

Nervousness fills my seat
When I pull down the safety bar
Click! Click! Click!

I see the sign
Blinking
"Are you ready?"
Go!

I feel amazing
Wind in my hair
Like skiddeling through space

It's so fast
"More!" I think
Then the ride slows down
Wow!

Again!
Natalie Helfrich, Grade 3

My Jordans

I like wearing Jordan's on my feet,
when I walk down the street

As I walk I draw a crowd,
which makes me really proud

I feel so big and tall,
all I need is a basketball

My Jordan's are truly the best,
they're better than all the rest
Angel Calvo, Grade 3

Love

Reflect my heart
Golden rule
Pretty tunes
Red running blood reminds me of love
When I think of it, it's like a dream
A sweet touch
A smooth touch
A touch that makes me feel special
Everyone loves someone, just someone
Love is like a volcano about to erupt
It's like a red heart pumping with joy
The whole world is like a bucket of love
Everlasting love
Someone that loves you
Lauren Vince, Grade 3

Basketball

A colossal hole
My heart pounds like a dribbling basketball
A gaping shot
The ball soars like a wandering eagle
A loud swoosh
Glory falls upon me
Glory
I run with a successful breeze
Confidence rises up
The land of winners
Winners
Victorious
Silence strikes upon the crowd
The impossible shot
Tre Henning, Grade 3

Yellow

I like yellow shoes.
I like yellow dye.
I like everything yellow.
I don't know why.

I like yellow crayons.
Mom will make yellow dots.
Dad will do it on white paper
I have to find a spot.

I love yellow paper.
Sis loves a yellow shoe.
She loves a yellow basket.
Mom loves yellow too.
Kychaun Goode, Grade 3

My Mom

I love my Mom.
She is helpful, nice, kind,
sweet, caring and a good cook!
I love my Mommy.
Mikaela Manalaysay, Kindergarten

Blue

Blue is the sound of rain falling.
Blue looks like the beautiful sky when it's clear.
Blue tastes like freshly picked, from the garden, blueberries.
Blue smells like just bought from the store blue paint.

Blue feels like me when I'm sad and depressed.
Blue makes me think of ocean waves crashing.
Blue makes me feel happy when I see the open, blue sky.
Blue is my most favorite color (even since I was a baby).

Skyy Batts, Grade 3

Blue

Blue looks like the ocean at the beach.
Blue tastes like blueberries picked from a garden.
Blue smells like crisp morning air.
Blue feels like the wind in the morning.

Blue sounds like the ocean; like when I wake up.
Blue makes me feel like a happy ballerina.
Blue is like a beautiful day at the beach.
Blue is my favorite color.

Isabella Florin, Grade 3

Red

Red is anger.
Red feels like scarlet fabric.
Red looks like blood.
Red sounds like loud screams.

Red tastes like Sour Patch Kids (p.s. Red is the most sour).
Red looks like the beautiful sunset.
Red reminds me of love.
Of your heart itself.

Dalton Tipton, Grade 3

Blue

Blue is my favorite color.
Blue is the color of the sky.
Blue is lighter than the water in the sea.
Blue is like a waterfall.

Blue smells like fresh blue raspberries from a farm.
Blue feels like a cloud.
Blue tastes like blueberry pie.
Blue makes me feel like I'm diving into water.

Aundrea Clark, Grade 3

Here Fall, Dear Fall

The leaves will fall we shall hear that fall is coming near.
The leaves are whirling and twirling.
The leaves are brown gold yellow and red.
Here fall will be we will not fear.
We hope you never leave.
HERE FALL
DEAR FALL

Shawn Neal, Grade 3

My Brother

My brother is so nice.
He is loving, funny, and cool.
My brother is the best in the world.
He has a phone and we can play together.
He comes over my house a lot, he is 13 years old.
He prays a lot, I love him so much.

Emily Neal, Grade 3

The Snow

The cold snow
Cold as ice, white ice
So cold we need big jackets
People are not walking up and down
Instead they are running to escape this horrible weather
It is winter.

Ka-nahya Peterson, Grade 3

What Cookie?

Baking in the oven was a spicy cookie.
It had M&M buttons.
This cookie is hard on your teeth.
When I bite into the cookie it is crunchy and has yummy frosting.
The cookie feels bumpy, rough, and flat.
Can you guess what cookie I made?

Amanda Gilmore, Grade 3

The Sweet Treat

Yum, a wonderful sweet smell fills the house.
I looked at the tan, brown gingerbread boy baking in the stove.
I took the flat cookie out of the stove.
I saw the frosted, small person-like cookie.
Crunch!
My teeth touched the ginger taste cookie and it filled my mouth.

Ryan Coleman, Grade 3

Thanksgiving

Pumpkin pie — As yummy as an ice cream sundae at the beach.
Feast — Like being in heaven
Happiness — Like bluebirds chirping in a tree.
Family — As rambunctious as soccer players trying to score a goal.
Love — As honorable as soldiers fighting for our country.

Luis Rocha Murillo, Grade 3

My Teacher

My teacher asks people to listen.
My teacher gives us homework.
My teacher teaches us about the Letter People, math, science.
I love my teacher.

Jakob Connolly, Kindergarten

Kyle

K nows a lot about four-wheelers
Y ummy popcorn with butter is my favorite snack!
L ikes candy
E specially likes to play soccer

Kyle Johnson, Grade 2

Turtles
Hard, slow
Swimming, snapping, eating
Hide in their shells
Animal
Jack Wescott, Grade 3

Blue
B lueberries
L evi jeans
U mbrellas
E yes
Daniel Gonzalez, Grade 2

Winter Day
Winter is cold
Winter is fun
Winter is a
Time to play and chill in the cold sun.
Aleeyah Tramel, Grade 3

Cats
C heetahs
A frican lions
T igers
S now leopards
Glenda Velez, Grade 2

Rosy
I have a dolphin
her name is Rosy
I like to cuddle with her when I go to bed
She keeps all the bad dreams away
Reyvalen Lozada, Grade 1

Cheetah
Are fast as lightning
They have yellow and black stripes
Are very sneaky
Mahady Rabbani, Grade 3

Riding Fast
I ride my jet ski
Flies over waves at the beach
It goes very fast
Nathan Roseberger, Grade 3

Mars
Red shiny planet
Orbiting the giant star
Mars, the next frontier
Daniel Dean, Grade 3

Vampire Bats
Not all bats are scary!
Vampire bats are not scary because they do not bite
Bats help save us,
They eat insects so that they will not bite us
Bats that eat fruits are called fruit bats
When bats have babies, people take them to wrap them up like a towel
Bats usually do not bite people, they bite animals
They never bother humans, unless you bother them
So you should not be afraid of bats!
Juelz Manzano, Grade 3

Smile Brother Smile
Hey there Bro, I really want to see you smile
You have been so down for quite a while.
College has taken you away from me and I feel sad
And then I hear your coming home and I start to feel glad.
You are my brother and I love you so much,
But you have been distant and moody and so hard to reach and touch.
I may be younger than you and really don't know everything going on,
But one important thing I do know brother is my world just isn't right when you are gone.
Come home to me and smile!
Emma Treber, Grade 2

Yummy Little Men
"Sniff, sniff."
Sweet ginger fills the air as I walk to the kitchen to see what it was.
When I got to the counter I saw a plate full of yummy little men covered in frosting.
I pick one up.
"It's very crumby," I said.
Then I ate it.
"Snap!"
Mmmm, mmm, mmm!
I love gingerbread cookies.
Emily Austin, Grade 3

Black
Black looks like a road.
Black smells like my black hair.
Black tastes like licorice Twizzlers.
Black feels like tar that has just dried.

Black sounds like my dad's new Ram truck.
Black makes me feel like I'm in my room under my nice, warm covers.
Safe in my bed.
I love black.
Nicole Rogers, Grade 3

A Christmas Delight
Mmmm! I smell something cinnamony and sweet baking in the oven.
I peek in and see a golden brown gingerbread man sitting on a tray.
Gingerbread men remind me of Santa coming to my house.
CRUNCH!!
I ate them all up!
They are so tasty!
Anabel Pozniewski, Grade 3

Please Don't Eat Me!

The turkey is on the kitchen table.
It is big and brown.
It reminds me of a meatball.
But he looks like he has a frown.
The turkey looks tasty
It makes me go crazy!
Finally, I get the last piece of turkey!
Daniel Mejia, Grade 3

Finding Charlie the Elf

There is Charlie on the
light post!
There is Charlie on the
stair!
Charlie likes to eat his
toast.
But never when I'm there.
Finnian MacLaughlin, Kindergarten

Penguin

I am short and warm
Even though I live in an icy cold place.

I have a long, sharp beak
Do you know who I am?

A Penguin!
Jada Cedie, Grade 3

My Dog

Oreo is my dog
We gave her that name
Because she is Furry, black and white.
She is a playful and nice dog,
Oreo is so fun.
I love her so much, I take good care of her
And let no one hurt her.
Juliet Buscemi, Grade 3

The Zoo Day

Hooray!
It is zoo day!
I love the elephants
and the lions and tigers too.
It is time for them to play,
so I really want to say "Hooray"
It made my day.
Surisaday Davila, Grade 2

Wolf

Wolf
Black, rough
Running, jumping, glistening
It is a carnivore
Mammal
Luca Stevens, Grade 3

Wolves

I am strong
Teeth sharp as an
Elephant's tusks.

I am a carnivore
I munch on fat, juicy meat.

You can find me in the forests.
Christian Emile, Grade 3

Dogs

Dogs jump like kangaroos.
Dogs play with puppies.
Dogs run like other dogs.
Dogs sleep like tigers.
Dogs leave in houses like people.
Dogs have names like cats.
Dogs walk like people.
Dogs play with other dogs.
Ariel Canales, Grade 3

Red

Red tastes like gobs of gum
Red smells like tomatoes
Red is the color of a baby's thumb

Red tastes like blood moon ice cream
Red feels like lemons
Red is my favorite color
Red is like a bed
Orren Gordon, Grade 3

Picking Flowers

One day I saw a flower and many more,
So I picked one.
Someone else was picking flowers,
So I helped them.
Then a boy joined his sister and they
picked almost the whole field.
We took them inside to put in a vase.
Then they got some juice.
Chaise Surley, Grade 3

Football in Fall

I play football in the fall.
Football is fun!
Buzz! Time runs out as I catch the ball.
I play football in fall.
When the colorful trees are tall.
We play at night and in the sun.
I play football in the fall.
Football is fun!
Campbell Barker, Grade 3

Blue

The sky is blue, your dress is blue,
The ocean and the rain are blue.
The cup is blue, the bucket is blue,
Water and flowers are blue.

Love is blue, glasses are blue,
Makeup and shoes are blue.
Your hair is blue, pants are blue,
Nail polish and waterfalls are blue.

Clothes are blue, paper is blue,
A ball is blue, sweaters are blue,
Books are blue,
Blue is a pocketbook.
Teairra Robinson, Grade 3

Green Is Beautiful

Green is the color of my yard
Green is the color of my tree
I wish green was the coolest color
I wish green was the color of a bee

Green is the color of my pencil
Green is the color of my room
Green is the color of my shirt
Green is the color of my broom

Green is the color of my book bag
Green is the color of my grass
Green is the color of my binder tab
Green is the color of some cash
Dillon Newton-Short, Grade 3

What Is Red?

Red is a strawberry.
Anger is red.
Red is an apple.
Red is the best I said.

Red is a soda and
The color of a rose.
Red is a shirt,
Also a nose.

Red is a heart.
Gum is red.
Red is a blanket
On my bed.
Sierra Gay, Grade 3

My Birthday

Bouncy house, cake
Friends, family, balloons
Presents.
Happy Birthday!
Caitlyn Pham, Kindergarten

Thanksgiving

Love as sweet as hugging and giving kisses to mom and dad.
Happy as having a great Christmas morning and spending time with your family.
Mom as nice as helping her clean because she doesn't need to do everything, kids need to help too.
Eat like eating and talking with friends and family.
Kind like being nice to one another and not making fun of anyone and being grateful.

Joana Gonzalez, Grade 3

My Garden

Birds fly in the sky,
Squirrels jump from branch to branch,
Collecting nuts as they go by,
Butterflies fly from flower to flower,
Sucking nectar as they go by,
All so busy in my garden.

Roses so red,
Violets so blue
Sunflowers so yellow,
All flowers so pretty,

Adding splashes of color to my garden.
Trees with green leaves,
Gently swaying in the wind,
Scattering to the ground,
Creating a yellow and green carpet in my garden.

Dog's barks heard far and wide,
Cats walking across the street,
Paws moving on the ground.
Tails are everywhere some are tucked,
Some wag, some stay straight,
There is so much activity around my garden.

Shivani Yadavalli, Grade 3

I Am

I am brave and sharing.
I wonder if my mom will get a car.
I hear people talking in the classroom.
I see pictures of people hanging on the wall.
I want toys that will build things.
I am brave and sharing.

I pretend to be a teacher.
I feel happy at home.
I touch my heart when my grannie and sister come.
I worry if my sister is going to be OK.
I cry when people hurt me.
I am brave and sharing.

I understand to tell people the truth.
I say I believe in my mom.
I dream about my mom getting a cool new car.
I try very hard to write.
I hope my dad feels better from his broken arm.
I am brave and sharing.

Ashley Villia Gonzalez, Grade 2

The Fall Leaves

The leaves of fall waiting for snow
Will they get it, we shall know
The leaves of fall wait to be jumped on
They can play in the leaves but can't play in the sea
The bright gold does glare at day
But red shines at night
They shine at night
It glares the sea

The sea prances and dances,
Rustles and hustles
The leaves at fall,
Fall to the floor,
Blowing here and there, and everywhere
Blowing into people who play and relax
Dear fall leaves
We love you so much
We like and love you!

The fall leaves falling down to the ground
Twisting and turning
Tumbling and fumbling

Brandon Baptiste, Grade 3

The Sun

The sun reminds me of happiness
The sun reminds me of life
The sun reminds me of happy little children
The sun reminds me of flowers
The sun reminds me of millions of smiling faces
The sun reminds me of love
The sun reminds me of laughter
The sun reminds me of a beautiful family
The sun reminds me of amazing summer days
The sun reminds me of crystals
The sun reminds me of a beach of happy people
The sun reminds me of animals
The sun reminds me of a fuzzy blanket
The sun reminds me of friendship
The sun reminds me of all those good times I had
The sun reminds me of angels
The sun reminds me of rainbows
The sun reminds me of greatness
The sun reminds me of all the amazing things you could do
The sun reminds me of all good things
And the sun reminds me of you

Sabrina Muche, Grade 3

United States

U nited States forever
N ever change your rights, because
I live in this special place where it
T ruly taught me to live freely.
E ndless history that
D oes not change my liberty.

S o many states with patriotism are
T ogether forever.
A merica you are my history
T hat is true to heart
E ven in every space, I am
S trongly a sacred citizen of this wonderful place.

Alizay Zia, Grade 3

United States

U nited States, United States
N orth and South,
I wonder how old you are
T en, fifteen, one hundred
E veryone counts on you
D allas, Indianapolis, everywhere

S ome of your people fought for you,
T ales of old folks, some are real,
A ll people wonder
T en, one hundred, fifteen
E agles are signs of freedom
S tates of America, you are so beloved to me!

Sara Mohamed, Grade 3

United States

U nited you stand
N ot alone, but together as a nation
I ncredible feeling to be in the United States
T ogether as a team
E very day we learn new historical facts; yet, some
D ifferent from the past

S uper patriotic presidents who were able to lead
T hank you so much for the freedom seed
A nd powerful peace
T errific United States do you hear how
E qually people are treated fairly in all of our
S acred United States.

Omar Elhalo, Grade 3

Christmas Crunch

I take out a tray from the oven full of colorful gingerbread men.
They have white chocolate chips as white as snow and icing.
Red, white, and a little blue.
I take a little bite of the cookie.
It tastes like ginger.
As I take a bite, I hear a crunchy sound.
I wait for Santa to eat my Christmas delight.

Layla Pirela, Grade 3

United States

U nited States my home
N ot just for me, but for all of you
I ntegrity and intelligence all around
T ogether we can make America proud, by learning about our
E lder founding fathers that we respect
D edicated duties we must practice for you in our heart

S hare cities and states together because it is our part
T hankful people sing with me:
A merica, America my home live with me, and we will totally be free
T errific love we have for one another
E ncourage our home to
S hine high with pride, I love you more than any other.

Fatima Siddiqi, Grade 3

United States

United States of America you are fascinating
Nothing can stop you from doing your job
If you my United States of America did not exist, I would feel so sad
Teaching citizens to stay together is your goal
Every day it feels great to be part of you in which I call my home
Dilligent people everywhere are working hard to call you their U.S.A.

South, north, east, and west regions of the United States
The American flag is special to you and me because
America is our beautiful land and country
The Star Spangled Banner is our eternity
Enjoy the American patriotic history because our
Stars and stripes are part of our American destiny.

Aleena Usmani, Grade 3

Nice Day

I wake up and get a feeling it is a nice day,
So I get up and go outside.
I feel good in the very outstanding temperature.
The flowers are dancing and are so pretty.
The day is so great and is covered with beauty.
The sun is shining bright.
I can't believe this!
Then there is a really bad stink so I look down.
It is so bad that I can't even open my eyes.
I slowly pick it up trying not to breathe through my nose.
I throw it in the trash and the smell is gone.
It's a wonderful day again.
I am happy!

Arron Spratley, Jr., Grade 3

The Best Teacher

My teacher never sits down
She is always helping others
She rewards us if we do our homework
She's one of the most inspirational people that I know
She teaches us what is wrong and what is right
She helps us grow
I hope you all have the chance to meet Ms. Betances

Michelle Barnes, Grade 3

United States

U nited States my special homeland
N orth America is where I love to live
I mportant history to learn each day,
T onight I will read the Constitution and
E ducate myself about the rights I have
D iscovered freely.

S haring rights so I can
T ell my friends about its beauty
A ll you need is freedom
T o learn, love, and live in America.
E veryone needs to hear the rights
S o that you will be free forever in the land of opportunity!

Sedeen Tutanji, Grade 3

United States

U nited States, United States
N eed not to cry at all, because we are
I n a happy country
T ogether we will work hard with everyone
E veryday fun is here and there, exploring the
D eclaration of Independence

S afe and sound for me
T olerating one another in our country is
A lways a democracy you see,
T elling me the true history is important
E qually for you and me, because we are the
S atisfying home of the free.

Yusuf Elliott, Grade 3

United States

U nited States, the United States
N ice native people here and there
I mportant citizens that show great care
T olerance is what they believe in, because they
E nded slavery with powerful leaders who
D iscovered the history of our past.

S tar regions, you know how important it is being
T ogether equally
A t a very strong amount
T errific talent of leadership roles who
E nded slavery and began new laws to become a
S acred state of the free.

Ameera Ahmed, Grade 3

Basketball

I like basketball
I know all the rules
I like to play basketball
With my dog
All he does is take it for himself
Or he bites on his leash
When he sees me with my basketball getting ready to shoot.

Stephan Picard, Grade 3

United States

U nited states of America, you
N ever let your states down because
I t feels incredible to be free
T ime passes as history grows
E veryone should learn about America's past
D o not be afraid to ask questions.

S top for once, to think about your rights
T ogether we will have eternal peace
A nd freedom.
T olerance is part of our unity
E veryone needs to portray it as a
S ign of our historical liberty.

Rami Hassan, Grade 3

My Daddy

Daddy is the warmth of the shimmering sun,
Daddy is the calm of the blue sea,
Daddy is the strength of my heart,
Daddy is the comforting side of night,
Daddy is the most generous hand,
Daddy is the wisdom of life,
Daddy is the power of a Majestic Eagle,
Daddy is the joy of spring breezes,
Daddy is the faith of a seed that grows love,
Daddy is the honesty that will tell you it straight,
Daddy is the depth of a family need,
And a Father's Day Masterpiece!!!
Happy Father's Day!!!

Aliza Baig, Grade 3

United States

U nited States you are my special country
N ever a dull day with you
I ndependence is who you are
T olerant states everywhere
E ndless historical facts to learn about and
D ifferent cultures to appreciate splendidly.

S outh, North, East, and West regions in all
T eaching people to be thankful for freedom
A nd the American dream
T errific nation who treats people
E qually in such a superb place with unlimited rights
I S where I always wanted to be.

Alysha Usmani, Grade 3

Aquarium

Dolphin as bright as the sun
Fish as fast as a cheetah
Jellyfish as slow as a frog
Sharks as strong as lightning
Shark whale as big as a skyscraper
Blue whale as strong as an elephant
Turtle as slow as a cloud moving across the sky

Yajaira Velasquez, Grade 3

I Am

I am crazy and smart.
I wonder if in the future they will make human robots.
I hear a wolf howling on a mountain.
I see a paperclip floating around inside my brain.
I want, when I'm older, a robot that will do anything I say.
I am crazy and smart.

I pretend to be a Celtic warrior.
I feel like I am a chef.
I touch a lizard trying to run away from em.
I worry about my family.
I cry when I get a sad face in school.
I am crazy and smart.

I understand that the world can never change.
I say God is real.
I dream about my friend and me finding a bear with a white beard.
I try really hard in school.
I hope that the human species will not get extinct.
I am crazy and smart.

Troy Gunnels, Grade 2

I Am

I am a scientist and a great helper.
I wonder about discoveries.
I hear noise inside the house.
I see too much fun.
I want to be smart.
I am a scientist and a great helper.

I pretend that I have super powers.
I feel good, like I want to do everything at once.
I touch unicorns outside in space.
I worry about my dad and my mom's job.
I cry when someone says mean stuff to me.
I am a scientist and a great helper.

I understand what people say.
I say I believe in God.
I dream of flying in the air.
I try to get to the final round and win.
I hope I can go to the places where I want to go.
I am a scientist and a great helper.

Joshua Cruz-Cervantes, Grade 2

I Am

I am a princess and I am nice.
I wonder if they will give me cake.
I hear my heart beeping.
I see a frog jumping in the water.
I want a chocolate bar.
I am a princess and I am nice.

I pretend that I am a teacher.
I feel sad when I'm in trouble with my mom.
I touch a cat. She is touching me, too.
I worry about God…that He doesn't like Halloween.
I cry when I am dreaming.
I am a princess and I am nice.

I understand math.
I say to stand up on your bed.
I dream that I am fairy princess.
I try to be good.
I hope we celebrate my birthday.
I am a princess and I am nice.

Valerie Rodriguez-Leon, Grade 2

I Am

I am happy and special.
I wonder where we are going sometimes.
I hear my mom's music playing.
I see the lights in my room.
I want another baby brother.
I am happy and special.

I pretend to be a princess.
I feel happy about the surprises my mom gives.
I touch the sand at the beach.
I worry about my dad when he is at work.
I cry when brother gets me in trouble.
I am happy and special.

I understand my teacher when she is teaching.
I say I believe in my friends.
I dream that I'm at school every day.
I try to plant my flowers.
I hope I get to go to Guatemala.
I am happy and special.

Ashley Recinos-Santos, Grade 2

Zeus

My dog is the one that always makes me happy,
Even when I am sad
My dog is the one that's always playful
My dog is the one that makes me laugh all of the time
He is funny
My dog is the one that always makes me not lose hope
My dog is the one that always makes me feel not alone
My dog is the one that makes me enjoy life
I love my dog Zeus!

Shesit Moreno, Grade 3

Mom and Dad

My mom and dad are sweet and wonderful!
My mom and dad go on magical journeys with me.
My mom and dad are as happy as a king and queen.
My mom and dad shine like the golden sun.
My mom and dad listen to the rain with me.
My mom and dad watch the sunset with me.
My mom and dad see the moon.
And hang out at night with me.
My mom and dad are cute and loving!

Abigail Hays, Grade 3

White Is All

White is the star when Jesus was just born
White is white rose I hold
White is the symbol of strength
White is for white ice cream that I sold

White is for the light when Jesus rose
White is for the dove that watches over me
White is the life for you and me
White is the cloud over me

White is the love that I share
White is the cotton I see
White is milk from cows I see
White is the glory of God
Makayla Connelly, Grade 3

Blue Is Pretty

Blue is the color of my bed
Blue is the color of the ocean
Blue is the color of the pretty blue sky
Blue is the color of the pretty blue bells

Blue is the color of my favorite shirt
Blue is the color of a piece of gum
Blue is a lunch box
Blue is a pencil box

Blue is a superman shirt
Blue is a rug
Blue is a cup
Blue is a bucket
Montaniq Fitzgerald, Grade 3

Gold Is

Gold is waves on the beach
Gold is my life
Gold is like a blossom flower
Gold is not a knife

Gold is smart
Gold as good as love
Gold is what wakes me up
Gold is a flying dove

Gold keeps me alive
Gold is where my heart begins
Gold loves me
Gold is where my heart ends
Harper Siefferman, Grade 3

Playing Soccer

I kick the ball
I pass to my teammates
The team mates score
Goal! We won!
Kevin Wagner, Kindergarten

Birds

Chirping sounds
High in the tree
I sit quietly
Listening
Under the big brown tree
The golden sun
Warming my face
As it shines on me
I gaze
At the colorful birds
Dashing and darting
Wings fluttering
All around me
They flutter and flap
Zip and zap
To another
Big brown tree
Jason Garbacz, Grade 3

A Beach Day

Wake up! Everybody get in the car.
Drive, drive, drive, we drive so far.
On the way to the sandy shore,
We stopped at a convenience store.
I had two cents to spare,
After buying a seashell so rare.
We finally arrived and everyone got out,
We stood in line when Dad started to shout.
The sun was so very bright,
We looked at the sea, a beautiful sight.
We ran down to the water,
I was thinking, can the day get any hotter?
I sat down and started to dig,
And built a sandcastle so large, so big.
It looked so tall it could touch the sky,
Up washed a wave, with a quick good-bye.
Vanessa Miller, Grade 3

A Sunny Day

One day I went to the beach.
On the way I ate a peach.
I arrived and jumped in the water,
Hoping to spot a sea otter.
I played in the golden sand,
Building a kingdom covered the land.
Mom remembered to pack some food,
Knowing hunger would be a bad mood.
With my brother we played Frisbee,
Running and catching with such glee.
Back in the water to play some more,
"Marco Polo" was fun for sure.
We dried off and feeling bored,
I kicked a beach ball till I scored.
Walking home after my win,
Now everything is the way it's been.
Mary Maloney, Grade 3

Basketball

Basketball is fun,
it makes you run,
You dribble you shoot,
you pass through the hoop.
You play on a team,
nobody should be mean!
You don't practice once,
you practice a whole bunch.
There are coaches and referees,
that you'll always need.
Basketball is fun,
I like to be number one.
Swish! I made it in.
Dribble, dribble I passed it again.
Buzzz! We won! We won!
We are number one!
Kendria Bynum, Grade 3

Bowling

A nine pound ball
Slips out
Of my hand
Slowly rolling
Down the alley
My mind is blank
I want a strike
A tumble tune
As it smashed against
A white mountain of pins

My eyes are shut
Slowly one pin falls
Then another
I think it's a strike
It's a STRIKE!
Aditi Sangishetty, Grade 3

Fishing

Orange sunrise
Far into the shadow
Far into the gloomy water
Far into the deep end
Whispers of the worm
Smelling of the bait
A silver point
Dip the hook
Dip the line
Open his mouth to gulp the bait
Magical tug
Right out of the water
Sound of the bubbles
Like a shiny, slimy pearl
He says goodbye freedom
A drop of excitement
Elizabeth James, Grade 3

Fall
Fall is as red as an apple.
Fall is as orange as a pumpkin.
Fall is as yellow as a leaf.
Madison Tracey, Kindergarten

Fall
Fall is as red as apples.
Fall is as orange as a pumpkin.
Fall is as yellow as a bus.
Dylan O'Connell, Kindergarten

Fall
Fall is as red as an apple.
Fall is as orange as a giant pumpkin.
Fall is as yellow as the sun.
Benedek Martinez, Kindergarten

Fall
Fall is as red as a caramel apple.
Fall is as orange as a pumpkin.
Fall is as yellow as a leaf.
Gabrielle Green, Kindergarten

Fall
Fall is as red as an apple.
Fall is as orange as a leaf.
Fall is as yellow as a school bus.
Payton Parson, Kindergarten

My Birthday
Balloons, presents, cake
Guests, games
Happy Birthday to me!
Elizabeth O'Neill, Kindergarten

I Love My Dog
Dukie is a white German Shepherd.
I throw a ball and Dukie catches.
My dog is my friend.
Brooke Raffle, Kindergarten

Ice Cream
I like ice cream.
I eat it at Mom Mom and Pop Pop's house.
The ice cream there is always yummy!
Julia Montag, Kindergarten

Thanksgiving
Happy as having a new kid at school.
Family as sweet as chocolate candy.
Apple pie as delicious as a sunrise.
Alyssa Diaz, Grade 3

The Haunted House
The ceiling will leak.
The floor will creak.
The stairs will rumble.
That walls will tumble.
The goblin's belly will grumble.
The ghost will be up in the attic and scare you all night.
You can try hiding under the bed you when you hear boo! You're dead.
Be careful when you go under the bed because it might fall on your head!
The only way to defeat the house, is to run like a mouse, get the trophy they said
Just make sure nothing falls on your head.
You're welcome to spend the night just be sure you're not going to cry.
Just remember…
The ceiling will leak.
The floor will creak.
The stairs will rumble.
That walls will tumble.
The goblin's belly will grumble.
So when you come to my house be prepared to get scared.
Shh, we don't want to wake up the monsters downstairs.
Melanie Solera, Grade 3

The Extraordinary Ice Cream Cone
I scoop, 2 scoop, very big scoops!
Oh how extravagant, — it's going to be big as an elephant.
3 scoops, 4 scoops, 5, 6, and 7 scoops.
Layers on top of layers, oh so many flavors!
8, 9, and 10th scoops, plus add three, —
13 scoops it's almost as tall as me!
14, 15, and 16 scoops, — tall as a tree.
17 and 18 scoops, might as well make it twenty.
20 scoops as big as can be,
Heaver than my whole family.
Stacked up, cone rivers dripping to the ground.
It's got me drooling like a hound.
Don't forget my chocolate syrup, some sprinkles falling like snow
I'm so excited I can't stand it!
Someone please hold the door, so my ice cream doesn't end up on the floor.
SPLAT!
Oh no! I guess we'll just have to make one more.
Chloe Roberts, Grade 3

United States
U nited States is our America
N ow let us explore our past.
I n many different times, I dream about what it was like
T o know the true history of
E veryone who was part of building America definitely
D eserves a clap!

S tay with me always United States,
T o remember my history.
A merica I love you, let us always be
T ogether
E ducational facts of
S uccess, survival, and sacrifice is what will always make you bigger and better!
Anas Farhan, Grade 3

Puppies

I am brave
I am growl
I am strong and fast
I am naughty but unique
I can run
Also I am lots of fun
I have sharp teeth because that's me.
I could be any color
I could be red like a cherry
Or yellow like honey
I could lick people's cheeks
I could make people comfortable I could listen and sniff
I could drink from a bowl or dig a hole.
I could dress up in style
I could run for miles
You can find me as a Pit bull
Digging deep holes
Finding treasures like bones.

Sade Clarke, Grade 3

Getting Lucy

She nips at my nose and kissed my cheek
Her eyes glimmering in the sunlight
She rises in my arms
Lucy's paws
Are like a giant pointy mountain
She jumps
She soars through the air
Like a Bald Eagle
She dashes and darts around me
She hops in the car
She lays on my lap
She shivers
I get a blanket as hot as hot lava
Now she's nice and toasty
She drifts off to sleep
She roars in her sleep
She barks and I think that was a happy bark
She found a forever home

Connor Basile, Grade 3

United States

U nited States is incredible
N orth, south, east, and west regions too
I ndependent people who are free, simply learn
T o live together in liberty
E ducate everyone about the past so that we
D iscover important facts.

S tories of our amazing America
T housands tell these patriotic stories in
A merica
T o share our history in
E very special way possible
S o that we continue to celebrate our freedom train.

Zaynah Khan, Grade 3

I Am

I am smart and responsible.
I wonder if a castle is real.
I hear a bird in a tree singing.
I see a frog jumping over a branch.
I want a phone.
I am smart and responsible.

I pretend to be a teacher.
I feel happy whenever I'm in school.
I touch a bird in a garden.
I worry if I will get burned.
I cry when I get a shot.
I am smart and responsible.

I understand that I have to be clean.
I say I can raise $90 to pay for a bouncy house.
I dream that someday I will be an artist.
I try to get 100% on tests.
I hope I have a beautiful house.
I am smart and responsible.

Kheily Nieto-Corona, Grade 2

The Fire Falcon

Falcon 9 is a very tall rocket,
if a robot looks at it, it will burn it's socket…

When the nine Merlin engines helped it blast,
the rocket with satellites took off very fast.

Once it lifted up high with a roar,
the people on earth forgot about their chores.

When the satellite launching was over,
the rocket ship did not yet lower.

When Falcon 9 touched the ground,
it made a very LOUD sound.

Falcon 9 will go down in history,
people will remember this amazing victory!

Future Falcon rocket will go to the Mars,
and will collect the space dust in jars!

Himank Chhaya, Grade 2

PS131

School is fun!
You can do math, reading, social studies, and writing
You can play in the playground
You can watch movies in the auditorium
You can have lunch with your friends
I love PS131
The teachers help the students when they need help
The students help each other too!
Every one is nice

Amira Salokhidinova, Grade 3

Summertime

Heat, sun glasses,
Open pools
Not a lot of rain,
People sweating,
And lemonade.
Daniel Lonon, Grade 3

Headbands

Colorful, comfortable,
Soft, comfortable, pretty.
You can buy, give or receive them.
Some are hard, some are soft.
Headbands.
S'mya Maddox, Grade 3

The Lady with Gold

There once was a "Lady of Gold."
Whose beautiful clothes smelled of mold.
She bought some new clothes.
They're covered with bows.
Now she's the "Bow Lady" we're told.
Je'Keira Godette, Grade 3

Zebras

I am a herbivore
I have bright black and white stripes
I crunch on grass
I also live in zoos,
Grassland, and savannahs.
Michelle Lewis, Grade 3

Math Facts

Math facts are easy.
Math facts are hard.
You can do math facts at school.
You can do math facts at home.
Math facts rule.
Tamiyah Parham, Grade 3

Feast

feast
juicy, heavenly
cooking, eating, baking
I like turkey sandwiches most
dinner
Kaitlyn Wilson, Grade 2

Feast

feast
delicious, crowded
eating, drinking, sitting
families love to eat good food
banquet
Jocelyn Welch, Grade 2

Thanksgiving

Love as sweet as having a great Christmas and giving a kiss to my mom.
Happy like doing my spelling homework.
Sweet like helping your mom clean the house.
Thankful like mom for helping her make dinner.
Family as good as a sweet dinner.
Joselin Reyes, Grade 3

The Sick Day

Looks like a sick day.
Oh, what will I do?
No school for me,
I hope it's not the flu.

There's aches in my head
and pains in my throat.
I even have pains
that run to my toes!

The doctor checks for a fever
and looks at my nose.
My ears are the real culprit —
Guess that's how it goes.

Medicine from the doctor
is sure to help my head.
Like a bear in the winter,
I'm headed to bed!
Cameron Warner, Grade 3

My Cat

I love my cat
Even though she is fat.
She sits on a mat
While she plays with a rat.

When I give her her food
She gives me a me-eew
She steps in glue
I say, "Who knew!"

When I give her a treat
She starts to eat, eat, eat
She has tiny feet
And she loves meat.

She plays with an opossum
She is awesome

That is my awesome cat!
Cami Browne, Grade 3

Cats

Cats have long whiskers
They are lazy and grumpy
Kittens are playful.
Kylie Creedon, Grade 3

My Dog

A magical pet
A treasure to keep forever
The color of joy
Laying on silver grass
Sings of freedom
His tune is heard in my heart
Before the night has swept the sky
He says goodbye
And I know
That I will keep his memory in my heart
Forever

As the moon and stars shine bright
I dream of my dog
As he runs through the grass
And I know that he will always
Be with me
Because he is everlasting in my mind
Paige Geiger, Grade 3

A Great Summer Day

I wake up early and ready to go.
I jump in the car wearing a pink bow.
The shining sun is strong and bright.
The clouds are puffy and oh so white.
We get out of the car ready to play.
So excited and shout HOORAY.
As I climb into my tent.
I can smell a pine scent.
Next is to unpack my bag.
And go get my name tag.
In comes my new tent mate.
Introducing herself as Kate.
We head down to the boat.
Pushing it away from the dock we float.
Kate almost fell in the water.
And the day kept getting hotter.
We enjoyed the day in the sun.
We hope tomorrow will be as fun.
Theresa Kilburg, Grade 3

Girl Named Ellie

There once was a girl named Ellie,
Who scored nine balls one summer.
Nine is a good score,
but not good as ten.
So she lost. Well, she can't always win.
Skylar Crowder, Grade 3

I Am

I am kind and I pay attention.
I wonder if I can see the Big Dipper.
I hear people whispering my name.
I see the sun and I am flying in it.
I want good grades.
I am kind and I pay attention.

I pretend I am riding in a helicopter.
I feel excited about science.
I touch a shark in the water doing tricks.
I worry about my family.
I cry when I come home and my family isn't there.
I am kind and I pay attention.

I understand God.
I say He protects me.
I dream about moving to a new house.
I try my best to pass my test.
I hope I pass second grade.
I am kind and I pay attention.

Jae Paz-Domingo, Grade 2

I Am

I am smart and hardworking.
I wonder if I am going to be taller than my sister.
I hear water going into the sea.
I see a dog playing with me.
I want new shoes.
I am smart and hardworking.

I pretend I could be a super hero.
I feel pleasant.
I touch my heart.
I worry about my grades.
I cry on my birthday, when they give me stuff.
I am smart and hardworking.

I understand if I get a bad grade.
I say I believe in God.
I dream I will go to Heaven.
I try to help my dad at work.
I hope my mom won't get hurt.
I am smart and hardworking.

Jonathan Salvador, Grade 2

Halloween

H alloween is coming near
A ll the costumes on and ready
L ight the pumpkins
L ight the way
O n the streets we walk and walk
W hen we go to houses and say something special
E veryone yells, "Trick or treat!"
E veryone's bags are full and heavy
N ow we go back and start to rest

Alex Cotnoir, Grade 3

Fall

Fall is coming
Fall is near
It always brings a cheer

Fall is coming
Fall is near
The children are really sincere

Fall is coming
Fall is near
I wonder when school is going to come near

Fall is coming
Fall is here
I am near when fall is here.

Emily Buchanan, Grade 3

Sports

Oh, sports you have fun games!
Wins or losses are the claims.
Some sports you could be by yourself
Some sports you could be with twelve.
When you lose or get hurt, there can be sadness,
But when you win, there is always happiness.
Scores can be high or scores can be low
Sports can be fast or sports can move slow,
Some people like sports…some don't.
Some people play sports…some won't.
In sports there are different levels
And in sports there are a lot of rivals
Some games you get trophies for winning.
The lessons you can learn are just beginning.

Karson Cloninger, Grade 3

Little Gifts

Bubbly Bouncy Blue gift is waiting to be opened.
Jumpy Giant Green gift is trying out jumping jacks.
Perfect Purple little gift is showing it's perfect looks.
Little Orange gift is eating orange pie.
Lemon Yellow gift is fluffing her lemony looks.
Picky Pink gift is playing Peek-a-Boo.
Rosy Red gift is baking velvet cake.
Icky inky Indigo gift got messed up with ink.
Gifts and Gifts now, we can't wait to open 'em!

Roshini Chakkravarthi, Grade 2

Snakes

Slithers and slides
Goes into holes.
What animal is this?
It is a snake in the hole.
Where else can you find me?
In so many different environments!
Places so varied like deserts, savanna, forests, and even seas.
Those are some places where I live.

Khadesha Stephenson, Grade 3

Soccer

Songs of wind
Bring us together
Setting the field
Helping our friends
Defeating
The other team
Scoring with help
Working hard together
Winning
Sparks of gold
Happy feelings
Fill the field
Congratulations
Each other
Going with glory
Emma Hunter, Grade 3

Destinee — What I Like

I like girls,
I like boys,
I can play with all my toys.

I like science,
I like math,
I can play in my bath.

I like cats,
I like dogs,
I can fly as fast as hogs.

I like bats,
I like hats,
I can run as fast as rats.
Destinee Alicea, Grade 3

Golden Sunrise

Every morning
A magical thing
Awakens
Lovely gold
Beams are gold and bright
Shines in my window
Like a flame of gold
Sweet and wonderful
Gold
His golden face around
The sky turns bright
Like diamonds put forth radiance
As the sunlight
On the sill of my window
It wakes me up and brightens my room
Aubrey Gattinella, Grade 3

What Is Fall?

Fall is…
Halloween,
Hunting,
The leaves changing,
Thanksgiving,
And decorations.
Oliver Van Nostrand, Grade 2

Aubrey

A lways loves people
U sually having fun at school
B eing silly all the time
R eally likes rain
E specially loves to read
Y earns to not be afraid
Aubrey Ostrander, Grade 2

Rain

Whoosh! Goes the wind
As the rain drips upon my window pane
And thunder roars
And there is a yellow streak across the sky.
After the rain is done
The sun comes out of the sky!
Camille Bishop, Grade 3

Summer

S un shining
U mbrellas cooling
M arshmallows roasting
M oving waves
E vening bike rides
R ain drops falling
Kathyana Alicea, Grade 2

Boys

How do boys act?
How do boys draw?
What do boys do?
Do boys behave?
Are boys good?
Are you a boy?
Jadina Campbell, Grade 3

Drums

Fun, big
Loud, symbols, small
Drums are very loud
Heavy, teach, practice
Play, band
Instrument
Craig Phillips, Grade 2

Waterfalls

A secret waterfall
A bright blue waterfall
Sparkling whiteness
Falling to catch air
A secret feeling in my heart
Hearing the sound of drops dripping
A light blue waterfall
Carries the water
It warms my heart
Drops that floated
A bright blue dream
An everlasting stream
Ayeza Akhtar, Grade 3

Ocean

The ocean
Sprinkles all
Over.
The big waves
Will toss you
Forward and
Backward.
The ocean waves
Bounce.
The ocean
Waits till people
Come and play.
Anna Wheeler, Grade 3

Winter

Always snowing, always cold,
Everyone has to be bold.
We need to stand up to this weather,
No bird is around, not even a feather.
Each animal does a different thing,
Some hibernate until spring.
Others just stick around,
And some scurry underground.
We go sledding and skiing all day long,
Others might sing a Christmas song.
Winter is here for a good reason,
We all enjoy this wonderful season.
Grace Bergeron, Grade 3

Family

Family,
Many cousins, many aunts.
Family all around me.
Old, young, teen, grown up.
Nice, mean, kind, bad, glad.
My family
is the
WORLD
to
ME!
Ciara-J Link, Grade 3

Making That Frown Upside Down
My dad came home late
On my birthday
I made a frown and
Nobody can make it upside down
I just can't believe it
Before that day
He was early yesterday
Today he is not
I wonder why
Is he coming or is he not
I am so upset that
All I can do is sit and sit
It's my birthday
What a day!
It's supposed to be a happy day
Then when I was sitting upside down
Guess who I saw
My dad was here all day long
Now he made my frown upside down!
Ria Kamat, Grade 3

Fear
Fear is hard to conquer,
When your brain won't let you win.
When other people add to your fear,
It cuts as deep as a fish fin.

Fear crawls into your body,
Like bugs at night when you sleep.
It causes you to stay awake all night,
Scared and ready to weep.

Fear can be sad,
When you are trying to have joy.
But fear can be overcome,
So give God the glory.

Once you conquer your fear,
You will be so excited.
The joy will shine through,
And make your heart delighted.
Sarah Patricia Rhyne, Grade 3

The Snowman
There were kids in the snow.
One was looking for sticks.
The others were in the house
Getting a carrot and blueberries
For nose and eyes.
When they went back out,
They worked as a team to put
It together.
It looked so pretty because the
Fluffy white snow was glistening.
They loved their beautiful snowman.
Gabriayla White, Grade 3

Gabriel — What I Like
I like candy,
I like pink,
I can wash the plates in the sink.

I like books,
I like math,
I can take a bath.

I like Sponge Bob,
I like crabs,
I can ride in a cab.

I like cake,
I like to bake,
I can hear an earthquake.
Gabriel Quist, Grade 3

Nomar — What I Like
I like blue,
I like pink,
I can take a test and really think.

I like movies,
I like cats,
I can wear my favorite hats.

I like mail,
I like mice,
I can slip on slippery ice.

I like tag,
I like pillows,
I can turn anything yellow!
Nomar Rivera, Grade 3

Madisen — What I Like
I like books,
I like toys,
I can run as fast as the boys.

I like pink,
I like red,
I can read a book in bed.

I like reading,
I like a chipmunk,
I will run away from a skunk.

I like a test,
I like the west,
I can do a test the best.
Madisen Harris, Grade 3

Summer and Winter
summer
hot, sunny
biking, rollerskating, partying
sun, grass, snow, snowflakes
snowing, skating, sledding
cold, cloudy
winter
Alina Davila-Cruzado, Grade 3

Games
My favorite thing to do is play games
When I'm bored, I play games
I can play them on my phone
I always play them with my friends
We make sure to take turns
My friends love to play games with me
I LOVE GAMES!
Jacob Yoffe, Grade 3

Love
Love is great, it is in the air.
It is all around you. You can feel Love.
You cannot spend it,
It is for everyone.
You cannot see it,
But it is there for everyone.
So let everyone feel LOVE.
Claire Jefferis, Grade 3

My Puppy
My puppy is yellow,
Her ears are like velvet, her eyes hazel.
She is quite cute.
She has soft pink nose like a rose.
My puppy is fluffy and very friendly.
She gives you kisses when you
Come home.
Gabriel Ferraro, Grade 3

Sunset
Sun is going down
The time is 8:08
Mom calls, "Come on in."
I slouch down in my bed
The sun
Is setting
No more.
Magie Yeaton, Grade 3

Braids
Pretty, long,
Shake, heavy, light.
Beautiful, short, and more.
Curly, straight, wavy
Micros
S'Myria Bonner, Grade 3

What Is Purple?
Purple is closest to blue.
Also the color of my shoe.
Purple is the number two.
Purple is a grape.

Maybe a cape
Purple is a hurt eye,
But never the sky.
Purple is my lunch box.

Imagine purple polka dots,
And my book bag that looks bad,
Purple is a marker.
Purple is a loopy feeling.
Harmony Mendoza, Grade 3

Mother
She wraps her arms around me.
She kisses my round face, too.
She comforts me whenever I weep.
And she can cure any boo boo.

She's the best superhero there is.
Better than Batman, Spider-man, and Hulk.
She soars and flies to my rescue,
whenever she sees me sulk.

She's my North Star, my doctor, my pride.
She's more powerful than any other.
She's there for me when I cry.
She's my one and only mother.
Ivyann Shen, Grade 3

My Pets
Buster is my dog.
He rolls around in mud.
He's like a big, fat hog,
but he is my best bud.

Nala is my cat.
She eats a lot of food.
That's what makes her twice as fat,
but it puts her in a good mood.

My hermit crab is named Red.
He never moves a lot.
He looks like he is dead,
but he really is not!
Emily Morris, Grade 3

Popcorn
Yummy, salty, sweet
Making, popping, eating
It tastes good
Crunchy
Grace Carpenter, Grade 1

Horses
H eavy
O ut in the pasture
R ide on them
S it on them
E at hay
S leep in stalls
Trace Fulton, Grade 2

Colors
C rimson
O range
L ilac
O rchid
R ed
S ky blue
J'Leah Gonzalez Bier, Grade 2

The Book
The book, the book
Oh, how I love the book.
I love every page, word, and line.
It's full of adventures, mysteries, and more.
The book, the book
Oh, how I love the book.
Evan McCall, Grade 3

Calves
C ows mooing
A ttacking flies
L icking salt
V ets helping
E ating apples
S leeping in stalls
Angela Lenz, Grade 2

Green
G rass
R ocks with moss
E ggs and ham
E yes
N ickels

Carlos Pinet, Grade 2

Leaves
L arge and small
E legant
A utumn time
V ivid colors
E mpty trees
S ad to see them fall
Tyreese Live, Grade 2

jewelry
rings beautiful as rubies.
earrings like crystals hanging.
necklaces like pretty rainbows.
bracelets was wonderful as shiny marbles.
watches timing a count down.
Zytnia Otero, Grade 3

Mom
Mom
Laughing, happy
Cooking, working, sweeping,
My mom is cool
I love her
Chantel Montalvo, Grade 1

Fall Is Here!
Fall is here!
Leaves are changing.
Trees are twisting and turning.
It is getting cooler and darker.
We are getting ready for winter.
Skylar Cottingham-Stewart, Grade 3

Fall
Fall
Red, orange
Falling, raking, crunching
Playing in falling leaves
Autumn
Emily Inesti, Grade 1

Dog
Dog
Yellow Lab
Running, sniffing, barking
He eats my food
Toby
Brody Apholz, Grade 1

Snow
Snow
White, cold
Rolling, building a snowman
Writing letters in the snow
Winter
Nathan Kalinowski, Grade 1

Dog
Dog
Brown, white
Playing, sitting, jumping
My dog plays with me and mommy
Dallas
EmmaLynne Lasher, Grade 1

Fish

They are colorful
They use their fins for swimming
They are really small.
Tommy McHugh, Grade 3

Giraffes

Tall, long neck, black tongue
He stretches up to the sky
Eats a lot of leaves
Jonathan Bonebrake, Grade 1

Sea Turtle

Sea turtle sleeping
In the bright and shining sun
She will soon lay eggs
Grace O'Brien, Grade 3

Whales

Intelligent whales.
They speak a secret language.
Smart amazing whales.
Oscar Weinik-Brewer, Grade 3

Cheetah

Cat that is spotted
Antelope are food for him
Hides in the tall grass
Vincent Lisandrelli, Grade 3

Ducks

Have feathery wings
They live in ponds
They have beaks to peck.
Preston Farrington, Grade 3

Fall

Fall is as red as a cherry.
Fall is as orange as a pumpkin.
Fall is as yellow as fire.
Kameryn Rogers, Kindergarten

Fall

Fall is as red as an apple
Fall is as orange as a pumpkin.
Fall is as yellow as a school bus.
Leah Perez, Kindergarten

Fall

Fall is as red as a crab.
Fall is as orange as a pumpkin.
Fall is as yellow as the sun.
Ryan Lauff, Kindergarten

United States

U nited States, United States,
N not just good, you are great!
I nside I feel so happy to live here, my brothers and me,
T ogether we share amazing memories!
E very day I step another step on you,
D oing things that I normally do.

S pecial to me, you are,
T o me, you are a lucky star!
A mazing country, and I live here,
T ell your history to the young,
E qual we are, having fun!
S pectacular, stupendous, splendid and more

These are just words that aren't enough to say, Thank you for every single day!
Jannah Ahamat, Grade 3

Roller Skates

Roller skates have four wheels
They make the riders really squeal
Eekkkkk!
They are lots of fun and you can ride them in the sun
Weeeeeeeeeeeeeeeeeee!
They come in many magnificent colors
Red, orange, yellow and green
When I ride, I let off steam
Some wheels are made of steel, my favorite color skates are teal
When I ride them in my house, my dog chases me like a cat does a mouse
Sometimes I tremble when I'm heading towards the wall
Because, I think I'm going to fall
My mom always watches me in awe
My skates make me look really tall
If there are things scattered on the floor, I have to be careful or I will end up sore!
Ella Ticknor, Grade 3

Friends

Friends are people who always have your back.
They never let you down and they always help you up.
True friends will never push or bully you.
Also, true friends will never ignore you but they always help you with something.
Friends never leave your sight and always stay with you.
One reason why you have a friend is so that they will always stick to you.
That is what I think friends are supposed to do.
Last, they always never let you feel bad.
That is all about FRIENDS!
Teiresias Jones, Jr., Grade 3

Mmmmm!

'Do I smell a cookie?'
I looked in the oven to see if there was a tasty treat ready to be eaten.
'Yummy!' I said.
I heard my taste buds screaming 'yeah!'
It was a gingerbread man.
Crunch! Mmmmmm!
That tastes good!
Charlie Hudak, Grade 3

Why I Love Park

W onderful
H appy to play out
Y uppie

I love the slides and tunnels

L ots of fun
O ur family will have fun
V ery cool
E xciting

P lay hide and seek
A wesome to see squirrels around
R ide on bike to ride on sea horse
K ind to other kids to take turns on swings
Architha Reddy Varakantam, Grade 2

The Beach

At the seashore
I run down to the sea
And dip my feet in the ocean
The yellow sand disappears
Wishes and feeling
Fly through my head
As I go on the surf board
Sweet silver trumpets
Sing to me
As a magical journey comes
Lightning flashes
Mountains like thunder crashes
I listen to the rain
Everlasting waves come
As I go again
Maddy Coombs, Grade 3

Art

Art is beautiful, nothing is sloppy
Art is making, whatever you want.
Art is colorful, with bright colors,
When the design is so neat.
I like to draw, and love what I do,
Because art is what I really want to do.
Julianna Aguilar, Grade 3

Reading

In my uncertain fingers
An open book
The first sentence was exciting
It got scary
The second sentence was hard
The third sentence was unbelievable
Feelings surround me
Feelings hit me
Reading is challenging and exciting
A wonderful journey
Mason Benner, Grade 3

The Haunted Holiday

Vampires, witches, scary claws,
Where is jolly old Santa Claus?
Creepy monsters under your bed
Shouting boo…just cover your head!
Trick or treating, candy galore
But monsters think this is a bore.
They want little children, little feet
And little toes for them to eat.
Bloodsucking vampires just want a snack
While Frankenstein has to attack!
Halloween is fun my dear,
You just have to cover your fear…
Wait, where are you going,
Come back here!
Kathleen Rebillot, Grade 3

Pink

Pink is a pig,
Lemonade is pink.
Pink is a card
Don't you think?

Pink is a box,
There are shades of pink.
Pink can be a top
Being washed in a sink.

Pink is a jacket.
Roses are pink.
Pink is gum
I chew with a wink.
Abigail Nadeau, Grade 3

Elephant

I am big
I have two big white tusks
I have no predators
My little ones do —
Lions, hyenas, leopards, and
Crocodiles.

Humans can only threaten me
But nothing else

I have a long trunk
I use it to get bark,
and buds off trees.
Sanai Miller, Grade 3

Jacob

J oyful
A thletic
C onfident
O bedient
B oy
Jacob Ruiz, Grade 2

Presents

P resents are amazing
R ight presents are awesome
E veryone is happy
S eeing everyone so jolly
E veryone so excited
N o one sad
T errific presents
S eeing love in the air
Jeilanie A. Carmenaty, Grade 3

Ice Cream

ice cream ice cream
what a galore
ice cream ice cream
one or more
ice cream ice cream
sea or shore
ice cream ice cream
is all over the world
Gretchen Smith, Grade 3

The Beauty of Nature

The beauty of the trees
The gentleness of air
All the things around me are miracles
The little birds tweet
The trees sway
The leaves are colorful
This world is a beautiful place
So I'll never forget nature
Irene Li, Grade 3

Playing with My Friends

Playing with my friends is always fun
especially when we can run
We play some basketball at the court
at night we build a fort
Riding the golf cart can be tricky
my friends can be really picky
They come over every day
it's so much fun that we can play
Isaiah Jacobsen, Grade 3

Rohan

Excited, hard working, happy
Sibling of Vaiga
Lover of fast cheetahs
Who fears the dark
Who needs to be good at basketball
Who gives happiness
Who would like to see Niagara Falls again
Jayakrishnan
Rohan Jayakrishnan, Grade 2

Moises — What I Like

I like animals,
I like pets,
I can take them to the vet.

I like math,
I like games,
I can have lots of names.

I like basketball,
I like sports,
I can get a pig to snort.

I like food,
I like books,
I can help my mom cook.
Moises Martinez, Grade 3

Justice — What I Like

I like science,
I like math,
I CANNOT Take a bath.

I like pizza,
I like rainbows,
I CANNOT wear a bow.

I like books,
I like tools,
I can swim in my pool.

I like dogs,
I like cats,
I can buy my cat some mats.
Justice Gras, Grade 3

Wilberto — What I Like

I like books,
I like toys,
I can throw the ball farther than the boys.

I like games,
I like pets,
I can wish to be on a jet.

I like gym,
I like math,
I can give my dog a bath.

I like friends,
I like cats,
I can fly on a mat.
Wilberto Gutierrez, Grade 3

The Sun

Sweating Sun
The sun makes
the city sultry.
The sun swirls
with warmth.
The sun stands
up with pride.
The sun vanishes
when he goes to sleep.
The moon is awake.
Good-bye sweating sun!
Brody Schuh, Grade 3

Blue

Blue is the color of my shirt
That got dirt on it.
Blue is the flag
That we pledge to.
Blue is the color
That is overhead.
Blue is the color of my doll's dress
That is a mess.
Blue is a great color that
I know for art.
Blue is so great.
Kinyiah Scott, Grade 3

Piano Recital

I burst out the door to go to piano
My mom kisses my cheek
Before I go onstage
I shiver when I go on stage
The room is filled with people
I am nervous
I have butterflies in my tummy
Come see what I am playing on the piano
My mom's face is so happy
That I am playing the piano
On stage
Marina Breunig, Grade 3

My First Holy Communion

Angels fly around me
My dress sits like silk along my spine
My heart flutters happy
A wonderful sight of Christ
My uncertain fingers
His body in my hands
Like showers of gold
Grains of the golden Christ sit inside me
He lives within my heart
And he will always be with me
Alexandra Engart, Grade 3

Lilyrose

Lilyrose is my new baby sister.
She has a little red hair.
I hold her every morning
Before I leave for school.
Sometimes I feed her.
I love my baby sister!
Shawn Rynkiewicz, Kindergarten

Fall

Leaves are falling, Leaves are falling,
Colorful they are all on the ground.
We rake the leaves and put them aside,
Until they are picked up.
Fall is a nice season, with beautiful trees,
Only those who like fall, can appreciate all.
Peyton Klein, Grade 3

My Sister

Nice, smart
Playful, careful, unbeatable
Joyful, happy, cool, working hard
Jealous, funny, angry
Lovable, cute
Good
Marquez Thomas, Grade 3

Candy

Sweet, colorful.
Eat, lick, chew.
Sometimes lose, sometimes sticky.
Hard, cracks, slips.
Round, tasty.
Lollipop.
Asia Spralling, Grade 3

Clouds, Clouds

White and all dry.
And some are all so dark black.
These clouds are so beautiful.
Clouds blocking the sun.
That means it's springtime.
I love clouds a whole lot.
Jacob Maddy, Grade 3

Cupcakes

Cupcakes make me smile,
I love them, they are so sweet.
The Icing is creamy and so good,
It melts in my mouth.
When I make cupcakes I eat them.
I love cupcakes.
Julia Beach, Grade 3

My Best Friend

My dog is my best friend
He makes me happy when I am sad
When I want to play, he's there to play with me
When I am sad, he's there to lick my tears away
I sometimes get mad at him because he's a bit crazy
But he is still my best friend forever!

Ileyana Xicali, Grade 3

Trees

Trees are so big
They have different leaves.
Yellow orange and green.
Trees are very peaceful,
They give you shade and breeze
Fruits also grow on trees, that is why I like trees.

Gavin Friel, Grade 3

Thanksgiving

Respectful as a child helping mom.
Happy as a bird tweeting in a tree.
Enjoying like a child eating apple pie.
Peaceful as a baby sleeping.
Love as big as the world
Food as delicious as a juicy turkey on the table.

Paola Soto, Grade 3

Spring

Spring is like a butterfly that feels like silk.
Just going through the forest,
listening to tweeting birds.
It's sweet when they meet and find their pals.
Spring looks like a heart with a melody that never stops beating.
That's what Spring is.

Tanaya Gore, Grade 3

Scary Nightmares

Ah! Scary noises are coming from my room.
I think they are zombies.
I need a weapon!
I grab the book from the shelf and follow the sound.
I am frightened. I think the zombie is ugly and bloody.
Oh no! It is only my big brother joking with me.

Michelle Montero, Grade 3

Thanksgiving

Respectful as when you're at the dinner table
Helpful like a counselor helping kids.
Happy as a kid opening his birthday presents.
Important like having food, shelter, and family.
Sweet as candy in your mouth.
Caring like people are when you fall down.

Monze Mendoza Duran, Grade 3

Lost

Time merely lost,
destroyed in a cauldron
of burning light.
This invisible matter
eats stars.
And when in its belly,
Science, an understanding of what we know,
is destroyed by the great black hole.

Siobhan Milton, Grade 3

Fall Is Near

Fall is near
It is getting cold.
Animals are storing food.
Squirrels are fattening up.
School has started, leaves are falling.
Kids are staying inside.
People are raking leaves.
Fall is here.

Benjamin Richard, Grade 3

Gold of a Century

The shimmering gold of Golden Clutch will be revealed
from under rock and soil.
For all the mine bosses over the fields of all men
working for all, might start their mining business.
All the gold from Golden Clutch will be mined from
day to night and night to day.
All the beer shiny as gold will be drunk at dusk and
every man, every soul will have gold in their hands.

Nate Kirkland, Grade 3

Halloween

It's October in the cold night
When wolves howl and when bats come out to play
In the night, the children say,
"It's Halloween, it's Halloween!
Let's go dress up!"
But what they don't know is that
Ghosts are watching and the goblins are hunting.

Jacob Hughes, Grade 3

The Ocean

The ocean sparkles with light.
The ocean waves kiss the fragile sand.
The ocean animals swim with happiness.
The ocean swirls like a whirlpool.
The ocean uncovers beautiful smooth sea shells.
The ocean floor is as dark as the midnight moon.
The ocean sings a beautiful song.

Gregory Walpole, Grade 3

I Want to Be a Nurse
I want to be a nurse
I like to help people stay well
I want to work in a hospital
I will take very good care of sick people
I will be a special nurse
I will do my best every day.
Promise Lide, Kindergarten

My Teacher
My teacher is special to me
She helps me learn what I cannot see
My teacher is kind
She helps me keep learning on my mind
My teacher is my friend
With my teacher, I will always win.
Amillyan Autry-Cooper, Kindergarten

My School
I like my school it is the best
I can learn but I don't get much rest
I like my teacher she is fun
She makes me get all my work done
I like my friends at school
They are really cool
Kiara Burroughs, Kindergarten

Cars
Small, fast,
Moving, controlling, driving,
Moves in the street.
Rolling, turning, leaving,
Short, wide,
Dodge.
Traeveon Butler, Grade 3

Summer
S un for most of the day
U mbrellas might go away
M ore time to play
M an, it's great!
E nvironments change from erosion
R ead in bed
Charlotte Spence, Grade 3

My Little Sister
My little Sister is 6 years old,
She is so cute. Her name is Adeline,
And she is in first grade.
Adeline is smart and she is sweet,
She can read chapter books, all by herself.
I love my little sister Adeline.
Sofia Bompensa, Grade 3

Goal!
I kick the ball, BAM!
Into the net it slams.
My coach yells, "Hooray!"
He is excited about my play.
The crowd cheers and claps.
Then, my teammates give my hand a slap.
I am feeling happy!
So, my mom took me for a treat —
Something quite delicious to eat!
Emma Rose Taylor, Grade 3

Chihuahua
C ompanion
H appy with toys
I ntelligent
H unter
U nusually small
A lert
H yper
U nique colors
A dventurous
Jesus Cardona, Grade 2

Lions
Big as an elephant
Sharp, sharp teeth
Strong legs like a cheetah
Eyes as sharp as a bat's
I a like no other animal.
I use all my adaptations to
Survive especially in the jungle.
You guessed right!
I am King of the Beasts
Jalieo Tang, Grade 3

My Potions
I think that when
I get a little bigger,
A professor of potions I'll be.
Ice potions,
Lava potions,
Acid potions, too.
Potions that explode,
Potions that grow, stink, and
Turn people to gold.
Urias Bland, Grade 3

Karyssa
K angaroos are my favorite animal
A nd I love going to pick apples
R abbits are also an animal that I like
Y earns for a phone
S chool is one of my favorite places
S nakes are awesome!
A pples are my favorite fruit
Karyssa Johnson, Grade 2

Funnel Webbed Spider
Creep face
Small ball eyes
Kill people
With venom

Brown or black
I eat horses, dogs, pigs, and cats

If you want to fight me
Pick up a twig
But if you get too close
I might give a DEADLY bite.
Kaden Francis, Grade 3

What Is Fall?
Fall is…
Halloween,
my birthday,
butterflies flying South,
black cats,
animals migrating,
leaves changing,
coming back to school,
picking pumpkins,
picking apples,
picking out costumes,
and carving jack-o'-lanterns.
Ryleigh Ralph, Grade 2

Lions
Dark
Brown
Eyes
Shine
So
Bright
Like
The
Sunset
In
The
Sky.
Neveah Samuels, Grade 3

Heaven
Kingdom of God
Up in a cloud tree
Sky blue butterfly
Soul where you stand
Seeking with memory
Summoning an empty room
Rise again
My heart hung low
They are in a better place
They remember me
Cate Decembrino, Grade 3

Birthday Parties

Birthday parties
Fun, nice
Eating cake, opening presents, blowing candles
Friends come to my birthday
July 14
Spencer Stride, Grade 1

Christmas

Christmas Eve is very exciting, joy, and laughter.
So, when Santa comes down the chimney
He'll put down my presents
Walk out the door letting us people snore.
Ava Bartlett, Grade 3

Erasers

Erasers, erasers. Erase, erase.
Going along to fix my mistakes.
As pink as a pig,
As clean as a line,
You're definitely always going to be mine!
Sometimes I mess up, but that's just O.K.!
You come in and fix up all my mistakes.
Julia Garrido, Grade 3

Izabella — What I Like

I like gymnastics,
I like toys,
I can sing with Christmas joy.

I like trees,
I like math,
I can give my dog a bath.

I like cats,
I like pink,
I can walk while I wink.

I like school,
I like dance,
I can go to France.
Izabella Bartman, Grade 3

Beach

Splash! Splash! Splash!
I am swimming
In the water

Click! Clack! Cluck!
I am walking out of the water

Dlesh! Dlesh! Dlesh!
I am eating
Fish and bread.
Barbara Bouloute, Grade 3

The Eagle

Swoops through
Mountains like thunder

Flies like
A glistening wonder

Its shadow
Sweeps the ground

Black eyes keep
A sharp look out

Its wings make
The wind howl

Its talons are like
A silver blade

Slipping silver
Talons through its fish

Hovering and darting
Over its prey

Wings spread out
Singing of freedom
Dylan Lockhead, Grade 3

Roaring Rain

Leaving all outdoors
While first raindrop
Whispers through my fingers
I hear the loud sound
The steady sound of the roaring rain

Wherever I go
There is the roaring rain
Coming down
Pounding from the sky

Rain
Like a cycle
That goes and never stops
Rain pounding on the ground
Like a hammer
Hitting the strongest metal

Rain
When the rain
Hits my head to my toes
I feel the calm on my body
On the tips of my warm fingers
Like a fireplace
Thomas Michael Fedesco, Grade 3

The Darkness
Bars of fright
The walls crumble down
A wicked scream
Fear screams in my mind
My untaken soul
I panic
My room was filled with horror
Fear shrieks in the black, crumbled walls
I see a blade of unknown blood
I see a reaping from the backyard
I lock my door
When I hear knocking
I peek through the keyhole
I let none enter
Trent Melchior, Grade 3

Dancer
I am like a dancer.
All dressed in pink
Dancing through the stars.
Up, up and away.

I am like a ballerina.
I am twice as tall.
I am twirling on my toes.
I am trying not to fall.

Like the wind,
I sway back and forth.
Dancing through the stars.
I'm off to explore!
Kayton Houser, Grade 3

Dolphin, Dolphin
Dolphin, dolphin, in the sea
The dolphin speaks, "eeeh, eeeh"
I love the way they jump and leap!
They are so beautiful in the deep.

I love the way they sing.
They soar like they have wings.
They are the color of gray.
They're having fun while they play.

Dolphins have always fascinated me.
I like dolphins as you can see.
They are friendly, they are smart.
Dolphins are really off the chart.
Stacia Dell Cowan, Grade 3

My Puppy
Bella is my new puppy.
She is black and brown.
Runs, barks, jumps.
This is Bella!
Adriana Coreano, Kindergarten

Seasons
Leaves fall here and leaves fall there
  and at the fair.
Yellow, red and orange leaves
  fall from the trees.
But soon they shall go
  and next comes the snow.
And the snowflake shall fly
  and then dry.
And then we shall have the flower
  and the longer hour.
The children shall run
  in the hot sun.
John Beaupre, Grade 3

Airplane Riding
Flying above the treetops,
looking down at my town,
it looks like a doll's.
Tiny cars look like a
kid is pushing them.
Houses and buildings
are like miniature displays.
Finally soaring higher into the clouds,
it is beginning to turn dark.
See the sunset like a fire
underneath the clouds.
Hours pass and we are landing.
Alana Samson, Grade 2

Pink as It Is
Pink is a cool color
Pink is like my baby cousin's thumb
Pink is the color of my bubble gum
Pink is peaceful

Pink is a smart color
Pink is smooth
Pink is the color of my room

Pink is the color of my bear
Pink is the color of my mom's hair
Aaron Johnson, Grade 3

About Fall
We play at fall.
We trick or treat at fall.
Leaves fall in fall.
Color changes at fall.
Trees sleep at fall.
The sun rises late at fall.
The sun sleeps early at fall.
We pick pumpkins at fall.
Its cold at fall.
The cold wind blows leaves at fall.
Animals get ready to hibernate at fall.
Sujitha Muralidharan, Grade 1

Hawaii
Burning mountain
Temple of heat
Blood red lava
Pouring over
The volcano
Smoke everywhere
Screams ahead
The distance
Isn't so quiet anymore
Then boom a lightning flash
Boom! Boom! Two more

Then it's quiet
No more lightning
No more screams
Then clouds are pouring out rain
As if the clouds
Are crying in pain

Lava stop pouring out the volcano
But I know another cycle
A new cycle will start again
BOOM!
Nate Manley, Grade 3

Sunrise
The golden sun
Wakes up from the dark
Like words of freedom
The cold creeps as fire dies
As I awake
The sun awakens
Like a flame
Lovely yellow and orange

Like a pot of gold
Shimmering in daylight
You can't miss
It going over the sky
With beautiful colors
It's not an everyday sunrise
You always see in the morning
It's like a magical sunrise
I can't ever forget
I will never forget
Never
Never
Never
Emerson Tooley, Grade 3

Huskies
Huskies have long,
fluffy tails with glowing blue eyes.
In front of the moon
the booming howl makes them seem wise.
Callie Delemarre, Grade 1

Green

Green is...
Leaping lizards and evil grin of an elf
Mounds on the hills and meadow field
Ivy clinging to itself.

A bumpy amusement park ride
A foe not a friend
Who has jealousy not pride.

Sweet tastes like green
Except yucky peas
There is apple bubble gum and a lime jelly bean.

Emerald crown for a dizzy queen
The smell of fresh cut grass in a garden
Recycling and reusing is also green!

David Deacle, Grade 2

Roller Coasters

We ride on a track and go up up and away!
Weeeeee!
We go down. Hooray! We made it!
I am so scared that I'm quavering with fear!
We are close to the front of the line, we are super near!
Ahhhhhh!
Here we go upside down. Wow! That was magnificent!
I can't see because of the sun, here comes the next one.
It kind of looks scary.
Creeek!
Up we go the eerie track.
This one is scary for a fact.
We go down so fast, I'm free at last.
My satin cape fell off, my cape was oh so soft.
Let's gather our group, my mom says let's go troops.
We head to the next ride.

Molly Hughes, Grade 3

Summer Vacation

Vacation is the best time of year.
I love to swim, play and have no fear.
I love to lie in the warm sun.
Building sand castles is so much fun.
The waves spread across the sand,
As I grab the grains in my hand.
I like to play paddle ball,
As I even hit it against the wall.
I like swimming in the pool,
For the splashing water is very cool.
I like lying on a raft or doing flips,
As my friends and I take turns taking dips.
Going to the boardwalk or riding the Ferris wheel,
And dinner there for my favorite meal.
Visiting the Candy Kitchen where the fudge is best,
Far better and above all the rest!

Maria Pasquinelli, Grade 3

Bow

I love bows, bows, bows.
Big ones little ones I don't care.
Red ones, white ones, blue ones too,
Pink with polka dots I love you.
Look close and you will see bows galore can't you see.
Bows on my braids and pony tails too,
Bows in my hair oh bows how I love YOU.

Omyriah Herbert, Grade 2

My Dog

I love my dog, she is the best,
She listens to my orders well,
especially when I call her to bed.
She loves to play, she likes to sleep,
But most of all she likes to eat.
We named her Mello because it rhymes with Jello.
I love my dog, she is the best.

Asher Lomax, Grade 3

Heroes Don't Always Wear Capes

Heroes don't need a cape to save lives.
Physicians save you from hives.
Firefighters fight fires forgetting fears.
Teachers teach lessons forever needed in life.
Soldiers protect you with their knives.
Lives get saved... with no capes.

Madelyn White, Grade 3

My Best Teacher

My teacher, Ms. Betances, is the best!
She teaches us math, reading, and writing
She gives us things like shirts
She helps us learn new things
She makes a lot of charts to let us focus on all subjects
She is an excellent teacher

Jennifer Liang, Grade 3

Just a Dream

I had a dream about a mysterious girl
In my house sneaking in my room,
Trying to get my money from my piggy bank.
I was trying to catch her,
But I woke up.
It was just a dream.

Tate Johnson, Grade 3

My Cat

Siamese onyx cat
Fur as black as night
I see a dark fluffy cloud in the morning
He welcomes me when I get home from school
When I get up he runs as fast as lightning
Together or apart I love my cat

Tommy Lynch, Grade 3

The Curious Vase of Secrets

The gods of Olympus were acting
as if the Olympians were criminals.
They asked Hephaestus to make Pandora.
He scratched his dirty chin;
he didn't think it was a sin.
So he took a black kettle and set to work,
sculpting her like a living doll.
She was white, with gazing eyes.
Aphrodite made her hair golden without age.
Hera gave her curiosity so she would open the vase.
All because Prometheus had discovered fire
against their will.

Lev Bitterman, Grade 3

Ginger Delight

Mmmmm!
The kitchen smells so good.
I was baking a gingerbread girl.
The cookie girl had chocolate eyes and a tan body,
With M&M buttons, licorice hair and lots of icing.
I took the delicious cinnamon-y cookie off the steaming hot tray.
"Ouch!" I said as I took it out.
I was ready to eat her.
Crunch!
I ate her all up.
That was the end of the gingerbread girl.

Lily Major, Grade 3

JurassiCraft

I like to play *JurassiCraft*!
There are dinosaurs
And you can make and collect dinosaur eggs
In creative, you can make armors and weapons
Sometimes you get hurt, but you do not lose lives
Sea crabs can hurt you by pinching you
You get to live in two kinds of worlds,
Island world and a whole world
The worlds are both filled with dinosaurs
I like to play *JurassiCraft* with my cousins
It is very fun!

Geo Anthony Fragoso, Grade 3

I Feel Free in a Tree

The breeze in my face the sweet sweet smell
My hair flowing side to side I get higher
And higher
Like a huge ladder going up to the sky
I follow the birds,
I hang upside down and look directly at the ground
I go down the tree
Find another,
And right when I touch it
All of it starts over again.

Violet Falvey, Grade 3

Backyard Fun

A summer's day I went outside,
The sun was so bright with no place to hide.
The first thing I did was a ride on the swing,
I flew back and forth and started to sing.
As the day went on it got really hot,
I needed to cool down with the sprinkler I thought.
Turn on the hose and the water will fly,
Jump through the spray while my dog ran by.
Then I will kick a soccer ball,
I'm just go glad that it's not fall.
Getting hungry I called my dad,
Needing food really, really bad.
Wanting my dad to make a milkshake,
I know it would be one minute to make.
And now the long day is really done,
I had a lot of fun in the sun.

Chelsea Standish, Grade 3

Halloween

Pumpkins big and round seen all over town
scary masks and bats up high
with twinkling stars in the sky
it must be Halloween.
Kids are yelling "trick or treat"
many leaves are falling crisp and red
Lilly wears cat ears upon her head
it must be Halloween.
The wind is blowing with a chill
as I climb back up the hill.
So many treats in my bag mostly candy not to brag
it must be Halloween.
Eight o'clock most lights out
time for home but some kids pout.
Kids had fun this we know for the smiles that they show
it is Halloween!

Nalah Rey, Grade 3

The Last Day of School

The last sentence of excitement
A final dash home
The joy of summer
Sings of freedom
Every returning summer the flowers start to bloom
I see a flock of geese
Specks of pollen blow in the wind
My heart has an amazing feeling
A golden hot sun
A golden hot sun burns on me
I see my house in the distance
I feel safe and sound because I'm almost there
My heart has an exciting feeling
It's safe
The long journey is over

Olivia Coates, Grade 3

Monkeys

Monkeys can jump high
Monkeys like to eat bananas
Monkeys swing from tree to tree
Monkeys can play hide and seek
Monkeys can sleep
Monkeys can run very fast
Monkeys are cool.
Jameson Robinson, Kindergarten

Waffles

W heat
A dd milk
F lour
F iber
L ard
E ggs
S ugar
Justin Torres, Grade 2

Snowy Winter

Winter is cold.
Snow is falling along with the leaves
The wind is getting stronger.
The most beautiful things are the trees.
There are no animals on this winter night,
just the ground which is clear white.
Taya Xu, Grade 3

Falling Leaves

Leaves fall down without a care.
They come out, out of nowhere.
Sometimes the wind blows them away.
To where the people always play.
Or somewhere else far away.
But it's not my fault, it's fall today!
Crystal Graham, Grade 3

Tree

Look up there, at the tree,
I look at it, it looks at me.
The roots, the trunk, the limbs, the leaves,
All of those I love to see.
You're my favorite place to be,
Tree, oh tree, oh tree, oh tree.
Benjamin Scamardella, Grade 3

I Follow the Wind

When the wind blows
I fold
I will follow the wind wherever it goes
Through the forest
Through the grass
I will follow the wind wherever it goes
David Sagoua, Grade 2

Tigers

Has black stripes
Loves to bite

Orange skin
Camouflages in surroundings

Lives in zoos
Likes forest food.
Essence Haynes, Grade 3

Life

Life, life is not even.
Life is sometimes good.
Life is sometimes bad.
But it is life.
It is yours.
It is ours.
For eternity.
It is a gift from God.
Christian Smith, Grade 3

African Lion

I have quite sharp teeth
I only much on meat
I am a carnivore you see
I live in zoos to educate
Children that I meet.
I may also live on grassy plains
Savannas, open woodland,
And in shrub country places.
Danielle Turner, Grade 3

The Sun

The sun bouncing off the earth.
The sun swirls in the sky.
The sun opens our love.
The sun spies on us.
The sun's smile is warm.
The sun kisses us with happiness.
The sun sprints GOODBYE in the night.
The moon shakes HELLO.
Ava O'Keefe, Grade 3

If You Try

Everybody thrives
All throughout their lives.
If you try, you can fly.
I know it, because I show it.
It has happened in my life, too.
Really, it's true.
You can do it, my friend,
All the way to the end.
Charley VanWie, Grade 3

A Really Bad Hair Day!

I woke up with bad, bad, hair!
No one really cared.
My hair is frizzy.
I makes me dizzy.
I brush it
I comb it, curl it, cut it.
I twirl it, tie it, and can't tame it.
My hairs is a big as a bear!
No one cares.
It IS a really bad, bad hair day.
Marley Treadaway, Grade 3

Happy and Exciting Birthday Parties!

Presents wrapped like happiness.
Cakes yummy as sweets.
Streamers hanging like icicles.
Piñatas hit like baseballs.
Songs full as joy.
Bounce Houses like bouncy air.
Balloons float like clouds.
Candy too sweet like the salty ocean.
Food delicious like part treats.
Goodie Bags cool like happiness treats.
Victoria Candela, Grade 3

Dad

Dad walks in the door
He gives me a warm glittering look
    I run to him
Fast as green lightning
Into the welcoming arms of my dad
My dad looks
Deep into my eyes
    And gives me the biggest everlasting
Hug I could ever
    Imagine
Olin Chamberlain, Grade 3

My Favorite Day

I dream of playing
With Michael
Remember
Remember
Remember
We are as happy as kings
With lightning fast controllers
And scores and levels
As high as the golden sun
Sweet, wonderful Saturday
Christopher Blazo, Grade 3

Elephants

They pound on the ground
Female elephants are large
Loud gray elephants
Eva Getty, Grade 3

Jayla

Smart, beautiful, caring,
Sister of Travis, Jamaal, Taylor.
Who loves shopping, drawing, dancing,
Who feels that everyone should be treated equally.
Who needs shelter, water, clothes,
Who gives toys, love, knowledge.
Who'd like to see the Grand Canyon,
Who dreams of having a million dollars.
A student who works hard.

Jayla Moore, Grade 3

A Beautiful World

My world is beautiful. How about yours?
I love when the rain pours.
Don't take it in vain, just be plain.
I like to make music. It is so soothing.
Just like moving and amusing but not refusing.
A year is fair. It gives you time to chime into your surroundings.
Let love flow from your heart.
Be thankful for your blow and how you glow.
Be of one part with your heart.

Emilia Samuels, Grade 3

Art

Art is something that you can express.
You can show happiness or sadness anger or disgust.
You can show many ways that you feel.
Some people think that art anything is feelings or friends.
You can make art anything like; cats, dogs, people, and books.
Some people think art is a disgrace to the world.
My sister and I did some art yesterday.
We used chalk to make numbers.
I love art it makes me feel happy.

Gabrielle Roberts, Grade 3

A Gingery Cookie

Yum! I smell a spicy scent coming from the kitchen.
Ding! I hear an oven's bell go off and I run into the kitchen.
All of a sudden I see a gingerbread man!
I pick him up and turn him over in my hands.
He feels rough.
Then I take one little bite.
He's spicy and strong.
That's a gingery cookie.

Anna Paszkiewicz, Grade 3

My Classroom

My classroom is fun
There are lots of things to be done
I like to read
So that I will succeed
My classroom has lots of things for me to do
Like writing, reading, and learning math too
I like being in my classroom each day
I leave it when I go outside to play.

Vincent E. McNeil Jr., Kindergarten

A Christmas Delight

What is that spicy smell?
Is it a gingerbread boy?
I see a sign from heaven.
A dark beige gingerbread girl out of the oven
with snowcap buttons and frosting of white, green and red.
When they come out they feel smooth and hot.
Mmm! They're so good I could explode from the taste.
I bite on it.
It is crunchy and is a Christmas delight!

Addison Evans, Grade 3

Vampire Bats

Big eyes
I am small
I am a herbivore
I munch on fruits
I believe I am stronger than a big black bear.
Beware!
Because I just might be right there
Or in your closet doing what I do best
Beware! Because once again I might be right there.

Kyle Passard, Grade 3

My Pumpkin

My pumpkin is orange
My pumpkin is white
I like to play
by day and night
I have a pumpkin
It is a boy
My pumpkin is round and never frowns
He sits on my doorstep and lights up the night
He is waiting to greet on Halloween night

Jariel Pagani-Viteri, Grade 2

African Lions

A land with orange grass or
Is that an African lion?
Be careful of an African lion because
They are carnivores
Which means they eat meat.
Since you are juicy meat
Watch out for African lions!
No matter where you are you better look closely
He know how to be the master of disguise.

Aamal Ghaleb, Grade 3

Fall

Fall smells like a maple leaf falling from the tree;
and apple pie.
With Halloween hats and ghosts.
Fall looks like a tree with leaves on it;
and pumpkins.
Fall sounds like wind going from side to side on the trees;
and birds chirping.

Avonny Watson, Grade 3

Ocean

We arrive!
Excitement pumps through my heart
Tired from travel
I nestle in bed

I twist to my side
To see the ocean
Reflections of moonbeams
Making light to the beach
I hear the waves
As dreams fill the air

I awaken
To a new day
Ocean crashing!
Ocean bashing!
Like a symphony of cymbals
Charlie Roomberg, Grade 3

Bees

Makes honey
For money.

Fuzzy bodies
Buzzing sounds.

Stingers sharper than a pin
They can be soooo painful!

But bees won't hurt you
Only if you bother them.

Flies from flower to flower
Collecting pollen.

Lives in hives
Protecting the queen.
Thijs Timkee, Grade 3

Julissa — What I Like

I like basketball,
I like trees,
I can eat up all my peas.

I like math,
I like dishes,
I can make all my wishes.

I like school,
I like work,
I can eat with a fork.

I like sports,
I like books,
I can catch fish in a brook.
Julissa Rodriguez, Grade 3

My Dog

My dog is fun
I like to play with him day and night
He sits on my step
and waits for me to open the door
So he can jump on me
and give me his paw
and I love him
more and more
Emily Dewitt, Grade 2

Christmas and Thanksgiving

Christmas
presents, tree
giving, opening, thanking
family, dinner, play, celebration
gathering, cooking, eating
Pilgrims, turkeys
Thanksgiving
Chloe Crandall, Grade 3

Summer and Winter

summer
hot, sunny
sliding, swinging, swimming
sun, heat, ice, snow
freezing, sledding, playing
icy, cold
winter
Christopher Moore, Grade 3

Winter and Summer

winter
cold, fun
sledding, snowing, falling
jacket, boots, sandals, t-shirts
camping, playing, sweating
hot, fun
summer
Jomayra Hernandez, Grade 3

Bear and Bull

bear
claws, teeth
hibernating, hunting, attacking
furious, strong, big, scary
running, riding, attacking
furry, horns
bull
Yazleen Brace, Grade 3

Sad Mad Glad

Sometimes I am mad and sad
But I am glad right now
And sometimes I'm sad and mad
But right now I should be glad
Alayna Garvin, Grade 1

Future

My life stands beyond
I lay in my bed
Think about the next day
I am everlasting
I think about my future
My life finds me
Minutes go by
Light leads me through
And the sun rises
My parents follow me
Because my parents are the light
My future goes on
And my shadow follows me
I walk in my future
And my parents lead the way
Taylor Walls, Grade 3

The Shiny Sea

A big ball of flame
Comes up
From the starry night

Days at the sea
Reflecting
Like a sparkling mirror
The water puts forth
Radiance

A glowing
Twinkle hits my heart
My heart twinkles
A stream of happiness
Is everlasting
Trevor Coates, Grade 3

Campfire

A spark
Hits dry kindling
Whoosh it goes
Feed it
Dry wood

Fire turns into a
Temple of heat
A mountain of heat
Burns my eyes

Last red arrowheads
Fly up as the fire dies
The fire turns into
Heavy black ashes
Luca Barnabei, Grade 3

Football
Every morning
Starts a new day
I get my ball
And start to play

I throw the ball
And it pops
Into place
When they catch
The ball

They slip it under
Their arm
And start to run
Down the field
Fast as light
Evan Meenen, Grade 3

Lions
Moving through grass
Growling
Teeth as sharp
As kitchen knives

Hunts as a group
Called a pride

You can find me in savannas,
In Africa's forests
You can also find me in zoos
Why?
Even though I have
This environment
I am impressed with
Educating humans.
Ayden Smartt, Grade 3

Hurricane!
A circular storm
Spiraling across the sea
Pressure drops quickly!
Liam Gregg, Grade 3

Index by Author

Index by School

Blackrock School
Coventry, RI
Allen Benevides 15
Anthony Benevides 15
Emma Boulanger 93
Lauren Boulanger 134
Ashley Brookshire 93
Claire Carroll 90
Alec Castle 65
Emily Cronin 68
Logan D'Arezzo 104
Austin Denomme 151
Christopher Duncan 57
Abigail Fratus 119
Sonia Johnson 65
Maya Kaplun 90
Dakotah Saddow 104
Mitzie Westgate 42

Boiling Springs Intermediate School
Boiling Springs, SC
Benjamin Ashby 58
Bodey Barwick 153
Emma Kate Beheler 88
Gabriel Blanton 136
Brandon Boling 13
Emily Cantrell 66
Makenna Carothers 62
Morgan Carver 31
Jaelyn Charles 31
Ethan Collins 49
Mason Collins 88
Gavin Darity 149
Jake Diaz 33
Calvin Fritts 56
Lucas Gaines 117
Makayla Gardner 13
Parmdeep Ghataora 55
Orlando Hess-Tharpe 56
Tyce Hill 88
Shaydon Hinson 117
Ethan Horne 56
Olivia Ireland 101
Anslee E Johnson 88
Zachary Johnson 149
Cameron Jones 18
Elijah Jones 162
Arissa Katemba 136
Kylee Keller 31
Nazarii Klymiuk 13
Michaelyn Knight 31
Pierce Koreniuk 58
David Loftis 18
Ben Mabry 49
Jocelyn Madden 28
Kara McGowen 122
Sarah Reilly McMahon 101
Matthew Mills 31
Emma Mize 31
Reagan Moore 121

Messiah Moring 30
Chloe Moyers 58
Trisha Nguyen 38
Palmer Parrish 149
Jackson Reel 58
Coleman Roberts 117
Abigail Robertson 101
Devin Roe 20
Addison Sapp 28
Andrew Schmidt 121
Jadyn Sharick 162
Colby Smart 56
Steven Sparks 136
Caleb Sturgill 165
Adisyn Thornton 122
Sydney Threatt 66
Allyson Ward 38
Garrett Watson 88
Brendan Young 88

Boonsboro Elementary School
Boonsboro, MD
Camille Donovan 96
Gabrielle Donovan 107
Charlotte Elliott 118
Icie Favata 31
Colin Fulmer 96
Caroline Grubb 32
Madryn Hanser 116
Lucy Juedemann 54
Ryan Perry 143
Anaya Teye 27
Riley Troxell 13
Alyssa Webber 72
Sierra Wilcox 143
Jillian Zimmerman 54

Booth Hill School
Trumbull, CT
Sophia Molnar 43

Boyce Middle School
Upper St Clair, PA
Eddie Albert 38
Aidan Besselman 33
Bear Bottonari 114
Anna Cancilla 23
Phoebe Chen 129
Sophie Chen 147
Alyana Childs 45
Christian Chiu 158
Kaitlyn Clougherty 67
Anthony DeNoon 97
Zoe Dvorin 25
Maggie Lowden 63
Delaynie McMillan 28
Matthew Naumann 75
Lucas Pash 134
Erin Payne 116
Emma Pribanic 145
Sofia Putorti 124
Shana Reddy 19

Samuel Scalzo 113
Ritvik Shah 110
Sujay Shah 89
Nitish Sharma 162
Jillian Shaw 64
Anoushka Sinha 52
Evan Tefft 63
Alex Teresi 45
Daniel Wang 140

Brentwood Elementary School
Fayetteville, NC
Amillyan Autry-Cooper 196
Kiara Burroughs 196
Promise Lide 196
Vincent E. McNeil Jr. 202
Jameson Robinson 201

Bridge School
Lexington, MA
Angie Leung 22

Broad Rock Middle School
South Kingstown, RI
Kathryn Barrus 26
Jack DeMetrick 21

Buckingham Elementary School
Furlong, PA
Anika Keshri 114

Cantiague Elementary School
Jericho, NY
Aishani Sreejith Komath 120

Cardinal Charter Academy
Cary, NC
Marissa Love 61
Sophia Ly 46
Siri Mudunuri 49
Nicole Rangel Capelle 87

Carolina Friends School
Durham, NC
Amelia Posner-Hess 84

Caroline G Atkinson School
Freeport, NY
Angel Avendano 128
Karla Azucar 38
Yanelyse Cruz 120
June Cumento 156
Luca Gentile 106
Justin Hopkins 81
Brianny Luna 42
Kayla Robb 28
Elisabet Tapia 157
Nia Thornton 106
Andre Wilkes 106
Patrick Williams 68

Catherine A Dwyer Elementary School
Wharton, NJ
Andrew Azar 39
Connor Bourdon 107
Scarlett Brookes 94
Olivia Cammon 74
Kiley Cannon 35

Elbridge Gale Elementary School
Wellington, FL

Elizabeth Davis Middle School
Chester, VA

Elizabeth Elementary School
Shelby, NC

Emmanuel Children's Mission School
Mount Vernon, NY

Ethel M Burke Elementary School
Bellmawr, NJ

Ettrick Elementary School
Petersburg, VA

Author Autograph Page

Author Autograph Page